# ECUMENISM

**Recent Titles in**
**Bibliographies and Indexes in Religious Studies**

# ʹECUMENISM,

## A Bibliographical Overview

COMPILED BY

# MICHAEL A. FAHEY

Bibliographies and Indexes in Religious Studies, Number 23
G. E. Gorman, *Advisory Editor*

**Greenwood Press**
Westport, Connecticut • London

**Library of Congress Cataloging-in-Publication Data**

Fahey, Michael A. (Michael Andrew).
    Ecumenism : a bibliographical overview / compiled by Michael A.
    Fahey.
        p.    cm.—(Bibliographies and indexes in religious studies,
    ISSN 0742-6836 ; no. 23)
        Includes indexes.
        ISBN 0-313-25102-9 (alk. paper)
        1. Ecumenical movement—Bibliography.    I. Title.    II. Series.
    Z7845.1.F34   1992
    [BX8.2]
    016.2708'2—dc20        92-28449

British Library Cataloguing in Publication Data is available.

Library of Congress Catalog Card Number: 92-28449
ISBN: 0-313-25102-9
ISSN: 0742-6836

First published in 1992

Greenwood Press, 88 Post Road West, Westport, CT 06881
An imprint of Greenwood Publishing Group, Inc.

Printed in the United States of America

10 9 8 7 6 5 4 3 2 1

In Memoriam
**William J. Wolf**
(1918-1990)
Professor, Ecumenist, Anglican Observer at Vatican II
with gratitude and esteem

# Contents

# Foreword

Can we suppose, after studying the original testimony of the Bible, that the Church of God could be a jostling confusion of larger and smaller *ecclesiae*, which accuse one another of erroneous beliefs, rites and orders? Can the one great people of God ever be split up into an ugly plurality of larger and smaller tribes, which although they have abandoned hot war and open rivalry for cold war and undercover competition, still continue to make a mockery of belief to the detriment of mankind?

-Hans Küng, *The Church*

"No," responds Dr. Küng to this largely rhetorical question, for the overwhelming evidence of the New Testament proves that the church is a single entity, one spiritual creation unified in the Body of Christ. And yet this supposedly seamless fabric has been rent from its earliest days by heresies, schisms and divisions; indeed, one could argue that the history of the church is almost classically Hegelian in its sometimes antithetical denominationalism which has not yet achieved anything like a consensual synthesis.

It is this painful dichotomy between the truth of theological understanding and the imperfection of historical reality that has led in the twentieth century to the emergence of the ecumenical movement, which one dictionary economically defines as "the movement in the Church towards the recovery of the unity of all believers in Christ, transcending differences of creed, ritual and polity."[1] More expansively (and more comprehensively), the author

---

1 F.L. Cross and E.A. Livingstone (eds.), *The Oxford Dictionary of the Christian Church*. 2nd ed. Reprinted with corrections and revisions (Oxford: Oxford University Press, 1983), p. 443.

of the present volume describes ecumenism as "the exploration among Christians of different confessions about the history of their separations and the underlying doctrinal and social reasons so that ways may be found to overcome estrangement. Ecumenism comprehends all the activities and theological efforts to facilitate the unity of the churches that are separated by anathemas or psychological excommunications." It is a movement, in other words, that seeks historical, theological and social understanding of differences that traditionally separate Christian groups so that greater unity can be achieved. Movement implies process, and in this instance the process is a development of mutual respect and willingness to focus on major commonalities rather than minor differences.

For many Christians this process need not necessarily result in a single, unified *ecclesia* (a "single numerator" in Küng's terms) but rather lead to a greater awareness of life within a common denominator that permits varieties of expression. "What we can have is unity in the sense of the living *koinonia* of the Scriptures, which is unity in *diversity*, unity in a variety of rites, languages, customs, modes of thought and action and prayer. Such unity is more perfect than uniformity." [2] It is this unity in diversity that for many of us has been the most exciting development in inter-church relations during the latter half of this century; how well I recall the almost deafening applause at a 1966 theological conference in Boston that followed a Lutheran pastor's admission that he was "a Catholic of the Lutheran persuasion" -- a Protestant equivalent of the recognition in *Unitatis Redintegratio* that "...some, even very many, of the most significant elements and endowments which together go to build up and give life to the Church itself, can exist outside the visible boundaries of the Catholic Church: the written Word of God; the life of grace; faith, hope and charity, with the other interior gifts of the Holy Spirit, as well as visible elements."[3]

Ecumenism, then, is the process by which Christians of various persuasions recognize that, despite our divisions, there are many bonds that continue to unite us; "...we confess the same faith in the one true God; we have received the same Spirit; we have been baptized with

---

2 Hans Küng, *The Council and Reunion*. Trans. by Cecily Hastings (London: Sheed and Ward, 1961), p. 279.

3 Vatican Council II, *Unitatis Redintegratio*, no. 3.

the same baptism; and we preach the same Christ."[4] More than that, however, it is also a recognition that, while Christian unity may not have been destroyed by our separation, it certainly has been grossly impaired. In our view, therefore, reunion in some outwardly visible manifestation must be an aim of ecumenism, and probably a reunion more concrete than many would feel comfortable with.

On more than one occasion Pope John XXIII spoke of reunion by degrees, beginning with *avvicinamento* (the initial approach), moving through *riaccostamento* (coming together) and resulting eventually in *unità perfetta* (perfect unity). [5] In the twentieth century alone we have experienced *avvicinamento* for more than eighty years, beginning as early as the Edinburgh Missionary Conference in 1910, which recognized the counter-productive effect that denominational divisions were having on missionary activity in non-Christian countries. And we have also seen *riaccostamento* occurring in a variety of guises, sometimes in formal acts of union (the Church of South India, the Uniting Church in Australia, for example), in regular but informal participation in major Christian gatherings (non-Catholic observers at Vatican II, Catholic observers at the World Council of Churches), and most often in interconfessional dialogues of increasing value (Anglican-Roman Catholic, Lutheran-Roman Catholic, Orthodox-Roman Catholic, Anglican-Methodist, etc.).

At the same time, efforts at *riaccostamento* continue to fail, the most widely reported breakdown recently being the splits in the Anglican Communion, with "continuing" or "Catholic" branches appearing in Canada, the United States, South Africa and Australia. If individual traditions continue to disintegrate, what hope is there of any kind of inter-church *unità perfetta* in this life? To answer this we return to the concept of ecumenism as process -- a process which is in constant flux, with new understanding and new movements beginning even as old ones succeed or fail. Ultimately we view it as a hopeful process because of the essential unity from which all Christian activity springs. Perhaps the failures are merely a reminder that human pride and imperfections continue to stand in the way, or perhaps they are due to our failure to start from first principles. "...The first step in healing the breach must be an admission of guilt

---

4 Anglican-Roman Catholic International Commission, *The Final Report, Windsor, September 1981* (London: SPCK and Catholic Truth Society, 1981), p. 5.

5 See, for example, Küng, *op. cit.*, p. 278.

and a plea for forgiveness addressed both to God, the Lord of the Church, and to our brothers.... In asking for forgiveness, we ask for the healing of the division and in asking for forgiveness we declare that we are ready to do whatever is God's will to remove the division."[6] In recent years there have been precious few admissions of guilt and still fewer pleas for forgiveness -- there is a message here for all ecumenists.

The ecumenical process is not finished; in fact it has barely begun, for the most part straining to achieve even a basic *riaccostamento*. But it is also spreading and gaining momentum and in the next decade or two will, I am convinced, achieve some major breakthroughs (and result in some further divisions, to be sure). To assist not only those actively engaged in the spread of ecumenism but also those attempting to stand back from the process and chart its growth we approached Dr. Michael Fahey, S.J. (currently Dean of the Faculty of Theology at the University of St. Michael's College, Toronto) with a request to prepare a volume that would document the developments and trends in ecumenism. (On a personal note I find the institutional provenance of this work most satisfying, for my own ecumenical experience began in a classroom at "St. Mike's" with a seminar class on Puritanism taught by the Protestant scholar, Herbert Richardson, to a group of Anglicans and Catholics.) Dr. Fahey's own credentials are impeccably ecumenical, spanning three decades of dialogue, both formal and informal, with Christians from various traditions. During a peripatetic eight years Fr. Fahey has pursued his bibliographic course through the world's major ecumenical collections in Europe and North America, resulting in a carefully culled and annotated collection of 1,345 references.

As this important bibliographic volume shows, Dr. Fahey is well versed in literature from around the world on all aspects of ecumenism. Following his useful overview of the literature in Chapter 1, Dr. Fahey in seven additional chapters guides us through the plethora of publications on ecumenism with a scholarly precision that will assist ecumenists for many years into the future. All of the major historical treatments are here, as are the significant confessional accounts of ecumenism and works of and about interconfessional dialogues. In my view, however, the greatest contribution of this work lies in Chapter 8, which enumerates and annotates works on the doctrinal issues that are central to ecumenical understanding. In this

---

6 Hans Küng, *The Church*. Trans. by Ray and Rosaleen Ockenden (New York: Sheed and Ward, 1967), p. 284.

chapter one has a listing and treatment of all major works on the key doctrinal areas of ecclesiology, sacraments, doctrine and related issues. This chapter will be of special value to scholars.

Taken together, these eight chapters provide a careful and judicious survey that is both accessible to the student and useful to the scholar. It is commendable not only for its broad treatment of all aspects of ecumenism but also for its logical arrangement and scholarly assessment of the most important books in the field. Therefore, I am pleased to commend Michael Fahey's detailed work as a worthy addition to Bibliographies and Indexes in Religious Studies. It will shortly be complemented by Alan Black's forthcoming volumes entitled *The Quest for Church Union*.

The Rev. Dr. G. E. Gorman, FLA, FRSA
Advisory Editor
Charles Sturt University - Riverina
Wagga Wagga NSW Australia

# Preface

This bibliography is devoted to ecumenism, the exploration among Christians of different confessions about the history of their separations and the underlying doctrinal and social reasons so that ways may be found to overcome estrangement. Ecumenism comprehends all the activities and theological efforts to facilitate the unity of the churches that are separated by anathemas or psychological excommunications. I understand ecumenism in the strict sense and do not include works on interfaith dialogue in which Christians with members of other religious faiths, especially Judaism, search for understanding. These fruitful interfaith exchanges will hopefully be covered in future volumes of this series.

The time-frame for this bibliography on ecumenism is largely the years from the 1950s to the early 1990s. Two specific events led to an explosion of theological literature during these years: the first was the formal establishment of the World Council of Churches (WCC) at its inaugural general assembly in Amsterdam in 1948; the second was the convocation of the Second Vatican Council (1962-1965). The year 1910 is often cited as the beginning of modern ecumenism, the year of the Edinburgh World Missionary Conference. The establishment of the Faith and Order movement and its early meetings in Lausanne (1927) and Edinburgh (1937), as well as the Life and Work movement with meetings in Stockholm (1925) and Oxford (1937), contributed to the early stages of modern ecumenism. When I sometimes reach back into literature of the 1920s, 1930s or 1940s, it is to highlight important pioneer ecumenical works that either prophetically anticipated what was to come or perhaps fostered attitudes at first unpopular in official church circles.

My bibliography is annotated or critical in the sense that I make judgments about the relative value of specific volumes. Works that have a devotional or very basic instructional character are not included. My interest has been in works that have advanced the goals of ecumenism (or made its progress more difficult) and enriched theological or historical knowledge. Some works may have been omitted simply because they were not available to me in the many library collections I consulted. The bibliography is limited to books and excludes journal articles. However, I do provide a section that identifies the major ecumenical journals and the helpful bibliographical lists of periodical literature.

This bibliography obviously does not survey the whole field of modern theology. There are notable achievements of contemporary theology that remain unmentioned here. Important theological publications such as Karl Barth's *Dogmatics* or Jürgen Moltmann's *Theology of Hope* or Bernard Lonergan's *Method in Theology*, or major publications by Hans Urs von Balthasar or Juan Luis Segundo are not included here because, in my judgment, they have not emerged specifically from within an ecumenical matrix. Since the mid-1960s no Orthodox, Protestant or Catholic theologian worthy of serious consideration can conceive of theology in total confessional isolation from ecumenical awareness. I restrict myself to works that are the product of a conscious interchange or a simultaneous comparison of doctrine, or to works that have been elaborated to promote ecumenical exchange.

How did I go about this task? At every stage I worked directly in libraries studying books shelf after shelf. Chronologically this began at Rome's Centro pro Unione library and the library of the Pontificio Istituto Orientale. From there I went on to work in Geneva at the WCC's library. My work continued in Belgium and Germany and was brought to an end in North America. In Toronto I have been able to run computer searches and availed myself of the WilsonDisc database which uses the US Library of Congress system of classification. I consulted *Religion Index Two* to be assured that I had not omitted important *Festschriften*. Only in a few rare cases (as for instance some works in Polish) have I cited a book that I have not personally reviewed. I have not included Russian or, with a few exceptions, Greek material.

This bibliographical overview is organized into eight chapters. Chapter 1, written last, describes the various types of ecumenical publications and situates the historical events that occasioned their production. Here I offer my provisional assessment of what ecumenical literature has achieved especially for the development of theology. In this chapter the numbers in brackets refer to the entry numbers of the bibliographical citations.

The bibliography proper begins in Chapter 2, starting with

reference materials including older bibliographies, as well as collections of documents, encyclopedias, handbooks, journals or periodicals on ecumenism, and descriptions of research centers specializing in ecumenism.

Chapter 3 describes historical accounts of the ecumenical movement, both general accounts and studies concentrating on the twentieth century. In this section I include works that treat the foundation of the WCC, its general assemblies, and the meetings of the Faith and Order Commission. In this chapter I then describe works that report on Vatican II (1962-1965), its four sessions, commentaries on its teachings about the church and ecumenism, reactions by Orthodox, Protestant and Anglican observers, and recent retrospectives from the perspective of twenty or twenty-five years. The work of the Joint Working Group of the Roman Catholic Church and the WCC is noted. I also note a number of biographies or autobiographies of personages have been central to the modern ecumenical movement.

Chapter 4 gathers together accounts given by members of various Christian confessions to explain their own church's understanding of ecumenism. These are arranged according to the churches that identify themselves as Catholic, both Western and Eastern, Orthodox, Oriental Orthodox, Anglican, Lutheran, Reformed, Methodist, Baptist, Pentecostal and Charismatic.

Chapter 5 assesses publications that describe the various bilateral or multilateral consultations and agreed statements between or among Christian churches. Chapter 6 discusses works that approach ecumenism from a geographical perspective: Europe, North America and the Caribbean, the Middle East and Asia, Africa, and South America. Included here is reference to publications of the Ecumenical Association of Third World Theologians. Chapter 7 is devoted to literature generated by three documents that, for one reason or another, have received particular attention in recent years: the Augsburg Confession (1530), the Leuenberg Agreement of 1973, and the *Plan of Union* of COCU.

Chapter 8, the lengthiest chapter, addresses specific doctrinal issues, chief of which is the very nature of visible unity. There are studies on dialogue as a methodological tool for theology. Next comes a section on ecclesiology or the nature of the church followed by specific studies on justification, faith, the Bible, Christ, Holy Spirit, prayer and the saints. There is also a subsection on sacraments or Christian ordinances with special attention to recent ecumenical works on baptism, eucharist (or the Lord's Supper), and ordained ministry. Many books recording reactions to the Faith and Order Commission's Lima document (1982) entitled *Baptism, Eucharist and Ministry* are gathered into a special section. Doctrinal studies also included reflections on marriages between Christians of different confessional traditions (ecumenical marriages or "mixed" marriages). Then, under the rubric of authority, there are books treating "reception," Petrine ministry, papacy, and councils. The final doctrinal sections treat evangelism (more commonly called evangelization by Catholics) and mission, women in society and church, and ethical questions in ecumenical perspective with particular attention to peace, justice, and the church in the modern world.

How does one insure that a bibliography on ecumenism will be ecumenical in focus? The confessional background of any compiler inevitably colors the presentation of the material. I hope that my training as a theologian during and after Vatican II as well as my years of teaching in ecumenical consortia will have helped me at least partially to recognize emphases central to Orthodox, Anglican or Protestant theologians. From 1960 to 1965 I served as managing editor of *New Testament Abstracts* where I was introduced to a wide spectrum of journals and books from a variety of Christian perspectives. My doctoral studies in theology at the University of Tübingen (1965-1970) provided me with opportunities to follow courses not only in Catholic theology but also in the Faculty of Evangelical (i.e. Lutheran) Theology where I studied under Ernst Käsemann, Heiko Oberman, Gerhard Ebeling, Jürgen Moltmann, and others. Paradoxically, Tübingen had the luxury of two ecumenical institutes, one directed by Hans Küng, the other by Jürgen Moltmann. When I returned to North America in 1970, I was invited to serve as a theologian on the official Orthodox/Roman Catholic Consultation on which I have continued to serve for the last twenty-two years. I have also learned much as an ecumenical partner in the Inter Church, Interfaith Relations Committee of the Anglican Church of Canada, and as a consultant theologian in official conversations with the United Church of Canada. My association with the Boston Theological Institute and the Toronto School of Theology has, I trust, sensitized me to the multi-faceted nature of ecumenism.

*     *     *     *     *

A number of persons helped me in the preparation of this bibliography. I acknowledge first of all the generous assistance and patience of the general editor, Dr. G.E. Gorman. My special thanks to Sever J. Voicu of the Centro pro Unione, Rome, and to James Lee Dugan, librarian of the Pontificio Istituto Orientale, as well as to Professor Robert Taft of that same institution. At the library of the World Council of Churches in Geneva I was assisted by the librarians Ans J. van der Bent and Pierre Beffa. I also wish to thank Dom

Emmanuel Lanne and the Benedictine Community at Chevetogne for their assistance. The library staffs at the Hauptbibliothek of the Eberhard-Karls-Universität, Tübingen, and the Faculté de Théologie, Université de Louvain la Neuve, were also helpful. In the United States I was assisted by James Dunkly, librarian of the Episcopal Theological School/Weston School of Theology Library, Cambridge, Massachusetts, and by Mary Cronin, Head Librarian of the O'Neill Library, Boston College. Closer to home I was aided by the director of the Canadian Centre for Ecumenism, Thomas Ryan, and especially its librarian, Bernice Baranowski. The library staff of St. Paul's University, Ottawa, made their excellent collection available to me. In Toronto at the Kelly Library of the University of St. Michael's College, Toronto, Evelyn Collins provided valuable assistance. I profited from the ecumenical collection at Emmanuel College, Victoria University, Toronto, which is well supplied with publications of the World Council of Churches, and I found the Robarts Library of the University of Toronto well supplied with holdings especially in German.

Readers who wish to share with me their reactions or to point out inaccuracies are invited to contact me at the Faculty of Theology, University of St. Michael's College, 81 St. Mary St., Toronto, Ontario M5S 1J4, Canada.

# ECUMENISM

# 1

# Ecumenical Literature

## Basic Orientations

Most historians consider that the modern ecumenical movement originated in the year 1910 at the World Missionary Conference held in Edinburgh. The Protestant organizers of that international meeting were convinced that missionary endeavors by the European and American churches especially in Africa and Asia were being seriously hampered by the countersign of a divided church. But the modern ecumenical movement owes its origins not only to these farsighted missionaries but also to persons such as Bishop Charles Brent and his associates who organized the first international Faith and Order conference at Lausanne in 1927 to explore dividing doctrinal issues, and Archbishop Nathan Söderblom who founded the Life and Work movement in 1925 at Stockholm to discuss not doctrinal but practical questions since "doctrine divides, service unites." These original initiatives and their initial follow-up were inspired by Protestant, Anglican and Orthodox church leaders. Gradually, these three streams of ecumenical mission, doctrine and service merged into the formation of the World Council of Churches (WCC) already in formation before World War II but formally inaugurated at its first general assembly only in 1948 when it pondered "Man's Disorder and God's Design."

The leadership of the Roman Catholic Church, especially its popes in the early decades of the twentieth century, was suspicious of these models of "pan-Christian" unification because it perceived them as marred by indifferentism, false irenicism, or even syncretism. The Counter Reformation mentality of Catholicism, with its rigid theological categories formulated by controversialists and by the Council of Trent in the sixteenth century, and with its pervasive ecclesiastical triumphalism, legalism and clericalism created many obstacles to participation in the burgeoning ecumenical movement.

The religious shift in Catholicism and Christianity in general from polemics to dialogue and from tolerance to admiration was facilitated by the shared trauma of World War II, by population relocations that occurred after the War, and by adoption among Christians of historico-critical methods for interpreting the Scriptures and gradually even the creeds and decisions of ecumenical councils. All of this helped Christians put its existing practices into better perspective. The New Testament came to be read as a unified message to be sure but one that was expressed by varying, complementary theologies about the mission of Jesus, the role of the church, and apostolic ministry. This inevitably led to changes in attitudes towards one's own church and those of others. Some believers asked whether denominational differences might not be understood as expressions of different currents of spirituality already adumbrated in the New Testament.

Ecumenism is a recent phenomenon with a short history. What is truly amazing is the staggering amount of literature the ecumenical movement has produced, its numerous monographs, journals, and even devotional literature. The history of the ecumenical movement is a modest one, spanning to date at the most eighty-two years but probably, more realistically, only fifty years. In an extended sense, one could argue that the search for unity begins in the New Testament. Again the mutual anathemas exchanged in the year 1054 between Rome and Byzantium or Luther's posting of theses in 1517 gave impetus to theological exchanges, but these polemic and controversial debates hardly fostered mutual ecumenical exploration. Even in recent memory when ecumenism was emerging it produced simultaneous soliloquies rather than serious dialogue.

This bibliography, besides attempting to identify the more significant publications on ecumenism in this century, also tries to classify the movement's literary production into seven general categories. The literature generated by ecumenism, the modern movement among Christians to understand the divided nature of historical Christianity and to heal its divisions, is vast and complex. No attempt to classify books on the ecumenical movement by literary genres and thematic concerns does justice to the richness of literary production. What is here offered and what justifies the structure of this bibliography is one attempt at classification made with the realization that boundaries are sometimes fuzzy and divisions overlap.

The first proposed classification of ecumenical literature would be "basic orientations." Among these would be classified reference works such as bibliographies, encyclopedias, dictionaries, as well as journals or periodicals, and descriptions of ecumenical research centers. In this present volume, basic reference materials include some twenty-nine bibliographical resources which list books and articles on the ecumenical movement. These resources are available in the best theological libraries and now, with the advent of computer data-banks, it is now possible for persons with access to appropriate electronic hardware to consult bibliographical listings even without consulting printed sources.

The well-known distinction between an annotated bibliography and a non-annotated bibliography is basically the difference between a mere listing as opposed to a descriptive evaluation of an entry. In ecumenism, as in other fields of learning, mere lists of titles offer only very limited usefulness for the researcher. The problem is further compounded when the lists are not organized systematically. Without some brief description of contents and a hint at the relative importance of a bibliographical citation, listings may only confuse and frustrate the researcher. In the field of ecumenism annotated bibliographies are rare. One notable exception is the short and somewhat impressionistic bibliography prepared by Sutfin and Lavanoux [27]. One of the special benefits of this present series, *Bibliographies and Indexes in Religious Studies*, is its commitment to providing pointed judgments and to contextualizing research against specific historical backgrounds. The bibliographical studies by G. E. Gorman and Lyn Gorman [13, 14] which initiated this series are valuable examples of this kind of scholarship.

Among the bibliographical listings in modern ecumenism, one of the best for works published between 1962 to 1977 is the *International Ecumenical Bibliography* [16]. Unfortunately this research tool ceased publication in 1983. Another instrument for identifying published works in ecumenism is the printed catalogue from the library of the Geneva headquarters of the WCC that lists all its monographs up to the year 1981 [29]. For articles published in ecumenical journals the ongoing coverage of *Religion Index One* is invaluable [23]; ecumenical essays in books with multiple authors or *Festschriften* are catalogued in *Religion Index Two* [24] and reviews of new books are noted in *Index to Book Reviews in Religion* [15]. These three publications prepared under the auspices of the American Theological Library Association have expanded coverage in the last several years to include more European journals and more foreign language publications. For bibliographical data on continuing ecumenical dialogues and publications promoting mutual understanding among churches the listings by Puglisi [22], with the semi-annual follow-up in the *Centro pro Unione Bulletin* [8], are indispensable. The pre-history of modern ecumenism, specifically from the sixteenth to the nineteenth centuries, has been generally neglected by bibliographers. One notable exception that is particularly welcome is the survey of "irenic literature" by

Swinne [28]. Besides comprehensive bibliographical listings covering multiple areas of ecumenism, a number of specialized bibliographies have been produced on specific topics such as ecumenical marriages, reactions to the Lima document on the sacraments, eucharistic hospitality, or a host of other church-unity issues. Beyond the formal bibliographies, readers often discover helpful references to significant ecumenical publications from footnotes, reading lists, or book reviews. The suggested readings, for instance, at the end of the principal entries in the *Dictionary of the Ecumenical Movement* [72] or, from a Catholic perspective, in *The New Dictionary of Theology* [67] are useful resources.

One of the distinctive aspects of the modern ecumenical movement has been the joint production of numerous agreed statements or consensus documents which unfortunately have only infrequently been made easily accessible to the general public. The need for collections of such documents is still acute. Among rare compilations of ecumenical documents are George Bell's collections of texts spanning the years 1920-1957 [30]. A more recent series, *Ecumenical Documents*, is being published (at a very slow pace) by the Paulist Press [33, 38, 40, 682] which covers international and national bilateral statements, albeit selectively and partially. A useful model for other collections would be the handy two-volume ecumenical enchiridion published in Italian [86]. Most ecumenical documents still appear only in pamphlet format or in generally unaccessible journals and hence receive minimal attention. Lists of where ecumenical bilateral documents have been published are available in Puglisi [22] and in the *Centro pro Unione Bulletin* [8]. Without such lists, readers would waste valuable time trying to track down documents in periodicals or newsletters. This may well be one reason why ecumenical consensus texts are so rarely read except by those who compose them or by those who want to verify their orthodoxy.

Other published material in the area of "basic orientations" include encyclopedias, dictionaries or handbooks. The production of comprehensive encyclopedias or reference works that remain abreast of ecumenism is a formidable task. Encyclopedias typically become dated in short order. Four reliable works in this category can be noted. In German the completely revised edition of the *Evangelisches Kirchenlexikon* [58], still in production, and the mammoth *Lexikon für Theologie und Kirche* [70] are dependable. In English the *New Catholic Encyclopedia* [77] is uneven, although its supplementary volumes show more ecumenical sensitivity; the more theologically focused *Sacramentum Mundi* [82], which appeared simultaneously in several European languages, has aged well.

Among handbooks four remarkable publications can be singled

out: a three-volume work on the history of dogma and theology edited by Andresen [43], the new *Dictionary of the Ecumenical Movement* [72] published in 1991 (a veritable gold mine of information), the Barrett world encyclopedia of Christianity [46], and the Krüger ecumenical lexicon in German [68]. One particularly neglected genre of publication, especially in English, is the high-level general introduction suitable for use in schools or parishes. German ecumenists have tended to be more attentive to the need for this kind of pedagogical aid [61, 63, 64].

One can point to some eighty-five journals or periodicals sponsored by a variety of countries and churches that have a strong ecumenical focus [91-175]. Some of these publications regularly report on church-related events pertinent to the ecumenical movement, especially the ongoing bilateral conversations. It is impossible to keep abreast of the ecumenical movement without regularly consulting these journals. These periodicals often formulate insights that appear perhaps only a year later in book format. Most of the world's ecumenical centers, if they do not publish a journal, at least print a newsletter. Several centers even sponsor publication of book series.

The number of ecumenical centers or research institutes world wide is significant, but only a few are well known except by specialists. Among the centers that have made notable contributions to ecumenism are the Monastery of Chevetogne in Belgium, the Bari Institute in southern Italy, the various ecumenical institutes connected with German universities or funded by church agencies, and the Institute of Ecumenical Research in Strasbourg. Many centers have been strongly influenced by the charisms of their founder, as for example Lyon's Centre Unité established by Paul Courturier. Some ecumenical centers, such as the Centre Orthodoxe du Patriarchat Oecuménique located in Chambésy, a suburb of Geneva, organize an annual ecumenical symposium and publish the scholarly papers delivered at such conferences. The Monastery of Taizé, located near the site of the medieval monastic foundation at Cluny in Burgundy, founded in 1940 by its prior, Brother Roger Schutz, to promote reconciliation among churches and people, is perhaps the best known ecumenical center [176, 178, 180, 181, 183, 185].

The category of ecumenical publications here described as basic orientations typically contain those works that a student or scholar will first consult for comprehensive treatment and information on the movement for Christian unity. What is sought in these sources is generally information about publications, dates, committees, meetings, centers and personnages.

# Historical Accounts

Historical accounts of modern efforts to achieve church unity have produced another category of publications, the narrative history. These accounts treat the modern ecumenical movement either globally with descriptions of its immediate antecedents and present agencies or specifically with emphasis on one vehicle of reform such as the World Council of Churches or the Second Vatican Council (1962-1965). More highly specialized works will trace, for example, the history of the Joint Working Group composed of Catholics and members of the WCC. An especially rich category of historical publications has been biographies and autobiographies of major personages who have had a notable impact on the ecumenical movement.

Among the thirty-four general histories of the ecumenical movement recommended in this bibliography, some cover several centuries, some concentrate uniquely on the twentieth century. The classic history of ecumenism remains the two volumes edited by Rouse [204] and Fey [213] spanning the years 1517 to 1968. These two volumes contain, besides the specialized essays composed by experts, excellent bibliographical orientations. Briefer historical accounts in this category, at the introductory level in English, include the volume by Brown [190] or the more global coverage by Vischer [207]. Although unabashedly British in focus, the historical account by Till [206] is informative and rewarding. For use in high school or university courses, teachers could use Desseaux [195]. The stout-hearted may wish to tackle a massive specialized work such as the study by Fouilloux on attitudinal shifts among French-speaking Catholics toward church unity since the nineteenth century [196]. Congar's historical account of the major causes for estrangement between Christians of the East and West [192] is thorough but accessible. The history of Catholic ecumenical pioneers written by the American Methodist Minus [486] is an excellent introduction. Also recommended is Baum's analysis of primary sources recording papal hesitations about certain models of church unity [209]. Among Catholic studies that antedate and anticipate Vatican II, the historical work by the Louvain professor Thils [216] merits special recommendation.

Historical studies of the WCC have been numerous. The recent fortieth anniversary of the first general assembly in Amsterdam in 1948 occasioned the publication of several interesting historical accounts [220, 227, 246]. Readers can obtain a good sense of the scope of the WCC's involvements by consulting the catalogue or *Verzeichnis* of its statements up to the year 1978 [222]. Also useful is the WCC's *Handbook of Member Churches* [224] with a more recent update [244].

Because the WCC frequently initiates internal restructuring, readers will profit from an updated account of its organizational chart such as the one provided by Van Elderen [244]. Several recent studies have been highly critical of the WCC on the grounds that it has lost its evangelical thrust and become entangled in political and social ideologies [221, 226, 238, 242, 245, 529]. Another group of literature, small in scope, comprehends Catholic assessments of the WCC. Given the reluctance of the Vatican to apply for full membership in the WCC (apart from membership in the WCC's theological right arm, the Faith and Order Commission), it is interesting to read sympathetic evaluations of the WCC by individual Catholics such as the 1956 study by the Jesuit Duff [230], the 1972 study by Chenu [228], or the 1985 study by McDonnell [239].

Each general assembly of the WCC, Amsterdam in 1948, Evanston in 1954, New Delhi in 1961, Uppsala in 1968, Nairobi in 1975, Vancouver in 1983, and Canberra in 1991, has generated a sizeable amount of ecumenical literature, not only the official proceedings and reports but penetrating theological assessments [249-263]. Ecumenists seek to explain the reasons for the choice of a general assembly's theme. Other ecumenists examine the growing tensions in the world organization between First World and Third World priorities. The excellent reports and position papers formulated at the general assemblies often remain buried in these acta without receiving the attention they merit. Not only the professional historian or theologian but even the general readers could profit from consulting the proceedings of the various WCC's Faith and Order Commission meetings which span the years 1927 (Lausanne) to 1989 (Budapest). The Faith and Order Commission has published a wide range of "Faith and Order Papers" usually in three or four language versions. The two other international ecumenical groups that amalgamated with the WCC, namely the Life and Work movement and the International Missionary Council, have also produced a small corpus of ecumenical studies. More information on publications by these earlier ecumenical organizations can be found in Neill's concise dictionary [1272], Rouse [204] or the *Dictionary of the Ecumenical Movement* [72].

Although the Roman Catholic Church was late in officially participating in many aspects of the modern ecumenical movement, particularly in undertakings sponsored by the WCC, its attitude at the official level changed after the convocation and convening of the Second Vatican Council which met in four sessions from 1962 to 1965. To be sure, numerous individuals and groups prepared for this shift, and their pioneering work is coming to be recognized more and more. Basic familiarity about the accomplishments of the Council, its texts, reactions to it by non-Catholic official observers, and about how the

Council has been judged in the light of twenty or twenty-five years' perspective, is a necessary prerequisite even for non-Catholic ecumenists. Vatican II's documents have had a notable impact, especially the Dogmatic Constitution on the Church (*Lumen Gentium*), the Decree on Ecumenism (*Unitatis Redintegratio*), and the Pastoral Constitution on the Church in the Modern World (*Gaudium et Spes*).

These conciliar statements, especially their judgments about the Orthodox Church, the Anglican Communion and the Protestant churches, had been adumbrated in the pioneering works of Catholic individuals such as Pribilla, Congar, Gille, Beauduin, and others. The Council accepted and ratified attitudes that had earlier been promoted by certain bishops, theologians and others, but whose views were classified as "unofficial" or "out of favor". This change among Catholics towards dialogue with other Christians was facilitated through three kinds of *ressourcement*, the return to Scripture, the return to patristics, and the return to early liturgical sources.

After Pope John XXIII's formal announcement in 1958 of his intention to convene a council, Küng's *The Council, Reform and Reunion (Konzil und Wiedervereinigung)* [310], translated into a number of languages, awakened wide interest in its potential for healing rifts in the church. Küng's book was followed by other publications that helped his church better appropriate the insight of the Reformers that the church continually needs reform (*ecclesia semper reformanda*). The Council helped its members appreciate that, even with the help of the Holy Spirit, the church has to contend with its own shortcomings: a lack of proper order or balance in doctrinal affirmations, a sacramental theology that contained mechanistic and extrinsicist elements, failures in the proper use of authority, a subtle clericalism, harshness in the face of diversity, cultural isolation, liturgical passivity, and neglect of the Scriptures. The growing awareness of the need for reform, together with a more acute historical consciousness, helped Catholics formulate more positive attitudes toward change and development in their own church and explains the paradigm shift from polemics to ecumenical sharing.

Within a remarkably short period of time after the close of Vatican II, fifty-one folio Latin volumes containing the complete acts of the Council, containing its "antepreparatory", preparatory, and conciliar stages, were published [286]. This accomplishment in a brief time-lapse is one of the extraordinary publishing achievements of this century. These acta will continue to be closely studied by experts for generations to come in order to situate the preliminary submissions or subsequent *modi* (proposed emendations) made from the Council floor. What has already become clear in the preliminary historical assessments is the astounding discrepancy between, on the one hand, the timid, even lifeless *postulata* (recommended agenda items) submitted in advance by dioceses, seminaries, or theology faculties as the burning issues facing the church and, on the other hand, the relatively progressive decisions and strategies adopted by the Council. Researchers who wish to consult the acta but who are somewhat intimidated by the sheer bulk of the material can be assisted by a detailed user's guide prepared by Lefeuvre [286]. Research on the final documents is facilitated by two concordances of all the Latin words contained in the sixteen documents [297, 313]. The two English translations of the sixteen documents of Vatican II, Abbott [284] and Flannery [302], continue to be widely consulted.

Various chronicles or daybooks on the Council, such as Anderson [288] or, in Italian, Caprile [294], describing the daily agenda items, spoken or written interventions, voting procedures, etc., constitute another subdivision of historical publications. Even two photographic essays of the Council's four sessions have provided visual life to the ceremonial aspects [304, 319].

The best comprehensive commentaries on the sixteen conciliar documents are found in the five-volume English translation of the original German text, edited by Vorgrimler [321]. Besides this influential publication, a number of commentaries on the three most important Council documents can be noted: on the dogmatic constitution on the church (*Lumen Gentium*) [287, 289, 300, 306, 307, 316, 321, 326, 1091], on decree on ecumenism (*Unitatis Redintegratio*) [292, 300, 305, 307-309, 311, 318, 321, 326, 1341]; and on the pastoral constitution on the church in the modern world (*Gaudium et Spes*) [300, 307, 321, 326, 1341].

Orthodox, Anglican and Protestant official observers, usually theology professors or ecumenical officers within their own churches or representatives of worldwide ecclesiastical alliances, were invited to Vatican II as guests of the Secretariat for Promoting Christian Unity. A complete listing of these experts is published in the Council's acta [286]. Many of these ecumenical observers subsequently produced assessments of the sessions of Vatican II. Special interest in particular has been registered for the evaluations by Barth [323], Cullmann [330-331], Schlink [350], and Vischer [355]. Another specific volume bears noting, namely the assessment of the late dissident Roman Catholic archbishop, Marcel Lefebvre, who came to judge the Council as a betrayal and who was eventually excommunicated by the Vatican [318].

A number of retrospective studies, written mostly by Catholics, have been published to mark the tenth, twentieth, or twenty-fifth anniversaries of the Council. These form an additional group of literature described as post-conciliar assessments. Some of these are markedly pessimistic [361, 367], referring to the slowing down of reform and the cooling of ecumenical relations as a "new ice age" [363]. Others are self-congratulatory. The best of these assessments are not the collaborative studies but individual evaluations, such as those by Congar [357], Grootaers [362], and Thils [381]. One team effort, edited by Hastings, stands out as unusually well informed about the years 1965 to 1990 [364]. The lengthiest, three-volume assessment, edited by Latourelle [368], is surprisingly notably weak in ecumenical insight.

In 1965 the Joint Working Group of the WCC and the Roman Catholic Church was established as an official consultative forum to initiate, evaluate and sustain ecumenical collaboration. The publications of this Joint Working Group have been notable for the sharpness of their perception: "Catholicity and Apostolicity" (1968), "Common Witness and Proselytism" (1970), and "Common Witness" (1980) [382]. Two of the group's recent studies, "Hierarchy of Truths" (1990) and "The Church: Local and Universal" (1990), address some of the critical theological issues of the present [385]. Descriptive reports on the activities of the Joint Working Group are published regularly in *The Ecumenical Review*.

Biographies or autobiographies have been a particularly popular form of historical studies on ecumenism. For persons unfamiliar with the history of ecumenism these narratives may well offer the best introduction, especially since they capture the passion and drama in the lives of many who helped to shape the ecumenical movement since 1910. Another group of historical publications are sketches of "ecumenical pioneers" or *Vorläufer*, some of whom lived as early as the start of the Enlightenment [28, 389, 398, 402-404, 407-409, 416, 418, 429, 438]. Of particular note among the (auto)biographies of modern ecumenists are accounts of the lives of the Protestants, J.R. Mott [411], N. Söderblom [401, 433], W.A. Visser 't Hooft [439]; the Catholics, A. Bea [388,431], L. Beauduin [392, 428, 435], Y. Congar [397, 414, 427]; and Athenagoras I, the late Orthodox Ecumenical Patriarch [395, 406].

The historical studies of the modern ecumenical movement are as varied as its many strands but offer fascinating insights into the determination and convictions of the individuals and churches committed to church unity.

# Confessional Views

Although ecumenism is an attitude that transcends confessionalism, one can speak of a Catholic ecumenism, an Orthodox ecumenism, a Protestant ecumenism, at least inasmuch as a particular church or one of its members will articulate, in a typically characteristic way, the need for church unity, specify the goals of ecumenism, or identify previous notable achievements of a specific communicant. One group of publications gives expressions to the ecumenical vision of a distinctive church affiliation. These confessionally inspired works are a mixture of history, doctrine and theology. They are distinguished from specifically doctrinal reflections on the nature of church unity, which form another category of publications noted later. Obviously, within a church community and even within the leadership of a church, there will be a variety of emphases. One's country of origin also plays a factor. Some ecumenical attitudes are cautious, others more venturesome, some conservative, some progressive, some optimistic, some gloomy, some "official", some personal. What is often relevant is the date of publication.

Special insights can be drawn from the study of forerunners in ecumenism who anticipated the formal teaching of their churches. Among Catholics the pre-Vatican II publications by Pribilla in 1929 [491], Gille in 1934 [464], Congar in 1937 [453], van de Pol in 1948 [489], Laros in 1950 [474], Boyer in 1951 [448], and Leeming in 1957 [476] are all notably significant. They contributed to the gradual shifts in Catholic attitudes toward other churches. An American Methodist, Paul M. Minus, Jr. has described what he calls a Catholic rediscovery of Protestantism [486]. Henry St. John, a British Dominican priest, published a series of ecumenical articles, considerably ahead of their time, appearing in *Blackfriars* from 1928 to 1954 and then reprinted as a book [496]. Another Catholic, the director of the Canadian Centre for Ecumenism, Ryan, responding to the growing disappointments with the slow progress of change in the mind-set especially of many in his church, has sketched the outlines of a "survival guide" for ecumenically minded Christians [494].

Several writers have described the ecumenical experience of Eastern churches in full communion with the Church of Rome, notably the Melkite church [512-515]. However, the vast majority of Eastern or Byzantine Christians are members of the Orthodox church. Orthodox Christians have a distinguished history of responding positively to efforts intended to promote Christian unity. The 1902 patriarchal encyclical of Joachim III on ecumenism is a case in point. Yet, given the autocephalous character of the individual Orthodox churches, it is difficult to speak of *the* Orthodox view. Commitments to ecumenism were articulated at various Pan-Orthodox meetings. Especially notable for its ecumenical convictions has been the Ecumenical Patriarchate of Constantinople. For primary sources, in English translation, of this Orthodox commitment to ecumenism, covering the years 1902 to 1975, the collection of Patelos is indispensable [530]. For texts in Greek and French that record ecumenical relations between Constantinople and Rome the volume *Tomos Agapis*, edited by Papandreou, is useful [671]. Most of the documents in that collection (and several other texts) have been translated into English by Stormon [682]. The Orthodox have formulated their understanding of ecumenism, especially as it affects their relationship to the WCC, a relationship which has occasionally created problems for some Orthodox [517, 527, 529, 532, 538]. The Centre Orthodoxe du Patriarchat Oecuménique, located in Chambésy near the WCC headquarters, sponsored a symposium in 1985 to explore Orthodox involvement in the ecumenical movement [519]. Finally, another sector of Eastern Christians, the non-Chalcedonian churches, also known as the Oriental Orthodox churches and the Assyrian Church of the East, has articulated its attitudes toward ecumenism [544].

Among Anglicans various reports of the Anglican Consultative Council are notable resources [548, 556, 558, 566, 646, 1269]. Individual Anglican authors such as Bell [551], Howe [556], Neill [560], and Runcie [563] have provided authoritative accounts of the commitment to ecumenism.

Given the rich tradition of dogmatic or systematic theology among Lutherans, it is not surprising to note their significant contributions to ecumenism. Coordination by the Lutheran World Federation has facilitated international dialogue that has made important contributions to Christian unity [572]. Individual Lutherans in Germany, such as Asmussen [569, 570] and Lackmann [576], have also given helpful contributions to church unity from European perspectives; Quanbeck wrote from the perspective of an American Lutheran [579]. Also, the five hundredth anniversary of the birth of Martin Luther observed in 1983 occasioned several publications, usually papers given at symposia as noted in Geisser [574], the Chambésy meeting under Orthodox sponsorship [571], and Lehmann [577]. To these should be added a series of books illustrating how Luther as a churchman has recently been re-evaluated in a much more favorable light by Catholics [480, 583, 584].

With regard to the Reformed or Calvinist tradition, the relatively early studies of Cullmann [589] and of Torrance [602] are particularly notable. The principal agency for coordinating their dialogues is the World Alliance of Reformed Churches whose history is well outlined [599].

Other Protestants such as the Methodists, Baptists, Pentecostals/ Charismatics have described their particular approach to church unity. John Wesley's famous letter written in Dublin to Roman Catholics during the year 1749 has been edited with a commentary by an Irish

Jesuit and founder of the Irish School of Ecumenics [605]. Four volumes published by Baptists aim to dispel popular misconceptions about their attitudes to church unity. Two Catholic ecumenists, Mühlen [617] and McDonnell [694], provided a series of primary ecumenical sources on charismatic renewal [617]. Davis's study on charismatic renewal and the ecumenical movement for which van der Bent provided an eleven-page bibliography is another confessional statement [614].

One of the most fruitful forms of ecumenical exchange since the 1960s has been the emergence of bilateral dialogues, theological conversations between two churches, that have been mandated by official headquarters and facilitated by the Faith and Order Commission and the Pontifical Council (formerly Secretariat) for Promoting Christian Unity. These bilaterals have been held at the international level and, often even more successfully, at various national levels. In a few cases these dialogues are multilateral in the sense that three or more parties are involved. For the years 1959-1974 these bilateral exchanges are described in Ehrenström [621]. The WCC sponsored several forums to assess the importance of these conversations [625, 622]. In the 1980s the French Catholic ecumenist Desseaux [620] reported on the bilaterals and provided a succinct description of their themes: church, ministry, eucharist, unity models, etc. In conjunction with its journal *Mid-Stream*, COCU published in 1986 an analysis of the bilateral dialogues [619]. Likewise, the Orthodox Centre in Chambésy devoted its 1984 symposium to theological reflection on the process and the results of the bilaterals. It is not easy for the ecumenist to locate published texts of these bilateral dialogues. The Puglisi volume [22] lists where these texts were published in journals and classifies them chronologically. Twenty-seven international bilateral texts appear in English in the Meyer-Vischer collection [38] and texts from national dialogues in the USA are reproduced in the Burgess-Gros collection [33].

Professional ecumenists have recognized several of the many modern ecumenical consensus statements as particularly important. Among these is the *Final Report* of the Anglican/Catholic international dialogue, ARCIC-I [632], that summarizes over ten years' careful study on the principal issues separating the two communions. The six agreed statements of the US Lutheran/Catholic dialogue [660, 1015, 1109, 1218, 1243] have also had a strong impact even beyond North America and have been translated into a variety of languages. Also particularly notable in light of the millennium of estrangement between the churches of Rome and Byzantium are the various agreed statements of the Orthodox/Catholic international consultation. These have not yet been published in a single English publication but an

Italian collection of all the statements does exist [680]. The agreed statements of the Orthodox/Roman Catholic consultation in the United States reflect the harmonious relationships that exist between Orthodox and Catholics in the New World. Some of these texts, at least those produced before 1980, have been published in a book with a short historical introduction [669]. Lastly, scholars have recognized the six consensus statements produced by the Groupe des Dombes, the European French-speaking Catholic/Reformed consultation, as highly important ecumenical documents [1114, 1158, 1157, 1057, 1247, 698]. A useful historical and theological study on the dialogues by the original Groupe des Dombes from 1937 to 1955 provides a handy background study [717].

Another way of classifying ecumenical publications is to do so according to their geographical focus. Europe continues to dominate the field of published works. Because of the shifts in the Eastern European countries and the demise of the former Soviet Union, there has emerged a particular interest about those churches, formerly under Socialist or Communist control [709, 713, 718, 720, 724]. Also the influence of the annual ecumenical colloquia held at the Monastery of Chevetogne (1942-1983) has been evaluated by Verdoodt [729]. A promising exchange of ideas has been developing between the Conference of European Churches, those Protestant and Orthodox churches affiliated with the WCC, and the Council of Catholic Bishops' Conferences in Europe [715].

Within North America, including both Canada and the United States, there has not been a comprehensive study on ecumenism since the 1970s. Cavert's volume covering the years 1900-1970 [734] is a standard source, though its scope excludes Orthodox and Catholics. A more recent work by Cuthbert on the Caribbean concentrating on the years 1957 to 1977 appeared in 1986 [735]. The North American Faith and Order Conference held in Oberlin in 1957 was an important American event but lacked follow-up [738, 872].

For Asia and the Middle East in particular there are several important publications. Ecumenical activities within India [745, 746, 748] are also well documented. The particular challenges of ecumenism in Asia where Christianity (apart from the Philippines) is a minority religion are documented [740, 741, 743, 747]. Two volumes, one by Zoghby [515] and one by Corbon [742], explore the particular characteristics of ecumenism in the Middle East against the background of Muslim societies. Thanks to the efforts of the publishing house of the Maryknoll community, Orbis Books, a complete record in English has been made available of the first seven theological consultations of EATWOT (Ecumenical Association of Third World Theologians) [753-759], an organization which has contributed to lessening the dominance of North Atlantic theology in ecumenism.

Three documents produced in different settings have had a notable impact on recent ecumenical exchange. To mark the 450th anniversary of the Reformation document known as the Augsburg Confession (*Confessio Augustana*) of 1530 a number of symposia were held especially in Germany and America [760-800]. It was hoped that the Roman Catholic Church might recognize as doctrinally acceptable the teaching of the Augsburg Confession. Publications describing these discussions are numerous. The ultimate reluctance of the Catholic leadership to make this gesture which many considered an ideal opportunity for ecumenical rapprochement was the start of chilly disillusionment that marked Catholic ecumenism's entering a wintry season. The cool reaction of the Vatican's Congregation for the Doctrine of the Faith to bilateral statements such as the *Final Report* has also contributed to a feeling of frustration among ecumenists. A second document known as the Leuenberg Agreement, completed in 1973, is not widely known in the English-speaking world. It is a declaration of church fellowship among the Lutheran, Reformed and United churches in Europe. The translation and English commentary edited by Rusch and Martensen [785] is the only major English guide to its genesis and significance. But especially in the German-speaking churches the text received close analysis. Finally, a third text, a specifically American venture, is the original 1970 *Plan of Union* drawn up by the Consultation on Church Union (COCU). After failure to obtain widespread Protestant support for the original proposal the plan was reworked into an agreement on covenanting [791]. In 1985, Moede, one of the main supporters of the COCU union plan, published a clear account about the various stages of the process [797]. Another ecumenical text, the Lima document on *Baptism, Eucharist and Ministry*, has occasioned more ecumenical publications than any other multilateral text in modern times. Literature relating to the Lima document is described later in the doctrinal section on sacraments.

# Doctrinal Issues

Not surprisingly, nearly one third of the publications cited in this bibliography, some 545 books, are classified under the general heading of "doctrinal issues" [801-1345]. Some 115 entries, or forty percent in this category [801-915], are theoretical explanations of unity, specifically visible unity. Several publications concentrate especially on what unity meant for the authors of the New Testament [801, 832, 834, 864]. Some address the New Testament concept of communion or fellowship (*koinonia*) [808, 828, 830, 891, 892], a concept that appears again in studies on ecclesiology. Several books on unity are especially interesting because of the relatively early dates of publication, for instance, one edited by Casper published in war-torn Vienna in 1940 [827] and another composed in 1948 by Lambert Beauduin, the founder of Chevetogne, during Catholicism's pre-ecumenical days [811]. Works by two other progressive pre-Vatican II Catholics are notable: Adam [803] and Aubert [806, 807]. Another early contribution from Protestants is the publication of the proceedings of the North American Conference of Faith and Order held in Oberlin, Ohio, in 1957, *The Nature of the Unity We Seek* [872].

In recent years one concrete proposal for achieving visible unity has received notable attention, the volume jointly authored by Fries and Rahner [841] *Unity of the Church - An Actual Possibility* (original German in 1983). This work outlines eight theses that, if agreed upon, could (so argued the authors) achieve reunion of the churches. A common strand that runs through this book and most of the other books in this category is that unity is both a given (*Gabe*) and a task to be achieved (*Aufgabe*) [850]. In 1989 Raiser argues that a paradigm shift had emerged in the 1980s resulting in a new way of perceiving church unity [886]. A familiar theme is the necessary coexistence of unity amid diversity argued by Congar [828] and Cullmann [834], though Kinnamon [854] has recently stressed the limits of diversity. The publication by Lengsfeld [862] may ultimately be recognized as one of the principal works in the theology of ecumenism from the twentieth century.

Ecumenical literature has also produced notable theological reflections on the dialogic process as such, studying how the practice of dialogue increasingly influenced the way theology has been done in the second half of this century. Two major theologians representing the Protestant and Catholic traditions, Barth and von Balthasar, appealed to the concept of dialogue as the organizational principle for their corresponding reflections [918]. The model of theological dialogue contrasts dramatically, as Brosseder notes [924], to the flawed models of polemics, irenicism and prosyletism. The title of Wacker's *Theologie als ökumenischer Dialog* [958] expresses succinctly the new model.

Special interest has been expressed for dialogue in "local ecumenism" [921, 922]. In the earlier days of ecumenism, certainly before Vatican II, the more typical method consisted of comparative theology whereby theologians of two churches would independently express their own traditions' views on Scripture, church, justification or whatever. Typical examples of this "double soliloquy" approach are noted [926, 931]. *Festschriften*, by the very nature of their literary genre, tend to promote this model. Nine such multi-authored volumes are listed in this section [916, 925, 936, 937, 944, 945, 948, 949, 960].

Among the books on dialogue as theology, some basic study guides are suitable for group discussions, in English [938, 939, 962] and in German [956]. Books that provide the best insights into dialogue tend to be the works of individual theologians rather than joint explorations. Two of the best are Thils in 1960 [954] and Sesboüé in 1990 [953]. More rare are reflections on the trans-cultural nature of the dialogic process, with one notable exception being the volume by the Indian Christian M.M. Thomas [955]. Another unique study on dialogue written by Willaime, a sociological analyst from Strasbourg [961], is one that accounts for non-theological factors in the search for unity and the quest for identity.

Fifty-two notable books on the nature of the church or ecclesiology have been identified. This area of investigation is heavily dominated by Catholics. Some of these studies that enrich the ecumenical movement explore the reality of church in the New Testament [963, 986]. Others use the Eastern or Orthodox insights into eucharistic ecclesiology as a starting point. The ecclesiology of communion is highlighted in the study on the writings of the Orthodox theologian John Zizioulas [966] and in two comprehensive studies on the church in Orthodoxy [981, 998] (all three written by Roman Catholics). Communion ecclesiology is analyzed in depth by the well-known ecumenist Tillard [1009]. Recently two new ecclesiological interests, especially among Catholics, partly because of the influence of communion ecclesiology, have been the exploration of the "local" (or "particular") church [858, 972, 989, 997, 1002] and the church understood as "sacrament" [990, 1001]. Catholic theologians have also found themselves obliged to compare the ecclesiologies of Vatican I and Vatican II and to explain continuity amid discontinuity [969, 976, 977, 982]. Another special interest of ecumenical ecclesiologists has been the exploration of the "catholicity" of the church [968, 979, 984]. Among the publications on ecclesiology, two have received wide attention and favorable reception, the volumes by Küng [991] and Dulles [980]. Probably no other area of contemporary theology better reflects the shift from polemics to mutual dialogue than the field of ecclesiology.

Doctrinal literature has concentrated on specific themes, some of which have been at the center of disagreements among Christians for centuries. Recent ecumenical studies on justification or righteousness by ecumenical consultations were anticipated by the studies of Moeller and Philips [1017] and by the monograph by Küng comparing the teaching on justification in the Council of Trent and in Barth [1016]. In 1985 the Lutheran and Catholic Consultation in the USA published an important agreed statement and background papers on "justification by faith" [1015] which prompted further reflections on its New Testament foundations [1019] and its connection to Luther's views [1021]. The newly reconstituted international Anglican/Roman Catholic Commission (ARCIC-II) published a similar, if somewhat less comprehensive, study on "salvation" in 1987 [1020].

The WCC general assembly in Vancouver (1983) reflected on the meaning of "a common understanding of the apostolic faith" and urged its Faith and Order Commission to give high priority in the future to a study "Towards the Common Expression of the Apostolic Faith Today." Works connected with this project have been appearing [1022-1038]. Linked to this undertaking are several studies on the ongoing significance of the second ecumenical council of Constantinople (A.D. 381) whose sixteenth centenary was celebrated in 1981 [1023, 1024, 1031, 1035, 1055]. An earlier attempt of expressing jointly today the apostolic faith was the Feiner and Vischer "common catechism" (or more accurately *Neues Glaubensbuch*) published by a team of Protestant and Catholic theologians [1027]. At a higher level *Ökumenische Dogmatik* [1036] by the distinguished Lutheran professor Edmund Schlink (with help from an Orthodox and a Catholic) is a model of how apostolic faith might be freshly articulated in modern categories.

Strange to say, given the centrality of the Bible for Christian belief, there has been a paucity of ecumenical studies on the role of Scripture. Only six publications are noted, two of which might be judged as making an important contribution to the topic [1040, 1041]. Also useful are the acts of the 1986 symposium organized by the Orthodox Center in Chambésy. However, this publication focused exclusively on the Old Testament and included ecumenical reflections on the biblical accounts of creation [1039].

Two additional categories of doctrinal studies are devoted to theological elaboration on the persons of Christ and the Holy Spirit. The Lund meeting of Faith and Order (1952) urged the preparation of a study for Montreal (1963) on "Christ and the Church" [1052]. One author, Simonson, has argued that a notable shift in Faith and Order Christology occurred at Lund [1050]. The Lutheran World Federation sponsored a lengthy study from 1964 to 1969 to explore "The Quest for True Humanity and the Lordship of Christ" [1045]. Despite the fact that members of the Ancient Oriental Orthodox churches have for centuries been dubbed "monophysites" by other Christians, modern research, reflected in the symposium on "Christ in East and West" held in New York (1985), has effectively shown that the label is a misnomer [1047]. Ecumenical discussions on the Holy Spirit have also been fruitful in the last several decades. A particularly useful investigation, sponsored by the WCC, has addressed the thorny problem of the *filioque* addition to the Nicene-Constantinopolitan creed [1060]. Also the Groupe des Dombes produced a far-reaching document on the Holy Spirit, the church and the sacraments [1057]. Likewise an Australian theologian has studied how documents of the Faith and Order Commission from 1927 to 1983 have described the role of the Holy Spirit in the church [1058]. Several international congresses have been held to discuss the relationship of the Holy Spirit to the church [1054, 1055, 1059]. The Societas Oecumenica of Europe devoted its second consultation in 1983 to the theme "The Holy Spirit and the Unity of the Church" [1061].

Interest in "spiritual ecumenism" has generated another corpus of doctrinal literature. Paul Couturier, about whom several biographical accounts exist [400, 436, 437], is considered the father of "spiritual ecumenism" [1076]. Other publications on spiritual ecumenism have expanded on the notion [1062, 1070, 1078]. Although traditionally Protestants have shied away from the term "spirituality," the concept has now been addressed by a WCC consultation held in 1984 [1074], by individual Protestant writers [1071], and even by contributors to a dictionary of Christian spirituality under the auspices of a Protestant publishing house [1080]. Some writing on prayer and spirituality is related to the charismatic renewal movement [1073], some to the writings of the Taizé monks Schutz [1072] and Thurian [1075]. The Faith and Order Commission promoted study of intercessory prayer [1079] and urged all its member churches to adopt an ecumenical prayer cycle [1067, 1081] to ensure that each week the needs of various parts of the world community would be commemorated.

Publications on sacramental theology and specifically on baptism, the Lord's Supper, and ordination number have been central to doctrinal studies from an ecumenical perspective. Despite a scarcity of full-length ecumenical studies on sacramental theory or on the theology of worship, some volumes can be noted. Hotz, a Swiss Jesuit, published a study in 1979 that contrasts the different ways in which sacraments are understood in churches of the East and West [1095]. Addressing a directly pastoral challenge, an Orthodox hierarch and a Catholic professor jointly published a concise handbook which outlines for German-speaking congregations the distinctive convictions and differing legislations of their churches regarding sacramental sharing and practices. A Catholic priest published a sympathetic study on the views of sacramental theology of Thurian, sub-prior at Taizé. The Swiss Reformed theologian von Allmen has written about what he calls *prophétisme sacramentel* [1093]. But the leading work in this domain is a Heidelberg dissertation by Hempelmann which outlines the concept of sacramental theology in the Lutheran/Catholic dialogues [1094].

On baptism, possibly because a broad consensus on its significance already exists, there have been few ecumenical studies, apart from reactions to the baptism section of the Lima document. One exception is the work by Wainwright, a British Methodist now teaching in the USA, whose treatment of Christian initiation is thoroughly ecumenical [1104]. Two of the Regensburg ecumenical symposia, largely exchanges between Orthodox and Catholics, explored baptism and chrismation (confirmation) [1103] as well as penance and confession of sins understood as a second baptism [1102].

The literature on the eucharist or the Lord's Supper and eucharistic hospitality or intercommunion is more extensive. *Modern Eucharistic Agreement* [1118] reproduces four ecumenical consensus statements. Five Anglican critiques of these agreements appeared shortly thereafter [1107]. The Groupe des Dombes [1114] and the US Lutheran/Catholic Consultation [1109] both published influential statements on the eucharist. A total of seven distinct bilateral dialogue groups in the USA have published consensus statements on eucharist [1126]. Several studies return to the New Testament for elucidation of eucharistic teaching [1113, 1120]. And the much debated sense in which the eucharist is a "sacrifice" continues to prompt arguments even into the twentieth century especially by Reformed and Lutheran theologians [1105, 1115, 1116, 1127]. The clearest and most comprehensive theological exposition on eucharistic theology by an individual ecumenist is the publication by Thurian [1127]. Publications on the Lord's Supper tend to be expositions of specific ecclesiastical legislation. Orthodox and Catholics have published widely on this topic often in the attempt to articulate their churches' official opposition to table-fellowship prior to unanimity of dogmatic beliefs. Some individual Catholic theologians, such as Fries [1135] and Murray [1137], have argued that their church's official views seem unnecessarily rigid.

Closely connected with the ecumenical topic of eucharist and eucharistic sharing is the notion of ordained ministry (*Amt*) which in some churches is identified as ordination to the priesthood. Writing on ordained ministry was originally formulated in the mind-set of what the Germans call *Kontroverstheologie*. It has produced its own literature including agreed statements [1149-1171] that seek to explain the nature of ordained ministry. A handy collection of four agreed statements on ordained ministry was published by the SPCK [1161]. Within this central ecumenical topic, one specific problem has troubled the churches since the Reformation, namely, one church's "recognition" of ordinations effected in a separated church. Older terminology asked whether or not a person can be considered to have been ordained "validly." The decision by Pope Leo XIII not to recognize Anglican Orders, despite the recommendation by his team of experts that he should have done so, has remained a troublesome irritant. Recently Tavard, a Catholic theologian, published a clear account of the historical and theological issues of recognition of ministries and attempts to show how Leo's decision has failed to gain acceptance within the broader *sensus fidelium* [1168]. In 1973, the Groupe des Dombes formulated a specific proposal for the mutual recognition of orders [1158]. Also six ecumenical institutes in Germany published a similar joint proposal in that same year [1166].

Among the "episcopal" churches, concern about the specific ministry of the bishop (*Bischofsamt* or *Amt der Einheit*) has produced its own considerable literature. Common explanations on the origin of this ministry have argued that, in the course of history, bishops became identified with the persons in the New Testament who were said to exercise a ministry of oversight (*episkopé*). The Groupe des Dombes published a far-reaching agreed statement which expands the notion of *episkopé* to include not only modern bishops but other pastoral workers in the church [1157]. The Faith and Order Commission published a collection of essays on *episkopé* in ecumenical perspective [1154]. Gassmann and Meyer edited several statements on both this form of ministry and papal ministry [1156]. Episcopal ministry is a dialogue topic where commonly shared conclusions have emerged, through the use of similar methodologies for interpreting the New Testament and the practices of the early church.

Whether or not women are "validly" or appropriately ordained to the ministerial priesthood is a sensitive and much debated issue especially among the Orthodox, Anglicans and Roman Catholics. From a growing corpus of literature, especially in journals, we have signalled out three books as especially relevant since they address the question ecumenically [1172-1174]. For a comprehensive list of ecumenical publications (mostly articles), some of which are complete ecumenical consensus statements or at least segments of agreed statements, one will need to consult specific bibliographies. The WCC has tried to broaden the topic by identifying this question as part of a larger issue, the "Community of Women and Men in the Church" which is described later in this chapter.

The 1982 Lima document *Baptism, Eucharist and Ministry* [1175] adopted by the Faith and Order Commission has generated more subsequent literature than any single ecumenical text of this century. After the text's adoption for study, the Commission asked churches to respond regarding "the extent to which your church can recognize in this text the faith of the Church throughout the ages." Hundreds of official responses from WCC member churches have been received and have been reproduced in six volumes [1193] together with other responses, all part of that growing literature on reception of the Lima document [1176-1196].

One of the most urgent doctrinal and practical questions in church unity remains how to respond pastorally to those planning to enter or who have already entered into a "mixed marriage" or an ecumenical marriage where each spouse is a member of a different church. The issues relate not only to the celebration of the wedding ceremony itself, but to the ways in which the couple (and their children) will worship, participate in sacramental rituals, or be further instructed doctrinally. Reformed, Lutheran, Anglican and Catholic theologians, especially in Germany, have collaborated on ecumenical studies on marriage. The Irish School of Ecumenics has argued that in ecumenical marriages the churches need to advance "beyond tolerance" [1210]. Several studies also address the differing doctrines and disciplinary traditions regarding the possibility of divorce and second marriage [1201, 1202].

Another area that dominates modern publications is grouped together under the general heading of authority in the church, its sources and vehicles of expression. This was the issue addressed by ARCIC-I's *Final Report* in its so-called Venice statement [1222]. The US Lutheran/Catholic Consultation confronted this issue under the heading "Teaching Authority and Infallibility in the Church" [1218]. A topic related to authority which has seen a growth of interest is that of reception, in other words, how does the church at large "receive" what has been formulated by its leadership whether in councils, in doctrinal pronouncements or in statements formulating ethical judgments. This topic of reception has also been studied by the Lutheran World Federation [1227], the Societas Oecumenica of Europe [1226] and various Catholic theologians [1223, 1224].

Historically a much vexed issue has been the authority of the popes or those who understand themselves to be exercising in the church universal a "Petrine ministry," which is seen to be a service comparable to the kind of comprehensive pastoral care for the wider community associated with the Apostle Peter in the early church. Ecumenical literature has approached this from two angles: Petrine ministry [1228-1238] and papal primacy [1239-1260]. Whereas a surprising willingness among various churches has emerged in many quarters to accept the notion that there could or should be a kind of Petrine ministry even today, the concentration of this ministry in the papal office (*Papstamt*), especially as it has come to be expressed since the late nineteenth century in Roman Catholicism, is highly controverted. The elements of disagreement are outlined clearly, for instance, in the US Lutheran/Catholic agreed statement [1243], in the text produced by the Groupe des Dombes [1247], and quite recently in a document written in France by a mixed group of Orthodox and Catholic theologians [1255]. Works published by individual theologians such as, among Catholics, the volume by Tillard [1259], two works by Granfield [1245, 1246], and the study by Ohlig [1253] as well as, among Orthodox, the collaborative volume [1251] are essential reading. Ecumenical books on papal infallibility, reacting to what Vatican I (1869-1870) formulated, remain part of the future agenda. The literature on authority concludes with reference to several works on councils, those "ecumenical" councils of the past as well as conceivable universal assemblies in the future [1261-1264]. Mühlen was among the first to imagine what might be the shape of a truly ecumenical council of all believers [1263]. A colloquium held in 1977 at the University of Notre Dame sketched what might be the tasks of an imagined Vatican III [1264].

# Mission and Ethical Issues

In additional to the large amount of publications on doctrinal issues, another growing area of ecumenical research focuses on the mission of the church and on ethical concerns related to a wide spectrum of issues including the role of women in church and society, international social justice, peace, and the protection of natural resources.

Even after the formal merger of the International Missionary Council with the World Council of Churches in 1961, mission concerns have continued to play a central role in ecumenical priorities of member churches and other churches. The WCC journal *International Review of Mission* [117] attests to a continuing lively interest in mission among Christians and provides valuable bibliographical information on world-wide missionary endeavors. The corpus of missionary literature reflecting ecumenical sensitivity includes a variety of Christian perspectives. One early, classic formulation of mission theology articulated in an ecumenical setting is the position paper adopted by the International Missionary Council at its Willingen meeting of 1952 [1270].

Since its merger with the WCC the responsibilities of the International Missionary Council has been subsumed under the WCC's Commission (formerly Division) of World Mission and Evangelism. Meetings of this commission in Melbourne (1980) [1280] and San Antonio, USA (1989) [1279] produced valuable reports and position papers that are paradigmatic of the best ecumenical mission strategy. In many ways these approaches have been influenced by two early publications that stressed the interdependence of mission and unity, namely those of Bishop Lesslie Newbigin [1273] and Van Dusen [1278]. It is informative that Emilio Castro, general secretary of the WCC, chose the theme of mission as the subject of his doctoral dissertation and other recent publications [1266, 1267]. For those searching for a general history of the missionary thrust within the ecumenical movement one can highly recommend the study by Seumois [1275]. To show how one's confessional allegiance influences one's understanding of spreading the Word of God, Stadler has compared the official statements on mission and dialogue that were independently formulated by the WCC and the Roman Catholic Church [1276]. Still a helpful reference work, at least for ecumenical developments up to the year 1971, is the *Concise Dictionary of the Christian World Mission* [1272].

Among the ethical concerns one of the foremost has been the condition of women. The 1981 Sheffield Report of the WCC on "The Community of Women and Men in the Church" was a milestone in ecumenical reflection on the status of women in church and society [1290]. The report's focus is much wider than access of women to ordination in the church which is a distinct issue [629, 642, 1172-1174, 1344]. Prior to the Sheffield Report there had been an important study in 1954 by Bliss reporting on the status of women in forty-five different countries [1282]. In 1965 the WCC held a consultation on the functions of the deaconess in various settings throughout the world. The Australian Council of Churches' Commission on the Status of Women published in 1977 a study with the provocative title *Deliver Us From Eve* [1291]. In the same year that the Sheffield Report was published there appeared a study showing what was the situation of women working for international ecumenical organizations, especially the WCC and the Lutheran World Federation [1287]. There was also a follow-up meeting to the Sheffield Consultation organized by the WCC in Prague, 1985, whose results were published [1281]. Several individual theologians published analyses and assessments of the Sheffield Report [1283, 1288]. The Women's Commission of the Ecumenical Association of Third World Theologians (EATWOT) addressed the topic of women in society and religion at its 1986 meeting in Mexico [1285].

A comprehensive, ecumenically balanced three-volume handbook on Christian ethics was jointly prepared by Protestant and Catholic publishing houses [1294]. Two other dictionaries of Christian ethics appeared between 1967 and 1979 which reflect ecumenical concerns [1296, 1300]. As Raiser [886] astutely observed, greater emphasis on social and ethical concerns has been characteristic of the paradigm shift that occurred both in the ecumenical movement as a whole and more specifically within the WCC. The history of the WCC's involvement in political or economic matters is quite complex and somewhat controversial. Those desiring further information on those matters can find appropriate entries in the *Dictionary of the Ecumenical Movement* [72]. As recent disagreements within the WCC illustrate, not all Christians feel comfortable with ecumenical activities that seem to opt for one or another political or economic options. Publications by ethicists with ecumenical credentials such as Preston [1322] and Hudson [1335] have eloquently defended such involvement.

Peace studies has been another rich area for research by associations such as the WCC [1305], the Conference of European Churches [1307], the Evangelische Kirche in Deutschland [1304, 1310], the Centre Orthodoxe du Patriarchat Oecuménique in Chambésy [1303], the Moscow Patriarchate [1311], and the Italian Ecumenical Association [1308, 1309]. Two leading ecumenists of their day representing the Catholic and Reformed traditions respectively, Bea and Visser 't Hooft, collaborated in 1966 on a major ecumenical publication entitled *Peace Among Christians* [1302].

As early as 1946 the WCC, still in the process of formation, and the International Missionary Council established a Commission of the Churches on International Affairs which received consultative status with the United Nations. This Commission held an important meeting at St. Pölten in 1974 on human rights and Christian responsibility. This was followed up in 1977 by a symposium in Gilion, Switzerland, on militarism. The quadrennial reports of the Commission of the Churches on International Affairs have been published [1332] and van der Bent published a brief account of that commission's history [1329]. The WCC's Commission on the Churches' Participation in Development that was established in 1968 has produced several important publications [1321, 1323, 1326, 1338]. Within the framework of the Commission on the Churches' Participation in Development an Advisory Group on Economic Matters was established in 1979 that has published several studies in a new series entitled "An Ecumenical Approach to Economics" [1312, 1313, 1320, 1321]. These volumes argue for Christians' need to be involved in the new world order. Likewise, the Commission (formerly Division) on Inter-Church Aid, Refugee and World Service established in 1944, has been deeply involved in *diakonia* [1325]. Also informative is the history of the agency established by the See of Rome and the WCC known as the Joint Committee on Society, Development and Peace (SODEPAX) which functioned from 1968 to the end of 1980 when it was terminated by mutual agreement. The dramatic account of the successes and failures of SODEPAX has been admirably narrated by Derr [1315]. Since the WCC general assembly in Vancouver in 1983 there has been a WCC Commission on Justice, Peace and the Integrity of Creation which understands these three as one reality.

Another ethical concern that has received ecumenical attention is racism. In 1969 the WCC Central Committee mandated the establishment of a Programme to Combat Racism in response to the urging of the Uppsala general assembly. Its work was helped by some earlier studies on the evil of racism that had been published in 1954 for UNESCO by Visser 't Hooft [1327] and by the WCC collecting ecumenical statements on race relations from 1937 to 1964 [1318].

Since the founding of the WCC there have been two World Conferences on Church and Society, one held in Geneva in 1966 [1330, 1345] and a second at the Massachusetts Institute of Technology in Cambridge, Massachusetts, in 1979 which discussed Faith, Science and the Future [1333, 1334]. These conferences continued discussions that were close to the heart of the Life and Work conferences held in Stockholm in 1925 and in Oxford in 1937 [1337]. In Roman Catholicism continued interest in the relationship of the church to the modern world has been promoted by studies on Vatican II's Pastoral Constitution on the Church in the Modern World (*Gaudium et Spes*) [1341]. The Italian [Catholic] Ecumenical Association has discussed such issues in six different  sessions [1299, 1308, 1309, 1324, 1339, 1340]. The Vereinigte Evangelisch-Lutherische Kirche Deutschlands has also addressed these matters [1328].

# Past as Prelude

The scope of ecumenical research has now become so vast that it is impossible for a single individual to aspire to mastering all its dimensions. The literature of ecumenism comprehends publications devoted to information data, to historical accounts of its emergence, to confessional descriptions of its nature, to bilateral explorations, to accounts of subtle variations in different geographical settings, to analyses of classical and modern texts, to reflections on the meaning of doctrines, and to Christian outreach in mission and in the modern world. This bibliographical tool aims at reclaiming the best of what the past has produced as a stimulus for discovering new ecumenical possibilities.

# 2

# Reference Materials

## Bibliographies

[1] American Theological Library Association. *The Ecumenical Movement: A Bibliography Selected from the ATLA Religion Database.* Chicago: American Theological Library Association, 1983.

> This computer generated author and subject index is drawn from the data available electronically in the publications *Religion Index One* [23] and *Religion Index Two* [24]. Printed supplements after 1983 have not been generated but persons with library access to the Wilson disk or online data can obtain this information updated each year. Subject classification is that of the US Library of Congress.

[2] *Bibliografia Missionaria.* Vol. 1- . Vatican City: Pontificia Università Urbaniana, 1937- ; annual.

> Published by the Pontificia Biblioteca Missionaria of the Vatican's Congregation for the Evangelization of People, this bibliography includes a section on "Ecumenical Dialogues and Missions". The well-indexed listings include useful information about a wide variety of churches in various countries. Also included is a section on dialogue with living faiths.

[3] *Bibliografía teológica comentada del área iberoamericana.* Vol. 1- . Buenos Aires: ISEDET, 1973- ; annual.

> This valuable bibliographical tool for Latin America is published by the Instituto Superior Evangélico de Estudios Teológicos. It

divides data into six sections: social sciences, practical theology, Church history (including ecumenical history), Bible, biblical background, and systematic theology. [ISEDET, Camacuá 282; 1406 Buenos Aires, Argentina].

[4] *Bibliographia Internationalis Spiritualitatis (BIS)*. Vol. 1- . Rome: Pontificium Institutum Spiritualitatis O.C.D., 1966- ; annual.

Although the main focus is on the history of spirituality, each year has a section of some 200 items on ecumenism, Orthodoxy, Protestantism, etc. The well-indexed publication is produced by the Carmelite order at the Teresianum in Rome. [Piazza S. Pancrazio 5A; I-00152 Rome].

[5] Brandreth, Henry R. T. *Unity and Reunion: A Bibliography*. 2nd ed. London: Adam and Charles Black, 1948.

The first edition of this valuable reference work appeared in 1945. This is a non-judgmental survey of ecumenical literature since the nineteenth century. This book provides evidence of how Catholics conceived of ecumenism in the mid 1940s.

[6] *Bulletin Signalétique: Histoire et Sciences des Religions.* Vol. 1- . Paris: Centre de Documentation Sciences Humaines, 1961- ; quarterly.

Formerly known as *Bulletin Signalétique: Sciences Religieuses*, this bibliographical tool reports on the French-speaking world quite well. Its system of indexing and of cross-referencing is highly idiosyncratic, but serious students will profit from using this reference aid critically. Beginning with vol. 45 (1991) it is now known as *FRANCIS: Bulletin Signalétique*.

[7] *Catholic Periodical and Literature Index*. Vol. 1- . Haverford, PA: Catholic Library Association, 1930- ; bi-monthly with annual cumulations.

Previously known as *Catholic Periodic Index* and *Guide to Catholic Literature*, this bibliography is less comprehensive than *Religion Index One* [23] or the *Bulletin Signalétique* [6]. One specific advantage is its coverage of leading North American Catholic newspapers and devotional publications.

[8] *Centro Pro Unione Bulletin*. No. 1- . Rome: Centro pro Unione,

1969- ; bi-annual.

This truly remarkable bibliographical tool covers the latest periodical and monograph publications with special attention to bilateral and multilateral consulations. The bulletin regularly updates the material found in Puglisi [22]. It also lists Centro's latest acquisitions (classified according to Geneva's WCC library). The autumn 1981 edition (no. 20), subsequently updated, provided an international directory of ecumenical research centers and a list of ecumenical and theological journals. It also updates material listed in Kelliher [182]. The Centro Pro Unione operates a first-rate research library in Rome under the Franciscan Friars of the Atonement. [Via S. Maria dell'Anima, 30; I-00186 Rome].

[9] Crow, Paul A., Jr. *The Ecumenical Movement in Bibliographical Outline*. New York: National Council of the Churches of Christ in the USA, 1965.

This much cited bibliography of books and articles has become outdated but still serves a purpose by its references to earlier literature. The material was carefully organized around ten headings. No critical judgments are included. The compiler aims to improve upon Brandeth [5] and Senaud [26].

[10] Delfs, Hermann. *Ökumenische Literaturkunde*. Ed. D.F. Siegmund-Schultze. Schriften des ökumenischen Archivs Soest, Bd. III. Soest: Mocker & Jahn, 1966.

The bibliographical material cited here is carefully organized into some 100 categories, stressing the history of the ecumenical movement, the pre-history of the WCC, various church traditions, and unity efforts country by country. There is a comprehensive index of subjects and names.

[11] Dulles, Avery, and Granfield, Patrick. *The Church: A Bibliography*. Wilmington, DL: Michael Glazier, 1985.

The two American Catholic theologians prepared this bibliography of books and articles for some fifty-one areas of ecclesiology. The works cited are written by members of most confessions. Although they disclaim covering the ecumenical movement (p. 77), a large number of references pertain to church unity.

[12] García Cortés, Carlos. *Selección bibliográfica sobre ecumenismo en lengua española*. Repertorios bibliograficos 5. Salamanca: Instituto Pontificio San Pio X, 1969.

This critical bibliography of Spanish publications (many of which appeared first in other languages) organizes its selection as follows: general studies; church denominations; ecumenical movement; and the practice of ecumenism.

[13] Gorman, G.E., and Gorman, Lyn. *Theological and Religious Reference Materials: General Resources and Biblical Studies*. Bibliographies and Indexes in Religious Studies, Number 1. Westport, CT and London: Greenwood Press, 1984.

The first volume in this series of bibliographical aids has set the standard for subsequent volumes. The first section of the book includes a number of general works that sometimes directly, sometimes indirectly, can assist researchers in ecumenism. See also the companion volume [14].

[14] Gorman, G.E., and Gorman, Lyn. *Theological and Religious Reference Materials: Systematic Theology and Church History*. Bibliographies and Indexes in Religious Studies, Number 2. Westport, CT and London: Greenwood Press, 1985.

The second volume in this series includes a special section on "Missions/Ecumenism" (pp. 289-318) which contains helpful material for the ecumenist. Some of the books cited in the doctrinal theology and the church history sections pertain to church unity also. See also the companion volume [13].

[15] *Index to Book Reviews in Religion (IBRR): An Author, Title, Reviewer, Series and Annual Classified Index to Reviews of Books Published in and of Interest to the Field of Religion*. Vol. 1- . Evanston, IL: American Theological Library Association, 1986- ; quarterly with cumulative volume.

Currently edited by Edwina A. Schaufler, this invaluable biliographical tool is a offshoot of *Religion Index One* [23] which previously also included book reviews. The classified index section 150 in the cumulative volume edition lists the newest books on ecumenism. The ATLA Religious Database is available online through Wilsonline or WilsonDisc. [820 Church St., Suite 300, Evanston, IL 60201-3707].

[16] *International Ecumenical Bibliography; Internationale ökumenische Bibliographie, 1962-77.* 16 vols. Munich: Kaiser; Mainz: M. Grünewald, 1967-1983.

The first double volume (1/2), published in 1967 by the University of Tübingen's library, covered publications of the years 1962-63. Vol. 15/16 appeared in 1983 and covered the years 1976-77. Each volume surveyed books, articles, and contained first-rate indexes of authors and subjects in four languages. Its disappearance from the scholarly scene was an enormous loss.

[17] Istavridis, Vasilios T. *Bibliographia tis Ikoumenikis Kiniseos, 1960-1970.* Athens: Theologia, 1972.

This 78 page bibliography on the ecumenical movement first appeared in the journal *Theologia*. The entries are predominantly in Greek but there is also a selection of works in other European languages. For a more complete bibliography of Eastern churches see Santos Hernández [534].

[18] Kasch, Wilhelm F., *et al. Ökumenische Bibliographie: Religionsuntericht, Religionspädagogik, Christliche Erziehung.* Paderborn: F. Schöningh, 1976.

Some fifty ecumenical collaborators prepared this guide for teaching religion in the German school system. It provides information about reference materials, journals, historical accounts, theory and praxis, use of media, institutes, etc. Some of the data is useful even beyond the confines of Germany.

[19] Lescrauwaet, Josephus Franciscus. *Critical Bibliography of Ecumenical Literature.* Bibliographia ad usum seminariorum 7. Nijmegen: Bestel Centrale, 1965.

This bibliographical series was undertaken by the Dutch Association of Seminary and Monastery Libraries. Section one concentrates on general literature of the churches; section two cites works on the ecumenical movement. Only 300 works are cited and extend only up to 1964.

[20] Nielsen, Johannes Albert. *Dansk okumenisk bibliografi 1910-1974: med et udvag of nordisk litteratur.* Copenhagen: Det okumenische Fallesrad, 1978.

This bibliography of the ecumenical movement covers Danish publications dating back to 1910.

[21] *Oecumene* 1. *International Bibliography 1975-1976* (=RIC Supplément 31-34). Eds. Marie Zimmermann, *et al*. Strasbourg: CERDIC, 1977.
*Oecumene* 2. *International Bibliography 1977* (=RIC Supplément 43-44), ibid., 1978.
*Oecumene* 3. *International Bibliography 1978-1980* (=RIC Supplément 53-56), ibid., 1980.
*Oecumene* 4. *International Bibliography 1980-1983* (=RIC Supplément 80-83), ibid., 1983.

Part of the RIC (Répertoire bibliographique des institutions chrétiennes) computer-driven bibliographical information published at the University of Strasbourg's CERDIC (Centre de Recherches et de Documentation des Institutions Chrétiennes), these volumes include evaluations of articles, identification of authors' confessional affiliation, authors' country of origin, etc. Although the indexing system is idiosyncratic, it merits the effort to master. The range of literature includes English, French, German, Italian and Spanish. See also Pigault [1141] for eucharist.

[22] Puglisi, James F., and Voicu, Sever J. *A Bibliography of Interchurch and Interconfessional Theological Dialogue*. Rome: Centro pro Unione, 1984.

Published under the same auspices as the *Centro Pro Unione, Bulletin* [8] which regularly updates this volume, this bibliographical tool succeeded *A Workbook of Bibliographies for the Study of Interchurch Dialogues* (1978). It indexed articles in more than 100 journals and reported on over 130 ongoing bilateral dialogues.

[23] *Religion Index One: Periodicals: A Subject Index to Periodical Literature Including an Author / Editor Index and a Scripture Index*. Ed. by Don Haymes. Vol. 1- . Evanston, IL: American Theological Library Association, 1949- ; semi annual fascicles with cumulative volume every two years.

Formerly known as *Index to Religious Periodical Literature* (1949-1976), this electronically produced survey increases in value year by year as the number of journals surveyed is 500. The material for 1949-1959 (vols. 1-4) has been revised to follow

*RIO*'s current standards. See also [15, 24]. The ATLA Religious Database is available online through Wilsonline or WilsonDisc. [820 Church St., Suite 300, Evanston, IL 60201-3707].

[24] *Religion Index Two: Multi-Author Works*. Vol. 1- . Ed. by Erica Treesh. Evanston, IL: American Theological Library Association, 1980- ; annual.

This twin publication of *Religion Index One* [23] was originally known as *Religion Index Two: Festschriften.* It provides excellent international coverage of multi-author works (of more than three authors), *Festschriften*, proceedings or regularly or irregularly published series and annuals. The ATLA Religious Database is available online through Wilsonline or WilsonDisc. [820 Church St., Suite 300, Evanston, IL 60201-3707].

[25] *Répertoire bibliographique des institutions chrétiennes: Bibliographical Repertory of Christian Institutions*. Strasbourg: CERDIC Publications, 1968- ; annual.

This computer-driven bibliographical source is published at the University of Strasbourg's CERDIC (Centre de Recherches et de Documentation des Institutions Chrétiennes). The coverage of literature now includes English, French, German, Italian and Spanish with a large section on ecumenism. See also *Oecumene* [21]. [9 place de l'Université, F-67084 Strasbourg].

[26] Senaud, Auguste, ed. *Christian Unity: A Bibliography*. Geneva: YMCA, 1937.

Although not useful for contemporary literature this early bibliography provided selected titles about international relations between the churches as well as refrences to the international Christian movements. This is still useful for earlier developments.

[27] Sutfin, Edward J., and Lavanoux, Maurice. *A Selected, Annotated Bibliography on Ecumenical and Related Matters*. Haverford, PA: Catholic Library Association, ca. 1968.

The 56 page critical bibliography up to 1966 appeared as a special issue of the journal *Liturgical Arts* (date not given). Although limited in scope it illustrates well how two Catholics evaluated publications on the ecumenical movement in the mid 1960s. Some of the annotations are very astute.

[28] Swinne, Axel Hilmar, ed. *Bibliographica Irenica, 1500-1970: Internationale Bibliographie zur Friedenswissenschaft, kirchliche und politische Einigungs- und Friedensbestrebungen, Oekumene und Völkerverständigung.* Studia Irenica 10. Hildesheim: Gerstenberg, 1977.

> For early literature ranging from the sixteenth to nineteenth century, this bibliography is a valuable source of information. The published books are arranged alphabetically by author but there is no index of subjects.

[29] World Council of Churches. *Classified Catalogue of the Ecumenical Movement.* 2 vols. Boston: G.K. Hall, 1972; *First Supplement*, 1981.

> The 1972 volume includes some 19,000 entries on ecumenism. The first supplement added another 13,000 entries. The indexing is arranged by name of the authors. Persons with computers are now able to have on-line access to the data-bank in Geneva that covers over 50,000 titles. See also [108].

# Documents and Texts

[30] Bell, George K. A., ed. *Documents on Christian Unity.* 4 vols. London: Oxford University Press, 1924-1958.

> The famous British ecumenist George Bell (1883-1958) prepared these classic collections of ecumenical texts, beginning with the early part of the twentieth century. Volumes 1 and 2 cover the 1920s and include 221 documents of Faith and Order, Lambeth Conference of 1920, and other texts of Catholic, Orthodox, Anglican interest. Volume 3 covers 1930-1948 and volume 4 the years 1948-1957. See also the series *Ecumenical Documents* sponsored by the Paulist Fathers [33, 38, 40, 682].

[31] Böhme, Kurt, ed. *Texte zur Geschichte der ökumenischen Bewegung: Verlautbarungen der weltkirchenkonferenzen 1910-1947.* Berlin: de Gruyter, 1948.

> This small publication (96 pp.) offers a useful collection of German and English texts from 1910 to 1947 drawn from the World Missionary Conference, the Life and Work Movement, Faith and Order and preparatory work for the WCC assembly in Amsterdam.

[32] Boyer, Carlo [Charles], and Belluci, Dino, eds. *Unità cristiana e movimento ecumenico.* Vol. 1. *1864-1961*; Vol. 2. *1961-1973.* Testi et Documenti 2, 10. Rome: Studium, 1963, 1975.

These two volumes contain documents from the See of Rome, from the WCC and various Anglican and Orthodox sources translated into Italian. There is no commentary or assessment. The first volume contains 42 documents or parts thereof, the second 112. There are brief chronological tables in each volume.

[33] Burgess, Joseph A., and Gros, Jeffrey, eds. *Building Unity: Ecumenical Dialogues with Roman Catholic Participation in the United States.* Ecumenical Documents IV. New York: Paulist, 1989.

This collection gives a cross section, though not complete publication, of recent official statements produced by American Catholics in dialogue with Anglicans, Baptists, Disciples of Christ, Lutherans, Methodists, Orthodox, Oriental Orthodox, and Presbyterian-Reformed. There are also three documents published by the National Council of the Churches of Christ in the USA. See also [38, 40, 682].

[34] Ehrenström, Nils. *Ecumenical Documents 1930-1983: Collected by Nils Ehrenström with a Bibliography by Habteab Tesfay.* Nordisk Ekumenisk Skriftserie 16. Uppsala: Nordisk Ekumeniska Institutet, 1987.

In 239 pages the author presents a wide cross-section of ecumenical texts spanning the years 1930 to 1983. The author served on the staff of the WCC for many years.

[35] Jaeger, Henry-Evgard. *Zeugnis für die Einheit: Geistliche Texte aus den Kirchen der Reformation.* 3 vols. Mainz: M. Grünewald, 1970-1972.

The volumes discuss in sequence the Reformation churches stemming from Lutheranism, Calvinism, and Anglicanism. The publication provides the reader with important primary sources.

[36] Krüger, Hanfried. *Ökumenische Bewegung 1963/64, 1964/68, 1969/72, 1973/74.* Beihefte zur Ökumenischen Rundschau, 3/4, 12/13, 28, 29. Stuttgart: Evangelisches Missionsverlag, 1966-1979.

These four volumes provide detailed accounts of ecumenical

activities from 1963 to 1974. The series was later discontinued. Although prepared for the Evangelische Kirche in Deutschland (EKD), the texts were addressed to a wider ecumenical audience.

[37] Meyer, Harding; Urban, Hans Jörg; and Vischer, Lukas, eds. *Dokumente wachsender Übereinstimmung: Sämtliche Berichte und Konsenstexte interkonfessionelles Gespräche auf Weltebene, 1931-1982.* Paderborn: Bonifatius; Frankfurt: O. Lembeck, 1983.

Published by the Faith and Order Commission in Geneva and ecumenical centers in Strasbourg, Paderborn and Rome, this valuable collection of worldwide ecumenical texts is more or less the equivalent of *Growth in Agreement* [38], the English text that unfortunately has numerous errors in production and indexing.

[38] Meyer, Harding, and Vischer, Lukas, eds. *Growth in Agreement: Reports and Agreed Statements of Ecumenical Conversations on a World Level.* Ecumenical Documents II. Faith and Order Paper 108. New York: Paulist; Geneva: World Council of Churches, 1984.

The twenty-seven documents from the 1970s and early 1980s are reproduced in their entirety in English translation where necessary. The texts are drawn from twelve different international bilateral dialogues as well as the Faith and Order's Lima Document *Baptism, Eucharist and Ministry.* Among the lengthiest and far-reaching texts are those of the Anglican-Roman Catholic and the Lutheran-Roman Catholic Commissions. There are production errors in the footnotes and indexes. See the other volumes in the series [33, 40, 682].

[39] Schweigart, Hans Günther, ed. *Weltweite Christenheit: Ein Quellenheft zur Ökumene und Weltmission.* Göttingen: Vandenhoeck und Ruprecht, 1965.

This high-level source book is designed for use by teachers and students in formal religious education classes of German Protestants. The documents are divided into four sections: the history of the ecumenical movement; new churches and mission today; conversation with Roman Catholicism; and dialogue with Judaism.

[40] Stransky, Thomas F., and Sheerin, John B., eds. *Doing the Truth in Charity: Statements of Pope Paul VI, Popes John Paul I, John Paul II, and the Secretariat for Promoting Christian Unity 1964-1980.*

Ecumenical Documents I. New York: Paulist, 1982.

This first of a multi-volume series of English texts covers 16 years since Vatican II's decree on ecumenism (1964). The volume contains official documents from various popes, the Roman Curia, especially the Vatican Secretariat for Promoting Christian Unity (SPCU). Some eighty pages are devoted to contacts with the Orthodox Church. There is an historical sketch on the growth of the SPCU. The volume has been justly criticized for frequently giving only excerpts from documents rather than citing the whole text. This is avoided in later volumes in the series [33, 38, 682]. See also, on texts of Orthodox-Catholic relations, Patelos [530], Garó [667], and Papandreou [671].

[41] Thon, Nikolaus. *Quellenbuch zur Geschichte der Orthodoxen Kirche*. Sophia 23. Trier: Paulinus, 1983.

This collection in German translation of 158 documents dating from the Edict of Milan (A.D. 313) to statements of Metropolitan Irenaios (1979) is a valuable sourcebook. It also contains a wealth of statistical information, lists of patriarchs for Constantinople, Alexandria, Antioch and Jerusalem. Of special ecumenical interest are the sections "G" through "K" that survey Orthodox ecumenical involvement in theological dialogues. See also Patelos [530].

# Reference Works

[42] Algermissen, Konrad. *Konfessionskunde*. 8th ed. Rev. by Heinrich Fries, Wilhelm de Vries, Erwin Iserloh, Laurentius Klein and Kurt Keinath. Paderborn: Bonifatius, 1969.

Sponsored by the Johann Adam Möhler Institute for Ecumenics in Paderborn, this latest edition of a comprehensive (886 pages) work was originally published in 1930 as *Christliche Sekten und Kirche Christi*. It contains historical and theological accounts of: the Roman Catholic Church; the Orthodox and Oriental Orthodox Churches; the churches of the Reformation; Anglican and Old Catholic churches; Free Churches and sects. Although written by Roman Catholics, the essays are ecumenically sensitive and well informed about other churches. The bibliographies are excellent and the volume well indexed.

[43] Andresen, Carl, ed. *Handbuch der Dogmen- und*

*Theologiegeschichte.* Bd. 1: *Die Lehrentwicklung im Rahmen der Katholizität.* Göttingen: Vandenhoeck und Ruprecht, 1982; Bd. 2: *Die Lehrentwicklung im Rahmen der Konfessionalität,* 1980; Bd. 3: *Die Lehrentwicklung im Rahmen der Ökumenizität,* 1984.

This three-volume scholarly collection is itself a splendid product of ecumenical collaboration. Volume one, the work of five authors, treats doctrinal developments in the early church as well as in the Orthodox Church of Byzantium, and in the West up to Scholasticism. Volume two, in six sections, discusses the impact of Luther, Zwingli, Calvin, and Henry VIII on the Reformation; further sections describe the Council of Trent and the beliefs of the Orthodox from the 16th century to the present-day. Volume three studies the role of humanism, Protestant doctrines from the eighteenth through the twentieth centuries, and modern Catholicism. Of special interest to ecumenists is the lengthy essay by R. Slenczka on "Dogma and Church Unity" (III, pp. 425-603).

[44] *L'Année religieuse dans le monde 1983.* Paris: Cana, 1984.

Published by the journal *L'Actualité religieuse dans le monde* [91] which after March 1983 replaced *Informations catholiques internationales,* this volume recalls major religious events that took place on five continents in the year 1983. The happenings are arranged by calendar date. There are indexes by country, persons, events. [163 boulevard Malesherbes, F-75859 Paris CEDEX 17].

[45] *L'attività della Santa Sede. Pubblicazione non ufficiale.* Vol. 1 -. Città del Vaticano: Libreria Editrice Vaticana, 1941-; annual.

Each year this publication provides day-by-day accounts of Vatican activities, photographic chronicles of events sponsored by the Roman Curia. Of special interest is the section outlining the work of the Pontifical Council [formerly Secretariat] for Promoting Christian Unity.

[46] Barrett, David B., ed. *World Christian Encyclopedia: A Comparative Study of Churches and Religions in the Modern World A.D. 1900-2000.* Oxford: Oxford University Press, 1982.

One of the great ecumenical publications of its decade, this mammoth (1010 pages) undertaking, compiled by 500 experts in 190 countries, includes fourteen sections on living faiths: their status; chronology; methodology and terminology; culture; evangelization; codebook; survey of religions in 223 countries; statistics; dictionary of controversial terms; bibliography (pp. 857-862); atlas; who's who; directory of organizations' names and addresses; indexes. See also Krüger [68] and Littell [71].

[47] Bent, Ans J. van der, ed. *Doctoral Dissertations on Ecumenical Themes: A Guide for Teachers and Students*. Geneva: World Council of Churches, 1977.

The former head librarian at the WCC's Geneva headquarters provides suggested topics for university research on general and specific issues or personnages and a list of completed dissertations available in the WCC library.

[48] Bent, Ans J. van der. *A Guide to Essential Ecumenical Reading*. Geneva: World Council of Churches, 1984.

Although only 44 pages long, this booklet contains a wealth of information especially helpful for beginners. The bibliography proper (pp. 29-44) focuses on the years from 1948 to 1984, excluding bilateral consultations but including dialogues with people of other living faiths. Material published in journals is not included.

[49] Bent, Ans J. van der, comp. *Major Studies and Themes in the Ecumenical Movement*. Geneva: World Council of Churches, 1981.

The major studies and themes addressed since the foundation of the WCC in 1948 are listed. Provided are lists of studies by the Council's units and subunits (including the Joint Working Group, the Ecumenical Institute in Bossey, and the German Kirchentage) as well as themes of the various assemblies. The work is meticulously indexed.

[50] Bent, Ans J. van der. *Six Hundred Ecumenical Consultations 1948-1982*. Geneva: World Council of Churches, 1983.

This reference book contains brief descriptions of and bibliographical information on 633 ecumenical consultations organized by various divisions and departments of the WCC. The volume is carefully indexed according to several categories.

[51] Bent, Ans J. van der. *Vital Ecumenical Concerns: Sixteen*

*Documentary Surveys*. Geneva: World Council of Churches, 1986.

> This 333 page reference work provides selections of official statements promulgated at six general assemblies of the WCC, at meetings of its Central Committee, and at other ecumenical conferences since 1948. Passages from Vatican II are also cited. The scope includes Asia and Africa. Sixteen topics concerned with church unity are covered. Each section has a brief bibliography.

[52] Berthier, René, *et al.*, gen eds. *2000 [Deux Mil] Ans de Christianisme*. 10 vols. Paris: AUFADI, 1975-1976.

> This ambitious, handsomely produced encyclopedia, contains numerous color plates, art reproductions and photos in addition to weighty articles. Within the ten volumes there are thirty different dossiers, each covering the past and the present. Produced by the Société d'histoire chrétienne, it includes in vol. X (dossier no. 28) a detailed treatment of ecumenism. Although lacking a general index, the work has been privately indexed (20 pp.) at the WCC's library in Geneva.

[53] Brierley, Peter, ed. *UK Christian Handbook* [1985/86 edition]. London: Evangelical Alliance; Bible Study; Marc Europe, 1984.

> The volume provides background information on churches in the UK. The directory section gives lists of religious publishers, missionary societies, and the like.

[54] Catholic Church. Congregation for the Eastern Churches. *Oriente cattolico: Cenni storici e statistiche*. 4th ed. Vatican City: S. Nilo, 1974.

> Although much of the data in this directory is outdated, the brief accounts of the historical origins, geographical distribution, and ecclesiastical institutions of Eastern Catholics are still useful. A new edition is needed.

[55] Catholic Church. Congregation for Catholic Education. *De Oriente Christiano*. Rome: Libreria Editrice Vaticana, 1975.

> Originally published as a special issue of *Seminarium*, the volume includes contributions in Italian, English, French and German. From its Catholic perspective, there are useful accounts of historical, canonical, spiritual, dogmatic, and liturgical aspects of

ecumenism. Special attention is given to the Christian East including a bibliography on its specific character.

[56] De Groot, A. T. *Church Unity: An Annotated Outline of the Growth of the Ecumenical Movement.* Fort Worth, TX: Texas Christian University, 1969.

The information here is outdated but the book is still a valuable historical record of unity efforts. The handbook contains lists of ecumenical institutes in Europe and North America, as well as data regarding denominational mergers. The text suffers from numerous misprints.

[57] *Enchiridion Vaticanum.* 10 vols. Bologna: Dehoniane, 1980- .

This source book gives texts in the original languages (usually Latin) plus an Italian translation. The texts begin with Vatican II and then cover subsequent official texts of the See of Rome. The last published volume at time of publication was volume 10, covering documents up to 1989.

[58] *Evangelisches Kirchenlexikon: Internationale theologische Enzyklopädie.* 3rd rev. ed. Ed. by Erwin Fahlbusch, *et al.* 5 vols. projected. Göttingen: Vandenhoeck und Ruprecht, 1986- .

This completely reorganized lexikon is a scholarly updating of a wide area of theological learning and events. As of February 1992 eight fascicles had been published (up to the letter "P"). The entries for "Ökumenismus" and cognates are excellent. This edition draws widely upon experts in the English speaking world also.

[59] Fahlbusch, Erwin. *Kirchenkunde der Gegenwart.* Theologische Wissenschaft, Bd. 9. Stuttgart: W. Kohlhammer, 1979.

The reference book treats: the Roman Catholic Church especially in the post-conciliar period; other Christian churches in Germany; and the "ecumenical context" with relationship to the WCC and the bilateral consultations. There is a good bibliography of works in German.

[60] Felmy, Karl Christian, *et al.*, eds. *Kirchen im Kontext unterschiedlicher Kulturen: Auf dem Weg ins dritte Jahrtausend.* Göttingen: Vandenhoeck und Ruprecht, 1992.

For this massive 1060 page volume, the editors enlisted a cross section of confessionally and culturally diverse experts to describe the challenges to church and theology of contextualization and globalization in the next millennium. The three major sections of the handbook are: the challenge of the Enlightenment to the churches, the unity of the church and the multiplicity of nations, and religious language and sacral symbols in a secularized world.

[61] Gleixner, Christina. *Ökumene heute: Eine Orientierungs-hilfe.* Vienna: Herold, 1980.

This high-level basic orientation for Christians regarding ecumenical matters was first formulated for the Catholic archdiocese of Vienna. It contains an historical account of divisions and various appendices (pp. 117-232) containing statistics, excerpts from documents, etc. See also Trautwein [956].

[62] Gründler, Johannes. *Lexikon der christlichen Kirchen und Sekten, unter Berücksichtigung der Missionsgesellschaften und Zwischenkirchlichen Organisationen.* 2 vols. Vienna: Herder, 1961.

Undertaken under Roman Catholic auspices, this publication identifies some 2000 ecclesial communities and sects. Although the statistical data is quite outdated, the historical background regarding these churches is still reliable.

[63] Hasselhoff, Friedrich, and Krüger, Hanfried, eds. *Ökumene in Schule und Gemeinde: Ein Arbeitsbuch.* Stuttgart: Evangelisches Missionsverlag, 1971.

Designed for parish and teachers at the local level, this volume however is not a primer but a sophisticated, detailed source book written by several major ecumenists. The three sections, with many sub-divisions, discuss the ecumenical movement, the basic theological questions, and ecumenical responsibility.

[64] Honecker, Martin, and Waldenfels, Hans. *Zu Gast beim Anderen: Evangelisch-katholischer Fremdenführer.* Graz: Styria, 1983.

This practical guide is intended to provide Protestants or Catholics with information they would need when visiting a church building of another confession. Thus the Catholic (Waldenfels) explains objects such as a tabernacle, a sanctuary, statues, etc. The Lutheran (Honecker) comments on the pulpit, baptismal font, etc. There are forty-nine illustrations sketched by Roland Pirker of Graz.

[65] IDOC-C. *Un nouvel âge oecuménique*. L'Eglise en son temps 10. Paris: Le Centurion, 1966.

Published by the international center IDOC-C (Information et documentation sur l'Eglise conciliaire), the volume has three parts: studies on the WCC, on Orthodoxy (essays by A. Schmemann and N. Nissiotis), and on Roman Catholic ecumenism. See companion volume [708].

[66] Ivánka, Endre von; Tyciak, Julian; and Wiertz, Paul, eds. *Handbuch der Ostkirchenkunde*. Düsseldorf: Patmos, 1971.

Sixteen international authors, both Orthodox and Catholic, collaborated on this 839 page handbook. The detailed bibliography is arranged thematically (pp. 766-817). Part one is a descriptive, historical section. Part two treats the theological, liturgical and spiritual traditions of the Eastern churches.

[67] Komonchak, Joseph A.; Collins, Mary; and Lane, Dermot A., eds. *The New Dictionary of Theology*. Wilmington, DL: Michael Glazier, 1987.

This one-volume (1112 pp.) encyclopedia of theology published by a team of some 160 Catholics provides a current description of progressive, theological research most of which has been heavily influenced by ecumenical dialogue. Twenty-four of the principal themes are given lengthy treatment. Bibliographies are first rate.

[68] Krüger, Hanfried; Löser, Werner; Müller-Römheld, Walter, eds. *Ökumene Lexikon: Kirchen, Religionen, Bewegungen*. 2nd ed. Frankfurt: O. Lembeck; J. Knecht, 1987.

This is a well conceived modern lexicon provided with excellent bibliographies, interesting archival photos, and biographies of ecumenical personages. The emphasis is on developments from 1953 to 1987. The articles were written by an ecumenical team of experts. A first edition appeared in 1983. See also Barrett [46] and Littell [71].

[69] Küng, Hans, ed. *Schema zum Forschungskatalog über die theologische Literatur seit 1945*. Tübingen: Institut für ökumenische

Forschung, 1967.

This publication gives the categories used by the Tübingen Ecumenical Institute for classifying books and articles on ecumenical topics.

[70] *Lexikon für Theologie und Kirche*. 2nd rev. ed. Ed. by Josef Höfer and Karl Rahner. 11 vols. plus 3 vols. supplement. Freiburg: Herder, 1957-67.

This Catholic encyclopedia, largely the brain child of Karl Rahner, was nearing completion when Vatican II (1962-1965) required three supplementary volumes with Latin and German conciliar texts and excellent commentaries. The commentaries have been translated into English in Vorgrimler [321].

[71] Littell, Franklin H., and Walz, Hans Hermann. *Weltkirchen Lexikon: Handbuch der Ökumene*. Stuttgart: Kreuz, 1960.

The statistics in this lexicon are outdated but there is still much of value in this publication. Besides providing a dictionary of ecumenical terms, the work includes numerous photographs, maps and charts. See also Barrett [46] and Krüger [68].

[72] Lossky, Nicholas; Bonino, José Miguez; Pobee, John; Stransky, Tom; Wainwright, Geoffrey; Webb, Pauline, eds. *Dictionary of the Ecumenical Movement*. Geneva: World Council of Churches; Grand Rapids: Eerdmans, 1991.

This is a milestone in modern ecumenical research. The 1196 page dictionary contains over 600 entries, often lengthy and detailed accounts of ecumenical themes, events, organizations, personalities and theological positions. The numerous contributors include many prestigious ecumenists. The brief bibliographies are excellent.

[73] Martineau, Suzanne. *Pédagogie de l'oecuménisme*. Tours: Mame, 1965.
This sizeable 416 page book is rich in documentation and well organized for teaching purposes. Arranged into two parts, it describes both the ecumenical dimension of Christian faith and practical means already taken by major churches to achieve unity. See also [483].

[74] Moderow, Hans-Martin, and Sens, Matthias, eds. *Orientierung Ökumene: Ein Handbuch.* E. Berlin: Evangelische Verlagsanstalt, 1979.

Besides its narrative on the modern ecumenical movement, the volume contains a useful account of ecumenism in what was formerly East Germany (DDR).

[75] Neuner, Peter. *Kleines Handbuch der Ökumene.* Düsseldorf: Patmos, 1984.

The professor of fundamental theology and ecumenical coordinator for the Catholic diocese of Passau intends this short work to be an introduction to the necessity of efforts to achieve church unity.

[76] Neuner, Joseph, and Dupuis, Jacques, eds. *The Christian Faith in the Doctrinal Documents of the Catholic Church.* 3rd ed. Bangalore: St. Peter's Seminary, 1978. Rev. ed. New York: Alba, 1982.

This collaboration between professors from Delhi and Pune led to publication of this English adaptation of the sixth edition of J. Neuner and H. Roos's *Der Glaube der Kirche.* The collection contains conciliar documents dating back to the early church arranged according to the system used by Denzinger.

[77] *New Catholic Encyclopedia: An International Work of Reference on the Teachings, History, Organization and Activities of the Catholic Church and on All Institutions, Religions, Philosophies and Scientific and Cultural Developments Affecting the Catholic Church from Its Beginning to the Present.* 17 vols. Gen. ed. William J. McDonald. New York: McGraw-Hill, 1967-1979.

The first fifteen volumes (including an index) appeared shortly after the conclusion of Vatican II. Two supplementary volumes 16 (1974) and especially 17 (1979) bring the material more up to date. Ecumenical coverage is generally good especially in vol. 17. The short bibliographies are reliable.

[78] *Oecumenica: An Annual Symposium of Ecumenical Research.* 6 vols. Eds. by Friederich Wilhelm Kantzenbach and Vilmos Vajta. Minneapolis: Augsburg, 1966-1972.

Published for six years under the aegis of the Institute for Ecumenical Research at Strasbourg, the yearbook began with a wide range of articles, but gradually came to focus on specific topics. The 1970 volume was entitled *Gospel and Sacrament* (ed. by Günther Gassmann and Vilmos Vajta) and the 1971/72 volume was entitled *Tradition in Lutheranism and Anglicanism*.

[79] Piepkorn, Arthur Carl. *Profiles in Belief: The Religious Bodies of the United States and Canada*. 4 vols. in 3. New York: Harper and Row, 1977-1979.

The Lutheran scholar died before the enterprise was completed, but for Christianity the coverage was finished. The historical and doctrinal information covers Roman Catholic, Orthodox, Protestant, and holiness churches. How these groups emigrated to North America and adapted to the new environs is clearly explained.

[80] Richardson, Alan, and Bowden, John, eds. *A New Dictionary of Christian Theology*. London: SCM, 1983.

First published in 1969 as *A Dictionary of Christian Theology*, this volume contains brief articles often with short bibliographies. The contributors represent a spectrum of ecumenical backgrounds, mostly from Britain but some from the USA.

[81] Roberson, Ronald G. *The Eastern Christian Churches: A Brief Survey*. 3rd rev. ed. Rome: Pontifical Oriental Institute, 1990.

The directory is a listing of the four branches of Eastern Christianity: the Orthodox, Oriental Orthodox, Assyrian, and Eastern Catholic. Brief historical accounts together with statistics and names of ecclesiastical heads are provided.

[82] *Sacramentum Mundi: An Encyclopedia of Theology*. 6 vols. Gen. ed. Adolf Darlap. New York: Herder and Herder; London: Burns and Oates, 1964-1970.

After Vatican II one of the major achievements of the international Catholic scholarly community (especially German and French) was the publication of this theological encyclopedia which also appeared in Dutch, French, German, Italian and Spanish editions. The treatment of ecumenical issues is sensitive and well informed (see especially II, pp. 191-212). Each article has a short bibliography.

[83] Sánchez Vaquero, José. *Ecumenismo: Manual de formación ecuménica*. Salamanca: Centro Ecumenico Juan XXIII, Universidad Pontificia, 1971.

Despite the size of this 635 page manual, the overall impression is disappointing. The essays explaining Orthodox and Reformation theology are clearly biased in favor of Catholicism.

[84] Troyanovskiy, Igor, ed. *Religion in the Soviet Republics: A Guide to Christianity, Judaism, Islam, Buddhism and Other Religions in Today's Soviet Union*. San Francisco: Harper, 1991.

This reference work completed in September 1991 provides a recent account in a rapidly evolving society of historical documents of religion in the former USSR, legislation on religion, and detailed descriptions of religious groups including all the major branches of Christianity as well as Judaism, Islam and Buddhism. The author was chief of the religious section of *Novosti*, the Soviet information agency.

[85] Urban, Hans Jörg, and Wagner, Harald, eds. *Handbuch der Ökumenik*. 3 vols in 4. Paderborn: Bonifatius, 1985-1987.

The two ecumenists from Paderborn and Marburg edited this comprehensive analysis for the Johann Adam Möhler Institute of Ecumenics. Volume one treats the meaning of the term ecumenical as well as the origins of Christian disunity in the early church and between East and West; volume two gives the history of the ecumenical movement in the twentieth century; volume three, in two parts, gives a panoramic view of doctrinal issues under current discussion.

[86] Voicu, Sever J., and Cereti, Giovanni, eds. *Enchiridion Oecumenicum: Documenti del dialogo teologico inter-confessionale*. Vol. 1: *Dialoghi Internazionali 1931-1984*. Bologna: Dehoniane, 1986; Vol. 2: *Dialoghi Locali 1965-1987*. Bologna: Dehoniane, 1988.

This work gives the full text in Italian translation of all the major international dialogues from 1931 to 1984. Volume two is especially valuable since its coverage is so wide. Texts are arranged by country and include locations such as Australia, Canada, Hong Kong, Philippines and the USA. The indexes, including ones for sources, Scriptural citations, and topics are excellent.

[87] Vischer, Lukas, ed. *Die Einheit der Kirche: Material der ökumenischen Bewegung.* Theologische Bücherei Bd. 30. Munich: Kaiser, 1965.

> The publication provides statements on church unity articulated by various general assemblies of the WCC, world conferences of Faith and Order Commission, the WCC's Central Committee, and other Faith and Order meetings.

[88] Ward, Hiley. *Documents of Dialogue.* Englewood Cliffs, NJ: Prentice-Hall, 1966.

> This 525 page collection of documents on ecumenism has limited value since it fails to weigh the relative importance of the 262 texts cited. Official ecclesiastical statements are given the same importance as individual remarks by well intentioned observers. Nor is the material organized thematically. There is a bibliography for Protestant/Catholic dialogue (1956-1966) and a glossary.

[89] World Council of Churches, Language Service. *Ecumenical Terminology. Terminologie oecuménique. Ökumenische Terminologie. Terminología Ecuménica.* Geneva: World Council of Churches, 1975; with a supplement, 1983.

> The volume and supplement provide in parallel columns English, French, German and Spanish language equivalents for words used to identify major ecumenical events and assemblies from 1910 to 1975 and the theological terminology used in modern dialogue.

[90] Wyrwoll, Nikolaus, ed. *Orthodoxia 1988-1989.* Regensburg: Ostkirchliches Institut, 1990.

> Produced by the Ostkirchliches Institut [Ostengasse 31; D-8400 Regensburg], this carefully prepared listing of canonically recognized hierarchs of the Orthodox and Ancient Oriental churches identifies their baptismal or monastic names, patriarchal affiliation, and other factual information (birth, ordination, etc.). This information is regularly updated.

# Journals on Ecumenism

[91] *L'Actualité religieuse dans le monde.* No. 1- . Paris: Malesherbes Publications, 1983- ; monthly.

This monthly documentary publication was preceded from 1955 to 1983 by the journal *Informations catholiques internationales*. It broadened its coverage to include news pertinent beyond Catholicism. For professional treatment of religious texts and events, this publication is excellent. [163 Boulevard Malesherbes; F-75859 Paris CEDIX 17].

[92] *Archivum Historiae Pontificiae*. Vol. 1- . Rome: Facultas Historiae Ecclesiasticae, Pontificia Universitas Gregoriana, 1963- ; annual.

This yearly publication contains some 700 pages of articles and shorter reports. Its "Bibliographia Historiae Pontificiae", edited by Paulus Arató, S.J., includes a section on ecumenism, chronicling initiatives of modern popes. The multi-lingual bibliography of Vatican II is excellent and its indexes are painstakingly comprehensive.

[93] *Bausteine für die Einheit der Christen*. Vol. 1- . Gersfeld-Dalherda, Germany: Bund für evangelisch-katholische Wiedervereinigung, 1961- ; quarterly.

Published to promote Lutheran and Catholic reconciliation, this modest journal, edited by Dr. Max Lackmann, founder of the Bund für evangelisch-katholische Wiedervereinigung and promoter of the Sammlung movement, focuses mostly on ecumenical issues in the German-speaking world. [Gichenbacherstr. 9; D-6412 Gersfeld-Dalherda, Germany].

[94] *Bulletin de Théologie Africaine; Bulletin of African Theology; Boletin de Teología Africana*. Vol. 1- . Kinshasa, Zaïre: Association oecuménique des théologiens africains. 1979- ; twice a year.

This organ of the Ecumenical Association of African Theologians includes articles in English and French as well as valuable reports and bibliographies regarding theological and ecumenical initiatives in sub-Saharan Africa.

[95] *Catholic International*. Vol. 1- . Paris: Bayard, 1990- ; every two weeks.

This publication is the English edition of *Documentation catholique* produced in cooperation with the North American Province of the Assumptionists. It includes papal documents, texts from ecumenical and inter-faith dialogues, and provides statistical and background information. [3-5, rue Bayard, F-75008 Paris].

[96] *Catholica: Vierteljahresschrift für ökumenische Theologie.* Vol. 1- . Münster, Johann-Adam-Möhler Institut, 1932- ; quarterly.

This journal of the Johann Adam Möhler Institute for Ecumenics includes high level articles on controverted issues among the Christian churches. A cumulative index for the years 1932-1988 exists. [Leostrasse 19a; D-4790 Paderborn].

[97] *Catholica Unio: Ostkirchliche Zeitschrift.* Vol. 1- . Lucerne: Schweizerisches Katholisches Ostkirchenwerk Catholica Unio, 1932- ; quarterly.

Edited by the well-known Swiss ecumenist Raymund Erni, this journal contains short reflective articles on Eastern spirituality, liturgy, and historical issues that have separated churches of the East and West. [Adligenwilerstr. 13; CH-6006 Lucerne, Switzerland].

[98] *Het Christelijk Oosten.* Vol. 1- . Nijmegen: Instituut voor Byzantijnse en Oecumenische Studies, 1948- ; quarterly.

This journal is a model of *haute vulgarisation*. All articles are published in Dutch, with brief summaries added in English or French, but the contributors include an international spectrum of authors. Relevant documents and chronicles relating to various Eastern churches are also featured. [Louiseweg 12; NL-6523NB Nijmegen].

[99] *Christian Orient.* Vol. 1- . Kottayam, Kerala, India: Pontifical Oriental Institute of Kottayam, 1980- ; quarterly.

Described as an "Indian Journal of Eastern Churches for Creative Theological Thinking", the publication concentrates largely on the Syro-Malabar and Syro-Malankara churches, both of which are in full communion with the Church of Rome. Each issue includes documentation and chronicles about the Eastern Orthodox and Catholic communities in India. [Oriental Institute, Kottayam 686010, Kerala, India].

[100] *Der christliche Osten.* Vol. 1- . Würzburg: Catholica Unio Deutschlands, Österreichs, und der Schweiz, 1946- ; bimonthly.

For over 65 years old, the Catholica Unio, established by members of the Augustinian order in Germany, has published this journal containing theological articles for the general public. It includes photographic records of ecumenical life, chronicles of events, statistics, etc. Its principal interests are the Orthodox, Eastern Catholic and Ancient Oriental Orthodox churches. During its first three years of publication it was entitled *Der christliche Orient*. [Grabenberg 6; D-8700 Würzburg].

[101] *Contacts: Revue Orthodoxe de théologie et de spiritualité*. Vol. 1- . Paris: Centre Ecuménique Enotikon. 1949- ; quarterly.

This distinguished journal concentrates especially on Orthodoxy in France and its dialogue with other Christians living in France. Special attention is devoted to liturgy and theology. Current editor is Olivier Clément. Annual texts by the Congrès Orthodoxe en Europe occidentale are included. [43 rue du Fer à Moulin; F-75005 Paris].

[102] *Courrier oecuménique du Moyen Orient*. Vol. 1- . Beirut, Lebanon: Middle Eastern Council of Churches, Information Office, 1987- ; three times a year.

The publication appears to have replaced the earlier *MECC Perspectives*. The journal contains articles, ecumenical news items, documents and book reviews related to the Middle East and the diaspora. See also *MECC NewsReport* [131] and *al Montada* [134]. [B.P. 5376 Beirut, Lebanon].

[103] *Diakonia*. Vol. 1- . Scranton, PA: John XXIII Center, Scranton University, 1966- ; three times a year.

Originally published by the John XXIII Center, Fordham University, New York City (previously known as the Russian Center) but since 1986 by Scranton University, the journal addresses a wide audience of clergy, religious and lay educators. It provides accessible but well-researched articles. Also included are editorials, documentation (especially on the work of the Orthodox/Roman Catholic and Oriental Orthodox/Roman Catholic dialogues in the USA). For many years Prof. Thomas Bird, but later followed by Thomas Sable, S.J., provided a yearly chronicle about the Eastern Christian churches. [Scranton University, Scranton, PA 18510-4507].

[104] *Dialog: A Journal of Theology*. Vol. 1- . St. Paul, MN: Dialog Inc., 1962- ; quarterly.

This journal is published by the Lutheran schools of theology in the USA. Since its inception it has had a keen interest in ecumenical topics and issues. [2481 Como Ave., St. Paul, MN 55108].

[105] *Diálogo Ecuménico*. Vol. 1- . Salamanca: Centro de Estudios Orientales y Ecuménicos Juan XXIII, Universidad Pontificia, 1966 - ; three times a year.

This journal, sponsored by the Pontifical University of Salamanca, includes articles, notes, documentation, text, bulletins and book reviews. Although it covers much of the material found in other journals, it specifically narrates ecumenical activities in Spain. [Calle Companía 5, Apdo. 541; 37080 Salamanca].

[106] *ECNL (Eastern Churches News Letter): Journal of the Anglican and Eastern Churches Association*. New Series. No. 1- . London: The Anglican and Eastern Churches Association, 1975- ; twice a year.

The association itself was founded in 1864. The journal (which eschews volume numbers) began a new series in the autumn of 1975. Its publication provides valuable source of documentation and opinion on national and international efforts for church union between Anglicans and Orthodox. The newsletter is jointly sponsored by the Ecumenical Patriarch of Constantinople and the Archbishop of Canterbury. [St. Dunstan's in the West, 184 Fleet St., London EC4A 2EA].

[107] *Ecumenical Press Service (EPS)*. Vol. 1- . Geneva: World Council of Churches, 1933/1934- ; approximately 45 times a year.

Known as the *EPS*, this newsletter contains information not usually found in other sources. A service of the WCC in partnership with the World Student Christian Federation, the World Alliance of YMCAs and the World YWCA, the publication contains news items, "ecuviews", and "ecutexts". From 1933 until 1974 it appeared as *Ökumenischer Pressedienst (ÖPD)*. Also published now in French as *Service Oecuménique de Presse et d'Information (SOEPI)* [156]. [150 route de Ferney, CH-1211 Geneva 20].

[108] *Ecumenical Review*. Vol. 1- . Geneva: World Council of Churches, 1948- ; quarterly.

Besides a cross-section of important articles on ecumenical theology and history, the journal contains an ecumenical chronicle and diary, a survey of significant articles from ecumenical journals, and a well-organized Bibliographica Oecumenica. [150 route de Ferney, CH-1211 Geneva 20].

[109] *Ecumenical Trends*. Vol. 1- . Garrison, New York: Atonement Friars, 1972- ; eleven times a year.

This publication by the Graymoor Friars contains brief articles and documentation of bilateral dialogues especialy in the USA. Publication offices are currently located at Graymoor Ecumenical Institute, Garrison, NY 10524.

[110] *Ecumenism*. No. 1- . Montreal: Canadian Centre for Ecumenism, 1966- ; quarterly.

Published in both English and French [139] editions, the journal took on a new format in 1982 and now devotes each issue to a special theme. It provides short accounts also of ecumenical events in Canada. [2065 Sherbrooke St. W., Montreal, Que H3H 1G6].

[111] *The Ecumenist: A Journal for Promoting Christian Unity*. Vol. 1-29. Mahwah, NJ: Paulist; Montreal: Faculty of Religious Studies, McGill University, 1962-1991; bimonthly.

Founded by Canadian theologian Gregory Baum, the journal appeared for twenty-eight years, first emanating from the St. Michael's Faculty of Theology, Toronto, and then from McGill University. Each issue contained several short essays often stressing issues of faith and social justice.

[112] *Ekklêsia kai Theologia (Church and Theology)*. Vol. 1- . London: Archbishop of Thyateira and Great Britain, 1980- ; annual.

This hefty publication, averaging a thousand pages, is an ecclesiastical and theological journal sponsored by the Greek Orthodox Archbishop of Thyateira in London. Articles appear in Greek or English. [Thyateira House 5, Craven Hill, London W2, UK].

**[113]** *Episkepsis*. Vol. 1- . Chambésy-Geneva: Centre orthodoxe du patriarcat oecuménique, 1970- ; originally biweekly, now monthly.

Published in French from the Patriarch of Constantinople's Ecumenical Center near Geneva, the newsletter contains items and documents often difficult to find elsewhere. Frequently an issue will contain a "Bibliographie Orthodoxe" arranged alphabetically by author. Also appears in Greek. From June 1991 it has been experiencing publication delays due in part to financial problems. See also *Service Orthodoxe de Presse* [157]. [37 chemin de Chambésy; CH-1292 Chambésy-Geneva].

**[114]** *Greek Orthodox Theological Review*. Vol. 1- . Brookline, MA: Holy Cross Greek Orthodox School of Theology, 1954- ; quarterly.

This journal and its Orthodox Church in America's counterpart, *St. Vladimir's Theological Quarterly* [155], are leading English-language Orthodox theological reviews for America. This publication is sponsored by the Greek Orthodox Archdiocese of North and South America. The authors, almost always Greek Orthodox, address doctrinal issues sometimes with an ecumenical perspective. Besides articles and book reviews there are papers from meetings of the Orthodox Theological Society. [50 Goddard Avenue, Brookline, MA 02146].

**[115]** *Herder Korrespondenz*. Vol. 1- . Freiburg: Herder, 1946- ; monthly.

This useful German-language Catholic publication includes brief informational items, interviews, documents, and surveys of new literature relating not only to the international Roman Catholic community but to other Christian churches as well. It has some similarity to the Swiss *Orientierung* [147]. [Hermann-Herder-Strasse 4; D-7800 Freiburg].

**[116]** *Information Service*. No. 1- . Vatican City: Pontifical Council for Promoting Christian Unity, 1967- ; three times a year.

Together with its French edition, *Service d'Information*, this newsletter of the Pontifical Council [Secretariat] for Promoting Christian Unity contains valuable documentation regarding visits of delegations to and by the Vatican, ecumenical news, documents, reports on international bilateral consultations and on yearly activities by this Vatican office. [Via dell'Erba 1; I-00193

Rome].

[117] *International Review of Mission.* Vol. 1- . Geneva: World Council of Churches, Division of World Mission and Evangelism, 1912- ; quarterly.

Edited over the years by leading WCC ecumenists, the journal focuses on mission theology in a variety of settings. Unique to the journal is an indispensable "Bibliography on World Mission and Evangelism" (edited by A. F. Walls). A cumulative index for 1912-1966 is available.[150 route de Ferney, CH-1211 Geneva 20].

[118] *Internationale Kirchliche Zeitschrift.* Vol. 1- . Bern: Staempfli und Cie AG, 1911- ; quarterly.

The journal continues the *Revue internationale de théologie* (1892-1911) of the International Congress of Old Catholics (Lucerne). Over the years, besides its theological essays, it has included numerous installments of a chronological bibliography of Orthodox theology (now edited by B. Spuler).

[119] *Irénikon.* Vol. 1- . Chevetogne: Moines de Chevetogne, Belgium, 1926- ; quarterly.

This publication by the Benedictine monastery of Chevetogne is devoted to fostering reconciliation between Eastern and Western Christians and contains scholarly articles on theological and ecumenical themes as well as book reviews. It also includes detailed accounts of ongoing contacts between different Christian communions and chronicles of church events. Current editor is Emmanuel Lanne, O.S.B. [Monastère Bénédictin, B-5590 Chevetogne, Belgium].

[120] *Istina.* Vol. 1- . Paris: Centre d'Etudes Istina, 1954- ; quarterly.

This successor to *Russie et Chrétienté* (1934-39, 1946-50), is now published under the title *Istina* ("truth"). The journal, sponsored by French Dominicans, contains articles centered on ecumenical problems of East and West, documents, book reviews and an annual ecumenical chronicle covering periodical literature. [45 rue de la Glacière, F-75013 Paris].

[121] *Journal of Ecumenical Studies.* Vol. 1- . Philadelphia: Temple

University, 1964- ; quarterly.

This important ecumenical journal of North America contains a wide cross-section of articles as well as book reviews, brief news items, and abstracts of periodical articles from many specialized ecumenical journals including those in Slavic languages. [Temple University, Philadelphia, PA 19122].

[122] *Journal of Moscow Patriarchate.* Year 1- . Moscow: Russian Orthodox Church, 1971- ; monthly.

The Russian edition of this official publication, *Zurnal Moskovskoj Patriarkhii*, began in 1931 and has continued with several interruptions. The English edition dates from 1971. It contains a wide range of articles, sermons, reports on current events, photographs, and editorials. The clarity of the English translation often leaves much to be desired. [Box 624, Moscow 119435].

[123] *Kirche im Osten: Studien zur osteuropäischen Kirchengeschichte und Kirchenkunde.* Vol. 1- . Göttingen: Ostkirchenausschuss der Evangelischen Kirche in Deutschland (EKD) und das Ostkirchen-Institut der Westfälischen Wilhelms-Universität Münster, 1958- ; annual.

Each year, in addition to scholarly essays probing issues of pertinence to East European churches, there is a chronicle reporting on events of church life in that part of the world.

[124] *Kirche im Sozialismus. Zeitschrift zu Entwicklungen in der DDR.* Vol. 1- . Berlin: Berliner Arbeitsgemeinschaft für Kirchliche Publizistik, 1973- ; six times a year.

This journal reports on the activities of the Bund der Evangelischen Kirchen as well as those of the Vereinigte Evangelische Lutherische Kirche. Prior to the reunification of Germany it was being published in West Berlin. [Bachstrasse 1-2; D-1000 Berlin 21].

[125] *Kosmos + Oekumene.* Vol. 1- . The Hague: St. Willibrord Vereniging, 1962- ; ten times a year.

Originally known as *Oecumene*, this Dutch publication of the St. Willibrord Association for Ecumenism reports on ecumenical life in the Netherlands and beyond. [Walpoort 10; NL-5211 DK The Hague].

[126] *Le Lien: Revue du Patriarcat Grec-Melkite Catholique.* Vol. 1- . Beirut: Greek Melchite Catholic Patriarchate, 1936- ; bimonthly.

Founded in Cairo in 1936, the journal has appeared out of Beirut since 1968. It contains news of the Antioch Catholic patriarchate, one of the more active among the Middle Eastern churches in communion with the Church of Rome. The journal contains an account of ecumenical activities in the Middle East. [B.P. 50076, Beirut, Lebanon].

[127] *Lutheran World / Lutherische Rundschau.* Vol. 1-24. Geneva: Lutheran World Federation, 1954-77; quarterly.

Both the English and German editions of this publication ceased in 1977 and have been replaced partly by the bulletins *LWF Documentation* and *LWB Dokumentation.* [150 route de Ferney, CH-1211 Geneva 20].

[128] *LWF Documentation.* No. 1- . Geneva: Lutheran World Federation, 1978- ; irregular.

The publication provides useful information on the activities of the Lutheran World Federation. Each issue is normally devoted to a particular theme. It also is published in German as *LWB Dokumentation.* [150 route de Ferney, CH-1211 Geneva 20].

[129] *Lutherische Monatshefte.* Vol. 1- . Hannover: Lutherisches Verlagshaus, 1962- ; monthly.

For information on the German ecumenical scene, especially prior to German reunification, this publication is indispensable. Similar to *Herder Korrespondenz* [115] among Catholics in Germany, it covers church, culture and politics by means of reports, analyses, interviews, documentation, brief overviews of theological journals. Particularly good for accounts of the Evangelische Kirche in Deutschland (EKD) and the DDR Kirchenbund. [Knochenhauer Str. 42; D-3000 Hannover].

[130] *Materialdienst des Konfessionskundlichen Instituts.* Vol. 1- . Bensheim: Konfessionskundliches Institut des Evangelischen Bundes, 1950- ; bimonthly.

Serving the German Reformation churches in a way similar to the Swiss Catholic *Orientierung* [147], this publication contains articles, documents, editorials, book reviews of international but especially European interest. Sponsored by the Evangelische Kirche in Deutschland, this newsletter includes ecumenical news about the Roman Catholic Church. [Eifelstrasse 35; D-6140 Bensheim 1].

[131] *MECC NewsReport*. Vol. 1- . Limassol, Cyprus: MECC Communication Department, 1988- ; ten times a year.

The English language newsletter, until recently published in Beirut, provides church-related information from and about the Middle Eastern churches. See also [102, 134]. [P.O.Box 4259, Limassol, Cyprus].

[132] *Media Development*. Vol. 1- . London: World Association for Christian Communication, 1954- ; quarterly with occasional extra issues.

This journal which continues the earlier *WACC Journal* is devoted to an ecumenical coverage of effective ways to communicate church unity achievements through modern means of communication. [357 Kennington Lane, London SE11 5QY, UK].

[133] *Mid-Stream: An Ecumenical Journal*. Vol. 1- . Indianapolis, IN: Council on Christian Unity of the Christian Church (Disciples of Christ), 1961- ; quarterly.

Edited by the American ecumenist Paul A. Crow, Jr., and supported by the Consultation on Church Union (COCU) [787-800] this publication contains essays, addresses, papers of general ecumenical interest besides recent consensus statements. It also records ecumenical events, book reviews and yearly reports of the National Workshop on Christian Unity held in the USA. Beginning with vol. 14 (1975) its title was changed by adding its present subtitle. An index of vols. 1-22 (1961-83) is available. [P.O.Box 1986, Indianapolis, IN 46206].

[134] *al Montada*. No. 1- . Beirut: Middle East Council of Churches, 1967- ; bimonthly.

The newsletter in Arabic, whose title means "The Forum", is published by the MECC, the regional council linking Oriental

Orthodox, Eastern Orthodox, Evangelical Reformed and Episcopal churches in the Middle East. It contains documents and news items pertinent to Antioch-centered Christians, but also reports on dialogue with Islam. See also [102, 131]. [P.O.B. 5376, Beirut, Lebanon].

[135] *Neue Stimme: Ökumenische Monatschrift zu Fragen in Kirche, Gesellschaft und Politik.* Vol. 1- . Mainz: Neue Stimme, 1974- ; monthly.

Originally entitled *Neue Stimme: Evangelische Monatschrift*, the journal has substituted the adjective *ökumenische* since January 1980. Similar to *Herder Korrespondenz* [115] and *The Ecumenist* [111], it focuses mainly on social and economic issues. [Postfach 3805; D-6500 Mainz 1].

[136] *Nicolaus: Rivista di teologia ecumenico-patristica.* Vol. 1- . Bari, Italy: Istituto di teologia ecumenico-patristica, 1973- ; twice a year.

Edited by the Institute's director, Salvatore Manna, O.P., the journal is a valuable source of information on international consultations between Roman Catholics and Orthodox. It contains articles, notes, shorter communications in Italian, Greek and French. [Via Bisanzio e Rainaldo 15; I-70122 Bari].

[137] *Notizie Ortodosse. Bolletino mensile d'informazione.* Vol. 1- . Rome: Comunità Ortodossa Ellenica in Roma, 1979- ; monthly.

This Italian-language newsletter comparable to *Episkepsis* [113] and *Service Orthodoxe de presse* [157] contains items of ecumenical interest relating to the Eastern churches. Sponsored by the Greek Orthodox community in Rome, its scope is nonetheless quite wide. It includes documents difficult to find elsewhere. Also provided occasionally are theological supplements that give useful bibliographical references to Orthodox theology, which unfortunately are poorly indexed. [Via Albricci 4/30; I-00194 Rome].

[138] *O Odigos (La Guida).* No. 1- . Bari: Ecumenical Center S. Nicola of the Dominican Fathers, 1982- ; quarterly.

The ecumenical center located in Bari, southern Italy, aims to specialize in matters of importance to the Eastern churches and to promote understanding between churches of the East and West.

This is a good source of information about current Orthodox/Catholic dialogue. [Largo Abate Elia 13, I-70122 Bari].

[139] *Oecuménisme*. No. 1- . Montreal: Canadian Centre for Ecumenism, 1966- ; quarterly.

Published in both French and English [110] editions, the journal took on a new format in 1982 and now devotes each issue to a special theme. It provides short accounts also of ecumenical events in Canada. [2065 Sherbrooke St. W., Montreal, Que H3H 1G6].

[140] *Oecuménisme Informations*. No. 1- . Paris: Commission luthéro-réformée, 1974- ; eighteen times a year.

This bulletin published by the Lutheran Reformed Commission for contacts with Catholics and with the Joint Orthodox Committee of Bishops gives useful information about dialogues in France, especially Paris, involving the Reformation churches. [8 rue de la Ville l'Evêque; F-75008 Paris].

[141] *Ökumenische Rundschau*. Vol. 1- . Frankfurt: Deutscher Ökumenischer Studienausschuss, 1952- ; quarterly.

One of the best German-language resources on contemporary ecumenical research, this journal contains articles, excerpts of consensus statements, chronicles, overviews of journals and new books. Its companion series, *Beihefte zur Ökumenischen Rundschau*, began in 1985 and now numbers some 50 volumes. [Leerbachstrasse 42; D-6000 Frankfurt 1].

[142] *Ökumenisches Forum: Grazer Hefte für konkrete Ökumene*. Vol. 1- . Graz: Institut für ökumenische Theologie und Patrologie der Theologischen Fakultät Graz und Interkonfessioneller Arbeitskreis Ökumene in der Steiermark, 1977- ; irregular.

This Austrian Catholic publication, edited by Professor J. B. Bauer, contains information about many Christian churches. It reports especially on ecumenical activities in Austria including its Ökumenische Akademie. This is a good source of information on activities of the Pro Oriente Foundation. [Universitätsplatz 3; A-8010 Graz].

[143] *Oikoumenikon: Rassegna sull'ecumenismo*. Vol. 1-18. Rome:

Oikoumenikon, 1961-1978; monthly, then bimonthly.

After 270 issues the publication ceased with vol. 18 (1978). The journal had been edited by Mons. Giulio Penitenti and was originally called *Oikoumenikon: Rassegna sull'ecumenismo cattolico*. It contained installments of an ecumenical dictionary which had reached the entry "Silvestro". Its contributors were representative of most major churches.

[144] *One in Christ*. Vol. 1- . Turvey, Bedfordshire, UK: Vita et Pax Foundation for Unity, 1965- ; quarterly.

This journal is successor to *Eastern Churches Quarterly* which published sixteen volumes from 1936 to 1964. Each fascicle contains four or five major articles on ecumenical research. This is one of the better sources for keeping abreast of activities in the UK. Sometimes it translates the statements of dialogues such as the Groupe des Dombes. Together with *Sobornost* [159], this is among the best British journals on ecumenism. [Turvey Abbey, Turvey, Bedfordshire MK43 8DE].

[145] *One World*. Vol. 1- . Geneva: Communications Department, World Council of Churches, 1974- ; ten times a year.

This valuable monthly magazine brings first-hand information about the WCC and the churches throughout the world in an accessible manner with photographic documentation also. [150 route de Ferney; CH-1211 Geneva 20].

[146] *Oriente cristiano*. Vol. 1- . Palermo: Associazione Cattolica Italiana per l'Oriente Cristiano, 1963- ; quarterly.

A useful source of information on relations between Roman Catholics and Orthodox, especially in Sicily, this publication is similar in concept to *Information Service* [116]. It provides articles, documentation, chronicles and even photographs. Some issues are devoted to single themes. [Piazza Bellini 3; I-90133 Palermo].

[147] *Orientierung*. Vol. 1- . Zürich: Jesuits of Switzerland, 1936- ; every two weeks.

This high level journal of opinion reports on European and international church life and ecumenical initiatives.

[Scheideggstrasse 45; CH-8002 Zürich].

[148] *Ostkirchliche Studien*. Vol. 1- . Würzburg: Ostkirchliches Institut der deutschen Augustiner, 1952- ; quarterly.

Sponsored by German Augustinians, the journal provides articles, documentation, reports and book reviews. It also contains short abstracts of articles from specialized journals including Russian-language material. There is an on-going bibliography of Eastern Christianity which unfortunately is extremely difficult to consult because of its poor method of organization and defective indexing. [Grabenberg 2, D-8700 Würzburg].

[149] *Pastoral Ecuménica*. Vol. 1- . Madrid: Centro Ecuménico 'Missioneras de la Unidad', 1984- ; quarterly.

Especially valuable for its coverage of Spain is this Catholic journal which draws upon Orthodox, Anglican and Protestant collaboration. It also includes correspondents from North and South America. For Spain see also [153]. [Pza. Conde Barajas 1; E-28005 Madrid].

[150] *PCR Information: Reports and Background Papers*. No. 1- . Geneva: World Council of Churches, Programme Unit on Justice and Service, Programme to Combat Racism, 1979- ; irregular.

This newsletter of the WCC's Programme to Combat Racism (PCR) first appeared in 1979 and changed its format in 1982. Each issue is devoted to a special theme, such as South Africa, Women and Racism, etc. [150 route de Ferney; CH-1211 Geneva 20].

[151] *Proche Orient Chrétien*. Vol. 1- . Jerusalem: Pères Blancs de Sainte Anne de Jérusalem, 1951- ; quarterly.

Published by the Missionaries of Africa (White Fathers), the journal covers articles, documents, chronicles and book reviews especially related to the Middle East. Individual fascicles are sometimes combined into a single issue. [Sainte Anne, BP 19079, Jerusalem].

[152] *Religion in Communist Lands*. Vol. 1- . Chislehurst, Kent: Centre for the Study of Religion and Communism, Keston College, 1973- ; quarterly.

Keston College is an educational center specializing in the study of religious communities in the Soviet Union and Eastern Europe. Articles have addressed issues such as: Orthodox churches behind the Iron Curtain, Protestantism in Russia. It also summarizes items from the Russian and other Eastern European secular press. [Heathfield Road, Keston, Kent BR2 6BA, UK].

[153] *Renovación Ecuménica*. Vol. 1- . Salamanca: Asociación Ecuménica Juan XXIII, 1968- ; three times a year.

Editor of this journal is José Sanchez Vaquero whose work *Cristianos, Reconciliaos!* is cited elsewhere [725]. The review follows the usual structure of articles, documents, short communications and ecumenical chronicles especially for Spain. For Spain see also *Pastoral Ecuménica* [149]. [Ramón y Cajal 15; E-37001 Salamanca].

[154] *Romanian Orthodox Church News*. Vol. 1- . Bucharest: Romanian Orthodox Patriarchate, 1971- ; quarterly.

Published in separate English and French editions, this quartrly is sponsored by the Department of Foreign Affairs of the Romanian Orthodox Patriarchate. Besides international reports, it contains valuable accounts of the Romanian Orthodox theology and ecumenical dialogue. The Romanian theologian Dimitru Staniloae has often contributed to this publication. [29 rue Antim, Bucharest 70666].

[155] *St. Vladimir's Theological Quarterly*. Vol. 1- . Tuckahoe, NY: St. Vladimir's Orthodox Theological Seminary, 1952- ; quarterly.

Together with its Greek Orthodox counterpart, *Greek Orthodox Theological Review* [114], this journal is a major voice for Orthodox in North America, especially the Orthodox Church in America (OCA). Originally known as *St. Vladimir's Seminary Quarterly*, it has featured English writings of the late Alexander Schmemann (1921-1983) and its present dean John Meyendorff. [575 Scarsdale Rd., Crestwood, Tuckahoe, NY 10707].

[156] *Service Oecuménique de Presse et d'Information*. Vol. 1- . Geneva: Conseil oecuménique des Eglises, 1934- ; 44 times a year.

This French edition of *Ecumenical Press Service* [107] had already by 1992 reached its fifty-ninth year of publication. The annual index is arranged in two major categories: one for geography and organizations and another for subjects. [150 route de Ferney; CH-1211 Geneva 20].

[157] *Service Orthodoxe de Presse (SOP)*. No. 1- . Courbevoie, France; Comité inter-épiscopal orthodoxe, 1975- ; monthly.

Similar in concept to *Notizie Ortodosse* [137] and *Episkepsis* [113], this newsletter focuses especially on Orthodox theology and ecumenical life in French-speaking Europe. It occasionally reprints brief articles from other sources, cites documents, and calls attention to recent books and articles. [14 rue Victor Hugo, F-92400 Courbevoie].

[158] *Servizio Informazioni per le Chiese Orientali (S.I.C.O.)*. Vol. 1- . Rome: Vatican Congregation for the Eastern Churches, 1946- ; six times a year.

Similar in concept to the Pontifical Council for Promoting Christian Unity's *Information Service*, this newsletter of the Vatican's Congregation for Eastern Churches includes material especially pertinent to the Middle East and India. The publication appears only in Italian. Agreed doctrinal statements and accounts of mutual exchanges between churches are regularly recorded.

[159] *Sobornost*. [seventh series] Vol. 1- . London: Fellowship of St. Alban and St. Sergius, 1979- ; twice a year.

First known as *Journal of the Fellowship of St. Alban and St. Sergius* (1928-34) and *Sobornost* (1935-78), this journal merged in 1979 with the publication *Eastern Churches Review* (1966-1978). The Fellowship promotes cooperation between Anglican and Orthodox churches and its journal includes essays, reports, obituaries and bibliographies. [52 Ladbroke Grove, London W11 2PB, UK].

[160] *Sourozh: A Journal of Orthodox Life and Thought*. No. 1- . Oxford: Russian Patriarchal Diocese of Sourozh, s.d.- ; quarterly.

This review was founded and edited by Metropolitan Anthony [Bloom] of Sourozh (Suros), who served as Exarch of Western Europe (1965-1974). [94a Banbury Rd., Oxford OX2 6JT, UK].

[161] *Star of the East*. Vol. 1- . Kottayam, India: Sophia Centre,

Orthodox Seminary, 1979- ; quarterly.

This Indian journal specializes in Oriental Orthodox and Eastern Orthodox theology and is directed by the Indian Orthodox ecumenist Metropolitan Paulos Gregorios [Paul Verghese]. [PO Box 98, Kottayam 686001, Kerala].

[162] *Stimme der Orthodoxie.* No. 1- . Berlin: Mitteleuropäisches Exarchat des Moskauer Patriarchates, 1961- ; monthly.

A useful source in German of activites of the Moscow Patriarchate especially during the years of Patriarch Pimen's tenure. The newsletter gives brief accounts of ecumenical dialogues especially between Moscow and the Evangelische Kirche in Deutschland. See also *Journal of the Moscow Patriarchate* [122]. [Wildensteinerstr. 10; D-1157 Berlin].

[163] *Studi Ecumenici.* Vol. 1- . Venice: Istituto di Studi Ecumenici S. Bernardino, 1983- ; quarterly.

A relatively recent newcomer to the ecumenical scene, the journal includes articles, documentation, news items and a brief coverage of new books. For ecumenism in Italy a most useful source. [Castello 2786; I-30122 Venice].

[164] *Studia i Dokumenty Ekumeniczne.* Vol. 1- . Warsaw: Instytut Pasy i Wydawnictw "Novum", 1984- ; quarterly.

This important source of information for Poland contains articles, reports, surveys, reviews of the press, and an ecumenical bibliography of Polish periodicals. The articles are in Polish only, but summaries in English and German are provided.

[165] *Una Sancta: Zeitschrift für ökumenische Begegnung.* Vol. 1- . Niederaltaich: Una Sancta Arbeitsgemeinschaft, 1946- ; quarterly.

*Una Sancta* is published by the Christkönigs-Institut Meitingen and the Ökumenisches Institut of the Benedictine Abbey in Niederaltaich. Catholics, Orthodox and Lutherans are included on the editorial board. Each issue focuses on a special theme of historical and systematic theology and news of the major churches. [Abtei, D-8351 Niederaltaich].

[166] *Union des Eglises - Unité de l'Eglise.* Vol. 1-15. Paris:

Secrétariat de l'Union des Eglises, 1922-1937; quarterly.

From 1922 to 1929 the journal was known as *Union des Eglises*. Conceived in Constantinople, this Catholic publication of the Assumptionist Fathers and period piece, illustrates the pre-ecumenical, "unionist" perspective of those Catholics bent on the return of "dissidents".

[167] *Unitas*. International Quarterly Review of Ecumenism. Vol. 1-20. Rome, London, New York, Unitas Association, 1949-1968; quarterly.
*Unitas*. Organ d'information oecuménique. Vol. 1-16. Paris: Association "Unitas", Section française, 1948-1970; quarterly.
*Unitas*. Organo dell'Associazione "Unitas". Vol. 1-6. Rome: Associazione Internationale "Unitas", 1946-1951; six times a year; and New Series, 1952- ; now quarterly.

All these versions of the influential Catholic journal were originally edited by the pioneer ecumenist Charles Boyer, S.J. (1884-1980). Only the Italian edition continues to be published. The present editor, Anselmo Aru, S.J., maintains the generally cautious character of the journal. [Via del Corso 306; I-00186 Rome].

[168] *Unité chrétienne*. No. 1- . Lyons: Association 'Unité chrétienne', 1970- ; quarterly.

This publication results from the merger of the French edition of *Unitas* (1948-1970) and *Pages documentaires*. Edited originally by the ecumenist Paul Couturier, the journal retained the title *Pages documentaires* up to no. 19 (August 1970). Each issue treats a specific theme and includes a comprehensive report of international ecumenical news. Specific fascicles treated topics such as ecumenism in Spain (no. 61) and in India (no. 65). [2 rue Jean Carriès, F-69005 Lyon].

[169] *Unité des Chrétiens*. No. 1- . Paris: Secrétariat national pour l'unité des chrétiens, 1971- ; quarterly.

This high-level ecumenical publication of France addressed to the non-specialist includes excellent articles of *haute vulgarisation*, news reports of ecumenical happenings especially in Eastern Europe. [17 rue de l'Assomption, F-75016 Paris].

**[170]** *Unity Trends*. Vol. 1-2. Huntington, IN: Our Sunday Visitor, 1967-1969; 25 times a year.

This now defunct publication appeared from November 15, 1967 to December 15, 1969. The newsletter was jointly sponsored by the Catholic Newspaper *Our Sunday Visitor* and the New York office of the Faith and Order Commission of the National Council of Churches. Although discontinued for financial exigencies it was replaced in 1972 by its roughly equivalent *Ecumenical Trends* [109].

**[171]** *Ut Omnes Unum*. Vol. 1- . Paderborn: Winfriedbund, 1938- ; six times a year.

The organ of the Winfriedbund (im Dienste der Einheit im Glauben), this publication includes articles on topics such as spiritual ecumenism and pastoral care of "converts". [Postfach 2807; D-4790 Paderborn].

**[172]** *Voice from the East*. Vol. 1- . Chicago: Assyrian Church of the East, 1982- ; quarterly.

Founded by His Holiness Khanania Dinkha IV, Patriarch of the Holy Apostolic Catholic Assyrian Church of the East, the publication is written mostly in Syriac but with some sections in English. [P.O.Box 25264, Chicago, IL 60625].

**[173]** *Wereld en Zending*. Vol. 1- . Amsterdam: Nederlandse Zendingsraad and Nederlandse Missieraad, 1972- ; quarterly.

This ecumenical journal for missiology and missionary praxis is produced under the auspices of Dutch and Belgian organizations. [Prins Henriklaan 37; NL-1075 BA Amsterdam].

**[174]** *WCSF Journal*. Vol. 1- . Geneva: World Student Christian Federation, 1979- ; monthly.

The WSCF is a federation of some 60 national Protestant ecumenical student movements most of whom are called Student Christian Movement (SCM). This newsletter is a useful source of information of its current activities. [150 route de Ferney, CH-1211 Geneva 20].

**[175]** *Yearbook / Annales / Jahrbuch*. Vol.1-14. Tantur-Jerusalem:

Ecumenical Institute for Theological Research, 1971-1984; annual.

The yearbook contained principally various addresses delivered that year at Tantur in a variety of languages as well as the annual report of the Institute's academic year. Also included some discussions related to inter-faith dialogue. After 1984 it seems to have ceased regular publication.

# Centers and Research Institutes

[176] Balado, José Luis G., *The Story of Taizé.* 3rd rev. ed. Collegeville: Liturgical Press, 1991.

The monastic community founded in 1940 in Burgundy has also become a meeting place for prayer and reconciliation of the churches. This volume by a Spanish journalist first appeared as *El Desafio de Taizé* (1980) tries to explain "the Taizé phenomenon." See also [178, 180, 181, 183, 185].

[177] Bauer, Johannes B., ed. *Fünfzehn Jahre Institut für ökumenische Theologie und Patrologie.* Gräzer Theologische Studien, Beiheft 1. Graz: Institut für ökumenische Theologie und Patrologie, 1982.

Originally known as the Institut für Dogmengeschichte und ökumenische Theologie, this research center, founded by Bauer in 1966, has played an important ecumenical role in the German-speaking world. This volume narrates its history and offers reflections by several collaborators: Manfred Kertsch, Wolfgang L. Gombocz, Grigorios Larentzakis and Justinus Greifeneder. It also contains a list of Bauer's publications.

[178] Brico, Rex. *Taizé: Brother Roger and His Community.* London: Collins, 1978.

The 220 page account of the establishment of the monastery at Taizé and its youth councils also gives biographical details on its founder Roger Schutz. Selections from the prior's writings are reproduced (pp. 151-175) and an interview with him (pp. 177-211) round off the work.

[179] Deemer, Philip, ed. *Ecumenical Directory of Retreat and Conference Centers.* Boston: Jarrow Press, 1974.

A listing (presumably some of the information is now obsolete) useful for individuals and groups choosing venues for conferences and workshops. The scope is ecumenical. The material for the USA is arranged by states and cities (pp. 13-199); Canada is also listed (pp. 203-222). Although published as volume one, apparently volume two never appeared. See also Kelliher [182].

[180] Grenier, Jean-Claude. *Taizé: une aventure ambiquë*. Paris: Editions du Cerf, 1975.

The young journalist composed this work for the non-specialist with a tinge of skepticism. It provides statistics and background information and also reports on the Taizé sponsored youth councils. See also [176, 178, 181, 183, 185].

[181] Heijke, John. *An Ecumenical Light on the Renewal of Religious Community Life: Taizé*. Duquesne Studies, Theological Series 7. Pittsburgh: Duquesne University, 1967.

Although some parts of this work need to be updated, the section on Taizé's ecumenical vocation (pp. 119-162) is excellent. The author, a Spiritan Catholic priest, first visited the monastery in 1959. See also [176, 178, 180, 183, 185].

[182] Kelliher, Alexander. *International Directory of Ecumenical Research Centers and Publications*. rev. ed. Rome: Centro pro Unione, 1986.

This most recent edition of the directory of ecumenical research centers and publications is prepared by one of the Atonement Friars of the Centro pro Unione, Rome. This listing is regularly updated in *Centro pro Unione: Bulletin* [8]. See also [179].

[183] Paupert, Jean Marie. *Taizé et l'Eglise de demain*. Paris: Fayard, 1967.

This is an interesting account about the origin of Taizé, the ecumenical monastery in Burgundy, and its contributions to ecumenism. It contains a map and even travel instructions. The writings of three of its members: Roger Schutz, Max Thurian and Pierre-Yves Emery are noted. See also [176, 178, 180, 181, 185].

[184] Siegmund-Schultze, D. F., ed. *Inventarverzeichnis des ökumenischen Archivs in Soest (Westfalen)*. Soester Wissenschaftliche Beiträge 22. Soest: Westfälische Verlagsbuchhandlung Mocker und

Jahn, 1962.

This specialized catalogue of the ecumenical archives in Soest might be of use for specialists who wish to investigate German ecumenism before, during and after the two World Wars. It also identifies documentation in support of ecumenical efforts for peace. The volume is meticulously indexed.

[185] *Taizé et les jeunes: Que se lève une confiance sur la terre.* Paris: Le Centurion, 1987.

Written in collaboration with several Taizé monks and young people from around the world, the volume seeks to explain the attraction of the meeting place. It also describes the various meetings (*rencontres*) that have been sponsored by Taizé around the world as well as John Paul II's visit there in October 1986. See also [176, 178, 180, 181, 183].

# 3

# Historical Accounts

## General History

[186] Alberigo, Giuseppe. *Nostalgia di unità: Saggi di storia dell'
ecumenismo.* Genoa: Marietti, 1989.

> The distinguished church historian from Bologna has here
> collected into one volume of 175 pages a cross section of his
> essays written between 1965 and 1988 on historic moments in the
> search for Christian unity.

[187] Arminjon, Pierre. *Le mouvement oecuménique: Efforts faits pour
réaliser l'union ou le rapprochement des Eglises chrétiens.* Paris: P.
Lethielleux, 1955.

> The author, professor at Geneva and Lausanne, judged when he
> wrote this volume at the age of eighty-six that there was no
> comparable French-language work available. While the recorded
> events are now widely known, the work served an important
> function at the time especially by apprising francophone readers
> of ecumenical activities taking place in the English- and German-
> speaking world. See also [505].

[188] Benz, Ernst. *Kirchengeschichte in ökumenischer Sicht.*
Ökumenische Studien 3. Leiden: E. J. Brill, 1961.

> Among the topics treated in this short work (147 pp.) are:
> ecumenical church history as a discipline, the relationships
> between European and American church history, and tensions
> between Christianity and non-Christian religions.

[189] Biot, François. *De la polémique au dialogue*. Vol. 1. *L'Eglise face aux chrétiens séparés*. Vol. 2. *Les chrétiens séparés face à l'Eglise*. Paris: Cerf, 1963.

These two volumes give an account of moves toward church unity from the Middle Ages to modern times. The first volume concentrates on Catholicism's actions; the second on initiatives of other Christian churches. See also his popularization for non-specialists [817].

[190] Brown, Robert McAfee. *The Ecumenical Revolution: An Interpretation of the Catholic-Protestant Dialogue*. 2nd rev. ed. Garden City, NY: Doubleday, 1969.

The first edition appeared in 1966. In this version many revisions are noted in chapters 12, 14, 17, 18 and 20. There is a section on the history of the WCC and of recent developments in Reformation and Catholic churches. The work has aged well and is still useful for pre-Uppsala developments.

[191] Conord, Paul. *Brève histoire de l'oecuménisme*. Paris: s.p., 1958.

The short volume (233 pp.) is handsomely illustrated with photos of ecumenical encounters. Much the same material is found elsewhere except for chapter 10 on "L'Eglise Réformée de France." There is a useful glossary of terms (pp. 194-216) and an introduction by W. A. Visser 't Hooft.

[192] Congar, Yves. *After Nine Hundred Years: The Background of the Schism between Eastern and Western Churches*. New York: Fordham University, 1959.

The English translation is from the French *Neuf cents ans après* which was extracted from the volume *1054-1954, L'Eglise et les églises* [665]. In four chapters and a conclusion Congar outlines the political, cultural, and ecclesiological factors that led to estrangement between East and West.

[193] Congar, Yves. *Essais oecuméniques: Le mouvement, les hommes, les problèmes*. Paris: Le Centurion, 1984.

This collection of twenty essays addresses mostly historical moments in the movement while singling out seven individual ecumenists for commendation. The final section focuses on theological issues.

[**194**] Dawson, Christopher. *The Dividing of Christendom*. New York: Sheed and Ward, 1965.

This early work is based on lectures given while the British philosopher held the Charles Chauncey Stillman Chair of Roman Catholic Studies at Harvard Divinity School (1958-1962). The approach is historical and begins with the medieval period.

[**195**] Desseaux, Jacques Elisée. *Twenty Centuries of Ecumenism*. Trans. by Matthew J. O'Connell. New York: Paulist, 1984.

This short book serves as a very basic introduction to the history of efforts to achieve church unity. The appendix contains a glossary and a list of important dates.

[**196**] Fouilloux, Etienne. *Les catholiques et l'unité chrétienne du XIXe au XXe siècle: itinéraires européens d'expression française*. Paris: Le Centurion, 1982.

This volume is one of the major achievements of the post-Vatican II period. Its length (1007 pp.) can be daunting but the work is well written and carefully indexed. The author notes a gradual progression among Catholics from problematic "unionism" to a healthy "ecumenism." Unionism flourished from 1878 to 1928; ecumenism began to emerge in the 1930s and during World War II; in the years 1945-1952 (the *terminus ad quem* of the study) there appeared the first spring of ecumenism. The author is professor at the University of Caen.

[**197**] Gavalda, Berthe. *Le mouvement oecuménique*. Que sais-je? 841. Paris: Presses universitaires de France, 1959.

A concise and well-informed account of pre-Vatican II attitudes towards ecumenism including Anglo-Saxon settings. The volume underestimates the role of Orthodox and Roman Catholic pioneers.

[**198**] Hajjar, Joseph. *Le christianisme en Orient: Etudes d'histoire contemporaine 1684-1968*. Beirut: Librairie du Liban, 1971.

The author who was born in Damascus is a Melkite Catholic and a noted historian of several Arab-speaking Eastern churches.

Much of the French text from the latter half of this volume appeared in a English translation as part of *The Church in a Secularised Society* (Christian Centuries 5; New York: Paulist, 1978).

[199] Iserloh, Erwin. *The Theses Were Not Posted: Luther Between Reform and Reformation*. Trans. by Jared Wicks. London: Geoffrey Chapman, 1968.

The book treats not only the events of October 31, 1517, but also Luther's involvement in the indulgences controversy. The well known Luther expert first published this volume in German as *Luther zwischen Reform und Reformation*. For Lutheran attitudes to ecumenism, see also [569-584].

[200] Kantzenbach, Friedrich Wilhelm, ed. *Einheitsbestrebungen im Wandel der Kirchengeschichte*. Gütersloh: Gerd Mohn, 1979.

Part of a series of textbooks designed for theology students, this particular volume covers a spectrum of historical moments from the early church, through A.D. 1054, to the Reformation and up to efforts at ecumenism in the nineteenth and twentieth centuries.

[201] Meinhold, Roger. *Kirchengeschichte im Schwerpunkten: Ein ökumenischer Versuch*. Graz: Styria, 1982.

The Protestant author covers the whole gamut of church history from Jesus to the twentieth century and tries to identify thirty key moments (*Schwerpunkte*) that have had ecumenical impact.

[202] Mönnich, Conrad. *Una Sancta: De Mogelijkheid der christelijke eenheid*. Amsterdam: Elsevier, 1947.

This 541 page volume describes in detail early, pre-Amsterdam efforts at church unity. This is a good source of earlier attitudes and convictions. See also Van der Linde [603, 728].

[203] Nash, Margaret. *Ecumenical Movement in the 1960s*. Johannesburg: Ravan, 1975.

From Cape Town comes this overview of the history of modern ecumenism and a plea for greater commitment among South African churches to the goals of ecumenism.

[204] Rouse, Ruth, and Neill, Stephen Charles, eds. *A History of the Ecumenical Movement, 1517-1948.* 3rd rev. ed. Philadelphia: Westminster; London: SPCK, 1986.

This book needs to be read with its companion volume two, edited by Harold E. Fey [213] which continues up to the year 1968. Some seventeen expert collaborators contributed to this historical narrative. The experiences of the Orthodox churches are included. In English there is still no rival to this publication.

[205] Tavard, George H. *Two Centuries of Ecumenism: The Search for Unity.* Trans. by Royce W. Hughes. Notre Dame: Fides, 1961.

This pre-Vatican II Catholic study is divided equally between accounts of nineteenth and twentieth century church unity movements. The volume is still a reliable description of events up to 1960.

[206] Till, Barry. *The Churches Search for Unity.* Harmondsworth, UK: Penguin, 1972.

Although somewhat overly focused on the British experience of church unity efforts, this descriptive volume is nonetheless a useful short account of the background, the beginnings and the contemporary scene of ecumenism.

[207] Vischer, Lukas, ed. *Church History in an Ecumenical Perspective.* Bern: Evangelische Arbeitsstelle Ökumene Schweiz, 1982.

The volume contains papers from an international ecumenical consultation held in Basel, October 1981. Besides the general theme, other essays treat the Council of Basel, church history from new horizons (such as Mexico, Fiji, India), and joint conclusions on church history from the Swiss theological faculties.

# Twentieth Century

[208] Aubert, Roger, ed. *Le Saint Siège et l'union des églises.* Brussels: Editions universitaires, 1947.

This short 160 page account narrates the Roman Church's understanding of church union prior to 1878 and then during the pontificates of Leo XIII, Pius X, Benedict XV and Pius XII. Some of this material appears also in the work edited by Shook [379].

See also [209].

[209] Baum, Gregory. *That They May Be One: A Study of Papal Doctrine (Leo XIII - Pius XII)*. London: Bloomsbury; Westminster, MD: Newman, 1958.

This book is an indispensable resource for understanding the shifting and developing attitudes of five modern-day popes on ecumenism. The period extends from Leo XIII's *Praeclara gratulationis* to statements by Pius XII in 1955. There is a chart of documents but not all the original texts are cited in full. See also [208].

[210] Brown, William Adams. *Toward a United Church: Three Decades of Ecumenical Christianity*. New York: C. Scribner's Sons, 1946.

W. A. Brown (1865-1943), after whom the Brown Library of Ecumenical Theology at Union Theological Seminary in New York City is named, wrote this personal account during World War II which was then updated after his death by Samuel McCrea Cavert. The book also contains an annotated ecumenical bibliography prepared by Paul Griswold Macy (pp. 234-256).

[211] Cutler, Donald R., ed. *The Religious Situation: 1968-1969*. 2 vols. Boston: Beacon Press, 1968-1969.

The reporting on religious events here is descriptive, journalistic, socio-political in focus. It notes events and trends that occurred in the two years noted. The scope is broader than Christianity.

[212] Davies, Rupert E. *The Church in Our Times: An Ecumenical History from a British Perspective*. London: Epworth, 1979.

The Methodist minister who played a notable role in ecumenical activities nationally and internationally gives an historical account of ecumenism with special stress on twentieth century Britain.

[213] Fey, Harold E., ed. *A History of the Ecumenical Movement*. Vol. 2: *The Ecumenical Advance 1948-1968*. Philadelphia: Westminster Press; London: SPCK, 1970.

This volume continues the study begun by Rouse and Neill [204]. There are fifteen chapters undertaken by various Protestant and Orthodox scholars. There is an excellent bibliography prepared by

Ans J. van der Bent to accompany each chapter (pp. 447-508). In English, it is hard to find a better collaborative study of these eventful twenty years.

[214] Goodall, Norman. *The Ecumenical Movement: What It Is and What It Does*. rev. ed. London: Oxford University Press, 1964.

The first edition appeared in 1961 and was followed three years later by this version. While quite outdated, the volume continues to serve as a faithful reflection of the situation in the mid 1960s as seen through the eyes of Norman Goodall (1896-1985). See also [215].

[215] Goodall, Norman. *Ecumenical Progress: A Decade of Change in the Ecumenical Movement, 1961-1971*. London: Oxford University Press, 1972.

This companion volume to the previous volume [214] focuses on the years 1961-1971 and features the wider impact of Vatican II and the enhanced role of Eastern Orthodoxy.

[216] Heiler, Friedrich. *Vom Werden der Ökumene: Zwei Vorlesungen*. Beiheft zur Ökumenischen Rundschau 6. Stuttgart: Evangelisches Missionsverlag, 1967.

Heiler (1892-1967) gave these two lectures in Munich and Marburg for his seventy-fifth birthday shortly before his death. The first concerns his own ecumenical encounters (pp. 5-26) and the second concerns the development (*"Werden"*) of ecumenism (pp. 27-55). See also [524, 846].

[217] Hope, Norman Victor. *One Christ, One World, One Church: A Short Introduction to the Ecumenical Movement*. Philadelphia: Church Historical Society, 1953.

The author was professor of church history at Princeton Theological Seminary at the time of this publication. The work is intended to complement W. Richey Hogg's *Ecumenical Foundations* (1952) and W. Adams Brown's *Towards a United Church* (1946). The discussion covers the period up to Amsterdam in 1948. Some of the book's views on the freedom of the Russian Orthodox Church at that time are rather naive. The focus of the book is notably Protestant.

[218] Neill, Stephen. *Towards Church Union 1937-1952: A Survey of Approaches to Closer Union Among the Churches*. London: SCM, 1952.

This is a record of movements for union or reunion among Protestant churches up to the 1950s. It treats organic mergers, establishment of intercommunion, and negotiations still in progress.

[219] Thils, Gustave. *Histoire doctrinale du mouvement oecuménique*. 2nd ed. Paris: Desclée de Brouwer; Louvain: E. Warny, 1963.

Although other histories of ecumenism are more complete, this work remains a Catholic classic because of its pioneering character (1st ed., 1955 [206 pp.]; 2nd ed., 1963 [338 pp.]). Part one discusses the origins and accomplishments of the WCC up to 1961; part two, the more original section (pp. 155-324), reflects an enlightened if somewhat cautious commitment to modern ecumenism.

# World Council of Churches
# General Studies

[220] *And So Set Up Signs... The World Council of Churches' First 40 Years*. Geneva: World Council of Churches, 1988.

This oversized commemorative volume contains numerous photographs recalling great moments in the WCC's history. The history and purpose of the organization are lucidly enunciated. The charts and schemata are helpful.

[221] Beach, Bert Beverly. *Ecumenism, Boom or Bust?* Washington: Review and Herald, 1974.

This sardonic book by a British churchman from St. Albans is one of several strong criticisms of the goals of the WCC. Its main objection is that the organization fails to promote evangelism.

[222] Beffa, Pierre; Bent, Ans J. van der; Homberger, C.; Poutalès, R. de. *Index to the World Council of Churches Official Statements and Reports: 1948-1978*. Geneva: World Council of Churches, 1978.

This list (104 pp.) of official reports of the assemblies, units and sub-units of the WCC is carefully indexed. At the end of the booklet there is reproduced the original index covering the years 1948-1967. The new index reshapes the previous material and updates it to 1978. Some 5221 printed pages of WCC documents are here indexed.

[223] Bent, Ans J. van der. *From Generation to Generation: The Story of Youth in the World Council of Churches*. Geneva: World Council of Churches, 1986.

With his usual thoroughness, the retired WCC librarian gives an account of youth activities in the WCC starting from the ecumenical youth commission (1933-1939) and the first world conference of Christian youth in 1939 (Amsterdam). There is an excellent bibliography and a list of conferences in the appendix.

[224] Bent, Ans J. van der. *Handbook: Member Churches, World Council of Churches*. Rev. ed., Geneva: World Council of Churches, 1985.

First published in 1982 the book gives lists of member churches of the WCC by continent, region and country, as well as names of church leaders, publications and a wealth of statistics. Especially useful are the lists of national and regional councils of churches (1-10) and the clear descriptions of the Christian world communions (11-29). For an update of membership list to May 1990, see Van Elderen [244].

[225] Bent, Ans J. van der. *The Utopia of World Community: An Interpretation of the World Council of Churches for Outsiders*. London: SCM, 1973.

The eight chapters of this popular introduction are addressed primarily to those who have only remote interest in church matters: marginal Christians, people of other faiths, adherents of a secular ideology.

[226] Carson, Herbert. *United We Fall: A Study of Current Ecumenical Pressures*. Haywards Heath, England: Carey, 1975.

The sixteen page booklet gives an account of the annual Evangelical and Reformed Conference in South Africa, held in Skoeghem, Natal, in 1973. The approach is strongly evangelical and critical of the WCC and the modern ecumenical movement in general judged to be a threat to true gospel values.

[227] Castro, Emilio, and Best, Thomas F., eds. *Commemorating Amsterdam 1948: 40 Years of the World Council of Churches*. Geneva: World Council of Churches, 1988.

This volume also appeared as a fascicle of *The Ecumenical Review* 40, nos. 3-4 (1988). There are numerous accounts of what happened at Amsterdam, what it has meant, its wider impact, and enduring issues.

[228] Chenu, Bruno. *La signification ecclésiologique du Conseil Oecuménique des Eglises, 1945-1963*. Paris: Beauchesne, 1972.

This dissertation directed by Joseph de Baciocchi at the Faculty of Theology, Lyons, contains twelve chapters outlining the early work of the WCC sometimes in a critical manner for its becoming overly institutionalized. The two final chapters are Catholic reflections raising the question of the WCC's ecclesiological status.

[229] Döring, Heinrich. *Kirchen unterwegs zur Einheit: Das Ringen um die sichtbare Einheit der Kirchen in den Dokumenten der Weltkirchenkonferenzen*. Munich: F. Schöningh, 1969.

This doctoral dissertation for the Catholic Theology Faculty at Würzburg (1967), directed by Josef Hasenfuss, is described as a phenomenological-theological reflection. Much of the text is devoted to WCC meetings from 1927 to 1968 but also to comparisons of Catholic and non-Catholic ecumenism.

[230] Duff, Edward. *The Social Thought of the World Council of Churches*. London and New York: Longmans, Green, 1956.

The American Jesuit who later served as one of the first Catholic official observers at a WCC general assembly (New Delhi, 1961) intended this to be not a theological study but an investigation of the ecumenical movement's criticism of the economic order, politicial institutions, and international developments of our times.

[231] Gaines, David P. *The World Council of Churches: A Study of Its Background and History*. Peterborough, NH: Richard R. Smith, 1966.

This monumental 1302 page volume by the pastor of the First Baptist Church in Waterbury, Connecticut, a long-time member of the WCC's Faith and Order Commission provides a detailed account of the WCC's history up to the third general assembly of New Delhi (1961). A long section discusses the pre-history of modern ecumenism and the WCC's formation. Also included is a lengthy bibliography (pp. 1265-81).

[232] Gentz, William H. *The World of Philip Potter.* New York: Friendship, 1974.

Potter (b. 1921) became general secretary of the WCC in 1972. This 96 page narrative of his life and accomplishments for church unity begins with an account of his attendance as a youth observer at the WCC general assembly in Amsterdam (1948).

[233] Groscurth, Reinhard, ed. *Wandernde Horizonte auf dem Weg zu kirchlicher Einheit.* Frankfurt: Otto Lembeck, 1974.

Eight collaborators from five countries (Argentina, France, Germany, Switzerland, USA) contributed to this working session of the Faith and Order Commission meeting in Salamanca, September 1973. All the essays are in German but originate from a cross-section of well-known European and North American professional ecumenists. They attempt to summarize the ecumenical situation prior to the WCC general assembly in Nairobi.

[234] Hoekstra, Harvey T. *The World Council of Churches and the Demise of Evangelism.* Wheaton, IL: Tyndale, 1979.

Published in the UK as *Evangelism in Eclipse: World Mission and the World Council of Churches* (Exeter: Paternoster, 1979), this work is typical of the publications that strongly critique the WCC. The author is opposed to the WCC's reconceptualization of mission seen to be at variance with classical, biblical mission.

[235] Howell, Leon. *Acting in Faith: The World Council of Churches since 1975.* Geneva: World Council of Churches, 1982.

The author is a free-lance American journalist based in Washington. Besides giving a description of the organizational structure of the WCC, he outlines its search for a just and sustainable society. He stresses the relationship between the unity of the church and the unity of humankind.

[236] Hudson, Darril. *The World Council of Churches in International*

*Affairs*. Leighton Buzzard: Faith, 1977.

The author praises the work of the WCC's Commission of the Churches in International Affairs for its stands on racism, peace, and economics in the third world. Unlike the work of Norman [242] and others, he sees this involvement as consistent with ecumenism. See also Hudson [1335].

[237] Lange, Ernst. *And Yet It Moves: Dream and Reality of the Ecumenical Movement*. Trans. by Edwin Robertson. Belfast: Christian Journals; Grand Rapids: Eerdmans; Geneva: World Council of Churches, 1979.

This book began as an evaluation of the Louvain (1971) meeting of Faith and Order but expanded into a probing analysis of the strengths and weaknesses of the ecumenical movement in general. Lange (d. 1974) served on the WCC and was a Lutheran minister in Germany.

[238] Lefever, Ernest W. *Amsterdam to Nairobi: The World Council of Churches and the Third World*. Washington: Georgetown University, 1979.

The author, director of the Ethics and Public Policy Center at Georgetown University, asks whether the WCC is an appropriate instrument for Christian action, whether it is active on behalf of decent causes, and whether it is indecently quiet about indecencies committed by regimes on the left. In his strong criticism he proposes eight recommendations to guide the WCC toward more enlightened engagement.

[239] McDonnell, John J. *The World Council of Churches and the Catholic Church*. Toronto Studies in Theology. Lewiston, NY: Edwin Mellen Press, 1985.

This doctoral dissertation covers the history of the WCC's relationship to the Catholic Church through the general assembly in Vancouver in 1983.

[240] Macfarland, Charles S. *Christian Unity in Practice and Prophecy*. New York: Macmillan, 1933.

Written between the Edinburgh International Missionary Conference (1910) and the first meeting of Faith and Order in

Lausanne (1927), this early work records the perspectives and fears of ecumenists at that time. A separate chapter on unity movements in the USA is included. For a more complete history see Rouse [204] and Fey [213].

[241] Müller-Römheld, Walter. *Zueinander-Miteinander: Kirchliche Zusammenarbeit im 20. Jahrhundert.* Frankfurt: O. Lembeck, 1971.

This short account of ecumenical efforts in this century gives special attention to the WCC. It lists all its member churches by date of entry and country and provides some fascinating archival photographs.

[242] Norman, Edward. *Christianity and the World Order.* Oxford: Oxford University Press, 1979.

In the Reith Lectures for 1978 the dean of Peterhouse, Cambridge University, critiques the modern politicization of religion and expresses his scepticism about the propriety of associating Christianity with any set of political values. The WCC is specifically singled out for blame.

[243] *Rencontre oecuménique à Genève.* Collaboration oecuménique 4. Geneva: Labor et Fides; Paris: Librairie Protestante, 1965.

Cardinal A. Bea's visit to the WCC headquarters (February 1965) is here described. Also included are comments on that occasion by W.A. Visser 't Hooft and M. Boegner and conferences given by N. Nissiotis and O. Cullmann.

[244] VanElderen, Marlin. *Introducing the World Council of Churches.* Geneva: World Council of Churches, 1991.

The author is also editor of the WCC's magazine *One World* [145]. In six chapters there is provided a good review of the WCC's history and goals. The appendix includes a useful explanation of the WCC's new organizational structure and a list of member churches updated to May 1990. The book is richly illustrated with archival photographs.

[245] Vermaat, J.A. Emerson. *The World Council of Churches and Politics 1975-1986.* Focus on Issues no. 6. Lanham, MD: University Press of America, 1989.

This polemic volume strongly criticizes the recent policies and decisions of the World Council of Churches and its Faith and Order Commission in particular. For a similar critique, see also Norman [242].

[246] Visser 't Hooft, W.A. *The Genesis and Formation of the World Council of Churches*. Geneva: World Council of Churches, 1982.

The special interest of this 130 page account about the WCC's foundation are the personal details provided by its former general secretary (1948-1966) who was connected with it from 1933 on. There are five appendices including the important Toronto Statement of the WCC's Central Committee (1950).

[247] Wegener-Fueter, Hildburg. *Kirche und Ökumene: Das Kirchenbild des Ökumenischen Rates der Kirchen nach dem Vollversammlungs-dokumenten von 1948 bis 1968*. Göttingen: Vandenhoeck und Ruprecht, 1979.

This doctoral dissertation at Göttingen studies the growth in the WCC's ecclesiology as reflected in its statements at general assemblies from Amsterdam (1948) through Uppsala (1968).

[248] Wind, A. *Zending en Oecumene in de twintigste eeuw: Handboek over de geschiedenis van zending en oecumene aan de hand van de grote conferenties en assemblées. Deel I: Van Edinburgh 1910 tot en met Evanston 1954*. Kampen: J.H. Kok, 1984.

This careful historical study, well documented with primary sources, aims to show the close relationship between mission and ecumenism especially as conceived by the WCC. The bibliography is extensive (pp. 384-412).

# General Assemblies

### Amsterdam 1948

[249] *Man's Disorder and God's Design: The Amsterdam Assembly Series*. New York: Harper and Brothers, 1949.

This publication contains the official report of the first general assembly, four books in one volume, covering the topics discussed: the universal church, the church's witness, the church and disorder of society, and the church and international disorder.

**Evanston 1954**

[250] Visser 't Hooft, W.A., ed. *The Evanston Report: The Second Assembly of the World Council of Churches, 1954.* New York: Harper and Brothers; London: SCM Press, 1955.

This volume contains the official proceedings of Evanston general assembly.

[251] *The Christian Hope and the Task of the Church: Six Ecumenical Surveys and the Report of the Advisory Commission on the Main Theme.* New York: Harper and Brothers, 1954.

This book contains the study preparations for the theme "Christ - The Hope of the World."

**New Delhi 1961**

[252] Visser 't Hooft, W.A., ed. *The New Delhi Report: The Third Assembly of the World Council of Churches, 1961.* New York: Association; London: SCM, 1962.

This publication contains the official proceedings of the New Delhi general assembly.

[253] *Evanston to New Delhi 1954-1961: Report of the Central Committee to the Third Assembly of the World Council of Churches.* Geneva: World Council of Churches, 1961.

Continuing its tradition, the Central Committee reported to the assembly about issues that emerged between the second and third general assemblies.

**Uppsala 1968**

[254] Goodall, Norman, ed. *The Uppsala Report 1968: Official Report of the Fourth General Assembly of the World Council of Churches, Uppsala, July 4-20, 1968.* Geneva: World Council of Churches, 1968.

Contained in this volume are the official proceedings of the fourth general assembly.

### Nairobi 1975

[255] Paton, David M., ed. *Breaking Barriers, Nairobi 1975: The Official Report of the Fifth Assembly of the World Council of Churches, Nairobi, 23 November-10 December 1975.* London: SPCK; Grand Rapids, Eerdmans, 1976.

In this publication are the official acta of fifth general assembly of the WCC.

[256] Johnson, David Enderton, gen. ed. *Uppsala to Nairobi 1968-1975: Report of the Central Committee to the Fifth Assembly of the World Council of Churches.* New York: Friendship; London: SPCK, 1975.

The report is intended to cover the years intervening between the fourth and fifth general assemblies.

[257] *Orthodox Contributions to Nairobi: Papers Compiled and Presented by the Orthodox Task Force of the WCC.* Geneva: World Council of Churches, 1975.

The booklet reproduces the final reports of five separate international meetings of Orthodox held between 1972 and 1975 to study the upcoming theme of the Nairobi assembly.

### Vancouver 1983

[258] Gill, David, ed. *Gathered For Life: The Official Report of the Sixth Assembly of the World Council of Churches.* Geneva: World Council of Churches, 1983.

Gill served as editor for the official final report of the sixth general assembly held in Vancouver in 1983.

[259] Lazareth, William H., ed. *The Lord of Life: Theological Explorations of the Theme "Jesus Christ - the Life of the World".* Geneva: World Council of Churches, 1983.

Prior to the general assembly in Vancouver an ecumenical group of theologians prepared individual reflections on the assembly's four sub-themes: life as a gift of God, life confronting and overcoming death, life in its fullness, and life in unity.

[260] *Nairobi to Vancouver 1975-1983: Report of the Central Committee to the Sixth Assembly of the World Council of Churches.* Geneva: World Council of Churches, 1983.

Besides the English edition of the report to the general assembly there are versions also in French, German and Spanish.

**Canberra 1991**

[261] Kinnamon, Michael, ed. *Signs of the Spirit: Official Report of the Seventh Assembly, Canberra, Australia, 7-20 February 1991.* Geneva: World Council of Churches; Grand Rapids: Eerdmans, 1991.

The proceedings of the seventh general assembly were published in remarkably short time after the conclusion of the meeting.

[262] Best, Thomas F., ed. *Vancouver to Canberra 1983-1990: Report of the Central Committee of the World Council of Churches to the Seventh Assembly.* Geneva: World Council of Churches, 1990.

Besides the report of the general secretariat there are reports from Faith and Witness, Justice and Service, Education and Renewal, and several appendices.

[263] Limouris, Gennadios, ed. *Come, Holy Spirit, Renew the Whole Creation: An Orthodox Approach to the Seventh Assembly of the World Council of Churches, Canberra, Australia, 6-21 February 1991.* Brookline, MA: Holy Cross Orthodox Press, 1990.

The volume gives the addresses and interventions of some twenty-five theologians meeting at the Inter-Orthodox Consultation of Eastern Orthodox and Oriental Orthodox Churches held on Crete, November 25-December 4, 1989, prior to the Canberra assembly. All the papers are in English.

# Faith and Order Commission

**Lausanne 1927**

[264] Bate, H.N., ed. *Faith and Order Proceedings of the World Conference, Lausanne, August 3-21, 1927.* New York: George H. Doran, 1927.

The proceedings include the daily schedule of events, the

documents received by the commission, and the text of addresses given at the public meetings.

### Edinburgh 1937

[265] Hodgson, Leonard, ed. *The Second World Conference on Faith and Order Held at Edinburgh, August 3-18, 1937.* New York: Macmillan; London: SCM, 1938.

Included here are the proceedings of the meeting, a theological report (pp. 220-269), and the proposal (270-274) to establish a WCC.

### Lund 1952

[266] Tomkins, Oliver S., ed. *The Third World Conference on Faith and Order Held at Lund, August 15th to 28th, 1952.* London: SCM Press, 1953.

This volume includes a report to the churches, an overview of the years from Edinburgh to Lund (1937-1952), and proceedings of the conference.

### Montreal 1963

[267] Rodger, P.C., and Vischer, Lukas. *The Fourth World Conference on Faith and Order, Montreal 1963.* New York: Association Press, 1964.

There is a Montreal diary by David M. Paton as well as section reports on Faith and Order projects underway. The volume also contains the official proceedings.

[268] *Faith and Order Findings: The Final Report of the Theological Commissions to the Fourth World Conference on Faith and Order.* Faith and Order Papers 37, 38, 39, 40. Minneapolis: Augsburg, 1963.

The volume contains four reports on: institutionalism, Christ and the church, worship, and tradition and traditions.

[269] Ehrenström, Nils, and Muelder, Walter G., eds. *Institutionalism and Church Unity: A Symposium Prepared by the Study Commission on Institutionalism, Commission on Faith and Order, World Council of Churches.* New York: Association Press, 1963.

Sixteen Protestant theologians provided theological papers and a series of case studies in preparation for the forthcoming Montreal Conference of Faith and Order.

### Louvain 1971

[270] Vischer, Lukas, ed. *Faith and Order: Louvain 1971: Study Reports and Documents*. Faith and Order Paper 59. Geneva: World Council of Churches, 1971.

The offical proceedings of the Louvain meeting contain the study reports presented to the commission and reports arising from the commission's meeting.

### Accra 1974

[271] *Uniting in Hope, Accra 1974: Reports and Documents from the Meeting of the Faith and Order Commission, 23 July - 5 August 1974, University of Ghana, Legon*. Faith and Order Paper 72. Geneva: World Council of Churches, 1975.

This volume contains the proceedings and reports from the 1974 meeting held in Accra, Ghana.

### Bangalore 1978

[272] *Sharing in One Hope: Bangalore, 1978: Reports and Documents from the Meeting of the Faith and Order Commission*. Faith and Order Paper 92. Geneva: World Council of Churches, 1978.

The proceedings contain reports on two themes: giving account of hope and growing together in unity.

### Lima 1982

[273] Kinnamon, Michael, ed. *Towards Visible Unity: Commission on Faith and Order, Lima, 1982*. 2 vols. Faith and Order Papers 112, 113. Geneva: World Council of Churches, 1982.

Volume one contains the minutes and addresses of the conference; volume two contains the study papers and reports relating to two themes: the common expression of the apostolic faith today, and the unity of the church and the renewal of human community.

### Stavanger, Norway 1985

[274] Best, Thomas F., ed. *Faith and Renewal: Reports and Documents of the Commission on Faith and Order, Stavanger, Norway, 13-25 August 1985.* Faith and Order Paper 131. Geneva: World Council of Churches, 1986.

Contained in this volume is an overview of Faith and Order activiites past, present and future as well as reports on BEM, apostolic faith today, and unity and renewal.

### Budapest 1989

[275] Best, Thomas F., ed. *Faith and Order 1985-1989: The Commission Meeting at Budapest, 1989.* Faith and Order Paper 148. Geneva: World Council of Churches, 1990.

The Commission's meeting held in Budapest in 1989 is here recorded together with the reports connected with the sessions.

### General Studies

[276] De Groot, Alfred Thomas. *An Index to the Doctrine, Persons, Events, etc. of the Faith and Order, Commission World Council of Churches, Given in the English Language Editions, Official, Numbered Publications, 1910-1948 and Check List Faith and Order Commission Official, Numbered Publications; Series 1: 1910-1948; Series 2, 1948-1970.* 3rd ed. Geneva: World Council of Churches, 1970.

The archivist from Texas Christian University, Fort Worth, Texas, carefully prepared this listing of Faith and Order publications up to the year 1970. The volume is indexed not only by name but also by theological or ecumenical concept.

[277] Gassmann, Günther. *Konzeptionen der Einheit in der Bewegung für Glauben und Kirchenfassung 1910-1937.* Forschungen zur systematischen und ökumenischen Theologie, Bd. 39. Göttingen: Vandenhoeck und Ruprecht, 1971.

Produced as a *Habilitationsschrift* at Heidelberg under the direction of Edmund Schlink, this study of the Faith and Order Commission includes background material of organic views of unity especially among Anglicans. The author identifies 1920 as the start of the movement's withdrawal from isolation. The volume does not go beyond the Edinburgh meeting of 1937.

[278] *Lausanne 77: Fifty Years of Faith and Order*. Faith and Order Paper 82. Geneva: World Council of Churches, 1977.

Fifty years after the first international meeting of Faith and Order in 1927, this commemorative volume was published. Contributions include articles by Y. Congar, J. Moltmann, N. Nissiotis, R. Schutz. Especially interesting are the historical reflections by W.A. Visser 't Hooft. The focus also includes theological reflections.

[279] Pathil, Kuncheria. *Models in Ecumenical Dialogue: A Study of the Methodological Development in the Commission on "Faith and Order" of the World Council of Churches*. Bangalore: Dharmaram, 1981.

In nine chapters this Roman Catholic author gives both a description of Faith and Order's comparative method and a critique which suggests preferable models. There is an extensive bibliography on Faith and Order (pp. 443-491) and a list of its leaders from 1910 to 1980 (492-503).

[280] Skoglund, John E., and Nelson, J. Robert. *Fifty Years of Faith and Order: An Interpretation of the Faith and Order Movement*. New York: Committee for the Inter-Seminary Movement of the National Student Christian Federation, 1963.

This presentation of Faith and Order is designed for the non-specialist. The authors are convinced that familiarity with the movement's history and goals is important for the wider public but especially for divinity students. Although designed for North American students it has an international prespective.

[281] Vischer, Lukas, ed. *A Documentary History of the Faith and Order Movement 1927-1963*. St. Louis: Bethany, 1963.

The volume contains the final reports of the first three Faith and Order meetings and the first three general assemblies. There are also three statements received by the Central Committee and several other reports. The official numbered publications of Faith and Order (Series 1, 1910-1948 and Series 2, 1948 [up to no. 35 in 1962]) are given.

## Life and Work Movement

[282] Journet, Charles. *L'Union des Eglises et le christianisme pratique*. Paris: Bernard Brasset, 1927.

This is one of the earlier Roman Catholic studies of the Life and Work movement's meeting in Stockholm in 1925. Its rather one-sided assessment shows that not only the Vatican but individual Catholic theologians harbored suspicions of the movement. For another early evaluation by a Catholic see Pribilla [491].

[283] Niederschlag, Heribert. *Für Alle: Der Beitrag der Life and Work Bewegung zur Begründung christlicher Weltverantwortung*. Frankfurt: P. Lang, 1982.

The present volume was accepted as a doctoral dissertation at the University of Würzburg in 1981 under the direction of G. Teichtweier. It covers the genesis, development and purpose of the Life and Work movement.

## Vatican II
## Sessions and Documents

[284] Abbott, Walter M., gen. ed. *The Documents of Vatican II*. trans. ed. Joseph Gallagher. New York: America Press, Guild Press, Association Press, 1966.

This widely used translation of Vatican II's sixteen documents is a generally reliable version but not without its shortcomings. It contains brief commentaries by Catholic, Orthodox and Protestant scholars. See also English version edited by Flannery [302].

[285] Abbott, Walter M. *Twelve Council Fathers*. New York: Macmillan; London: Collier-Macmillan, 1963.

During the course of Vatican II, Abbott published a series of interviews in the Jesuit weekly *America* with twelve prominent Council Fathers representing several continents: Paul-Emile Léger, Joseph Cordeiro, Léon-Joseph Suenens, Achille Liénart, Giuseppe Siri, Franziskus König, Laurian Rugambwa, Bernhard Alfrink, Ermenegildo Florit, G. Emmett Carter, Julius Döpfner and Richard Cushing. The interviews provide useful background for interpreting the Council's final documents.

[286] *Acta et Documenta Concilio Oecumenico Vaticano II*: Series I: *Antepraeparatoria*. 4 vols. in 12 folios, plus 2 appendices, and index; Series II: *Praeparatoria*. 4 vols. in 8 folios; *Acta Synodalia Sacrosancti Concilii Oecumenici Vaticani II*. 5 vols. in 25 folios, plus 2 vols. appendices, 1 vol. index. Vatican City: Vatican City Press, 1960-1989.

These numerous volumes are the official Latin records of Vatican II including the "antepreparatory" and preparatory stages as well as all four sessions of the Council. All speeches, interventions, *modi* (suggested emendations), preliminary drafts and final texts are included. The second volume of appendices for the *Acta Synodalia* lists all the official observers and guests of the Secretariat for Promoting Christian Unity and what churches or organizations they represented (pp. 231-287). The Index volume contains a list of the *periti* (pp. 279-798). Because of the complexity of using these primary sources, one could profit from consulting G. Lefeuvre's detailed user's guide in *Revue théologique de Louvain* 11 (1980) 186-200; 325-351.

[287] Alberigo, Giuseppe, and Magistretti, Franca, eds. *Constitutionis Dogmaticae Lumen Gentium Synopsis Historica*. Bologna: Istituto per le Scienze Religiose, 1975.

This complete chronology of the various drafts of Vatican II's *Lumen gentium* is presented in synoptic columns by Bologna's Institute for Religious Studies. All the various questions, animadversions and responses (*modi*) given orally or in written form at the Council are also included in Latin. The introduction to the volume is in English and Italian. Alberigo is professor of church history in Bologna.

[288] Anderson, Floyd, ed. *Council Daybook: Vatican II*. 3 vols. Washington: National Catholic Welfare Conference, 1965.

This work was prepared by the Rome office of the NCWC news service. All four sessions of the Council are included in a day by day account of the 168 general congregations and the ten plenary sessions. Because the volumes are so well indexed one would be well advised to begin locating a reference to a specific speech or text here first before consulting the bulky *acta*.

[289] Barauna, Guilherme, ed. *L'Eglise de Vatican II: Etudes autour de la Constitution conciliare sur l'Eglise*. 2 vols. Unam Sanctam 51b, 51c. Paris: Editions du Cerf, 1967.

The two volumes of commentary on *Lumen gentium* extend to 1442 pages and are part of the *Unam Sanctam* series (volume 51a contains only the Latin text and French translation). The commentaries are rich and detailed. Besides the some fifty Catholic contributors there are six essays by Orthodox, Anglicans and Protestants. Of special note is the blunt and astute conclusion by Yves Congar (pp. 1365-73).

[290] Bea, Augustin. *Ecumenism in Focus*. London: Geoffrey Chapman, 1969.

Published also in Italian (*Ecumenismo nel Concilio*, 1968) and German (*Der Ökumenismus im Konzil*, 1969), this volume by A. Bea (1881-1968), the Jesuit Cardinal and founder of the Vatican's Secretariat for Promoting Christian Unity, contains historical reflections on the period before Vatican II and on each of the four conciliar sessions, in addition to four essays about the post-conciliar period.

[291] Bea, Augustin. *The Way to Unity after the Council*. London: Geoffrey Chapman; New York: Herder and Herder, 1967.

The noted ecumenist published these analyses of seven of Vatican II documents: on ecumenism, revelation, the church, religious liberty, non-Christian religions, and the modern world.

[292] Békés, Gerard J. and Vajta, Vilmos, eds. *Unitatis Redintegratio: eine Bilanz der Auswirkungen des Ökumenismus-Dekrets*. Frankfurt: O. Lembeck, 1977.

These seven articles in German, French and English were composed by leading theologians to mark the tenth anniversary of the promulgation of Vatican II's Decree on Ecumenism. Catholic, Protestant and Orthodox views are included.

[293] Blondel, Maurice. *Attente du concile*. Paris: Editions du Cerf, 1964.

The publishers of Maurice Blondel (1861-1949) undertook this posthumous collection of various religious reflections mostly from unedited material on matters that later emerged as central concerns of Vatican II. In this way it is possible to illustrate how he anticipated much of the Council's preoccupations even in ecumenical issues.

[294] Caprile, Giovanni. *Il Concilio Vaticano II.* 5 vols. in 6. Rome: Civiltà Cattolica, 1965-1969.

One of the most comprehensive of all the chronicles of Vatican II, this series was prepared by the staff of the Jesuit journal *Civiltà Cattolica.* The analytical indexes are excellent, and even the coverage of the Council's preliminary commissions is comprehensive. For a simpler English guide see F. Anderson [288].

[295] Cereti, Giovanni. *Riforma della chiesa e unità dei cristiani nell'insegnamento del Concilio Vaticano II.* Biblioteca de Studi Ecumenici 1. Verona: Ed. Ecumenice, 1985.

This 461 page study is a notable historical and doctrinal study of early and later drafts of Vatican II's Decree on Ecumenism, *Unitatis redintegratio.*

[296] Congar, Yves. *Le concile au jour le jour.* 4 vols. Paris: Cerf, 1963-1966.

These four mini volumes are a chronicle of the four sessions of the Council whereas his volume *Le Concile de Vatican II* [357] is theological in character. Volume one has a useful list of the thirty-nine observers at the first session of Vatican II.

[297] Delhaye, Philippe, *et al.,* eds. *Concilium Vaticanum II: Concordances, index, listes de fréquence, tables comparatives.* Louvain: Centre de traitement electronique des documents, 1974.

This concordance of the principal words in the Latin texts of Vatican II is a highly valuable tool. Words are listed in the context of a phrase; frequency lists are included. This work is indispensable for any close word-study of Vatican II. See also Ochoa [313].

[298] Deretz, Jacques and Nocent, Adrien, eds. *Dictionary of the Council.* London: G. Chapman, 1968.

This dictionary, a translation of *Synopse des textes conciliaires,* is more theological than linguistic. Under various ecclesiastical and theological terms are collected relevant passages illustrating the Council's teachings.

[299] *Documents conciliaires: Concile oecuménique Vatican II*. 4 vols. Paris: Le Centurion, 1965-1966.

These volumes are of interest not for the French translation of the texts of Vatican II but for the excellent introductions by major French and Austrian (F. König) ecumenists.

[300] *Dokumente des Zweiten Vatikanischen Konzils*. 9 vols. Trier: Paulinus, 1965-1967.

Both the Latin original and a German translation are provided together with excellent but brief commentaries by leading German theologians. The commentary on the Constitution on the Church document was done by Wilhelm Breuning. See also Vorgrimler [321].

[301] Fesquet, Henri. *The Drama of Vatican II: The Ecumenical Council, June 1962 - December 1965*. Trans. by Bernhard Murchland. New York: Random House, 1967.

This 831 page diary of the Council was prepared by the religious news editor of the Paris daily *Le Monde* who had been a student of Jean Guitton and Yves Congar. His personal interpretations of the proceedings are also informative.

[302] Flannery, Austin, gen. ed. *Vatican II: The Conciliar and Post Conciliar Documents*. Collegeville: Liturgical Press; Northport, NY: Costello, 1975.

This more recent English translation than Abbott's [284] is the work of twenty-four different translators, mostly Irish. The volume also contains many post-conciliar directives promulgated to assist in the implementation of the Council's teachings. The translation is good but the order in which the two classes of documents is here presented is somewhat confusing. See also [303].

[303] Flannery, Austin, gen. ed. *Vatican Council II: More Post Conciliar Documents*. Northport, NY: Costello, 1982.

This companion to the previous volume adds another fifty-seven documents many of which are further implementations of the Council's decrees. Of special note is the text of the Secretariat for Promoting Christian Unity's "Ecumenical Collaboration at the

Regional, National and Local Levels (*Réunis à Rome*)", February 22, 1975 (pp. 153-182). See also [302].

[304] Galli, Mario von. *The Council and the Future*, with photographs by Bernhard Moosbrugger. New York: McGraw Hill, 1966.

The product of a four year collaboration between a Swiss Jesuit, von Galli, who wrote the text, and a professional photographer, this remarkable collection of photographs gives an intimate, behind the scenes view of the Council sessions. See also Vallainc [319].

[305] Gherardini, Brunero. *Cristianità in cammino: L'ecumenismo e la sua problematica*. Naples: Libreria Editrice Redenzione, 1969.

The professor of ecclesiology at the Lateran University, Rome, and seven others (including one Orthodox, one Protestant) collaborated for this study on ecumenism. The volume is largely an assessment of Vatican II's Decree on Ecumenism.

[306] Grootaers, Jan. *Primauté et collégialité: Le dossier de Gérard Philips sur la Nota Explicativa Praevia (Lumen gentium, Chap. III)*. Bibliotheca Ephemeridum Theologicarum Lovaniensium LXXII. Leuven: University Press, 1986.

During the third session of the Council, the third week of November 1964 was described as a "black week" because a problematic *nota explicativa praevia* was added to the text of the Constitution on the Church. This volume edits the private dossier of the Council *peritus*, Gérard Philips (1899-1972), which sheds much light on the origin and significance of this addition. See also [316].

[307] Hampe, Johann Christoph, ed. *Die Autorität der Freiheit: Gegenwart des Konzils und Zukunft der Kirche im ökumenischen Disput*. 3 vols. Munich: Kösel, 1967.

What might be described as a *summa theologica et historica* of Vatican II is this massive commentary on the drafts and final texts of the sixteen Council documents. The commentary on the Decree on Ecumenism appears in Vol. II (pp. 553-636) and is itself an ecumenical achievement. See also Vorgrimler [321].

[308] Jaeger, Lorenz. *A Stand on Ecumenism: The Council's Decree*.

Trans. by Hilda Graef. New York: P.J. Kenedy; London: Geoffrey Chapman, 1965.

Although not as detailed as the commentaries of Leeming [311] or Barauna [289], this volume published by a German Catholic is useful. The English translation of the Decree is defective, but the account of the document's pre-history is excellent. The author, cardinal and past president of the Johann Adam Möhler Institute for Ecumenics in Paderborn, also provided an appendix of sources used in the decree. The German original was entitled *Das Konzilsdekret* (1965).

[309] Javierre, Antonio M. *Promoción conciliar del diálogo ecuménico*. Madrid: Ediciones cristianidad, 1966.

This is the best Spanish commentary on the Decree on Ecumenism. It contains background material (pp. 55-74) and a detailed analysis (75-307). There is a lengthy bibliography (309-329). An Italian version of this book has also appeared.

[310] Küng, Hans. *The Council, Reform and Reunion*. Trans. by Cecily Hastings. New York: Sheed and Ward, 1961.

This volume which appeared on the eve of Vatican II in German as *Konzil und Wiedervereinigung* (1960) appeared in the UK under the title *The Council and Reunion*. It was widely read and contributed much to awakening popular interest in the coming Council.

[311] Leeming, Bernard. *The Vatican Council and Christian Unity: A Commentary on the Decree on Ecumenism*. New York: Harper and Row, 1966.

This is one of the more indepth analyses of the Decree on Ecumenism in the English language. The 333 page work by the veteran British ecumenist B. Leeming (1893-1971) contains background information not found in other works. Included is a list of official observers at Vatican II and the text of several pertinent speeches.

[312] Lefebvre, Marcel. *J'accuse le Concile*. 2nd ed. Martigny, Switzerland: Saint-Gabriel, 1976.

From his seminary at Ecône, Switzerland, the dissident French archbishop who eventually was excommunicated by the Roman Catholic Church for his rejection of the teachings of Vatican II here outlined his objections.

[313] Ochoa, Xaverius. *Index Verborum cum Documentis Concilii Vaticani Secundi*. Rome: Commentarium pro Religiosis, 1967.

While not as good as the Louvain computer generated concordance by Delhaye [297] still this concordance of almost all the Latin words appearing in the documents of Vatican II is a useful resource.

[314] O'Neill, Charles, ed. *Ecumenism and Vatican II*. Milwaukee: Bruce, 1964.

At the early stages of Vatican II this Jesuit professor from Fordham University organized a series of nine talks on Christian unity. Six are given by Catholics, but an Orthodox, Presbyterian, and a Jewish rabbi also speak from their perspectives. Especially prophetic is the talk of Flemish theologian Piet Fransen on "Episcopal Conferences: Crucial Problem of the Council" (pp. 98-126).

[315] Pattaro, Germano. *Corso di Teologia dell' Ecumenismo*. Strumenti 31. Brescia: Editrice Queriniana, 1985.

Noting the responsibility of the entire church to foster ecumenism, the author provides a popular guide for Italian study groups. He gives historical background and theological commentary on the results of Vatican II.

[316] Philips, Gérard, *L'Eglise et son mystère au IIe concile du Vatican. Histoire, texte et commentaire de la Constitution Lumen Gentium*. 2 vols. Paris: Desclée, 1968.

The special interest of this volume is that it is written by one of the principal theological architects of *Lumen gentium*. Philips was professor at the University of Louvain and active as a *peritus* at the Council. See also [306].

[317] Sayegh, Maximos, ed. *L'Eglise Grecque Melkite au Concile*. Beirut: Dar Al-Kalima, 1967.

This valuable collection of interventions at Vatican II by

Patriarch Maximos IV and various prelates of his church is arranged according to the themes of the conciliar decrees. See also his study [513].

[318] Thils, Gustave. *Le Décret sur l'oecuménisme: Commentaire doctrinal*. Paris: Desclée de Brouwer, 1966.

While this short work seems to be simply another standard commentary on *Unitatis redintegratio*, it holds special interest because of the author's pioneer involvement with ecumenism and his eventual direct impact on some of Vatican II's final formulations.

[319] Vallainc, Fausto. *Immagini del Concilio*. Vatican City: Vatican Press, 1966.

This oversized, largely photographic chronicle of Vatican II prepared by the director of the Vatican Press Office also contains a written essay on the antepreparatory, preparatory periods and the four conciliar sessions. There is also a valuable chronology of the Council. See also von Galli [304].

[320] Villain, Maurice. *Vatican II et le dialogue oecuménique*. Paris: Casterman, 1966.

This account of the four sessions of Vatican II by the successor to Paul Couturier includes a number of helpful observations. He also includes various reactions by Orthodox and Protestants and his reflections on the relationship of the Council to the WCC.

[321] Vorgrimler, Herbert, ed. *Commentary on the Documents of Vatican II*. 5 vols. New York: Herder and Herder; London: Burns and Oates, 1967-1969.

These commentaries were originally prepared in German for the supplementary volumes of the *Lexikon für Theologie und Kirche* [70]. Each paragraph of conciliar texts is analyzed closely with special attention to various emendations suggested and voted upon. The theological commentary is excellent and prepared by experts. In English there is no better comprehensive commentary.

[322] Yzermans, Vincent A., ed. *American Participation in the Second Vatican Council*. New York: Sheed and Ward, 1967.

This book contains English texts of Council speeches given by American bishops. The speeches are arranged according to sixteen sections corresponding to the decrees of Vatican II. The editor provides an historical introduction and experts offer theological analyses.

# Observers' Reactions

[323] Barth, Karl. *Ad Limina Apostolorum: An Appraisal of Vatican II*. Trans. by Keith R. Crim. Richmond: John Knox, 1968.

Barth had been prevented by ill health from attending Vatican II as an observer. After the Council he studied the sixteen documents and visited Rome from September 22-29, 1966, to take part in discussions. He subsequently conducted a seminar at Basel on Vatican II. His views are contained here especially in his "Thoughts on Vatican II" (pp. 65-79) and his list of questions about *Lumen gentium*.

[324] Berkhof, Hendrikus, *et al. Protestantse Verenningen na 'Vaticanum II'*. The Hague: Boekencentrum, 1967.

Ten essays by nine Dutch Protestants record their assessments of Vatican II's teachings on: Scripture and tradition ( C.A. DeRidder), early catholicism in the New Testament (G. Sevenster), justification (A.F.N. Lekkerkerker), nature and grace (G.E. Meuleman), church (H. Berkhof), ecclesial office (A.J. Bronkhorst), eucharistic sacrifice (W.F. Golterman), liturgy (H. Jonker), church and world (H. Berkhof), and unanswered questions (C.J. Dippel).

[325] Berkouwer, Gerrit Cornelis. *The Second Vatican Council and the New Catholicism*. Trans. by Lewis B. Smedes. Grand Rapids: Eerdmans, 1965.

This is a translation of *Vatikaans concilie en nieuwe theologie* (1964) written by the well-known conservative Dutch Reformed theologian, professor of systematics at the Free University of Amsterdam. Can the Roman Catholic Church, he asks, experience a radical change when it believes that the Holy Spirit has directed its entire history? The treatment here concentrates on the theological impact of the Council. See also his [445].

[326] Bosc, Jean, *et al. Points de vue de théologiens protestants:*

*Etudes sur les décrets du Concile*. Unam Sanctam 64. Paris: Editions du Cerf, 1967.

> As part of a multi-volume work on the texts of Vatican II, this volume holds particular significance since twelve Protestant collaborators here assess its principal theological texts.

[327] Bronkhorst, Alexander J. *Het concilie en de oecumene*. Baarn: Bosch & Keuning, 1962.

> The author, a professor at the Protestant Theology Faculty of Brussels, provided a popular study towards the beginning of Vatican II. The work taps a source (Flemish Protestantism) not easily available.

[328] Brown, Robert McAfee. *Observer in Rome: A Protestant Report on the Vatican Council*. New York: Doubleday, 1964.

> Dr. Brown served as an official observer for the World Alliance of Reformed and Presbyterian Churches at Vatican II but only for its second session (1963). He describes its ten weeks in detail especially the conciliar debates about ecumenism.

[329] Brun, Maria. *Orthodoxe Stimmen zum II. Vatikanum: Ein Beitrag zur Überwendung der Trennung*. Ökumenische Beihefte zur Freiburger Zeitschrift für Philosophie und Theologie 18. Fribourg: Universitätsverlag, 1988.

> This is a valuable record of Orthodox reactions to the Council with thoughtful conclusions. The material is organized around four themes: an "ecumenical" council, the nature of the church, the hierarchical structure of the church, and new ecclesiological perspectives.

[330] Cullmann, Oscar. *Vatican Council II: The New Direction*. New York: Harper and Row, 1968.

> Cullmann was personally invited by Rome to be a Protestant observer at Vatican II where his influence on certain textual formulations was observable. Collected here are seven important ecumenical articles he composed for a lectureship after the autumn of 1966.

[331] Cullmann, Oscar. *Vrai et faux oecuménisme: Oecuménisme après*

*le Concile*. Cahiers théologiques 62. Neuchâtel: Delachaux et Niestlé, 1971.

A major conviction of this 75 page book is that Protestants and Catholics have distinctive charisms to contribute to the global task of ecumenism.

[332] Helbing, Hanno. *Das Zweite Vatikanische Konzil: Ein Bericht*. Begegnung 10. Basel: F. Reinhardt, 1966.

This non-Catholic author served as a Council observer for the *Neue Zürcher Zeitung* at all four sessions. One of the first German language evaluations of the Council, it is based largely on the daily speeches given at the sessions.

[333] Horton, Douglas. *Towards an Undivided Church*. New York: Association; Notre Dame, IN: University of Notre Dame, 1967.

This work by the retired dean of Harvard Divinity School, who served as an official observer at Vatican II, treats problems relating to infallibility, papacy, veneration of saints, trans-substantiation, birth control, etc. Part two contains the texts of official talks addressed to Protestant and Orthodox observers from 1962 to 1965.

[334] Kantzenbach, Friedrich Wilhelm. *Aktion und Reaktion: Katholizismus der Gegenwart evangelisch gesehen*. Stuttgart: Steinkopf, 1978.

This useful follow up to an earlier work [343] explains in twelve chapters how a Lutheran relates to Roman Catholics one decade after the Council. He touches upon changes in the ecumenical scene, the evolving papacy, bilateral dialogues and theological research.

[335] Lackmann, Max. *Mit evangelischen Augen: Beobachtungen eines Lutheraners auf dem Zweiten Vatikanischen Konzils*. 5 vols. Graz: Styria, 1963-1966.

The Lutheran observer at all four sessions of Vatican II, founder of the Bund für evangelisch-katholische Wiedervereinigung, and editor of *Bausteine* [93] provided a day by day account of the Council. Beyond the purely human interest stories he has numerous insights into the theological issues.

[336] Lindbeck, George A., ed. *Dialogue on the Way: Protestant Report from Rome on the Vatican Council*. Minneapolis: Augsburg, 1965.

This work which also appeared in German and French was the first extended evaluation of Vatican II by a group of Protestants. It covered only the first three sessions of the Council. Sponsored by Strasbourg's Institute for Ecumenical Research, it provided nine contributions. Especially pertinent is E. Schlink's commentary on the Decree on Ecumenism (pp. 186-230). This volume is continued in [343].

[337] Lindbeck, George A. *The Future of Roman Catholic Theology: Vatican II, Catalyst for Change*. Philadelphia: Fortress, 1970.

This book originated in lectures given at Concordia Lutheran Theological Seminary, St. Louis, in August 1966. The conservative Missouri Synod Lutherans invited the liberal Lutheran to speak on five aspects of the Council at which he had been an official observer.

[338] Moorman, John. *Vatican Observed: An Anglican Impression of Vatican II*. London: Darton, Longman and Todd, 1967.

The Anglican bishop of Ripon who served as an observer for the Church of England to all four sessions of Vatican II here summarizes his impressions. Also included is an address of Pope Paul VI to the Council's observers (Dec. 4, 1965) and Moorman's response.

[339] Outler, Albert C. *Methodist Observer at Vatican II*. Westminster: Newman, 1967.

The late professor of theology at the Perkins School of Theology, Southern Methodist University, provided these insightful observations following his presence as an observer at all four sessions of Vatican II. See also his [607].

[340] Papandreou, Damaskinos, ed. *Stimmen der Orthodoxie zu Grundfragen des II. Vatikanums*. Vienna: Herder, 1969.

This important work presents the views of twelve leading Greek Orthodox theologians and churchmen regarding nine Council texts and a papal document on indulgences. The volume was sponsored by the Pro Oriente Foundation in Vienna.

[341] Pawley, Bernard C. *An Anglican View of the Vatican Council.*
New York: Morehouse-Barlow, 1962.

The Anglican canon of Ely who was to serve as personal
representative of the Archbishops of Canterbury and York at
Vatican II wrote these eight chapters prior to the opening of the
Council. See also [342].

[342] Pawley, Bernard and Margaret. *Rome and Canterbury: A Study
of the Relations Between the Church of Rome and the Anglican
Churches 1530-1981.* 2nd rev. ed. London and Oxford, Mowbray,
1981.

The former Archdeacon of Canterbury and his wife collaborated
on this comprehensive historical study of relations between the
Roman Church and the Anglican Communion. The second edition
includes additional material about the years 1973 to 1981. The
earlier edition (New York: Seabury, 1975) included an American
epilogue by Bishop Arthur A. Vogel which is omitted in the later
British publication. See also [341].

[343] Quanbeck, Warren; Kantzenbach, Friedrich Wilhelm; Vajta,
Vilmos, eds. *Challenge ... and Response: A Protestant Perspective of
the Vatican Council.* Minneapolis: Augsburg, 1966.

This continuation of *Dialogue on the Way* [336] covers the fourth
session of Vatican II. It appeared in German as *Wir Sind Gefragt*
and in French as *Rome nous interpelle* (ed. W. Kantzenbach).
There are seven Protestant evaluations of conciliar decrees and
five reflections including a postscript from H. Dietzfelbinger.

[344] Ricca, Paolo. *Il Cattolicesimo del Concilio: Un guidizio
protestante sul Concilio Vaticano II.* Turin: Claudiana, 1966.

An Italian Protestant gives an insightful assessment of Vatican II
in twelve chapters together with a glossary of technical terms. See
also Subilia [354].

[345] Rilliet, Jean. *Vatican II: Echec ou réussite? Le concile vu par un
protestant.* Geneva: Editions générales, 1964.

The religion correspondent for the newspaper *Tribune de Genève*,
Pastor Rilliet reports on sessions one and two of Vatican II. This
is a useful formulation of Reformation concerns about the

Council.

[346] Rostan, Ermano. *L'Unità della Chiesa a Nuova Delhi e a Roma*. Turin: Ed. Claudiana, 1963.

This is an account of the WCC 1961 general assembly meeting in New Delhi and the opening of Vatican II narrated by two Italian Protestants.

[347] Roux, Hébert. *Le Concile et le dialogue oecuménique*. Paris: Seuil, 1964.

The French Protestant pastor and well known ecumenist Hébert Roux (1902-1980) wrote these twelve essays between January 1963 and June 1964 during the first two sessions of the Council. See also his longer work [348].

[348] Roux, Hébert. *Détresse et promesse de Vatican II: Réflexions et expériences d'un observateur au Concile*. Paris: Seuil, 1967.

Commissioned by the World Alliance of Reformed Churches, this pastor wrote this assessment of all the sessions of Vatican II from the viewpoint of a committed Protestant. An earlier work *Le Concile et le dialogue oecuménique* (1964) covered only the first two sessions.

[349] Schatz, Werner, ed. *Was bedeutet das Zweite Vatikanische für uns?* Basel: Friedrich Reinhardt, ca. 1966.

Pastor Schatz of the Petersgemeinde in Basel hosted a series of lectures in 1966 delivered by members of the Protestant, Old Catholic, Catholic, Anglican Orthodox and Jewish communities. The common topic was the wider significance of Vatican II.

[350] Schlink, Edmund. *After the Council*. Trans. by Herbert J.A. Bouman. Philadelphia: Fortress, 1968.

The distinguished professor of systematic theology at the Evangelical Theological Faculty of Heidelberg University attended all four sessions of Vatican II and conveyed in these fifteen chapters his evaluation of the event. The German original was *Nach dem Konzil* (1966).

[351] Siegmund-Schultze, Friederich, ed. *Das zweite Vatikanische*

*Konzil: Vorträge katholischer und evangelischer Theologen über den Ökumenismus.* Schriften des ökumenischen Archivs Soest, Bd. IV. Soest: Mocker und Jahn, 1967.

This collection of nine German essays contains ecumenical talks given in Europe during Vatican II. The authors address the genesis and impact of the Decree on Ecumenism.

[352] Skydsgaard, Kristen E., ed. *The Papal Council and the Gospel: Protestant Theologians Evaluate the Coming Vatican Council.* Minneapolis: Augsburg, 1961.

The German title [*Konzil und Evangelium: Lutherische Stimmen*] gives a more accurate account account of the volume's contents. Collected are seven essays by Lutherans written before the opening of the Council in which they outline their hopes and fears regarding the forthcoming event.

[353] Sonntag, Frederick. *The Crisis of Faith: A Protestant Witness in Rome.* New York: Doubleday, 1969.

Written by the first Protestant ever to teach as visiting professor of philosophy at Rome's University S. Anselmo where he lectured in the academic year 1967/68, this personal account of his encounter with the church of Rome includes a sympathetic analysis of crises facing it: crises in vocations, in dealing with pluralism.

[354] Subilia, Vittorio. *Le nouveau visage du Catholicisme: Une appréciation réformée du Concile Vatican II.* Trans. by Emile Ribante. Collection oecuménique 6. Geneva: Labor et Fides, 1968.

This lengthy volume (395 pp.) by a Protestant professor in Rome appeared originally as *La nuova cattolicità del cattolicesimo* (1967). Part one discusses the ecclesiology of Vatican II; part two the theology of worship and the function and ministry of the ordained. See also Ricca [344].

[355] Vischer, Lukas. *Überlegungen nach dem Vatikanischen Konzils.* Zürich: EVZ Verlag, 1966.

The former secretary of Faith and Order who served as observer to Vatican II for the WCC published four of his assessments of the Council: kerygma and dialogue, visible continuity in the church, reform of canon law, and nature of an ecumenical council.

# Post Conciliar Assessments

[356] Bohn, Oluf, and Rasmussen, Niels Krogh. *Den katolske kirke efter 2. Vatikanerkoncil*. Copenhagen: Gyldendal, 1975.

Ten years after the close of the Council two Danish Catholics collaborated on this retrospective assessment of its major positions.

[357] Congar, Yves. *Le Concile de Vatican II: Son Eglise, Peuple de Dieu et corps du Christ*. Théologie Historique 71. Paris: Beauchesne, 1984.

From a perspective of some twenty years Congar published twelve essays that reviewed what the Council had stated about the church against the background of the wider history of ecclesiology.

[358] Defois, Gérard, ed. *Le Concile: 20 ans de notre histoire*. Paris: Desclée, 1982.

Twelve witnesses, including Y. Congar and J.E. Desseaux, describe the significance of Vatican II and its subsequent impact on French Christianity up to 1982.

[359] Fagin, Gerald M., ed. *Vatican II: Open Questions and New Horizons*. Theology and Life Series 8. Wilmington, DL: Michael Glazier, 1984.

From the perspective of some twenty years, four Catholic theologians (Stephen Duffy, Avery Dulles, Gregory Baum and Francine Cardman) and one Protestant (George Lindbeck) give their assessments of the Council and its impact.

[360] Floristan, Casiano, and Tamayo, Juan José, eds. *El Vaticano II, Veinte Años Despues*. Madrid: Ediciones Cristianidad, 1985.

This lengthy 475 page assessment of the post-Vatican II period contains fifteen essays organized around four themes: the significance of Vatican II; new ecclesial awareness; theological insights; basic unanswered questions.

[361] Greinacher, Norbert and Küng, Hans, eds. *Katholische Kirche - wohin? Wider den Verrat am Konzil.* Munich: R. Piper, 1986.

These thirty essays are by Roman Catholics who wish to argue that the initiatives of Pope John XXIII and Vatican II have been hampered by reactionary moves in the post-conciliar church. An English adaptation, *The Church in Anguish*, appeared the same year [367]. See also Halter [363].

[362] Grootaers, Jan. *De Vatican II à Jean-Paul II: le grand tournant de l'Eglise catholique.* Paris: Le Centurion, 1981.

The Flemish Catholic lay professor of theology at Leuven published this work simultaneously in French and in Dutch (*De onverwachte Wending*). Using conceptual framework drawn from the field of political science, he analyzed the impact of John Paul II's strong personality on shaping post-conciliar Catholicism.

[363] Halter, Hans, ed. *Neue ökumenische Eiszeit?* Zürich: Benziger, 1989.

The questions posed is whether the ecumenical movement has entered a new "ice age". Four Catholics (F. Annen, A. Gasser, A. Ebneter and R. Hotz) and two Protestants (L. Vischer and J. Flury) respond with a variety of nuanced replies. See also [361, 367].

[364] Hastings, Adrian, ed. *Modern Catholicism: Vatican II and After.* London: SPCK; New York: Oxford University Press, 1991.

This high level assessment of the state of Catholicism from the years 1965 to 1990 has been produced by an international team of Catholics and one "outsider" (Norman Thomas). Each conciliar document is re-evaluated, special issues are addressed and geographic contexts described. George Tavard provides an account of recent ecumenical relations (pp. 398-421).

[365] Kaufmann, Gisbert, ed. *Tendenzen der katholischen Theologie nach dem zweiten Vatikanischen Konzil.* Munich: Kösel, 1979.

This valuable overview of post-Vatican II Catholic theology was authored by eleven theologians born in the 1920s and 1930s. Especially useful are the articles by W. Beinert on the principal tendencies in Catholic theology today and by H.-J. Schulz on the role of the local church.

[366] König, Franz, ed. *Die bleibende Bedeutung des Zweiten Vatikanischen Konzils*. Schriften der Katholischen Akademie in Bayern, Bd. 123. Düsseldorf: Patmos, 1986.

For the twentieth anniversary of Vatican II's closing, seven Catholic theologians, including the editor who is Archbishop Emeritus of Vienna, composed essays on various theological issues. The contribution of Heinrich Fries describes the ecumenical hopes attached to the Council.

[367] Küng, Hans, and Swidler, Leonard, eds. *The Church in Anguish: Has the Vatican Betrayed Vatican II?* San Francisco: Harper and Row, 1986.

From among the thirty essays in the German original *Katholische Kirche - wohin?* [361] twelve were here translated into English and an additional fourteen new essays by American theologians were included. Besides the Catholic authors, R. M. Brown gives a Protestant assessment. See also Halter [363].

[368] Latourelle, René, ed. *Vatican II: Assessment and Perspectives Twenty-Five Years After (1962-1987)*. 3 vols. New York: Paulist, 1988-1989.

This mammoth theological commentary was carried out by sixty-seven professors (representing some twenty countries) teaching in the three Jesuit institutions of Rome (the Gregorian University, the Oriental Institute and the Biblical Institute). Oddly, apart from the study of Jared Wicks on Lutheran/Catholic dialogue from 1965 to 1985 (II, pp. 305-346), there is meager attention to ecumenical issues.

[369] Lubac, Henri de. *Entretien autour de Vatican II: Souvenirs et Réflexions*. Paris: Editions du Cerf, 1985.

This volume records an interview held in Paris in June 1985 between the late theologian Cardinal Henri de Lubac (1896-1991) and Angelo Scola first published in Italian in *30 Giorni*. He describes pre-Vatican II France, controversies around his book *Le surnaturel*, and the impact of the Council.

[370] Miller, John H., ed., *Vatican II: An Interfaith Appraisal*. Notre

Dame: University of Notre Dame, 1966.

Twenty-six scholars, mostly Catholic, contributed to this international consultation held at Notre Dame in March 1966. The volume also contains a "Who's Who" of Vatican II theologians.

[371] O'Connell, Timothy E., ed. *Vatican II and Its Documents: An American Reappraisal*. Theology and Life Series 15. Wilmington, DL: Michael Glazier, 1986.

From 1982 to 1984 a group of scholars from the Chicago area generated these papers to promote discussion on the impact of Vatican II within the North American setting. Thirteen documents are analyzed and the editor provides a summing up.

[372] O'Malley, John W. *Tradition and Transition: Historical Perspectives on Vatican II*. Theology and Life Series 26. Wilmington, DL: Michael Glazier, 1989.

The distinguished Jesuit church historian from the Weston School of Theology, Cambridge, Massachusetts, brings together a series of studies that place Vatican II in a broad context of paradigm shifts.

[373] Pattaro, Germano. *Per una pastorale dell' Ecumenismo: Commento al Direttorio ecumenico*. Brescia: Editrice Queriniana, 1984.

This 161 page commentary on the Vatican Ecumenical Directory (published in 1967 and 1970) includes an Italian version of the Directory itself. The author teaches at the seminary in Venice and at the Ecumenical Institute of Verona.

[374] Pro Oriente. *20 Jahre Ökumenismus des II. Vatikanischen Konzils*. Pro Oriente 8. Innsbruck: Tyrolia, 1985.

The Vienna based Pro Oriente Foundation published these retrospective studies by a cross section of European theologians to mark the twentieth anniversary of the closing of Vatican II.

[375] Rahner, Karl; Cullmann, Oscar; Fries, Heinrich. *Sind die Erwartungen erfüllt? Überlegungen nach dem Konzil*. Theologische Fragen Heute 7. Munich: Huebner, 1966.

The question raised by the Protestant observer, O. Cullmann, is whether our expectations of the Council have been fulfilled. The two Catholics ask: what was achieved, and have Christians come closer together?

[376] Richard, Lucien J., ed. *Vatican II: The Unfinished Agenda. A Look to the Future.* New York: Paulist, 1987.

Fifteen persons associated with the Weston School of Theology in Cambridge, Massachusetts, explore most of the Vatican II documents with a critical eye for the future. Visiting lecturer Karl Rahner offers a fundamental theological interpretation of the Council.

[377] Schner, George P. *The Church Renewed: The Documents of Vatican II Reconsidered.* Lanham, MD: University Press of America, 1986.

This symposium sponsored by the Jesuits of Regis College, Toronto, took place in May 1984. Canadian Catholic scholars provided retrospective commentaries on the major texts of Vatican II. Cardinal George Bernard Flahiff provided his own "Recollections of a Council Father."

[378] Seeber, David, ed. *Brauchen wir ein neues Konzil? Erfahrungen mit dem II. Vatikanum.* Herder Taschenbuch 1400. Freiburg: Herder, 1987.

The editor in chief of *Herder Korrespondenz* [115] edited these sixteen contributions mostly by lay Catholics to assess the impact of the Council from a perspective of twenty-five years.

[379] Shook, Laurence K., ed. *Theology of Renewal.* Vol. 1: *Renewal of Religious Thought*; Vol. 2: *Renewal of Religious Structures.* Montreal: Palm; New York: Herder, 1968.

This important congress on theology and renewal of the church was held at St. Michael's College, Toronto, to mark the centenary of Canadian federation (1867-1967). While more comprehensive than a simple commentary on Vatican II, there are numerous analyses of conciliar positions, some by Anglicans, Protestants, Orthodox and Jews. Of special note is R. Aubert's "Stages of Catholic Ecumenism from Leo XIII to Vatican II" (II, pp. 183-203). See also Aubert [208].

[380] Stacpoole, Alberic, ed. *Vatican II Revisited By Those Who Were There*. London: Geoffrey Chapman; Minneapolis: Winston, 1986.

> Some twenty-two theologians and hierarchs involved in the day-to-day unfolding of Vatican II collaborated on this retrospective view to analyze the impact of specific thinkers and the genesis of conciliar texts. Also included are reflections by representatives of the Anglican and Protestant communities.

[381] Thils, Gustave. *L'après-Vatican II: Un nouvel âge de l'Eglise?* Cahiers de la Revue Théologique de Louvain 13. Louvain-la-Neuve, Faculté de théologie, 1985.

> The professor emeritus from Louvain, a participant at Vatican II, addresses four post-conciliar themes: how the church is conceived, Roman centralization, relations with non-Catholics, and church and civil society.

# Joint Working Group

[382] *Common Witness: A Study Document of the Joint Working Group of the Roman Catholic Church and the World Council of Churches*. Commission on World Mission and Evangelism [CWME], Series 1. Geneva: World Council of Churches, 1981.

> The concept "common witness" is explored mutually by the Vatican's Secretariat for Promoting Christian Unity and by the CWME of the WCC.

[383] *Joint Working Group between the Roman Catholic Church and the World Council of Churches*. Geneva: World Council of Churches, 1966.

> This first report of the Joint Working Group (JWG), founded in 1965, appeared also in *The Ecumenical Review* 18, no. 2 (1966). This report covers the two meetings held in 1965.

[384] *Fifth Report of the Joint Working Group between the Roman Catholic Church and the World Council of Churches*. Geneva: World Council of Churches, 1983.

> This fifth report of the JWG appeared also in *The Ecumenical Review* 35, no. 2 (1983). This report covers the years 1975-1983.

[385] *Joint Working Group between the Roman Catholic Church and the*

*World Council of Churches: Sixth Report.* Geneva: World Council of Churches, 1990.

> The JWG recently celebrated its twenty-fifth anniversary. This booklet describes the work of the ecumenical committee from 1983 to 1990. Included are two study documents commissioned and received by the JWG: "The Church: Local and Universal" (pp. 23-37), and "The Notion of 'Hierarchy of Truths': An Ecumenical Interpretation" (pp. 38-46).

# Biographies and Autobiographies

[386] Anderson, Paul B. *No East or West.* Paris: YMCA, 1985.

> The American author was associated with the YMCA beginning in 1913 first in China and then in Russia where he was in prisoner of war service. After 1924 he moved to Paris where he founded the YMCA Press which publishes religious books in Russian. This is a personal account of his long ecumenical involvements.

[387] Angell, Charles, and LaFontaine, Charles. *Prophet of Reunion: The Life of Paul of Graymoor.* New York: Seabury, 1975.

> Two members of his community narrate the life of Lewis Wattson who became known as Father Paul of Graymoor (1863-1940). He established the Franciscan Friars of the Atonement and was the first inspiration behind the Week of Prayer for Christian Unity.

[388] *Atti del Simposio Card. Agostino Bea, Roma, 16-19 dicembre 1981.* Communio n.s. 14. Rome: Pontificia Università Lateranense, Istituto 'Ut Unum Sint', 1983.

> On the occasion of the 100th anniversary of the birth of Augustin Bea (1881-1968) a special symposium was held at which Johannes Willebrands gave a personal account of his dealings with the founder of the Secretariat for Promoting Christian Unity. There are three other presentations commenting on Bea's dialogue with Jews (J. Osterreicher), his views on religious freedom (P. Pavan), and his theology of baptism (E. Lanne).

[389] Beumer, Johannes, ed. *Auf dem Weg zur christlichen Einheit: Vorläufer der ökumenischen Bewegung von den Anfängen des Humanismus bis zum Ende des 19. Jahrhunderts: Ausgewählte Texte.*

Sammlung Dietrich 314. Bremen: Carl Schünemann, 1966.

The Jesuit professor at Sankt Georgen, Frankfurt, produced this valuable study of sixteen forerunners of the modern ecumenical movement (as early as the fifteenth century) with excerpts of their writings. Included are: Nicolas of Cusa, Erasmus, Georg Witzel, the authors of the Leipzig Reunion Proposal (1539), Michel de Montaigne, Franciscus Veronius, J.B. Bossuet, Beda Mayr, Johann Sebastian von Drey, Maximilian Prechtl, Johann Adam Möhler, Franz von Baader, Ignaz von Döllinger, John Henry Newman, and Vladimir Solovieff. See also [403, 404, 408].

[390] Bilheimer, Robert S. *Breakthrough: The Emergence of the Ecumenical Tradition*. Geneva: World Council of Churches; Grand Rapids: Eerdmans, 1989.

The author offers his own personal recollections dating back to 1910 about the early days of the WCC and other ecumenical activities. The ecumenist worked at the WCC from 1948 to 1963 and is an ordained minister in the Presbyterian Church USA.

[391] Boegner, Marc. *The Long Road to Unity: Memories and Anticipations*. Trans. by René Hague. London: Collins, 1970.

This translation of the autobiography *L'exigence oecuménique* (1968) by Marc Boegner (1881-1970) covers the period from his first introduction to ecumenism in 1905 up to 1967. The work is rich in details especially for the period 1939-1959. Several photos are reproduced including some of the 1948 WCC meeting in Amsterdam. See also [420].

[392] Bouyer, Louis. *Dom Lambert Beauduin: Un homme d'Eglise*. Tournai: Casterman, 1964.

The founder of the monastery of Chevetogne, Belgium, devoted to reconciliation between the churches of the East and West, Lambert Beauduin (1873-1960), is shown in this biography to be ahead of his time and ultimately vindicated before his detractors. See also [428, 435].

[393] Brackenridge, R. Douglas. *Eugene Carson Blake: Prophet with Portfolio*. New York: Seabury Press, 1978.

Blake served as general secretary of the WCC from 1966-1972

succeeding W.A. Visser 't Hooft and preceding Philip Potter. This sympathetic biography assesses his contributions to church life, social action, and international service.

[394] Chaillet, Pierre, ed. *L'Eglise est Une: Hommage à Moehler*. Paris: Bloud et Gay, 1939.

This remarkable volume edited by a Jesuit professor at the theologate of Fourvière, near Lyons, enlisted collaboration from a cross section of French and German Catholic theologians at a time when ecumenism was suspect in many quarters of their church. The publication helped to familiarize the French context with the writings of the proto-ecumenist Johann Adam Möhler (1796-1838).

[395] Clément, Olivier. *Dialogues avec le patriarche Athénagoras*. Paris: Fayard, 1969.

The former Ecumenical Patriarch and the well-known French Orthodox theologian here exchanged a spiritual dialogue. Besides biographical material the interview includes an ecumenical discussion on "Roma - Amor?" and on Orthodox relations with the pre-Chalcedonian churches. See also Gheorghina [406].

[396] Collins, Patrick. *Gustave Weigel: A Pioneer of Reform*. A Michael Glazier Book. Collegeville: Liturgical Priess, 1992.

This first major biography and assessment of the American ecumenist Gustave Weigel (1906-1964) fills a real gap. It traces his teaching in Chile and finally at Woodstock College and describes his involvement in the first two sessions of Vatican II before his untimely death. See also [424].

[397] Congar, Yves. *Une passion: L'Unité. Réflexions et souvenirs 1929-1973*. Paris: Editions du Cerf, 1974.

The Dominican ecumenist narrates the beginning of his ecumenical vocation from 1929 up to the post conciliar period. He offers a number of interesting details about his contacts with other ecumenists and the origin of certain publishing projects. See also Puyo [427].

[398] Cranny, Titus. *Franciscan Contributions to Church Unity*. Garrison, NY: Graymoor, 1962.

The pamphlet holds up as models for reconciliation: Francis Assisi, Anthony of Padua, Bonaventure and Laurence of Brindisi.

[399] Cranny, Titus, ed. *Pope Paul and Christian Unity.* 3 vols. Garrison, NY: Unity Apostolate, 1964-1966.

The author, an Atonement Friar, assesses Pope Paul VI's contributions to ecumenism up to the year 1966.

[400] Curtis, Geoffrey. *Paul Couturier and Unity in Christ.* London: SCM; Westminster, MD: J. William Eckenrode, 1964.

This biography of Paul Couturier (1881-1953) outlines his distinctive contributions to spiritual ecumenism and his founding of the Center for Christian Unity in Lyons. The author is a member of the Community of the Resurrection in the Church of England. See also Villain [436].

[401] Curtis, Charles J. *Söderblom: Ecumenical Pioneer.* Minneapolis: Augsburg, 1967.

The author is a Lutheran minister who researched this material for his Ph.D. dissertation at the University of Chicago. The focus is largely on Söderblomian theology, its relevance for today's ecumenism, and criticisms that are sometimes brought against his system. See also Sundkler [433].

[402] Davey, Colin. *Pioneer for Unity: Metrophanes Kritopoulos (1589-1639) and Relations between the Orthodox, Roman Catholic and Reformed Churches.* London: British Council of Churches, 1987.

In 1617 a Greek Orthodox priest arrived in Oxford at the invitation of King James I to study the Anglican and Reformed churches in Britain and to explore the possibility of closer links between the Orthodox and those churches. This biography serves as a useful background to present ecumenical discussions.

[403] Fleischer, Manfred. *Katholische und lutherische Ireniker, unter besonderer Berücksichtigung des 19. Jahrhunderts.* Göttingen: Musterschmidt, 1968.

This study of the nineteenth century elucidates several significant personages and events that helped shape the modern ecumenical movement.

**[404]** Fries, Heinrich. *Wegbereiter und Wege: Ökumenische Verantwortung.* Theologica publica 8. Freiburg: Walter-Verlag, 1968.

Among the theologians treated as ecumenical pioneers are: John Henry Newman, Karl Adam, Friedrich Heiler, John XXIII, Augustin Bea and Karl Jaspers. These essays were originally given as radio talks from 1963 to 1967. See also [389, 407, 408].

**[405]** Garcías Palou, Sebastián. *Ramon Llull en la Historia del Ecumenismo.* Barcelona: Herder, 1986.

The 403 page study of the medieval Catalan theologian Raymond Lull or Llull (1232-1316) presents him as one of the major precursors of modern ecumenism. He is shown to have had an acute concern about the West's estrangement from Byzantium and traveled widely in the Christian East to promote rapprochement.

**[406]** Gheorghiu, Virgil. *La vie du patriarche Athenagoras.* Paris: Plon, 1969.

This biography by a Catholic priest is based in part on interviews and personal associations with the late Ecumenical Patriarch. There is a wealth of detail in the 319 pages. See also Clément [395].

**[407]** Gloede, Günther, ed. *Ökumenische Profile: Brückenbauer der einen Kirche.* 2 vols. Stuttgart: Evangelisches Missionsverlag, 1961-1963.

Volume one presents thirty-six pioneers of ecumenism, mostly Protestant but some Orthodox and Catholics. Volume two features forty-two individuals. Most entries include photographs. The biographical material is slim but serves as a first-level introduction. See also [404, 408].

**[408]** Gloede, Günther, ed. *Pionere und Plätze der Oekumenischen Bewegung; Pioneers and Places of Ecumenical Movement.* Hamburg: Herbert Reich, 1974.

This companion volume to the previous entry contains seventy woodcut portraits of ecumenical pioneers by artist Karl Stratil and twenty-five pen sketches by Gerd Wilk of ecumenically important buildings. The brief written commentary is published in German and English.

[409] Guitton, Jean. *Dialogue avec les précurseurs: Journal oecuménique 1922-1962*. Paris: Aubier, 1962.

Guitton (b. 1901) here provided fascinating vignettes of several pioneers of the ecumenical movement: Charles Lindley Wood (Lord Halifax), Cardinal Désiré Joseph Mercier, Cardinal Jules-Géraud Saliège and Brother Roger Schutz of Taizé.

[410] Hebblethwaite, Peter. *Pope John XXIII: Pope of the Council*. London: Geoffrey Chapman, 1984.

The well-known Catholic journalist researched for many years a number of primary sources to prepare this biography. He describes how Angelo Roncalli, the future pope, developed his interest in ecumenism during his long diplomatic assignments in Bulgaria, Turkey and France.

[411] Hopkins, C. Howard. *John R. Mott: 1865-1955, A Biography*. Grand Rapids: Eerdmans, 1979.

This excellent account narrates the life of the man described as the leading ecumenical statesman of the Protestant world throughout the first half of the twentieth century. Among other accomplishments he was chairman of the Edinburgh World Missionary Conference of 1910 and played an important part in the first two world conferences of Faith and Order (Lausanne 1927, Edinburgh 1937).

[412] Jackson, Eleanor M. *Red Tape and the Gospel: A Study of the Significance of the Ecumenical Missionary Struggle of William Paton (1886-1943)*. Birmingham, UK: Selly Oak Colleges, 1980.

Among the post-1910 British ecumenists Paton ranks with George Bell, J.H. Oldham and William Temple. This 409 page biography traces his early involvement with the Student Christian Movement, the International Missionary Council and the WCC in Formation. He was a member of the Presbyterian Church in England.

[413] Jacques, André. *Madeleine Barot*. Trans. by Pat and Bill Nottingham. Geneva: World Council of Churches, 1989.

The 88 page biography narrates the highlights of the activities of Barot (b. 1909) a leading figure in the ecumenical youth movement, student and women's movements, as well as in the French Protestant aid organization CIMADE (Comité inter-mouvement auprès des évacués).

[414] Jossua, Jean-Pierre. *Yves Congar: Theology in the Service of God's People.* Trans. by Sister Mary Jocelyn. Chicago: Priory, 1968.

The biographical tribute to Congar by a fellow Dominican theologian first appeared in French. It contains a list of his 958 publications up to the year 1967 (pp. 189-241). See also [397, 427].

[415] Jungclaussen, Emmanuel, ed. *Die grössere Ökumene: Gespräch um Friedrich Heiler: In Zusammenarbeit mit Anne Marie Heiler.* Regensburg: F. Pustet, 1970.

This 101 page work, edited by the Benedictine abbot of Niederaltaich, contains a short biography of Friedrich Heiler described as an original thinker and pioneer ecumenist. There is also a study assessing his major works and their critical reception. See also [623].

[416] Kantzenbach, Friedrich Wilhelm. *Johann Michael Sailer und der ökumenische Gedanke.* Einzelarbeiten aus der kirchengeschichte Bayerns, Bd. 29. Nuremberg: Verein für bayerische Kirchengeschichte, 1955.

The Bavarian Catholic theologian J.M. Sailer (1751-1832) is presented here as a founder of ecumenical theology in the South German context. The biography describes his thought, his trips, his letters and his genius for friendships.

[417] Kantzenbach, Friedrich Wilhelm. *Das Ringen um die Einheit der Kirche im Jahrhundert der Reformation: Vertreter, Quellen und Motive des "ökumenischen" Gedankens von Erasmus von Rotterdam bis Georg Calixt.* Stuttgart: Evangelisches Verlagswerk, 1957.

This fascinating historical account of important ecumenists identifies the specific contributions of Luther, Erasmus, Melanchton, Butzer, Georg Witzer, Georg Cassander, and Georg Calixt (1586-1656), as well as lesser known individuals in the Roman Church.

[418] Kawerau, Peter. *Die ökumenische Idee seit der Reformation.*

Stuttgart: W. Kohlhammer, 1968.

The author, an expert on Eastern Christianity, here describes the contributions of nine pioneers of Christian unity: Melchior Hoffmann, Sebastian Franck, Erasmus, Kaspar Schwenckfeld, Johann Arndt, J.A. Comenius, J.K. Dippel, N.L. von Zinzendorf and Jonathan Edwards.

[419] Linden, Juhani. *Unity of All Christians in Love and Mission: The Ecumenical Method of Kenneth Scott Latourette.* Helsinki: Suomalainen Tiedeakatemia, 1990.

The Finnish scholar wrote this account of Latourette's ecumenical involvement in the early part of this century. He is shown to have had strong convictions about the difference between acceptable diversity and unacceptable division. The volume contains a list of his publications dating back to 1910 (pp. 353-360).

[420] Mehl, Roger. *Le Pasteur Marc Boegner 1881-1970: une humble grandeur.* Paris: Plon, 1987.

The biography is very detailed in its narration of the life of this member of the Académie française, Protestant observer at Vatican II and dedicated President of the WCC 1948-1954. See his autobiography [391].

[421] Neill, Stephen. *Men of Unity.* London: SCM, 1960.

Written for the non-specialist in a lively style, this book offers brief biographies of thirteen notable ecumenists of our time. In the USA the book was entitled *Brothers of the Faith* (New York: Abingdon, 1960).

[422] Neuner, Peter. *Döllinger als Theologe der Ökumene.* Beiträge zur ökumenischen Theologie 19. Munich: F. Schöningh, 1979.

The famous German theologian of the nineteenth century, Ignaz von Döllinger (1799-1890), is assessed as an apologist, opponent of Vatican I's decree on the papacy, ecumenist, and eventually as an Old Catholic. Details about the two Bonn Conferences (1874-1875), described as the most important ecumenical conversations of that century, are included.

[423] Newbigin, Lesslie. *Unfinished Agenda: An Autobiography.* Grand

Rapids: Eerdmans, 1985.

> The bishop who was so instrumental in the formation of the Church of South India narrates in this 263 page work the events and challenges that have marked his ecumenical ministry for the church. See also his [1273].

[424] *One of a Kind: Essays in Tribute to Gustave Weigel*. Introduction by John C. Murray. Wilkes Barre, PA: Dimension, 1967.

> The well-known American ecumenist Gustave Weigel (1906-1964) died during Vatican II. This collection of ecumenical essays and personal reminiscences in his memory was prepared by nine of his Catholic and Protestant colleagues. See also [396].

[425] Piffl-Percevic, Theodor, and Stirnemann, Alfred, eds. *Veritati in Caritate: Der Beitrag des Kardinal König zum Ökumenismus*. Pro Oriente 5. Innsbruck: Tyrolia, 1981.

> This tribute to the Archbishop Emeritus of Vienna Franz König (b. 1905) outlines his work with the Pro Oriente Foundation between 1964 and 1981. It describes his on-going dialogue with Orthodox, Oriental Orthodox, Protestant and Muslim leaders. The Latin title is an allusion to his coat of arms' devise "doing the truth in charity" (Eph 4:15).

[426] Porter, John F. and Wolf, William J., eds. *Toward the Recovery of Unity: The Thought of Frederick Denison Maurice*. New York: Seabury, 1964.

> The two editors cite 138 extracts from letters written by F.D. Maurice (1805-1872) in the second half of the nineteenth century to illustrate his pioneering ecumenical vision.

[427] Puyo, Jean. *Jean Puyo interroge le Père Congar: Une vie pour la vérité*. Paris: Le Centurion, 1975.

> Puyo is editor in chief of *Journal de la Vie*. In these 239 pages he publishes Congar's responses to a vast range of questions reviewing the Catholic ecumenist's life since his birth in 1904. A wealth of detail, expressed with astounding candor, is recorded. See also [397, 414].

[428] Quitslund, Sonya A. *Beauduin: A Prophet Vindicated*. New York:

Newman, 1973.

In fourteen chapters the author presents a lively account of the life of the Benedictine Lambert Beauduin (1873-1960), founder of the monastery of Amay-Chevetogne and forerunner of Catholic ecumenism. See also [392, 435].

[429] Romeu, Luis V., ed. *Ecumenical Experiences*. Trans. ed. Lancelot C. Sheppard. London: Burns and Oates, 1965.

Originally published as *Diálogos de la Christianidad* (1964), this fascinating book produced by the Pontifical University of Salamanca addressed two questions to twenty-eight pioneers of ecumenism from various confessions: why did you get involved in ecumenism and what hopes do you have for ecumenism now?

[430] Roux, Hébert. *De la désunion vers la communion: Un itinéraire pastoral et oecuménique*. Paris: Le Centurion, 1978.

Towards the end of his life Hébert Roux (1902-1980) composed these memoirs covering his ministry as a pastor of the Reformed Church and as an ecumenist while serving as an observer at Vatican II.

[431] Schmidt, Stjepan. *Augustin Cardinal Bea: Der Kardinal der Einheit*. Vienna: Styria, 1989.

This mammoth study of the life and work of Augustin Bea (1881-1968), the Jesuit ecumenist and cardinal who was the first president of the Secretariat for Promoting Christian Unity and major voice at Vatican II, was written by his long-time executive secretary and collaborator.

[432] Schmidt, William J. *Architect of Unity: A Biography of Samuel McCrea Cavert*. New York: Friendship Press, 1978.

Dr. Cavert (1888-1976), a prominent Presbyterian ecumenist, served as first general secretary of the National Council of Churches of Christ in the USA. He was also active at the WCC general assemblies at Amsterdam, Evanston, New Delhi and Uppsala. See also Cavert [733, 734].

[433] Sundkler, Bengt. *Nathan Söderblom: His Life and Work*. London: Lutterworth, 1968.

This biography of the ecumenist Söderblom (1866-1931) was written by the former bishop of Tanzania and professor of church history and missiology at Uppsala. The work quotes a rich collection of the ecumenist's personal papers, correspondence and diaries. See also Curtis [401].

[434] Thomas, Madathilparampil M. *My Ecumenical Journey, 1947-1975.* Trivandrum: Ecumenical Publishing Center; Geneva: World Council of Churches, 1990.

The Indian ecumenist and associate of the WCC staff narrates his own personal encounters with events and persons up to the Nairobi general assembly.

[435] *Veilleur avant l'aurore: Colloque Lambert Beauduin.* Chevetogne: Editions de Chevetogne, 1978.

On the occasion of the fiftieth anniversary of the founding of the monastery of Chevetogne (originally at Amay), a group of some forty friends, disciples and collaborators of its founder, the late Lambert Beauduin (1873-1960), held a symposium in his memory from August 30 to September 3, 1976. The contributions are arranged according to: anamnesis, liturgy, Christian unity, and monastic spirituality.

[436] Villain, Maurice. *L'Abbé Paul Couturier: Apôtre de l'unité chrétienne: Souvenirs et documents.* Tournai: Casterman, 1957.

This biography, composed by a close Dominican collaborator, describes Couturier's late vocation to ecumenism (after his fifty-second birthday!). Also included are a list of his publications (pp. 343-346), a variety of tributes to him, and some prayers he composed. See also Curtis [400].

[437] Villain, Maurice. *Vers l'unité: Itinéraire d'un pionnier 1935-1975.* Dinard: Groupement pour le Service Oecuménique, 1986.

Maurice Villain (1900-1977) narrates these memoirs covering the forty year period of time during which he collaborated with Paul Couturier (1881-1953) and others. Villain also served as a *peritus* at Vatican II.

[438] Visser 't Hooft, Willem A. *Die ganze Kirche für die ganze Welt: Ökumenischer Aufbruch; Hauptschriften.* 2 vols. Stuttgart: Kreuz, 1967.

These essays and addresses are drawn from the period 1948-1966 when the noted ecumenist was serving as general secretary of the WCC. Volume two focuses on fundamental issues; volume one includes among other topics a tribute to pioneers of ecumenism: Söderblom, Mott, Bell, Bonhoeffer and Queen Wilhelmina. See also his [911].

[439] Visser 't Hooft, Willem A. *Memoirs*. London: SCM; Philadelphia: Westminster, 1973.

The original Dutch version, *Mémoires: Een leven in de oecumene* (1971), has also been translated into French, German and Swedish. In thirty-eight chapters the former general secretary of the WCC (who died in 1985) outlined his life from boyhood in Haarlem until his departure from Geneva. Chapter 37 discusses "The Ecumenical Mobilization of the Roman Catholic Church."

[440] Zabriskie, A. *Bishop Brent, Crusader for Christian Unity*. Philadelphia: Westminster, 1948.

The biography of Charles Henry Brent (1862-1929), Canadian ecumenist who attended the Edinburgh meeting of the World Missionary Conference (1910), describes his profound impact on the Faith and Order movement as well as on Life and Work.

[441] Zenk, Georg. *Evangelisch in Katholizität: Ökumenische Impulse aus Dienst und Werk Hans Asmussens*. 2 vols. Frankfurt: P. Lang, 1977.

This study tries to reconstruct the ecumenical ecclesiology of Hans Asmussen (1898-1969) drawing from his publications. He is seen by many as an ecumenical embodiment of the Catholic Protestant. On Asmussen see also [569, 570, 805, 965].

# 4

# Confessional Views

## Catholic

[442] Alting von Geusau, Leo G. M., ed. *Ecumenism and the Roman Catholic Church*. Trans. by H.J.J. Vaughan, et al. Westminister, MD: Newman Press; London: Sheed and Ward, 1966.

> These seven essays focus largely on the development of ecumenism in the Roman Catholic Church and in the WCC.

[443] Baum, Gregory. *Progress and Perspectives: The Catholic Quest for Christian Unity*. New York: Sheed and Ward, 1962.

> This collection of nine essays by the Canadian scholar also appeared under two other titles: *The Catholic Quest for Christian Unity* (Glen Rock, NJ: Paulist, 1962) and *The Quest for Christian Unity* (London: Sheed and Ward, 1963). The appendix contains two important pastoral letters on ecumenism, one by Paul-Emile Léger of Montreal and one by Achille Liénart of Lille.

[444] Beaupère, René. *L'oecuménisme*. Paris: Le Centurion, 1991.

> The Dominican director of the Centre oecuménique Saint Irénée and member of the ecumenical Groupe des Dombes here offers in eleven chapters a popular history of ecumenism and some fresh suggestions for advancing its goals.

[445] Berkouwer, Gerrit Cornelis. *Nabetrachting op het concilie*. Kampen: J.H. Kok, 1968.

This volume appeared also in German as *Gehorsam und Aufbruch: Zur Situation der katholischen Kirche und Theologie* (1969). The Dutch Protestant ecumenist studies the Catholic Church in relation to issues such as renewal and continuity in the church, the Word of God, and ecclesial authority.

[446] Boyer, Carlo [Charles], ed. *Il problema ecumenico, oggi*. Brescia: Queriniana, 1960.

The French Jesuit Charles Boyer (1884-1980) was an early Catholic ecumenist and professor at the Gregorian University, Rome. Here he edited eighteen contributions, some from quite rigid thinkers, which reflect the cautious state of Catholic ecclesiology prior to Vatican II. The book's preface was written by Cardinal Montini of Milan, the future Paul VI.

[447] Boyer, Charles. *Le mouvement oecuménique: Les faits, le dialogue*. Rome: Gregorian University, 1976.

After a long and pioneering career in ecumenism Boyer composed the sixteen chapters of his most mature work shortly before his death. Partly historical, partly theological, the work reflects certain cautious attitudes. See also his earlier [448].

[448] Boyer, Charles. *Unus Pastor: Pour la réunion à l'Eglise de Rome des chrétiens séparés*. Toulouse: Apostolat de la Prière, 1951.

It would be an interesting study to compare this early work of Boyer with his book published twenty-five years later [447]. Even this book's title itself reflects a certain rigid concept of church unity. This volume also appeared in English as *One Shepherd: The Problem of Christian Unity* (New York: P.J. Kenedy, 1952).

[449] Brandenburg, Albert. *Einheit, Evangelium, Katholizität*. Der Christ in der Welt XVI.1. Aschaffenburg: Pattloch, 1973.

This volume, part of the massive encyclopedia under the general editorship of Johannes Hirschmann, S.J., offers 112 pages on ten aspects of the ecumenical movement. The concise text emphasizes the twentieth century and reflects a Roman Catholic perspective.

[450] Brinkman, Bruno R. *To the Lengths of God: Truths and the Ecumenical Age*. London: Sheed and Ward, 1988.

The author was a Jesuit professor of theology at Heythrop College, London, for many years. This personal account of his views on church unity is based on articles he published in the 1970s and 1980s. Among the themes treated are the hierarchy of truths, the eucharist, and justification.

[451] Butler, Basil Christopher. *The Church and Unity*. London: Geoffrey Chapman, 1979.

The Benedictine monk and bishop (b. 1902) devoted most of his life to fostering a deeper understanding of Christian reunion. These twelve mature essays give a strong Catholic thrust to ecumenical endeavors.

[452] *Le Christ et les Eglises*. Paris: Editions universitaires, 1961.

The fourteen articles do not seem to have emanated from a symposium but were simply contributed to this collaborative volume. The intended audience is the general public but the authors are recognized Catholic ecumenists. The material covers dealings with Orthodox, Reformation and Anglican churches as well as the WCC.

[453] Congar, M.-J. [Yves]. *Chrétiens désunis: Principes d'un "Oecuménisme" catholique*. Unam Sanctam 1. Paris: Editions du Cerf, 1937.

This pioneering ecumenical work was the center of much controversy in the 1930s. It appeared in an English version as *Divided Christendom* (1939) and in a reprinting of the French without changes in 1965. Its call for a bold shift in Catholic thinking was originally thought to be too radical.

[454] Congar, Yves. *Dialogue Between Christians: Catholic Contributions to Ecumenism*. Trans. by Philip Loretz. Westminster, MD: Newman Press, 1966.

This translation of *Chrétiens en dialogue* (1964) includes an autobiography of Congar written in 1963 (pp. 1-51) and various essays written in the 1940s and 1950s treating the principles of ecumenism as well as Orthodoxy, Anglicanism and relations with Israel.

[455] Congar, Yves. *Ecumenism and the Future of the Church*. Trans.

by John C. Guinness and Geraldine F. McIntosh. Chicago: Priory Press, 1967.

> Besides the historical and theoretical overview of ecumenism, one of the seven chapters offers a practical "School for Ecumenists." This is a translation of *Aspects de l'oecuménisme* and a chapter on the future of the church from a volume *L'avenir* (1963).

[456] Couturier, Paul. *Rapprochement entre les chrétiens au XXe siècle*. Le Puy: X. Mappus, 1945.

> This pamphlet appeared shortly after the trauma of World War II. In 47 pages Couturier (1881-1953) wrote of Roman Catholicism's relations with Anglicans, Orthodox, Calvinists and Lutherans. There is a very long citation on church unity from Romano Guardini (pp. 38-47).

[457] Cunneen, Joseph E., ed., *Looking Toward the Council: An Inquiry Among Christians*. Quaestiones Disputatae [English edition] 5. New York: Herder and Herder, 1962.

> Drawing upon the results of a questionnaire distributed prior to Vatican II, the essays record the principal concerns of Roman Catholics on the eve of the Council. Also included are essays by Catholics, Orthodox and Protestants. The postscript was composed by Asian and African laymen. Most of these essays first appeared in the journal *Cross Currents*.

[458] Ehrlich, Rudolf J. *Rome: Opponent or Partner?* London: Lutterworth Press, 1965.

> The Protestant professor at Edinburgh wrote this monograph to describe the shift in Roman Catholic attitudes to other churches. He identifies Louis Bouyer's *The Spirit and Forms of Protestantism* and Hans Küng's *Justification* [1016] as milestones in Catholicism's paradigmatic shift.

[459] Faynel, Paul. *L'Unité des Chrétiens*. Paris: Desclée, 1985.

> The author, a Sulpician priest, served for many years as ecumenical officer for the Catholic Archdiocese of Paris. His book is easily accesible to the general public but contains valuable reflections on ecumenism as the church's primordial task, on bilateral conversations, and on models of unity.

**[460]** Fiolet, Herman A. *Ecumenical Breakthrough: An Integration of the Catholic and the Reformation Faith.* Duquesne Studies, Theological Studies, no. 9. Pittsburgh: Duquesne University, 1969.

While visiting professor at Duquesne University, the professor at the Faculty of Catholic Theology in Amsterdam reworked two of his earlier Dutch publications *Onvermoed perspectief of de Oecumene* (1963) and *Dilemma doobroken* (1965) which provided a theoretical explanation of the need for ecumenism.

**[461]** Fiorenza, Francis Schüssler, and Galvin, John P., eds. *Systematic Theology: Roman Catholic Perspectives.* 2 vols. Minneapolis: Fortress, 1991.

This unusual publishing venture reflects the maturity of the ecumenical movement. The Lutheran publishing house invited twelve Roman Catholic professors to present a comprehensive systematic theology inspired by Catholicism yet addressed principally to members of the Reformation churches. The section on ecclesiology was written by Michael Fahey (II, pp. 1-74).

**[462]** Fox, Helmut. *Ökumene: Hoffnung oder Illusion? Eine katholische Bilanz.* Trier: Spee, 1974.

This collection contains descriptions of Catholic authoritative teachings regarding ecumenism, a list of activities in Germany from 1964 to 1971, and a final ecumenical balance sheet.

**[463]** Fries, Heinrich. *Wir und die Andern: Beiträge zu dem Thema: Die Kirche in Gespräch und Begegnung.* Stuttgart: Schwabenverlag, 1966.

The prolific writer and Catholic professor of ecumenical theology at Munich collected here a number of contributions about Christians' relations with members of other living faiths and with non-believers.

**[464]** Father Jerome [Gille, Albert]. *A Catholic Plea for Reunion.* London: Williams and Norgate, 1934.

This 75 page book was considered so daring when it first appeared that the Dutch Jesuit Albert Gille (1878-1950) published it under a pseudonym. Dedicated to Cardinal Mercier and Lord Halifax it called for a total corporate unity between

Anglicans and Catholics and a discouragement of individual conversions. Shortly after its publication the author resigned from the Jesuits.

[465] Girault, René. *L'oecuménisme, où vont les Eglises?* Paris: Le Centurion, 1983.

This Roman Catholic member of the Groupe des Dombes [699] and director of the journal *Unité des chrétiens* [169], outlines the notable shift of attitudes regarding ecumenism among Catholics from 1966 to 1980. This is established by analyzing the results of a questionnaire administered during the ecumenical segment of the 1981 Eucharistic Congress held in Lourdes.

[466] Grasso, Domenico. *Ci sara una sola Chiesa: è possibile l'unione delle Chiese?* Milan: Nuova Accademia Editrice, 1960.

Prior to Vatican II, an Italian Jesuit produced this text that provides a useful summary (160 pp.) of stages in the ecumenical movement and enumerates typical prejudices that exist among Christians.

[467] Heenan, John C., ed. *Christian Unity: A Catholic View: Being an Account of the First Official Conference Organized by the Bishops' Committee for Christian Unity (Heythrop, August 1962).* London and New York: Sheed and Ward, 1962.

The Jesuit theological college located at that time near Oxford was host to this congress convened on the eve of Vatican II. There are eight essays by British Catholic ecumenists and two by Augustin Bea. See also the second conference's proceedings [859].

[468] Herbst, Karl. *Jenseits aller Ansprüche: Neue ökumenische Perspektiven.* Experiment Christentum, 12. Munich: J. Pfeiffer, 1972.

The author, a Roman Catholic priest born in 1916, founded the Evangelisch-Katholischer Briefkreis in Germany. This idiosyncratic volume describes his exchange of letters with Lutheran ministers as well as his controversy with the Catholic Bishop's Office in Berlin that led to his suspension from the priesthood. The topics treated include: infallibility, primacy, celibacy and divorce.

[469] Heufelder, Emmanuel Maria. *In the Hope of His Coming:*

*Studies in Christian Unity.* Trans. by Otto M. Knab. Notre Dame, IN: Fides, 1964.

This book was written by the Benedictine Abbot of Niederaltaich Abbey, Bavaria, which, together with Taizé and Chevetogne, has served as an important monastic center for Christian unity. Nine prominent ecumenists contributed essays which stress European leadership in the years prior to Vatican II. The original German title was *Dass Alle Eins Seien* (1959-62).

[470] Hoffmann, Gottfried. *Der ökumenismus heute: Geschichte, Kritik, Wegweisung.* Aschaffenburg: Paul Pattloch, 1978.

This generally cautious, conservative presentation of ecumenical principles, is presented by the writer who is the son of Lutheran pastor but who later in 1952 became a Catholic. The historical section is rather predictable but the section on spiritual ecumenism useful.

[471] Huber, Georges. *Vers l'union des chrétiens: Nouveaux entretiens sous la colonnade de saint Pierre.* Paris: Le Centurion, 1962.

This is a popular introduction for Catholics on ecumenism, beginning with the foundation of the Secretariat for Promoting Christian Unity. The book is sequel to *Vers le Concile* (1961). The introduction is written by Augustin Bea.

[472] Iung, Nicolas. *Bilan de l'oecuménisme contemporain: les églises chrétiennes non romaines à la recherche de l'unité, l'action oecuménique de l'Eglise catholique, points de divergence et d'accord.* Paris: Mame, 1971.

The author of this interesting 334 page work is a Roman Catholic canon whose views are cautious but well informed. In three parts he describes ecumenical efforts among non-Catholics and Catholics as well as points of divergence and agreement.

[473] Jaeger, Lorenz. *Einheit und Gemeinschaft: Stellungnahmen zu Fragen der christlichen Einheit.* Konfessionskundliche und kontroverstheologische Studien 31. Paderborn: Bonifatius, 1972.

The founder of the Johann Adam Möhler Institute for Ecumenics in Paderborn published on the occasion of his eightieth birthday fifty-five essays and addresses given between 1941 and 1971.

[474] Laros, Matthias. *Schöpferischer Friede der Konfessionen: die Una-Sancta Bewegung, ihr Ziel und ihre Arbeit*. Recklinghausen: Paulus, 1950.

This early account by a Roman Catholic of the pioneering Una Sancta movement explains in 220 pages the possibility of the churches' "creative freedom" in moving toward unity. This forward looking, prophetic book anticipated much of Vatican II's attitudes towards other churches.

[475] Leclercq, Jacques. *La réunion des églises*. Tournai: Casterman, 1962.

Completed before Vatican II, this personal testimonial of a Catholic ecumenist reflecting on forty years of experience during a time of suspicion and fear makes fascinating reading.

[476] Leeming, Bernard. *The Churches and the Church: A Study of Ecumenism*. London: Darton, Longman and Todd; Westminster, MD: Newman, 1960.

This is another notable account of Catholic ecumenism before Vatican II published as the Lauriston Lectures for 1957, sponsored by the Catholic Truth Society of the Archdiocese of St. Andrews and Edinburgh. Leeming (1893-1971) taught theology for many years at the Jesuit theologate in Heythrop College, Oxon. Vatican II went beyond his hesitant recommendations. See also his study on Vatican II [311].

[477] Le Guillou, Marie-Joseph. *Mission et unité: Les exigences de la communion*. 2 vols. Unam Sanctam 33. Paris: Editions du Cerf, 1960.

This pre-Vatican II work is highly recommended. Volume one treats Christian communities (including Orthodox and Protestant ones) and the contemporary scene. Volume two discusses the Catholic Church and its relationship to other churches. Extensive bibliographies are included (I, pp. 223-277; II, pp. 273-324).

[478] Löser, Werner, ed. *Die römisch-katholische Kirche*. Die Kirchen der Welt 20. Stuttgart: Evangelisches Verlagswerk, 1986.

This volume is one in a series covering the churches of the world. Of special interest for ecumenical studies are the essays on: the concept of church in the documents of Vatican II (W. Beinert);

Roman Catholic understanding of ecumenism (W. Löser); relations with the Orthodox Church (H.J. Schultz); relations with the Reformation churches (A. Klein); and the Catholic Church and the WCC (B. Meeking).

[479] McDonnell, Kilian. *The Charismatic Renewal and Ecumenism.* New York: Paulist, 1978.

The American Benedictine president of the Institute for Ecumenical and Cultural Research, Collegeville, Minnesota, argues that charismatic renewal with its stress on prayer and its breaking down of ancient barriers holds an important key to achieving church unity. See also Davis [614], Mühlen [617], K. McDonnell [694].

[480] McSorley, Harry J. *Luther: Right or Wrong? An Ecumenical-Theological Study of Luther's Major Work, The Bondage of the Will.* New York: Newman; Minneapolis: Augsburg, 1969.

The North American ecumenist originally published this Munich doctoral dissertation in German. It provides a very detailed analysis of the concept of free will in scholasticism, Erasmus and Luther. The volume was an influential source for Catholic re-evaluation of Luther.

[481] Margerie, Bertrand de. *Vers la plénitude de la communion.* Paris: Téqui, 1975.

This strongly critical assessment of recent ecumenical consensus documents by a conservative French Catholic priest has little good to say about what has been achieved to date.

[482] Maron, Gottfried. *Das Katholische Lutherbild der Gegenwart: Anmerkungen und Anfragen.* Bensheimer Hefte 58. Göttingen: Vandenhoeck und Ruprecht, 1982.

For the Luther Year (1983) the author, professor at Kiel and president of the Evangelisches Bund, published this helpful booklet that traces the history of Catholic attitudes toward Luther, the present situation, and possible future developments.

[483] Martineau, Suzanne. *Vivre l'oecuménisme dans le quotidien de nos vies.* Tours: Mame, 1969.

The author, a Roman Catholic laywoman, provides a useful compendium of practical hints for advancing the goals of ecumenism day by day. See also her [73].

[484] Michael, J. P. *Christen suchen eine Kirche: die ökumenische Bewegung und Rom. Mit Dokumenten und soziographischen Beilagen.* Herder Bücherei 10. Freiburg: Herder, 1958.

This 188 page introduction to the ecumenical movement for Catholics was published prior to Vatican II. It reviews the major stages and issues in the history of divided Christianity. A second edition appeared under the title: *Christen glauben eine Kirche* (1962).

[485] Michalon, Pierre. *Oecuménisme et unité chrétienne.* Paris: La Cordelle, 1968.

The Catholic author served as a seminary professor at Viviers (Ardèche) and succeeded Paul Couturier as director of the Centre Unité Chrétienne in Lyons. This 128 page work insists on the need for spiritual conversion to achieve Christian unity.

[486] Minus, Paul M., Jr. *The Catholic Rediscovery of Protestantism: A History of Roman Catholic Ecumenical Pioneering.* New York: Paulist, 1976.

The Methodist church historian provides a fascinating narrative focusing on the ecumenical contributions of Catholics from John Henry Newman to modern times. This is one of the most accessible English language accounts of Catholic efforts for church unity.

[487] Mondin, Battista. *L'Ecumenismo nella chiesa cattolica prima, durante e dopo il Concilio.* 2nd rev. ed. Rome: Herder, 1966.

The author who served as a *peritus* at Vatican II and teaches in Milan gives an historical and doctrinal account of Catholic participation in ecumenism. Of special interest are the chapters on ecumenism in Italy (pp. 153-165) and in mission countries (167-185).

[488] Ohlig, Karl-Heinz, and Schuster, Heinz. *Blockiert das Katholische Dogma die Einheit der Kirchen?* Düsseldorf: Patmos, 1971.

This short (104 pp.) presentation for non-specialists grew out of discussions at the joint Catholic and Lutheran Kirchentag held in 1971. It treats Christian belief and the church, worship (including sacramental confession), and marriage.

[489] Pol, Willem Henrik van de. *The Christian Dilemma: Catholic Church - Reformation*. London: J.M. Dent, 1952.

This work appeared as *Het christelijk Dilemma* in 1948. The author was baptized in the Dutch Reformed Church but entered the Roman Catholic church in 1940 and became professor of the "phenomenology of Protestantism" at the University of Nijmegen. The final chapter anticipated much of what in fact happened subsequently.

[490] Pol, Willem Henrik van de. *De Oecumene*. Roermond: J.J. Romen, 1961.

This 137 page well-balanced and general overview written by a professor at the Catholic University of Nijmegen had considerable influence on Dutch ecumenism.

[491] Pribilla, Max. *Um kirchliche Einheit: Stockholm, Lausanne, Rom: Geschichtlich-theologische Darstellung der neueren Einigungsbestrebungen*. Freiburg: Herder, 1929.

The special interest of this book by the German Jesuit Max Pribilla (1874-1956) is its early date of publication. In 332 pages he gives a sympathetic account of the early Life and Work Movement and the Faith and Order Movement and cites a number of interesting primary sources from Rome to illustrate its negative reactions. See also [282].

[492] Ratzinger, Joseph. *Church, Ecumenism and Politics: New Essays in Ecclesiology*. Trans. by Robert Nowell. New York: Crossroad; Middlegreen, Slough: St. Paul, 1988.

The work originally published as *Kirche, Ökumene und Politik* (1987) includes several analyses of Vatican II's contributions to ecclesiology and three essays on ecumenism: an assessment of *The Final Report* of ARCIC-I [632], Luther and unity, and ecumenical progress.

[493] Rodriguez, Pedro. *Iglesia y ecumenismo*. Madrid: Rialp, 1979.

This 418 page introduction to ecumenical theory draws upon French and German Catholic sources but is weak on analyzing bilateral conversations. The Pamplona based author includes here reflections on church, ministry, papal primacy and eucharist.

[494] Ryan, Thomas. *A Survival Guide For Ecumenically Minded Christians*. Ottawa: Novalis; Collegeville: Liturgical Press, 1989.

The author, director of the Canadian Centre for Ecumenism in Montreal, wrote this frank assessment of the ecumenical movement during the late 1980s in an attempt to offer practical hints how to maintain optimism even when interest in ecumenism by officials seems to be waning.

[495] Ryan, Thomas. *Tales of Christian Unity: The Adventures of an Ecumenical Pilgrim*. New York: Paulist, 1983.

Prior to joining the staff of the Canadian Centre for Ecumenism, this Paulist Father undertook a year's visit to major religious centers of Orthodoxy, Protestantism and Anglicanism. He narrates his experiences in Eastern settings (Cairo, Jerusalem, Constantinople, Mount Athos) as well as in Geneva and Canterbury.

[496] St. John, Henry. *Essays in Christian Unity, 1928-1954*. Westminster, MD: Newman, 1955.

The British Dominican published most of these twelve articles first in *Blackfriars*. The volume contains a short autobiography (pp. xi-xix) in addition to the articles which show the author considerably ahead of his time.

[497] Sartori, Luigi. *Teologia ecumenica: Saggi*. Studi teologici 14. Padova: Gregorgiana, 1987.

The Italian Catholic ecumenist here provides some twenty-two essays on the re-appropriation of Vatican II, the ecumenical dimension of faith, and contemporary efforts at church unity including the Lima document.

[498] Sartory, Thomas A. *The Ecumenical Movement and the Unity of the Church*. Trans. by Hilda G. Graef. Oxford: Blackwell's; Westminster, MD: Newman, 1963.

This narrowly Roman Catholic conservative book on ecumenism contains many views that were subsequently rejected by Vatican II. The work is judgmental, polemic and sweeping in its condemnations.

[499] Sartory, Thomas A., ed. *A New Interpretation of Faith*. Trans. by Martha Schmidt. Westminster, MD: Newman, 1968.

This curious book which first appeared as *Eine neue Interpretation des Glaubens* (1967) calls for a shift in the agenda of ecumenism to focus on Jews and unbelievers rather than on Reformation Christians since traditional unity talks are stalled.

[500] Scheele, Paul-Werner. *Alle Eins: Theologische Beiträge II*. Paderborn: Bonifatius, 1979.

The author, auxiliary bishop of the Roman Catholic diocese of Paderborn, composed these fifteen essays on a wide spectrum of modern ecumenical issues.

[501] Segretariato Attività Ecumeniche, ed. *Ecumenismo, vocazione della chiesa [Atti della I Sessione di formazione ecumenica organizzata dal S.A.E., 1964]*. Brescia: Morcelliana, 1965.

The eight papers in this first volume of the Italian Ecumenical Association's annual congress are devoted to the origin and nature of the "ecumenical problem". All the contributions are written by Catholics.

[502] Spinsanti, Sandro. *Ecumenismo*. Rome: Istituto di Teologia a Distanza Centro "Ut Unum Sint," 1982.

A very basic but solid initiation to ecumenism for Italian Catholics, the work discusses various "pathways" toward unity, the churches in dialogue (those of Eastern Orthodoxy and the Reformed churches), and dialogue with Judaism.

[503] Swidler, Leonard, ed. *Dialogue for Reunion: The Catholic Premises*. New York: Herder and Herder, 1962.

The three addresses were delivered at Duquesne University, Pittsburgh, in 1962. They are: the impact of the ecumenical movement (John J. Wright); liturgy and ecumenism (Hans Ansger Reinhold); and holy tradition (George Tavard).

[504] Todd, John M. *Catholicism and the Ecumenical Movement.* London: Longmans, Green, 1956.

In six chapters Todd outlines a brilliant pre-Vatican II statement on ecumenism and illustrates how in several segments of Catholicism a notable paradigm shift was in process, moving from unionism to ecumenism.

[505] Tolédano, André D. *Les chrétiens, seront-ils un jour tous réunis?* Bibliothèque Ecclesia 17. Paris: A. Fayard, 1956.

This pre-Vatican II work is more informative than the comparable volume published by Arminjon [187] for the same general audience, although its historical section is rather weak. The book is notable for its generally irenic and clear approach.

[506] Viatte, Gérard. *Oecuménisme.* Les cahiers de Saint-Séverin. Tournai: Casterman, 1964.

This 215 page volume inaugurated a collection of studies sponsored by St. Séverin Church in Paris. The three sections address the biblical data, the historical divisions, and modern developments.

[507] Weigel, Gustave. *Catholic Theology in Dialogue.* New York: Harper, 1961.

The American Jesuit ecumenist Weigel (1906-1964) published these seven essays on ecclesiology and related themes in May 1961 just prior to Vatican II. The chapter "Catholic Ecclesiology in Our Time" is particularly notable. The British title read *Where Do We Differ? Catholic Theology in Dialogue* (London: Burns and Oates, 1962). For tributes to Weigel see [396, 424].

[508] Weigel, Gustave. *A Catholic Primer on the Ecumenical Movement.* Woodstock Papers 1. Westminster, MD: Newman; London: Geoffrey Chapman, 1963.

This 79 page introduction to ecumenism was one of the early American Catholic primers on the subject. It is divided between non-Catholic and Catholic ecumenism. The title in the UK was *The Ecumenical Movement: A Catholic Approach.* See also [396, 424].

[509] Willebrands, Johannes. *Mandatum Unitatis: Beiträge zur Ökumene.* Konfessionskundliche Schriften 16. Paderborn: Bonifatius, 1989.

> The distinguished Catholic ecumenist and cardinal (b. 1906) published these twenty-eight articles and speeches composed between 1965 and 1987. All are reproduced in German for this volume sponsored by the Johnan Adam Möhler Institute for Ecumenics in Paderborn. The work is indexed. See also [510].

[510] Willebrands, Johannes. *Oecuménisme et problèmes actuels.* Paris: Editions du Cerf, 1969.

> The Dutch ecumenist who served as A. Bea's executive secretary in the Secretariat for Promoting Christian Unity published this collection of twelve essays describing Catholic involvement in ecumenism. See also [509].

[511] Yarnold, Edward. *They Are in Earnest: Christian Unity in the Statements of Paul VI, John Paul I, John Paul II.* Middlegreen, Slough: St. Paul, 1982.

> The British Catholic ecumenist from Oxford draws upon little known speeches of the last three popes which he cites in excerpts to show the priority attached by them to Christian unity. The last chapter is a summary of papal principles of ecumenism.

# Catholic, Eastern

[512] Madey, Johannes, and Erackel, Stanislaus Thomas. *The Future of the Oriental Catholic Churches.* Tiruvalla, India: Santinilayam Publications; Paderborn: Ostkirchendienst, 1978.

> Jointly published by the Ecumenical Centre of the Malankara Catholic Eparchy of Tiruvalla (Kerala) and the Ostkirchendienst, Paderborn, this valuable study provides eleven essays that situate the history and polity of various Eastern Catholic churches in full communion with Rome.

[513] Sayegh, Maximos, ed. *The Eastern Churches and Catholic Unity.* Trans. by John Dingle. New York: Herder and Herder, 1963.

> Translated from *Voix de l'Eglise en Orient* (1963), the book, edited by Melkite Patriarch Maximos IV, contains thirteen essays

by Eastern Catholic hierarchs which focus on the distinctive character and concerns of those Eastern churches in full communion with the See of Rome. See also [317].

[514] *The Unity of the Churches of God.* Trans. with an introduction by Polycarp Sherwood, O.S.B. Baltimore: Helicon, 1963.

The volume is a valuable collection of five articles on the nature of Byzantine Catholicism published in various languages from 1957 to 1960 by two Melkite Catholics (Pierre K. Médawar and Oreste Kéramé) and three Latin Catholic theologians (M.-J. Le Guillou, Yves Congar and Bernard Schultze).

[515] Zoghby, Elias. *Tous Schismatiques?* Beirut: Heidelberg Press, 1981.

The Eastern Catholic Archbishop of Baalbeck, Lebanon, wrote this forceful account of his own church and its relationship to the Orthodox Church especially in the Middle East. He comments: "I love the Roman Church and I love the Orthodox Church just as much, and I would gladly lay down my life to witness to either one." See also Corbon [742].

# Orthodox

[516] Attwater, Donald. *The Christian Churches of the East.* 2 vols. rev. ed. Milwaukee: Bruce; London: G. Chapman, 1961.

The two volumes are subtitled: *Churches in Communion with Rome,* and *Churches Not in Communion with Rome.* These are revisions of two earlier works: *The Catholic Eastern Churches* (1935) and *The Dissident Eastern Churches* (1937). The writings of Attwater (1892-1977) were widely consulted in the 1930s and 1940s but nowadays are judged to be noticeably outdated in concept and statistical data. He outlines the origins of the churches as well as their liturgical and theological traditions. Volume two contains a brief section on reunion with the East. Both volumes contain a glossary and some photographs.

[517] Bria, Ion. *The Sense of Ecumenical Tradition: The Ecumenical Witness and Vision of the Orthodox.* Geneva: World Council of Churches, 1991.

The Romanian Orthodox theologian who has been an active staff member of the WCC and has recently served as interim convenor for its new program unit "Unity and Renewal" here interprets the special charisms of the Orthodox for achieving church unity.

[518] Calian, Carnegie Samuel. *Icon and Pulpit: The Protestant Orthodox Encounter*. Philadelphia: Westminster, 1968.

The author was baptized in the Orthodox Church but raised as a Protestant. He taught as professor at the University of Dubuque Theological Seminary. His volume contains a history of Orthodox and Protestant relations, a comparison of their differing ecclesiologies, and an account of their search for spiritual renewal.

[519] Centre Orthodoxe du Patriarcat Oecuménique, Chambésy-Geneva. *Orthodoxie et mouvement oecuménique*. Etudes théologiques de Chambésy 6. Chambésy-Geneva: Centre Orthodoxe, 1986.

The annual symposium held at Chambésy met May 4-27, 1985, discussed that year the contributions of the Orthodox to the ecumenical movement in general, through the WCC, and specifically through its work with Faith and Order. Protestant, Catholic and Orthodox views are reproduced.

[520] Dragas, George D., ed. *Aksum - Thyateira: Festschrift Archbishop Methodios of Thyateira and Great Britain*. London: Thyateira House, 1985.

The Greek Orthodox Archbishop was honored by this massive 700 page volume of essays. Besides a biography and list of his publications, a number of articles in English, German and Greek, some of which discuss dialogues between Roman Catholics and Orthodox, were submitted.

[521] Florovsky, Georges. *Ecumenism I: A Doctrinal Approach; Ecumenism II: A Historical Approach*. Gen. ed. Richard S. Haugh. *The Collected Works of Georges Florovsky*, vols. 13 and 14. Vaduz: Buchvertriebsanstalt, 1989.

Georges Florovsky (1893-1979) was a Russian Orthodox émigré who taught first in Paris and later at Harvard University. These collections of his ecumenical essays contain assessments of Orthodox ecumenism especially Russian Orthodox. There is also short account of his ecumenical contacts in Paris (1926-1928).

[522] Harkianakis, Stylianos. *Orthodoxe Kirche und Katholizismus: Ähnliches und Verschiedenes*. Munich: Kösel, 1975.

Metropolitan Stylianos of the Orthodox Institute in Saloniki, drawing upon his years of experiences as a graduate student in Germany, published this 88 page reflection on the similiarities and dissimilarities between Orthodoxy and Catholicism. There are sections on church structure, spirituality, and iconography.

[523] Hatzimichalis, Nektarios. *Orthodox Ecumenism and External Mission: Toward a Theology of Catholicity of the External Mission*. Athens: Patmos, 1966.

This is a series of introductory essays produced at the "High Ecclesiastical School" of Saloniki that outlines the principles of ecumenism in the Bible, in the Fathers and in our own era.

[524] Heiler, Friedrich. *Die Ostkirchen*. Munich: Ernst Reinhardt, 1971.

This 640 page book is a new edition of the author's *Urkirche und Ostkirche* (1937) published posthumously after Heiler's death in 1967. The three major sections discuss Orthodox churches, the pre-Chalcedonian "national" churches, and efforts at reunion. A lengthy bibliographical section is included (pp. 441-598) but is difficult to use since it is so poorly organized. See also the volumes [216, 846].

[525] Hummer, Franz, ed. *Orthodoxie und Zweites Vatikanum: Dokumente und Stimmen aus der Ökumene*. Vienna: Herder, 1966.

The editor provides an introduction on Orthodoxy and ecumenism. Part one includes a number of documents also found in the *Tomos Agapis* [671]. Part two cites ecumenical voices from Orthodoxy, Protestantism and Catholicism. The book contains neither index nor bibliography.

[526] Konidaris, Gerassimos J. *Ökumenischer Dialog ohne 'Konsensus': Wie kann die Una Sancta wiederhergestellt werden?* Würzburg: Köningshausen und Neumann, 1983.

The work of a Greek Orthodox theologian, this volume draws upon lectures given in Athens and Munich from 1956 to 1961. None of the eleven essays treat the early church. The author has harsh criticism for the WCC. Included is a bibliography (pp. 306-318) and an appendix in Greek.

[527] Limouris, Gennadios, ed. *Justice, Peace and the Integrity of Creation: Insights from Orthodoxy*. Geneva: World Council of Churches, 1990.

The Orthodox staff member of the WCC here publishes twelve essays for the ecumenical community on various aspects of the ethical concerns related to peace and ecology.

[528] Mihaita, Nicolae, ed. *Orthodox Youth and the Ecumenical Movement*. Geneva: World Student Christian Federation, 1978.

This 75 page booklet contains the papers from the International Consultation of Orthodox Youth and Students hosted by the Orthodox Church in Nicosia, Cyprus, September 1977.

[529] *The New Valamo Consultation: The Ecumenical Nature of the Orthodox Witness*. Geneva: World Council of Churches, 1977.

At an international gathering of thirty-six Orthodox theologians held in September 1977 at New Valamo, Finland, a number of troubling concerns about trends in the WCC since the Nairobi meeting of 1975 were formulated. The publication includes a five page statement by delegates and subsequent comments by non-Orthodox persons who, though not present, responded to the statement.

[530] Patelos, Constantin G., ed. *The Orthodox Church in the Ecumenical Movement: Documents and Statements 1902-1975*. Geneva: World Council of Churches, 1978.

These primary sources on Orthodox ecumenism in English translation are divided into four categories: patriarchal encyclicals from 1902 to 1973, two Pan Orthodox conferences held in 1961 and 1968, various official Orthodox interventions at Faith and Order (1927-1975), and personal statements by individual hierarchs and theologians. See also Thon [41] and Zernov [541].

[531] Patrinacos, Nicon D. *A Dictionary of Greek Orthodoxy*. New York: Greek Orthodox Archdiocese of North and South America, 1984.

This work which reflects solid ecumenical sensibilities was published by the Greek Archdiocese's Department of Education. It contains a compendium of Orthodox faith and liturgical practices. The entries on the ecumenical movement and on relations with Roman Catholics are enlightened.

[532] Sabev, Todor, ed. *The Sophia Consultation: Orthodox Involvement in the World Council of Churches*. Geneva: World Council of Churches, 1982.

On the invitation of the Bulgarian Orthodox Church, the consultation took place in Sofia from May 23-31, 1981. Purpose of the meeting was to articulate the Orthodox Church's understanding of ecumenism, its experiences and problems with the WCC, its contributions to WCC projects, and its reflections on the upcoming Vancouver general assembly's theme.

[533] Santos Hernández, Angel. *Iglesías orientales separadas*. Historia de la Iglesia, no. 30. Valencia: EDICEP, 1978.

This 734 page oversized volume by the Spanish Jesuit professor was prepared for the Fliche-Martin series. Although written by an expert, the work addresses the general public and provides useful charts, maps, photographs and detailed indexes. The text needs updating.

[534] Santos Hernández, Angel. *Iglesías de Oriente*. Vol. I: *Puntos específicos de su teología*; Vol. II: *Repertorio bibligrafico*. Santander: Sal Terrae, 1959-1963.

This work was written prior to Vatican II by a Jesuit professor from the Pontifical University of Comillas, Spain, and Rome's Gregorian University. Chapter 19 in volume one addresses the ecumenical movement and the Eastern churches. Volume two contains 2243 bibliographical entries of books and articles with brief summaries.

[535] Savramis, Demosthenes. *Ökumenische Probleme der neugriechischen Theologie*. Oekumenische Studien VI. Leiden: Brill, 1964.

The 118 page work reviews the origins and history of the modern ecumenical movement through New Delhi. It also contains an appendix on the Greek Orthodox Church and Vatican II. See also

Slenczka [536].

[536] Slenczka, Reinhard. *Ostkirche und Ökumene: Die Einheit der Kirche als dogmatisches Problem in der neueren ostkirchlichen Theologie.* Forschungen zur systematischen und ökumenischen Theologie, 9. Göttingen: Vandenhoeck und Ruprecht, 1962.

This rich theological analysis of contemporary Orthodox ecclesiology addresses in nine chapters first the unity of the church in classical doctrinal works of Eastern Orthodoxy and then ecumenical problems in this theology of church. The volume also stresses the pluralism of Orthodox ecclesiology. See also Savramis [535].

[537] Stephanopoulos, Robert G. *Guidelines for Orthodox Christians in Ecumenical Relations: Published by the Standing Conference of Canonical Orthodox Bishops in America [SCOBA] and Commended to the Clergy for Guidance.* New York: SCOBA, 1973.

Formulated by a theologian of the Greek Orthodox Archdiocese of North and South America and approved by the hierarchs of several Orthodox jurisdictions, this 66 page booklet gives both Orthodox ecumenical guidelines and a selection of eleven official documents.

[538] Tsetsis, Georges, ed. *Orthodox Thought: Reports of Orthodox Consultations Organized by the World Council of Churches, 1975-1982.* Geneva: World Council of Churches, 1983.

The book reports on some twelve seminars and consultations organized by the WCC Orthodox Task Force, several sub-units, and the Commission on World Mission and Evangelism.

[539] Wingenbach, Gregory C. *Broken, Yet Never Sundered: Orthodox Witness and the Ecumenical Movement.* Brookline, MA: Holy Cross Orthodox Press, 1987.

The volume aims to show how Orthodoxy's commitment to ecumenism is consistent with its normatives guides: Scripture, the ecumenical synods and fathers, the divine liturgy, and sacraments.

[540] Zander, Leo A. *Einheit ohne Vereinigung: Ökumenische Betrachtungen eines russischen Orthodoxen.* Trans. by Reinhard Slenczka. Stuttgart: Evangelisches Verlagswerk, 1959.

In this German translation from the original Russian, Zander offers an original account of the history of ecumenism and its hermeneutics. There is a long discussion of Orthodox contributions to ecumenism. This volume ranks among the very best Orthodox discussions on the goals of ecumenism.

[541] Zernov, Nicolas. *Orthodox Encounter: The Christian East and the Ecumenical Movement*. London: James Clark, 1961.

Composed largely in 1956 and revised before its publication, this work has aged well. It gives valuable information about Orthodox, especially Russian Orthodox, involvement in ecumenism and its rationale. The volume includes a section on collaboration between Anglicans and Orthodox. The author drew from his stay at Drew University in formulating his chapter on the Orthodox in North America.

# Oriental Orthodox

[542] Atiya, Aziz S., *A History of Eastern Christianity*. London: Methuen; Notre Dame, IN: University of Notre Dame, 1968; expanded and updated, with supplement to Part I, London: Methuen; Millwood, NY: Kraus Reprint, 1980.

The author, born in 1898, a member of the Coptic church, was professor of history at the University of Utah. He provides valuable information on the ancient non-Greek family of churches: Coptic and Ethiopic, Jacobite, Nestorian, Armenian, Indian, Maronite, as well as the vanished churches of Nubia and North Africa. He describes their institutional and cultural practices as well as their hierarchical organization. Shorter accounts are given on rites, art, architecture and literature. There are nineteen plates of illustrations and a detailed bibliography (pp. 449-456).

[543] Heyer, Friedrich. *Die Kirche Äthiopiens: Eine Bestandsaufnahme*. Theologische Bibliothek Töpelmann, Bd. 22. Berlin and New York: Walter de Gruyter, 1971.

In ten chapters the author illustrates the historical and theological specificity of the Ethiopian Ancient Oriental Church. Chapter nine describes its ecumenical relationships (pp. 283-325).

[544] Hill, Henry, ed. *Light from the East: A Symposium on the*

*Oriental Orthodox and Assyrian Churches*. Toronto: Anglican Book Centre, 1988.

> Anglican bishop and ecumenist Henry Hill edited this study of pre-Chalcedonian churches: Armenian, Copt, Ethiopian, Syrian (of Syria and South India), Assyrian, and their perception by early Lambeth Conferences. Bishop Hill provides concluding remarks.

[545] Hornus, Jean-Michel. *Introduction aux églises orientales*. Cahiers d'études chrétiennes orientales, no. 12. Paris: Foi et Vie, 1974.

> This 100 page supplement to the journal *Foi et Vie* (vol. 73, no. 1, 1974) gives a reliable, if somewhat dated, account of the Oriental Orthodox and Orthodox churches.

[546] Menachery, George, ed. *St. Thomas Christian Encyclopedia of India*. 2 vols. Trichur: St. Thomas, 1973-1982.

> These volumes are a precious source of information about the Thomas Christians. Volume two appeared first (1973) and treats Thomas, Kerala, Malabar Christians. Volume one (1982) outlines the different ecclesiastical jurisdictions in India. The editorial board included ecumenical consultants. The color photographs or Christian sites in India are stunning and the maps (pp. 145-160) are excellent.

# Anglican

[547] Amand de Mendieta, Emmanuel. *Anglican Vision*. London: SPCK, 1971.

> The author, a former Benedictine monk who was received into the Church of England in 1956, outlines his understanding of the Anglican Communion as a whole. In generally irenic tones, he presents eight chapters treating various aspects of Christian unity including an account of theological diversity. He also describes what would be an acceptable if reformed papacy.

[548] Anglican Ecumenical Consultation, ed. *The Emmaus Report*. London: Church House, 1987.

> This report describes a meeting held from January 27 to February 2, 1987 in preparation for the seventh meeting of the Anglican

Consultative Council (ACC) and the 1988 Lambeth Conference.

[549] *Anglicans in Dialogue: The Contribution of Theological Dialogues to the Search for the Visible Unity of the Churches in the 1980s*. London: Board for Mission and Unity, 1984.

Published for the General Synod of the Church of England, this booklet outlines the various bilateral international dialogues in which the Anglican communion is involved. There is a summary of convergences that have emerged and suggestions how best to study the agreed statements at the local level.

[550] Avis, Paul. *Ecumenical Theology and the Elusiveness of Doctrine*. London: SPCK, 1986.

The author is a parish-based theologian whose five rural congregations are located near Exeter, UK. In seven brief chapters (142 pp.) he outlines the characteristics of Anglican theology and exposes what he perceives to be the weaknesses in the ARCIC *Final Report* [632]. He also criticizes the flaws in methodology in certain ecumenical theology.

[551] Bell, George K.A. *Christian Unity: The Anglican Position*. London: Hodder and Stoughton, 1948.

These Olaus Petri lectures delivered in Uppsala, October 1946, narrate the history and goals of Anglican ecumenism as reflected in the relationships of the Church of England with other Christian churches.

[552] Buchanan, Colin, ed. *Unity on the Ground*. London: SPCK, 1972.

Six Evangelical Anglican theologians from the UK review the importance of local church initiatives of church unity in light of concerns of the Free churches. The book also contains the Keele Statement "The Church and Its Unity" published in April 1967 by the National Evangelical Anglican Congress.

[553] Dun, Angus. *Prospecting for a United Church*. New York: Harper and Brothers, 1948.

This irenic work by a member of the Anglican Communion was delivered in the William Henry Hoover Lectureship on Christian Unity at the University of Chicago. The volume anticipates later notions of healthy diversity and complementary models of church identity.

[554] Gardner-Smith, Percival, ed. *The Roads Converge: A Contribution to the Question of Christian Reunion by Members of Jesus College, Cambridge.* London: E. Arnold, 1963.

In the scope of 253 pages the scholars provide ten learned essays. After an introductory chapter there are three studies by New Testament exegetes, three by church historians (including R.L. Hale's notable "The Mediaeval Unity" demythologizing romantic notions of earlier oneness), and three by scholars on modern ecumenical issues.

[555] Griffiss, James E. *Church, Ministry and Unity: A Divine Commission.* Oxford: Basil Blackwell, 1983.

Professor of systematic theology at Nashotah House, Wisconsin, this Anglo-Catholic Episcopalian writer intends his book to commemorate the 150th anniversary of the Oxford Movement. He explains the heritage and vision of the Movement and its pertinence for today.

[556] Howe, John. *Highways and Hedges: Anglicanism and the Universal Church.* London: Church House, 1985.

Published for the Anglican Consultative Council, this volume describes the character of the Anglican family, its international conferences, and especially its concern for unity and ecumenism (pp. 109-151).

[557] Kingston, Temple, ed. *Anglicanism and Principles of Christian Unity.* Windsor, Ontario: University of Windsor, 1972.

This brief 38 page booklet contains four essays on principles of Christian unity (G. Fisher), the Canadian "Principles of Union" (E.L. Mascall), Anglicanism and ecumenism (J. Macquarrie), and dialogue in phenomenological perspective.

[558] *Many Gifts One Spirit: Report of ACC [Anglican Consultative Council]-7: Singapore 1987.* London: Anglican Consultative Council, 1987.

Among the many helpful reports prepared for ACC there is a

section on ecumenical relations as they affect the Anglican Communion (pp. 83-97).

[559] Mascall, Eric Lionel. *The Recovery of Unity: A Theological Approach*. London and New York: Longmans, Green, 1958.

The Anglican author is convinced that theological issues at the heart of Christian unity are more profound than commonly recognized. He cites as examples liturgy, ordained ministry and papal primacy. This book serves as a good example of a pre-Vatican II perception by someone with a high church vision.

[560] Neill, Stephen. *The Church and Christian Unity*. London: Oxford University Press, 1968.

In these Bampton Lectures, the Anglican bishop from Hamburg reflected on his forty years of ecumenical experiences among which was his rediscovery of the church's missionary vocation.

[561] Nicholls, William. *Ecumenism and Catholicity*. London: SCM, 1952.

This is an early effort by a member of the Church of England, to describe how ecumenism might be encouraged in the churches. This book received the Norrisian Prize Essay Award at Cambridge University for 1950.

[562] Pol, Willem Henrik van de. *Anglicanism in Ecumenical Perspective*. Trans. by Walter van de Putte. Duquesne Studies, Series 4: Theological. Pittsburgh: Duquesne University, 1965.

This is a sympathetic exposition of Anglican ethos and its ecumenical efforts vis-à-vis Catholicism and Protestantism in this century. It identifies four principal obstacles to church unity. The Dutch original was published in 1962.

[563] Runcie, Robert. *The Unity We Seek*. Comp. and ed. by Margaret Pawley. London: Darton, Longman and Todd, 1989.

This collection of speeches and pastoral letters by the former Archbishop of Canterbury has been organized around the themes of unity, service and healing.

[564] Staples, Peter. *The Church of England 1961-1980*. IIMO

Research Pamphlet 3. Utrecht: Interuniversitair Instituut voor Missiologie en Oecumenica, 1981.

Produced by the Utrecht-based Interuniversity Institute for Missiological and Ecumenical Research, this volume focuses on the years 1961-1980 in its attempt to interpret the Church of England for European readers. One section describes its relations with other churches (pp. 82-112).

[565] Stephenson, Alan M.G. *Anglicanism and the Lambeth Conferences*. London: SPCK, 1978.

The volume concentrates on the first ten Lambeth Conferences (1867-1968) which are held every ten years. The author describes each conference's agenda, personalities, decisions and results. The final chapter treats the years 1968 to 1978.

[566] *Steps Toward Unity: Documents on Ecumenical Relations Presented to ACC-6, Lagos, July 1984*. London: Anglican Consultative Council [ACC], 1984.

The volume contains a report of the Preparatory Group on Ecumenical Affairs about growing convergences. It included a proposed plan for unity by stages. Also described is the 1984 visit of Anglican ecumenical officers to the WCC.

[567] Tomkins, Oliver. *A Time for Unity*. London: SCM, 1964.

The Bishop of Bristol, England, addressed seven issues including reading the signs of the times, non-theological hindrances to ecumenism, and ordination in a divided church.

[568] Wright, J. Robert, ed. *A Communion of Communions: One Eucharistic Fellowship: The Detroit Report and Papers of the Triennial Ecumenical Study of the Episcopal Church, 1976-1979*. New York: Crossroad, 1979.

The report includes essays by Catholics, Orthodox and Protestants. Some of the questions raised are: toward what goals should Anglicans aspire, and what is the present state of ecumenism. The essays contain excellent reflections on the the theology of communion which is inspired by the New Testament notion of *koinonia*.

# Lutheran

[569] Asmussen, Hans. *Rom, Wittenberg, Moskau: Zur grossen Kirchenpolitik*. Stuttgart: Schwabenverlag, 1955.

The Lutheran theologian Hans Asmussen (1898-1969) divided his material into seven chapters: the international context; politics and the churches; history and the churches; Orthodox initiatives; dialogue with the East; Orthodox, Roman Catholic and Lutheran views of each other; orthopraxis in the churches. Writing during the 1950s, the author judged dialogue with the Russian Orthodox as problematic because of the severe restrictions on religion in the USSR. See revision [570] and also response by Fries [573].

[570] Asmussen, Hans. *Rom, Wittenberg, Moskau am Vorabend des Konzils*. Rev. ed. Stuttgart: Schwabenverlag, 1961.

Although the title resembles the 1955 publication [569] this book is in fact a completely new work that takes into account new developments, ongoing issues and new relationships.

[571] Centre Orthodoxe du Patriarcat oecuménique, Chambésy-Geneva. *Luther et la Réforme allemande dans une perspective oecuménique*. Etudes théologiques de Chambésy 3. Chambésy-Geneva: Centre Orthodoxe, 1983.

To mark the 500th anniversary of Martin Luther's birth, Geneva's Orthodox Center sponsored these lectures for some sixty professors and graduate students of theology. The twenty-six contributions in French, German or English touch upon: Luther's life and work; theological issues close to his heart; ecumenical assessments of Luther; and Luther and the unity of the Church. See also Iserloh [199], Geisser [574], and Lehmann [577].

[572] Duchrow, Ulrich. *Conflict over the Ecumenical Movement: Confessing Christ Today in the Universal Church*. Trans. by David Lewis. Geneva: World Council of Churches, 1981.

Written by one who from 1970 to 1977 served on the staff of the Lutheran World Federation (LWF) and later as ecumenical coordinator for a Lutheran church in Baden, the book asks whether the WCC is a fellowship of churches on the way to becoming the one church of Christ or a functional association. The importance of international confessional organizations such as the LWF is stressed. This is a translation of *Konflikt um die Ökumene* (1980). See also Schmidt-Clausen [581].

[573] Fries, Heinrich. *Antwort an Asmussen*. Stuttgart: Schwabenverlag, 1958.

In the first edition of his book *Rom, Wittenberg, Moskau* [569] Asmussen posed five questions to Roman Catholics: concerning word and sacrament, the role of philosophy, the notion of merit, the interpretation of "dead to the Law" (Rom 7) and mariology. The Catholic theologian from the University of Munich here responds. A French version of the work appeared as *Cinq réponses à un théologien luthérien*.

[574] Geisser, Hans Friedrich, *et al. Weder Ketzer noch Heiliger: Luthers Bedeutung für den ökumenischen Dialog*. Regensburg: F. Pustet, 1982.

In preparation for the 500th anniversary of Martin Luther's birth, seven authors (Protestant, Catholic and Orthodox) from the Katholische Akademie in Bayern and the Evangelische Akademie Tutzing at their 1981 conference explored in depth the shift in attitudes whereby Luther became for some a "father in faith" rather than a "prince of heretics."

[575] Klappert, Erich. *Dialog mit Rom: Zusammenarbeit und Zukunft der Mission auf ökumenischer Basis 450 Jahre nach Luther*. Wuppertal: Aussaat, 1967.

Written by a Lutheran pastor and religion teacher, the book reflects on new directions taken by Catholics regarding doctrine, practice and mission.

[576] Lackmann, Max. *Credo Ecclesiam Catholicam: Evangelische Bekenntnis gegen den Protestantismus*. Graz: Styria, 1960.

The Lutheran editor of the journal *Bausteine* [93] published this book to encourage Protestants to enter into closer dialogue with Catholics. He discusses the evangelical intent of the Reformation and compares catechetical material from Evangelical-Lutheran and Roman Catholic sources.

[577] Lehmann, Karl, ed. *Luthers Sendung für Katholiken und Protestanten*. Munich: Schnell und Steiner, 1982.

The Katholische Akadamie of the Archdiocese of Freiburg im Breisgau sponsored an event in 1982 to mark the 500th anniversary of Luther's birth. Catholics and Lutherans alike here assessed his significance for the contemporary churches.

[578] Manns, Peter, and Meyer, Harding, eds. *Luther's Ecumenical Significance: An Interconfessional Consultation.* Philadelphia: Fortress; New York: Paulist, 1984.

For this English version of *Ökumenische Erschliessung Luthers*, C. Lindberg and H. McSorley also collaborated. The volume contains papers from an ecumenical consultation held at the Rosenberg Academy (Speyer) in October 1982 in preparation for the Luther year.

[579] Quanbeck, Warren. *Search for Understanding: Lutheran Conversations with Reformed, Anglican and Roman Catholic Churches.* Minneapolis: Augsburg, 1972.

This somewhat dated account of Lutheran ecumenism as interpreted by a professor of theology at the Lutheran Seminary in St. Paul, Minnesota, still contains useful information.

[580] Schlingensiepen, Ferdinand, ed. *Union und Ökumene: 150 Jahre Evangelische Kirche der Union.* Berlin: Lettner Verlag, 1968.

This 175 page study outlines the major ecumenical moments in the history of the Evangelische Kirche der Union.

[581] Schmidt-Clausen, Kurt. *Reformation als ökumenisches Ereignis.* Berlin: Lutherisches Verlagshaus, 1970.

The author was former general secretary of the Lutheran World Federation. He publishes here an especially rich collection of essays on ecumenism written from 1954 to 1969. See also Duchrow [572].

[582] Schütte, Heinz. *Protestantismus: Sein Selbstverständnis und sein Ursprung gemäss der deutschsprachigen protestantischen Theologie der Gegenwart und eine kurze katholische Besinnung.* Essen: Fredebeul und Koenen, 1966.

This sizeable (573 pp.) study of modern Protestantism surveys contemporary theologians' views on its essence. Part two explores the origins and fundamental traits of Protestantism including a section called "Protestantismus sui ipsius criticus."

[583] Stauffer, Richard. *Luther as Seen by Catholics*. Trans. by Mary Parker and T.H.L. Parker. Ecumenical Studies in History No. 7. London: Lutterworth; Richmond: John Knox, 1967.

Written by a professor at the Protestant Faculty of Theology, Paris, originally entitled *Luther vu par les catholiques*, this volume surveys the older polemic critique of Luther by Catholics such as Heinrich Denifle and Hartmann Grisar as well as more recent reassessment of Luther in Germany and Anglo-Saxon countries. Although only 83 pages long, the work is very well conceived.

[584] Yule, George, ed. *Luther: Theologian For Catholics and Protestants*. Edinburgh: T. and T. Clark, 1985.

The professor of church history at the University of Aberdeen edited these eight chapters which show how Luther probed central areas of the Christian faith in ways that might still be pertinent to renewal by more than one church tradition.

# Reformed

[585] Abbot, Carolyn T. *One Church: A Grass-Roots View of the Protestant Ecumenical Movement*. New York: Exposition, 1967.

In the view of the author, a review of seventy years in the ecumenical movement among Protestants shows how individual choice has often been threatened by those who undermine personal religious freedom through pressure and political activism. A paradigmatic example of enforced organic union, she argues, is the 1957 merger of the Congregational Christian Churches and the Evangelical and Reformed Church in order to create the United Church of Christ.

[586] Brown, Robert McAfee, and Scott, David H., comps. and eds. *The Challenge to Reunion*. New York: McGraw-Hill, 1963.

On December 4, 1960, Eugene Carson Blake delivered a sermon entitled: "A Proposal Toward the Reunion of Christ's Church" addressed to mainline Protestant churches (text pp. 271-283). In this volume, twenty-one reactions to his proposal are recorded which serve as a cross-section of Protestant ecumenical perspectives. On Blake see also [393].

**[587]** *Called to Witness to the Gospel Today: Cairo Consultation 1984.* Geneva: World Alliance of Reformed Churches, 1983.

Originally a special issue of *The Reformed World* published by the World Alliance of Reformed Churches (Presbyterian and Congregational), the book summarizes discussions at a February 1984 study conference of the WARC and prints five lectures delivered there by churchmen from different parts of the world.

**[588]** Cherix, Philippe. *Pour un vivant oecuménisme.* Neuchâtel: Editions H. Messeiller, 1952.

This brief account on the principles of ecumenism by a Swiss Protestant is an interesting pre-Vatican II testimony.

**[589]** Cullmann, Oscar. *Message to Catholics and Protestants.* Trans. by Joseph A. Burgess. Grand Rapids: Eerdmans; London: Lutterworth, 1959.

This short piece (62 pp.) contains talks given before the convocation of Vatican II that outline practical proposals for realizing Christian solidarity. Here Cullmann proposed that Protestants and Catholics mutually exchange financial offerings collected during the Week of Christian Unity. The original German title was *Katholiken und Protestanten* (1958); the title in the UK was *Catholics and Protestants: A Proposal for Realizing Christian Solidarity.*

**[590]** Dumas, André, *et al. Actualité de la Réforme.* Geneva: Labor et Fides, 1987.

This volume contains twenty-four lectures given at Geneva's Faculty of Theology at a special Calvin symposium. Three in particular by N. Nissiotis, P. Duprey and E. Castro, discuss the ecumenical contributions of the Calvinist or Reformed churches.

**[591]** Huxtable, John. *A New Hope for Christian Unity.* Fount Paperback. Glasgow: William Collins, 1977.

The first moderator of General Assembly of the newly formed United Reformed Church reports on the new hope given to ecumenism by the propositions of the Churches' Unity

Commission "arising out of the ashes" of the Anglican-Methodist reunion plan. The Commission includes eight Christian bodies including the Roman Catholic Church. Several documents are included.

[592] Kinnamon, Michael, ed. *Unity in Each Place ... in All Places: United Churches and the Christian World Communions*. Faith and Order Paper 118. Geneva: World Council of Churches, 1983.

What is here presented is an account of the dialogue between the united churches and the Christian World Communions (CWC), formerly known as the World Confessional Families.

[593] Leuba, Jean-Louis. *A la découverte de l'espace oecuménique*. Neuchâtel: Delachaux et Niestlé, 1967.

The Swiss professor gathered in this 237 page volume a number of essays written prior to Vatican II on what Protestants hoped for from Catholics. The material is organized under biblical, historical, systematic and specifically ecumenical (pp. 171-233) headings.

[594] McLelland, Joseph C. *Toward a Radical Church: New Models for Ecumenical Relations*. Toronto: Ryerson, 1967; Edinburgh: Saint Andrew, 1969.

The author, a Scottish Presbyterian, who also served as Dean at the Faculty of Religious Studies, McGill University, Montreal, describes the desirability of non-organic unity, illustrated by the experience of Canadian churches since 1925.

[595] McNeill, John Thomas. *Unitive Protestantism: The Ecumenical Spirit and Its Persistent Expression*. Richmond: John Knox, 1964.

Most of the research for this book was done in the 1920s for lectures at Chicago and Toronto. The author draws upon the experiences of the United Church of Canada to illustrate the desire of Reformation Christians for a "unitive principle."

[596] Morrison, Charles Clayton. *The Unfinished Reformation*. New York: Harper and Row, 1953; Freeport, NY: Books for Libraries Press, 1968.

The focus of these lectures is largely American Protestantism though there is a comparison of modern Reformation and Catholic attitudes. His assessment of Catholicism is negative and polemic. Morrison was one of the forces behind COCU's plan of union [787].

[597] Routley, Erik. *Congregationalists and Unity*. London: A.R. Mowbray, 1962.

The 94 page booklet written by a minister in a Congregational church in Edinburgh is a personal statement of how he perceives the exigencies of Christian unity.

[598] Rycroft, W. Stanley. *The Ecumenical Witness of the United Presbyterian Church in the U.S.A.* Philadelphia: Board of Christian Education of the United Presbyterian Church in the USA, 1968.

These eight chapters give an account of the early missionary efforts of Presbyterians in Colonial America and elsewhere, their involvement in ecumenical associations, and the formation in 1958 of their Commission on Ecumenical Mission and Relations.

[599] Sell, Alan P.F. *A Reformed, Evangelical, Catholic Theology: The Contribution of the World Alliance of Reformed Churches, 1875-1982*. Grand Rapids: Eerdmans, 1991.

The World Alliance of Reformed Churches (Presbyterian and Congregational) is a family of 173 member churches that has been involved in international bilateral dialogues since 1970. This account of the WARC describes its conversations with Catholicism, the Baptist World Alliance, the Anglican Consultative Council, and the Lutheran World Federation.

[600] Swartz, Fred W. *All in God's Family: Brethren and the Quest for Christian Unity*. Elgin, IL: Brethren, 1977.

This is a 144 page account of the Church of the Brethren by one of its pastors based in Harrisburg, PA. It explains the origins of the Brethren's "sectarian defenses" which resulted from their illegal status in Europe. Special stress is placed on their new situation in North America.

[601] Tavard, Georges H. *The Catholic Approach to Protestantism*. Trans. by the author. New York: Harper, 1955.

Tavard personally translated this work of his from the French *A la rencontre du protestantisme* (1954). The work has historical value inasmuch as it shows how, in the years prior to Vatican II, one leading Catholic theologian regarded Protestantism. The treatment is generally sympathetic and urges reconciliation and "spiritual emulation."

[602] Torrance, Thomas F. *Conflict and Agreement in the Church.* Vol. 1: *Order and Disorder*; Vol. 2: *The Ministry and the Sacraments of the Gospel.* London: Lutterworth, 1959-1960.

These two volumes assemble various essays of the Edinburgh professor published in a number of sources including the *Scottish Journal of Theology.* Volume one is divided into part one, reports on various churches including the Roman Catholic Church about which he articulates some highly critical remarks; part two, reports on Faith and Order discussions. Volume two discusses ordination to ministry, as well as baptism and the Lord's Supper.

[603] Van der Linde, Hendrik. *De oecumene in een planetaire wereld.* Roermond: J.J. Romen, 1967.

This 395 page work is not so much an historical account of church unity efforts but a reflective theological essay by a Dutch Protestant who sees the ecumenical movement as a shifting paradigm.

# Methodist

[604] Davies, Rupert E. *Methodists and Unity.* London: A.R. Mowbray, 1962.

This work of an individual Methodist from Bristol, England, articulates his concern about Christian unity especially against the background of the need for unity between Methodists and members of the Church of England.

[605] Hurley, Michael, ed. *John Wesley's Letter to a Roman Catholic.* London: Geoffrey Chapman; Nashville: Abingdon, 1968.

Published by an Irish Jesuit, founder of the Irish School of Ecumenics, this edition with commentary of Wesley's letter to a Roman Catholic hopes to make better known the letter written and printed in Dublin in 1749.

[606] Minus, Paul M. Jr., ed. *Methodism's Destiny in an Ecumenical Age*. Nashville: Abingdon, 1969.

Nine essays authored by leading Methodist ecumenists illustrate the important contributions their church has made to bringing Christians together. The focus is thoroughly international in scope.

[607] Outler, Albert C. *The Christian Tradition and the Unity We Seek*. New York: Oxford University Press, 1957.

The late Methodist ecumenist gave these five lectures in 1955 at the University of Virginia (Charlottesville). The publication was a milestone in American ecumenism by one who later served as an observer at Vatican II. See also his reactions to Vatican II [339].

# Baptist

[608] *Baptists and Reformed in Dialogue: Documents from the Conversations Sponsored by the World Alliance of Reformed Churches and the Baptist World Alliance*. Studies from the World Alliance of Reformed Churches 4. Geneva: World Alliance of Reformed Churches, 1984.

This 56 page booklet contains an account of ten years' work by a group of Reformed and Baptist theologians culminating in informal conversations from 1973 to 1977. Co-chairmen of the discussions were Günther Wagner (Baptist) and Martin Cressey (Reformed).

[609] Champion, Leonard G. *Baptists and Unity*. London: A.R. Mowbray, 1961.

As part of a series of confessional descriptions of the goals of Christian unity this booklet gives a representative position from a British Baptist.

[610] Estep, William R. *Baptists and Christian Unity*. Nashville: Broadman, 1966.

This book explains why many Baptists have shunned membership in the WCC because of their convictions regarding religious freedom, independent local churches and believers' baptism. The author focuses on those Baptists who are willing to participate in the WCC and in national councils of churches.

[611] Roberts-Thomson, E. *With Hands Outstretched: Baptists and the Ecumenical Movement*. London: Marshall, Morgan and Scott, 1962.

This book provides an important corrective to show that all Baptists are not anti-ecumenical. It lists the variety of Baptist traditions and their various attitudes towards other confessions. At the 1948 WCC Amsterdam assembly, eight different Baptist conventions were represented. The author was formerly principal of Baptist Theological College, New Zealand, and of Baptist Theological College, New South Wales, Australia.

## Pentecostal/Charismatic

[612] Bittlinger, Arnold, ed. *The Church is Charismatic*. Geneva: World Council of Churches, 1981.

The volume provides descriptions of several meetings sponsored by the WCC's sub-unit on Renewal and Congregational Life from 1978 to 1980. Because it involves Christian across denominational lines, charismatic renewal is judged to be important for the goals of the WCC. The editor is a Swiss pastor.

[613] Centre d'Etudes Oecuméniques de Strasbourg. *Au-delà des confessions? Les mouvements transconfessionels*. Paris: Editions du Cerf, 1979.

Five collaborators from Strasbourg's Institute for Ecumenical Research explore the ecclesiological significance of various transconfessional Christian movements (such as the charismatic movement, groups focused on action) and their impact on classical ecumenism. This volume exists in a German version entitled *Neue trans-konfessionelle Bewegungen*.

[614] Davis, Rex. *Locusts and Wild Honey: The Charismatic Renewal and the Ecumenical Movement*. Risk, no. 2. Geneva: World Council of Churches, 1978.

An account of the modern charismatic renewal or neo-pentecostalism and its impact on church unity. Included is an annotated bibliography by A. van der Bent on "Charismatic Movements Today" (pp. 112-122). See also [479, 617, 694].

[615] Harper, Michael. *This is the Day: A Fresh Look at Christian Unity*. London: Hodder and Stoughton, 1979.

The author concentrates on English language material taken from the 1970s that illustrates how the charismatic movement within Protestant, Anglican and Catholic churches has influenced ecumenical dialogue. It contains the final reports of official Catholic/Pentecostal and Catholic/charismatic meetings 1972-1976.

[616] Meeking, Basil, and Stott, John, eds. *The Evangelical / Roman Catholic Dialogue on Mission 1977-1984: A Report*. Grand Rapids: Eerdmans; Exeter: Paternoster, 1986.

The booklet describes three meetings held in Venice (1977), Cambridge (1982) and Landévennec, France (1984) with Evangelicals of several denominations and Roman Catholics. While there is no agreed statement as such, there is an account of areas of common concern.

[617] Mühlen, Heribert. *Dokumente zur Erneuerung der Kirchen*. Mainz: M. Grünewald, 1982.

Three documents promoting the goals of charismatic renewal in the churches are here reproduced: a pastoral letter of the German Catholic Bishops' Conference; a WCC report from Bossey, March 1980; and an address of John Paul II on charismatic renewal, dated May 7, 1981. See also [479, 614, 694].

# 5

# Bilateral Dialogues

## General Studies

[618] Centre Orthodoxe du Patriarcat oecuménique, Chambésy-Geneva. *Les dialogues oecuméniques hier et aujourd'hui.* Etudes théologiques de Chambésy 5. Chambésy-Geneva: Centre Orthodoxe, 1985.

> Part of the annual series of conferences held at Chambésy, this 1984 symposium brought together Orthodox, Catholics and Protestants to evaluate bilateral and multilateral consultations as well as their reception. No one from North America was in attendance.

[619] Crow, Paul A., Jr., ed. *Fundamental Differences, Fundamental Consensus: The Impact of Bilateral Dialogues on the Ecumenical Movement.* Indianapolis: COCU, 1986.

> Originally published as a special issue of *Mid-Stream* vol. 25, no. 3 (1986), the small book contains six ecumenical studies of the bilateral conversations and a description of recent events in the ecumenical community.

[620] Desseaux, Jacques Elisée. *Dialogues théologiques et accords oecuméniques.* Paris: Editions du Cerf, 1982.

> This is one of the more useful accounts of the numerous bilateral conversations underway since the mid 1960s. The volume enumerates the principal themes of the dialogues (e.g., church,

ministry, eucharist, unity models).

[621] Ehrenström, Nils, and Gassmann, Günther. *Confessions in Dialogue: A Survey of Bilateral Conversations among World Confessional Families 1959--1974*. 3rd rev. ed. Faith and Order Paper 74. Geneva: World Council of Churches, 1975.

This careful, descriptive listing of the numerous bilateral conversations, at least up to 1974, is an indispensable tool for identifying dialogues and tracing common topics. For more recent classification, see the listings in *Centro pro Unione, Bulletin* [8].

[622] *Fourth Forum on Bilateral Conversations: Report*. Faith and Order Paper 125. Geneva: World Council of Churches, 1985.

Work on this sequel to the other three forums [625] began in March 1985 at Bossey. Twenty-six participants from ten churches and the Faith and Order staff were on hand. This volume covers bilateral conversations from 1980-1985. Of special note is the useful summary of convergences regarding the Lima document [1175].

[623] Heiler, Anne M., ed. *Inter Confessiones: Beiträge zur Förderung des interkonfessionellen und interreligiösen Gespräche*. Marburger Theologische Studien 10. Marburg: N. G. Elwert, 1972.

In this *Festschrift* honoring the late Friedrich Heiler (1892-1967), there is a tribute to the honoree and a bibliography of his writings, plus ten essays, two of which address ecumenical matters: ecumenism in Russian Christianity (N. von Arseniev) and Catholic and Orthodox ecumenical relations. On Heiler see also [415].

[624] Ristow, Helmut, and Burgert, Helmuth, eds. *Konfession und Ökumene: Aspekte - Probleme - Aufgaben*. E. Berlin: Evangelische Verlagsanstalt, 1964.

This collaborative work antedates the later bilateral conversations and is heavily European in focus. Still it is a good indication of the state of ecumenism in the mid 1960s. The list of ecumenical collaborators is long and includes Orthodox and Catholics.

[625] *The Three Reports of the Forum on Bilateral Conversations*. Faith and Order Paper 107. Geneva: World Council of Churches, 1981.

In the course of fifty-two pages the booklet covers highlights of three forums held in Switzerland between 1978 and 1980 to evaluate the ongoing work of the international bilateral conversations. See also [622].

[626] Valentini, Donato, ed. *Dialoghi ecumenici ufficiali: Bilanci e prospettive.* Biblioteca di Scienze Religiose 53. Rome: Libreria Ateneo Salesiano, 1983.

A cycle of six lectures was given in 1982 on the major conclusions reached by the various international bilateral dialogues. A further essay reflected on why young people are generally disinterested in ecumenism.

# Oriental Orthodox/Catholic

[627] *Wort und Wahrheit: Revue for Religion and Culture. Supplementary Issues 1-4.* Vienna: Herder, 1972-1978.

Under the sponsorship of the Pro Oriente Foundation, Vienna, four ecumenical consultations between theologians of the Ancient Oriental Orthodox churches and the Roman Catholic Church were held in 1971, 1973, 1976 and 1978. The now defunct journal *Wort und Wahrheit* published all the papers in English translation (the quality of which leaves much to be desired) and included final communiques on christology and on ecclesiology. See also [1035].

# Anglican/Orthodox

[628] *Anglican-Orthodox Dialogue: The Moscow Statement Agreed by the Anglican-Orthodox Joint Doctrinal Commission 1976.* Eds. Kallistos Ware and Colin Davey. London: SPCK, 1977.

Besides the text of the Moscow agreed statement (pp. 82-91), there are useful accounts of the history of the dialogue from 1920 to 1976 and reflections on the status of the documents produced.

[629] *Anglican-Orthodox Dialogue: The Dublin Agreed Statement 1984.* London: SPCK, 1984.

The booklet provides the text of the consensus statement on the mystery of the church, divinization, and worship. It also reproduces the Moscow agreed statement (1976) and the Athens report (1978) on the ordination of women.

**[630]** *Anglo-Russian Theological Conference, Moscow, July 1956: A Report of a Theological Conference.* Ed. H.M. Waddams. London: Faith Press, 1957.

> The report of a meeting between members of the Russian Orthodox Church and the Church of England provides ten essays reviewing the history of relations between the two churches and an overview of doctrinal issues perceived differently by the two communions. There was no agreed statement.

**[631]** Istavridis, Vasilios T. *Orthodoxy and Anglicanism.* Trans. by Colin Davey. London: SPCK, 1966.

> This translation from the Greek provides a history of relations between the two churches up to the year 1960. The carefully documented work touches upon doctrinal and pastoral issues and offers some practical suggestions. Also included is a specialized bibliography (pp. 161-166).

# Anglican/Catholic

**[632]** *The Final Report: Anglican-Roman Catholic International Commission, Windsor, September 1981.* London: SPCK/CTS, 1982.

> The booklet contains the concluding work of ARCIC-I that reproduces the original statements on eucharist (1971), ministry (1973), authority (1976), plus a series of complementary elucidations intended to clarify the original intent or to meet objections. See also the subsequent work of ARCIC-II [974, 1020].

**[633]** Avis, Paul. *Truth Beyond Words: Problems and Prospects for Anglican - Roman Catholic Unity.* Cambridge, MA: Cowley, 1985.

> The author, an ordained priest in the Church of England, calls for a new approach to Anglican and Roman Catholic dialogue, one that would be more apophatic, seeking a truth beyond the level of doctrine or formulas. He cites the approaches of Maurice, Newman, Rahner and Lonergan.

**[634]** Carey, George. *The Meeting of the Waters: A Balanced Contribution to the Ecumenical Debate.* London: Hodder and Stoughton,

1985. American title: *A Tale of Two Churches: Can Protestants and Catholics Get Together?* Downers Grove, IN: Intervarsity, 1985.

The author was rector of St. Nicholas Church, Durham, and then principal of Trinity College, Bristol. He restricts his narrative to interaction between English-speaking Protestants and Roman Catholics in the United Kingdom and North America. The stress is on "serious concern for truth and evangelical essentials."

[635] Clark, Alan C., and Davey, Colin, eds. *Anglican / Roman Catholic Dialogue: The Work of the Preparatory Commission*. New York: Oxford University Press, 1974.

The collection of eleven documents includes the Malta Report which summarized the work of ARCIC-I (1967-1968). It also contains various Lambeth resolutions on relations with Catholicism.

[636] Dick, John A. *The Malines Conversations Revisited*. Bibliotheca Ephemeridum Theologicarum Lovaniensium 85. Leuven: Leuven University Press, 1989.

The 278 page monograph reviews the ecumenical activities of Cardinal Désiré Mercier (1851-1926) and specifically the Malines Conversations which held five sessions between 1921 and 1926. These talks, between English representatives of the Anglican Communion and continental European theologians of the Catholic Church, launched a new era in ecumenical attitudes and helped Catholicism out of its anti-Modernist prejudices. Especially useful is a biographical index giving dates and salient information about individuals (pp. 233-253).

[637] Haase, Wolfgang, ed. *Rome and the Anglicans: Historical and Doctrinal Aspects of Anglican - Roman Catholic Relations*. Berlin: W. de Gruyter, 1982.

The work comprises four essays treating: relations between Anglicans and Roman Catholics in the sixteenth and seventeenth centuries; the English clergy, Catholic and Protestant, in the sixteenth and seventeenth centuries; relations from 1717 to 1980; and contemporary Rome and the Anglican Communion.

[638] Hale, Robert. *Canterbury and Rome: Sister Churches: A Roman Catholic Monk Reflects upon Reunion in Diversity*. New York: Paulist,

1982.

A Camaldolese monk from Berkeley, California, uses the biblical, patristic and medieval idea of "sister churches" to illuminate the relationship that can exist between churches that have not yet achieved full visible communion.

[639] Montefiore, Hugh. *So Near and Yet So Far: Rome, Canterbury and ARCIC*. London: SCM, 1986.

To promote further rapprochement between Anglicans and Catholics, the Anglican bishop of Birmingham, England, discusses unfinished business of the first international Anglican-Roman Catholic International Commission (ARCIC-I) relating to church authority, the laity, Mary, sexual ethics, and women's ordination.

[640] Ryan, Herbert J., and Wright, J. Robert. *Episcopalians and Roman Catholics: Can They Ever Get Together?* Denville, NJ: Dimension, 1972.

The volume summarizes the results of an unofficial symposium held at Graymoor, New York, May 8-12, 1972. Seven distinct areas of concern are explored by both an Anglican and Catholic theologian.

[641] *Vom Dialog zur Gemeinschaft: Dokumente zum anglikanisch-lutherischen und anglikanisch-katholischen Gespräch*. Ökumenische Dokumentation 2. Frankfurt: O. Lembeck; J. Knecht, 1975.

Although these six documents were originally written in English and are available elsewhere, readers of English would profit from studying the excellent introduction that situates the historical importance and uniqueness of these dialogues.

[642] Witmer, Joseph W., and Wright, J. Robert, eds. *Called to Full Unity: Documents on Anglican - Roman Catholic Relations 1966-1983*. Washington: United States Catholic Conference, 1985.

The publication contains a wealth of documents dated from 1966 to 1983. Comments by popes and archbishops of Canterbury, as well as all the ARCIC-I statements including *The Final Report* [632] are reproduced. Especially useful are statements by ARC-USA on the purpose of the church and on the ordination of women.

[643] Yarnold, Edward. *In Search of Unity*. Middlegreen, Slough: St. Paul; Collegeville: Liturgical Press, 1991.

The British Jesuit served as a member of ARCIC-I from 1970 until his replacement by ARCIC-II. In light of two decades of involvement he writes about remaining problems relating to the papacy, Mary, purgatory and indulgences, and the ordination of women.

# Anglican/Lutheran and Reformed

[644] *Anglican-Lutheran Dialogue: The Report of the European Regional Commission, Helsinki, August-September 1982*. London: SPCK, 1983.

The booklet reviews the history of the relationship between the Anglican and Lutheran churches in Europe and outlines the principal areas of doctrinal convergences and agreements.

[645] *Anglican-Lutheran International Conversations: The Report of the Conversations 1970-1972 authorized by the Lambeth Conference and the Lutheran Federation*. London: SPCK, 1973.

The small booklet describes the discussions relating to authority, church, word and sacraments, apostolic ministry, and worship. A series of recommendations are appended.

[646] *Anglican-Lutheran Relations: Report of the Anglican-Lutheran Joint Working Group, Cold Ash, Berkshire, England, 28 November-3 December, 1983*. London: Anglican Consultative Council; Geneva: Lutheran World Federation, 1983.

This brief study describes the period of remarkable convergence over the fifteen years prior to 1983. It gives historical background on the development of Anglican-Lutheran relations as well as an account of the goals of dialogue. Some statistics and a brief bibliography are included.

[647] *God's Reign and Our Unity: The Report of the Anglican-Reformed International Commission 1981-1984*. London: SPCK, 1984.

The international dialogue group first met in 1978 to review Anglican and Reformed relations. This was followed by a meeting in Woking, England, in January 1984, which produced this 90 page agreed statement.

[648] *Die Hoffnung auf die Zukunft der Menschheit unter der Verheissung Gottes.* Beiheft zur Ökumenischen Rundschau, no. 41. Frankfurt: O. Lembeck, 1981.

The volume records the results of the eighth theological meeting between members of the Russian Orthodox Church and the Evangelische Kirche in Deutschland (EKD), held in Odessa, October 10-13, 1979. Theme of the conference was eschatology.

[649] *The Niagara Report: Report of the Anglican-Lutheran Consultation on Episcope, Niagara Falls, September 1987, by the Anglican-Lutheran International Continuation Committee.* London: Church House, 1988.

In some ways this agreed statement compares closely to the document on *episkope* produced by the Group of Les Dombes [1157]. The consensus statement on the nature of episcopal ministry runs to 52 pages.

[650] Norgren, William A., and Rusch, William G., eds. *Implications of the Gospel: Lutheran-Episcopal Dialogue, Series III.* Minneapolis: Augsburg; Cincinnati: Foreward Movement, 1988.

The two American branches of the Lutheran and Anglican communions address here the eschatological grounding of the Gospel, as well as the Gospel's God, world, and mission.

[651] Norgren, William A., and Rusch, William G., eds. *"Toward Full Communion" and "Concordat of Agreement": Lutheran-Episcopal Dialogue, Series III.* Minneapolis: Augsburg; Cincinnati: Foreward Movement, 1991.

The culmination of some twenty years of collaboration the document "Towards Full Communion" indicates what are seen as the areas of theological consensus. Therefore, the consultation offers a proposed "Concordat of Agreement" for approval. Dissenting opinions are also included.

[652] *The Report of the Lutheran-Episcopal Dialogue Second Series 1976-1980.* Cincinnati: Forward Movement, 1981.

The small book presents the report of the five year dialogue in the USA, five joint statements, and a selection of papers presented at the meetings.

# Anglican/Old Catholic

[653] Huelin, Gordan, ed. *Old Catholics and Anglicans 1931-1981.* Oxford: Oxford University Press, 1983.

This volume commemorates the fiftieth anniversary of the Bonn Agreement of 1931 that established full communion between Anglicans and Old Catholics. Besides sections on the history and theology of the Old Catholic Church, there is a detailed account of ecumenical initiatives of the Old Catholics (pp. 141-163).

# Lutheran/Catholic

[654] Anderson, H. George, and Crumley, James R. Jr., eds. *Promoting Unity: Themes in Lutheran-Catholic Dialogue.* Minneapolis: Augsburg, 1989.

Eight Lutherans, under the editorial assistance of the chairs of the US Lutheran/Catholic and the International Lutheran/Catholic consultations, produced this *Festschrift* in honor of Johannes Willebrands for his eightieth birthday.

[655] Birmelé, André. *Le salut en Jésus Christ dans les dialogues œcuméniques.* Cogitatio Fidei 141. Paris: Cerf, 1986.

The author, a member of Strasbourg's Institute for Ecumenical Research, prepared this 520 page study as part of his doctoral studies. The longest section (pp. 19-315) discusses the Lutheran/Catholic international and national consultations. Other bilaterals are studied also. The bibliography is especially rich (pp. 475-501).

[656] Brandenburg, Albert. *Die Zukunft des Martin Luthers: Martin Luther, Evangelium und die Katholizität.* Münster: Aschendorff; Kassel: J. Stauda, 1977.

This is a sympathetic account of Lutheran and Catholic interrelatedness. In four essays the author outlines how modern Catholic theologians view Luther and how Catholic theologians could profit from further study of Luther's theology.

[657] Empie, Paul C. *Lutherans and Catholics in Dialogue: Personal Notes for a Study*. Raymond Tiemeyer, ed. Philadelphia: Fortress, 1981.

The co-editor of six agreed statements between US Lutherans and Catholics condensed and popularized the texts for study purposes and included some brief personal memoirs from the consultations before his death in 1979.

[658] *Facing Unity: Models, Forms and Phrases of Catholic-Lutheran Church Fellowship*. Geneva: Lutheran World Federation, 1985.

This pamphlet publishes one of the agreed statements by the international consultation known in German as *Einheit vor uns*. For another printing of the text together with several other agreed statements see the collection edited by Meyer [38].

[659] Fries, Heinrich, ed. *Das Ringen um die Einheit der Christen: Zum Stand des evangelisch-katholischen Dialogs*. Schriften der Katholischen Akademie in Bayern, Bd. 109. Düsseldorf: Patmos, 1983.

Described as a provisional summing up of ecumenical issues between Lutherans and Catholics, this volume discusses in four sections: the struggle for Christian unity; the major on-going controversies; differences in teaching and resulting consequences; the future. A separate section assesses the Lutheran/Catholic consensus statement "Ways to Community" (1980).

[660] *Lutherans and Catholics in Dialogue I-III*. Paul C. Empie and T. Austin Murphy, eds. Minneapolis: Augsburg, 1965-1967.

The first three agreed statements of the US Lutheran/Roman Catholic Consultation are here published together: "The Status of the Nicene Creed as Dogma of the Church" (1965); "One Baptism for the Remission of Sins" (1966); and "The Eucharist as Sacrifice" (1967). For subsequent agreed statements see also [1015, 1109, 1218, 1243].

[661] Meyer, Harding, ed. *Evangelium-Welt-Kirche: Schluss-bericht und Referate der römisch-katholisch/ evangelisch-lutherischen Studienkommission "Das Evangelium und die Kirche," 1967-1971*. Frankfurt: O. Lembeck; J. Knecht, 1975.

The book reports on five meetings that served as background to the final text "Gospel and Church" (the Malta Report) published jointly by the international commission of Lutherans and Catholics.

[662] Meyer, Harding. *Luthertum und Katholizismus in Gespräch: Ergebnisse und Stand der katholisch / lutherischen Dialogs in den USA und auf Weltebene.* Ökumenische Perspektiven 3. Frankfurt: O. Lembeck; J. Knecht, 1973.

The volume gives the pre-history (prior to 1971) of international and American consultations between Lutherans and Catholics. Then it studies the methodology and theological results of these exchanges in regard to gospel, eucharist, and church.

[663] Stone, Glenn C., and LaFontaine, Charles, eds. *Exploring the Faith We Share.* New York: Paulist, 1980.

To commemorate the 450th anniversary of the Diet of Augsburg, the two theologians outline the teachings of their respective churches on creed, baptism, eucharist, ministry, authority, and Scripture. The book is intended as a popular discussion guide.

# Orthodox/Catholic

[664] Barringer, Robert, ed. *Rome and Constantinople: Essays in the Dialogue of Love.* Sts. Peter and Andrew Lectures. Brookline: Holy Cross Orthodox Press, 1984.

These four lectures were delivered at St. Michael's College, University of Toronto, in 1982 and 1983 by Roman Catholic and Orthodox theologians. Two are especially pertinent to ecumenism: a survey of official relations between Rome and Byzantium (M. Fahey) and a study of Catholic and Orthodox bilaterals (R. Barringer).

[665] *L'Eglise et les églises. 1054-1954: Neuf siècles de douloureuse séparation entre l'Orient et l'Occident. Etudes et travaux sur l'unité chrétienne offerts à Dom Lambert Beauduin.* 2 vols. Chevetogne: Editions de Chevetogne, 1954-1955.

Beauduin (1878-1960), pioneer ecumenist and founder of the monastery of unity at Amay sur Meuse (1926) later transferred to Chevetogne (1939), was honored in these volumes that focus especially on Catholicism and Orthodoxy. Among the articles published in English, French and German, nine treat ecumenical themes (II, pp. 347-486).

[666] Fahey, Michael A., and Meyendorff, John. *Trinitarian Theology East and West: St. Thomas Aquinas and St. Gregory Palamas.* Patriarch Athenagoras Memorial Lectures. Brookline, MA: Holy Cross Orthodox Press, 1979.

In the first Patriarch Athenagoras annual lectures delivered on March 22, 1977, the Catholic and the Orthodox ecumenists point to similarities in the methods employed by the two classic theologians that are pertinent for modern ecumenism.

[667] Garó, Grigoriou, *Poreia pros ten enoteta. Marche vers l'unité.* 2 vols. Athens: Rossolatou, 1978.

Similar in scope to the *Tomos Agapis* [671] this collection of official texts in Greek (with a French introduction) records modern efforts to restore full communion between Rome and Byzantium. There are two bibliographies, one for Greek publications (pp. 640-664) and one for other languages (664-691).

[668] Kallis, Anastasios, ed. *Dialog der Wahrheit: Perspektiven für die Einheit zwischen der Katholischen und der Orthodoxen Kirche.* Freiburg: Herder, 1981.

Catholics and Orthodox collaborated in preparing this general account of recent ecumenical efforts aimed at promoting understanding and agreement between Orthodox and Catholics.

[669] Kilmartin, Edward J. *Toward Reunion: The Roman Catholic and the Orthodox Churches.* New York: Paulist, 1979.

Besides providing an overview of Orthodox-Catholic relations and an account of the current international dialogue (up to 1978), the Jesuit author gives a useful analysis of the early years of the fruitful Orthodox-Catholic Consultation in the USA, including the agreed statements. The volume needs updating.

[670] *The Nullification of the Anathema between the Churches and Its Effect on the Relations between the Greek Orthodox and Roman Catholic Churches.* New York: Greek Orthodox Archdiocese of North and South America, 1966.

Under the leadership of Archbishop Iakovos, the Greek Orthodox Archdiocese with headquarters in New York published this pastoral letter in English and Greek explaining the significance of the decision reached mutually in 1965 to lift the anathema of 1055.

[671] Papandreou, Damaskinos, and Duprey, Pierre, eds. *Tomos Agapis: Vatican - Phanar (1958-1970)*. Rome: Istanbul: Imprimeries Polyglotte Vatican, 1971.

The "tome of charity" publishes 284 primary documents in Greek and French (sometimes Latin) with corresponding translations as a record of the official ecumenical relations between the Sees of Rome and Constantinople over a twelve year period. Some of these texts appear in English in Storman [682]. See also Hummer [525] and Garó [667].

[672] Paplauskas-Ramunas, Antoine. *Dialogue entre Rome et Moscou: Vladimir Soloviev, porte-parole du mouvement oecuménique en Russie*. Ottawa: University of Ottawa, 1966.

This 244 page study of the Russian philosopher and theologian Vladimir Soloviev (1853-1900) compares him to John Henry Newman. He is described as one of the major precursors of modern Orthodox and Catholic dialogue. There is a lengthy but not well organized bibliography on ecumenism (pp. 201-241).

[673] Pro Oriente. *Am Beginn des theologischen Dialogs: Dokumentation des römischen, des Wiener und des Salzburger Ökumemismus: Zehn Jahre Pro Oriente Symposien 1982 bis 1985*. Pro Oriente 10. Innsbruck: Tyrolia, 1987.

This *Festschrift* in honor of the Pro Oriente ecumenist Theodor Piffl-Percevic contains addresses and proceedings of symposia that took place in Rome, Vienna and Salzburg between 1982 to 1985.

[674] Pro Oriente. *Auf dem Weg zur Einheit des Glaubens*. Pro Oriente 2. Innsbruck: Tyrolia, 1976.

This volume contains in German the talks and proceedings of the first ecclesiological colloquium between Orthodox and Catholic theologians held under the auspices of the Pro Oriente Foundation (Vienna) in April 1974. A French version was published in *Istina* vol. 20 (1975).

[675] Pro Oriente. *Im Dialog der Liebe.* eds. T. Piffl-Percevic and A. Stirnemann. Pro Oriente 9. Innsbruck: Tyrolia, 1986.

The publication, a continuation of *Ökumenische Hoffnungen* [678], contains German addresses given from 1971 to 1981 at nineteen separate symposia organized by the Pro Oriente Foundation (Vienna) on a vast range of ecumenical issues.

[676] Pro Oriente. *Konziliarität und Kollegialität als Strukturprinzipien der Kirche; Das Petrusamt in ökumenischer Sicht; Christus und seine Kirche - christologische und ekklesiologische Aspekte.* Pro Oriente 1. Innsbruck: Tyrolia, 1975.

The volume contains the addresses by Orthodox and Catholic scholars given in German at three separate theological conferences held between 1970 and 1971 in Vienna. The documentation is continued in the following volume [677].

[677] Pro Oriente. *Ökumene, Konzil, Unfehlbarkeit.* Pro Oriente 4. Innsbruck: Tyrolia, 1979.

Gathered in this one volume are German texts from two theological conferences held in 1972-1973 and from a meeting of the Ecumenical Academy in 1976 all held in Vienna. See also [676].

[678] Pro Oriente. *Ökumenische Hoffnungen.* Pro Oriente 7. Innsbruck: Tyrolia, 1984.

This volume by the Vienna based foundation for promoting dialogue between the Christian East and West reproduces a series of talks given during the first five years of the symposia (1965-1970). A second volume appeared as *Im Dialog der Liebe* [675].

[679] Rick, Hermann-Joseph. *Friede zwischen Ost und West: Rom und Konstantinopel in ökumenischen Aufbruch.* Münster: Verlag Regensberg, 1969.

A German Catholic journalist wrote this short history of East/West relations up to the mutual lifting of anathemas in 1965. A brief bibliography of German works is appended.

[**680**] Salachas, Dimitri. *Il dialogo teologico ufficiale tra la Chiesa cattolico-romana e la Chiesa ortodossa.* 2 vols. Eds. G. Distante and S. Manna. Vol. 1: *Iter e documentazione.* Vol. 2: *Le quarta assemblea di Bari 1986-1987.* Bari: Istituto di teologia ecumenico-patristica, 1984-1988.

Volume one includes the statements of the first three meetings (Patmos-Rhodes 1980, Munich 1982, and Crete 1984) of the official International Orthodox - Roman Catholic Consultation. Volume two covers the two Bari meetings 1986-1987. Besides the agreed statements there is a description of the consultation's goals and methodologies.

[**681**] Stawrowsky, Alexis. *Essai de théologie irénique: L'Orthodoxie et le Catholicisme.* Madrid: Taravilla, 1966.

In an attempt to heal the divisions between Orthodox and Roman Catholics, the author discusses in this 277 page volume five central issues: dogmatic formulations, doctrinal controversies, the *filioque* addition, church and papal infallibility.

[**682**] Stormon, E. J., ed. and trans. *Towards the Healing of Schism: The Sees of Rome and Constantinople. Public Statements and Correspondence Between the Holy See and the Ecumenical Patriarchate 1958-1984.* Ecumenical Documents III. New York: Paulist, 1987.

This volume is basically a translation of the Greek and French bilingual *Tomos Agapis* [671] which reproduced official ecumenical documents between Rome and Constantinople. But whereas the earlier work only covered up to the year 1970, this volume includes fourteen more years.

[**683**] Tretjakewitsch, Léon. *Bishop Michel d'Herbigny SJ and Russia: A Pre-Ecumenical Approach to Christian Unity.* Das östliche Christentum, NS 39. Würzburg: Augustinus Verlag, 1990.

This detailed account of the life of the Jesuit Michel d'Herbigny (1880-1957), former Rector of the Pontifical Oriental Institute in Rome and secretly consecrated as bishop for activities in Russia following the Bolshevik Revolution, is an informative chapter in the relationships between the Vatican and the Soviet Union. See also Wenger [686].

[**684**] Vasiliu, Cezar. *Le relazioni tra la Chiesa Cattolica e la Chiesa*

*Ortodossa, dall' annuncio del Concilio Vaticano II (gennario 1959) fino ad oggi (dicembre 1970): Punto di vista ortodosso.* Palermo: ACIOC, 1971.

Written as a doctoral dissertation for Rome's Pontificio Istituto Orientale by a Romanian Orthodox under the direction of W. de Vries and G. Dejaifve, the historical account of formal relations between the Orthodox and Catholics focuses on eleven critical years.

[685] Vries, Wilhelm de. *Orthodoxie et catholicisme.* Trans. by Jean Houel. Paris: Desclée, 1967.

The German original was entitled *Orthodoxie und Katholizismus* (1965). The material is divided between the two millennia, with special attention given to the causes of estrangement between East and West.

[686] Wenger, Antoine. *Rome et Moscou 1900-1950.* Paris: Desclée de Brouwer, 1987.

The complex and troubled relationships between Rome and Moscow before, during and after the Bolshevik Revolution are here chronicled in this lengthy study by a French professor and editor in chief of the French newspaper *La Croix.* See also Tretjakewitsch [683].

# Orthodox/Lutheran and Reformed

[687] George, K.M., and Hoefer, Herbert E., eds. *A Dialogue Begins: Papers, Minutes and Agreed Statements from the Lutheran-Orthodox Dialogue in India 1978-1982.* Madras: Gurukul; Kottayam, Kerala: Sophia, 1983.

Published jointly by the Gurukul Lutheran Theological College (Madras) and the Sophia Centre, Orthodox Theological Seminary (Kottayam), the volume analyzes the seven meetings from 1978 to 1982 of the Lutheran and Orthodox Dialogue Group in India. The volume is available from the Lutheran College, 94 Purusawalkam High Rd., Madras 600010. See also Hoefer [768].

[688] Mehedintu, Viorel. *Offenbarung und Überlieferung: Neue Möglichkeiten eines Dialogs zwischen der orthodoxen und der evangelisch-lutherischen Kirche.* Forschungen zur systematischen und

ökumenischen Theologie, 40. Göttingen: Vandenhoeck und Ruprecht, 1980.

Written as a doctoral dissertation by a Romanian Orthodox theologian, a protégé of D. Staniloae, and under the supervision of E. Schlink and R. Slenczka, the book compares the notion of revelation and tradition in Orthodox and Lutheran perspectives.

[689] Meyendorff, John, and McLelland, Joseph, eds. *The New Man: An Orthodox and Reformed Dialogue.* New Brunswick, NJ: Agora, 1973.

The members of the North American Orthodox-Reformed Consultation met three times from 1968 to 1970. The results of their deliberations are shared in the form of three "summaries." Nine papers delivered at the sessions are here reproduced. There is no single theme to the presentations.

[690] *The Orthodox Church and the Churches of the Reformation: A Survey of Orthodox-Protestant Dialogues.* Faith and Order Paper 76. Geneva: World Council of Churches, 1975.

This publication contains a survey of the dialogues (pp. 1-40) and ten personal statements from Orthodox and Protestant theologians (43-100).

[691] Torrance, Thomas F. *Theological Dialogue between Orthodox and Reformed Churches.* Edinburgh: Scottish Academic Press, 1985.

The volume reports on theological discussions underway between the World Alliance of Reformed Churches and the Ecumenical Patriarchate of Constantinople. Three consultations from 1979 to 1983 are described. Six essays by individual churchmen are included and a brief concluding affirmation or "agreed understanding" (pp. 157-158).

[692] Wendebourg, Dorothea. *Reformation und Orthodoxie: Der ökumenische Briefwechsel zwischen der Leitung der Wittenbergischen Kirche und Patriarch Jeremias II von Konstantinopel in den Jahren 1573-1581.* Forschungen zur Kirchen- und Dogmengeschichte, Bd. 37. Göttingen: Vandenhoeck und Ruprecht, 1986.

Research for this volume was done at the Faculty of Evangelical Theology at the University of Munich as a *Habilitationsschrift.* It gives a full account of the exchange of letters between Wittenberg church leaders and the Ecumenical Patriarch Jeremiah II (1536-1594) about the orthodoxy of the Augsburg Confession and related credal statements. See also Mastrantonis [774].

# Pentecostal/Catholic

[693] Bittlinger, Arnold. *Papst und Pfingstler: Der römisch katholisch-pfingstliche Dialog und seine ökumenische Relevanz*. Studien zur Interkulturellen Geschichte des Christentums 16. Frankfurt: Peter Lang, 1978.

> Summarized here are highlights of the Catholic and Pentecostal dialogue beginning with its pre-history (1970-1971), its official meetings (1972-1976), and valuable theological reflections on the relevance of the conversations. Included is a bibliography (pp. 230-293) of mostly German and English works.

[694] McDonnell, Kilian. *Presence, Power, Praise: Documents on the Charismatic Renewal*. 3 vols. Collegeville, MN: Liturgical, 1980.

> This massive undertaking was produced by a Benedictine monk of St. John's Abbey, Collegeville. The first two volumes give eighty continental, national and regional documents related to charismatic renewal (1960-1979). Volume three contains eleven international documents (1973-1980) including international Pentecostal/Catholic dialogues. See also [479, 614, 617].

[695] Sandidge, Jerry L., ed. *Roman Catholic / Pentecostal Dialogue (1977-1982): A Study in Developing Ecumenism*, 2 vols. New York and Frankfurt: P. Lang, 1987.

> This work grew out of the author's doctoral dissertation at the Catholic University of Leuven, Belgium. The first volume describes the historical antecedents during the years 1972-1976 and the first five international meetings of the consultation. Volume two covers the sixth to the tenth meetings (1977-1982) and includes some sixteen background papers and concluding statements.

# Reformed/Catholic

[696] Bosc, Jean; Guitton, Jean; Daniélou, Jean, *The Catholic*

*Protestant Dialogue.* Trans. by Robert J. Olsen. Baltimore: Helicon, 1960.

Bosc writes as a Protestant pastor and discusses with two Catholics the meaning of church and Incarnation. The essay by Daniélou is an excellent account of the impact of biblical studies on ecumenism. The original French title was *Le dialogue catholique-protestant* (1960). See also [717].

[697] *Ethics and the Search for Christian Unity: Two Statements by the Roman Catholic / Presbyterian Consultation.* Washington: United States Catholic Conference, 1981.

The Roman Catholic/Presbyterian Consultation in the USA published this statement in 1980. For a fuller documentation containing four agreed statements see above [33].

[698] Groupe des Dombes. *Pour la conversion des Eglises: Identité et changements dans la dynamique de communion.* Paris: Le Centurion, 1991.

The latest in the impressive series of agreed statements made by the Group of Les Dombes is this 113 page invitation to all church members to undergo a profound conversion to help achieve a real visible communion that also respects particularities. For earlier statements see also [699].

[699] *Pour la communion des Eglises: L'apport du Groupe des Dombes 1937-1987.* Paris: Le Centurion, 1988.

This volume traces the fifty year history of the French-speaking Catholic-Reformed Consultation and reproduces in one volume the twelve "theses" (1956-1970) and the valuable five documents (1971-1985) also listed separately in this bibliography on: the eucharist [1114], reconciliation of ministries [1158], episcopal ministry [1157], the Holy Spirit [1057], and the ministry of communion in the universal church [1247]. See also the newest text [698] as well as [717].

[700] *Reconsiderations: Roman Catholic / Presbyterian and Reformed Theological Conversations 1966-1967.* New York: World Horizons, 1967.

Six American theologians equally divided between Catholic and

Reformed offered reflections on Scripture and tradition, the development of doctrine, and ministry in the church.

[701] Roesle, Maximilian, and Cullmann, Oscar, eds. *Begegnung der Christen: Studien evangelischer und katholischer Theologen.* Stuttgart: Evangelisches Verlagswerk; Frankfurt: J. Knecht, 1960.

This 696 page *Festschrift* in honor of Otto Karrer on his seventieth birthday includes an autobiographical essay (pp. 13-24), a list of the honoree's writings (25-32), and essays arranged around seventeen doctrinal issues raised by ecumenical dialogue. For each topic both a Protestant and Roman Catholic give a separate account. Two essays discuss the Augsburg Confession and the Council of Trent.

[702] Unterkoefler, Ernest L., and Harsanyi, Andrew, eds. *The Unity We Seek: A Statement by the Roman Catholic / Presbyterian and Reformed Consultation.* New York: Paulist, 1977.

After a summary reporting on the work of the American dialogue group from 1965 to 1975 there is a lengthy agreed statement on unity (pp. 11-51). Also included are four background papers.

## Baptist/Catholic

[703] Broach, Claude U., ed. *Issues of Church and State: The Proceedings of a Dialogue between Catholics and Baptists.* Winston-Salem, North Carolina: Wake Forest University, The Ecumenical Institute, 1976.

These proceedings of an ecumenical conference on church and state held in November 1976 contain five major papers and a joint statement from the twenty-six Baptists and Roman Catholics who participated.

## Methodist/Catholic

[704] Frost, Brian, and Pyle, Leo, eds. *Dissent and Descent: Essays on Methodism and Roman Catholicism.* London: Epworth, 1975.

Five topics are treated jointly by British Methodists and Roman Catholics as an aid for sharing the results of recent dialogue between members of the World Methodist Council and the Roman

Catholic Church. Discussed were: church and society; the church; mission; worship and spirituality; dissent and descent.

[705] *Growth in Understanding: Report of the Joint Commission Between the Roman Catholic Church and the World Methodist Council.* Abbots Langley: Catholic Information Services; London: The Methodist Ecumenical Committee, 1976.

This report covers four meetings held during the years 1970-1974 and serves as an informational update since the so-called Denver Report, agreed to at the twelfth World Methodist Conference (1971). It provides a handy summary of the dialogue between these two churches.

[706] *Report of the Joint Commission Between the Roman Catholic Church and the World Methodist Council: Third Series 1977-1981.* Lake Junaluska, NC: World Methodist Council, 1981.

This pamphlet contains suggestions for a possible agreed statement on the Holy Spirit, reflections on authority and a study on Christian marriage.

[707] Stewart, Richard Louis. *Catholics and Methodists: An Introduction to the Work of the Joint Commissions Between the World Methodist Council and the Roman Catholic Church since 1967.* London: CTS, 1974.

This pamphlet contains the first Roman Catholic and Methodist statement, the so-called Denver Report (1971) and a call to joint action published in 1973. For fuller documentation see Meyer [38].

# 6

# Geographical Perspective

[708] IDOC-C. *La situation oecuménique dans le monde: Etudes.* L'Eglise en son temps 12. Paris: Le Centurion, 1967.

Originally prepared by the so-called IDOC Center, this study covers twelve regions of the world including Europe, Africa, the Middle East, India, the USA and Latin America. Especially informative is the report on Scandinavia by Catholic Bishop Hans Martensen. The volume is intended to complement *Un nouvel âge oecuménique* [65].

## Europe

[709] Bassarak, Gerhard, ed., *Ökumenische Diakonie: Beiträge über den Dienst der Kirche in sozialistischer Gesellschaft aus Bulgarien, der CSSR, Kuba, Polen, Rumänien, Ungarn und der UdSSR.* E. Berlin: Evangelische Verlagsanstalt, 1975.

Contained in this volume are eighteen essays that report on the religious situation of six socialist countries in the 1970s. Six of the writers are Orthodox (including Patriarch Pimen of Moscow) and nine Protestant, all from Communist countries.

[710] Birmelé, André, ed. *Konkordie und Kirchengemeinschaft reformatorischer Kirchen im Europa der Gegenwart.* Ökumenische Perspektiven 10. Frankfurt: O. Lembeck; J. Knecht, 1982.

This volume contains the proceedings of a congress held in Driebergen (Netherlands), February 18-24, 1981, to explore the relationships of European Protestant churches among themselves.

[711] Bläser, Peter, *et al. Dialog Konkret: Fragen und Antworten zwischen den Konfessionen.* Theologische Brennpunkte, Bd. 11. Bergen: Gerhard Kaffke, 1967.

This 82 page booklet begins with a question by a Roman Catholic (Bläser, a member of Paderborn's Johann Adam Möhler Institute), expressing his puzzlement about certain Protestant convictions. Three respondents from the Lutheran and Reformed traditions, including Peter Meinhold, respond to these inquiries.

[712] Boyens, Armin. *Kirchenkampf und Ökumene 1933-1939: Darstellung und Dokumentation.* Munich: C. Kaiser, 1969. *Kirchenkampf und Ökumene 1939-1945.* 1973.

Based on serious archival work, the author investigates the actions of the ecumenical movement and the Evangelische Kirche in Deutschland (EKD) during the Nazi period. Also included are studies on Christian attitudes towards Jews, the peace initiatives and totalitarianism. Both volumes contain a large number of official documents, many of them originally confidential.

[713] *The Churches in Eastern Europe and the Ecumenical Sharing of Resources.* Geneva: World Council of Churches, 1982.

This report of the Consultation on the Ecumenical Sharing of Resources with the Churches in Eastern Europe, held in Sofia, Bulgaria, May 24-26, 1982, describes situations that have notably changed in light of political developments in the 1990s.

[714] *The Churches in Italy.* Geneva: World Council of Churches, 1984.

This booklet of the WCC's Commission on Inter-Church Aid Refugee and World Service (CICARWS) presents the life and witness of the Protestant minority churches in Italy. A special entry is given for ecumenical activities.

[715] Conseil des conférences épiscopales d'Europe, Conférence des églises européennes. *Travailler pour l'unité et pour la paix: Rencontre oecuménique de Chantilly, 10 au 13 avril 1978.* Paris: Le Centurion, 1978.

For the first time ever the two organizations, the Council of Roman Catholic Bishops' Conferences in Europe (CCEE) and the Conference of European Churches (CEC/KEK), gathered representatives from all the European countries except Albania to discuss the mutual interdependence of church unity efforts and peace. Six talks by bishops and theologians are here reproduced.

[716] Daniélou, Jean, ed. *Unité des chrétiens et conversion du monde: thèmes de réflexion et de prière*. Paris: Le Centurion, 1962.

An important Paris-based ecumenical group known as the Cercle Saint Jean Baptiste met regularly in the pre-Vatican II era. This brief volume (85 pp.) emanates from the group as it discussed unity and mission in 1961. Five members' talks are reproduced: J. Daniélou, M. Villain, J. Rogues, M.-J. LeGuillou, M. Hayek.

[717] *Ecumenical Dialogue in Europe: The Ecumenical Conversations at Les Dombes (1937-1955) Inspired by the Abbé Couturier*. Ecumenical Studies in History 6. Trans. by W. Fletcher Fleet. London: Lutterworth Press; Richmond: John Knox, 1966.

The original French-speaking ecumenical Group of Les Dombes (named after a Trappist monastery near Lyons) was founded by Paul Couturier and met from 1937-1955. It later began a second creative period which has led to six agreed statements. The history of the early days of this Reformed and Catholic group is narrated by Maurice Villain. See also [699].

[718] Forest, Jim. *Religion in the New Russia: The Impact of Perestroika on the Varieties of Religious Life in the Soviet Union*. New York: Crossroad, 1990.

Published shortly before the dissolution of the Soviet Union, this volume needs to be updated in some ways, but its information is still quite pertinent. The author served for many years as General Secretary of the International Fellowship of Reconciliation.

[719] Frieling, Reinhard. *Ökumene in Deutschland: Ein Handbuch der interkonfessionellen Zusammenarbeit in der Bundesrepublik*. Göttingen: Vandenhoeck und Ruprecht, 1970.

After an overview of ecumenical efforts internationally, the author gives a detailed account of diocesan and local initiatives in Germany as they relate to myriad facets of life.

[720] Hebly, Hans. *Eastbound Ecumenism: A Collection of Essays on the World Council of Churches and Eastern Europe*. Amsterdam: Free

University; Lanham, MD: University Press of America, 1986.

Writing before the major political shake ups of the 1990s, the author describes a situation that has since evolved. Still his book correctly identifies some of the challenges and obstacles the WCC faced in Eastern Europe.

[721] Lejeune, Charles. *Le dialogue oecuménique en Belgique*. Etudes religieuses, 778. Brussels: La pensée catholique, 1967.

The monograph describes the historical evolution of Protestantism in Belgium and the growth of dialogue there between Catholics and Protestants. An example of cooperation was the establishment of the organization known as L'Eglise Chrétienne Missionaire Belge.

[722] Maron, Gottfried, ed. *Evangelisch und Ökumenisch: Beiträge zum 100 jährigen Bestehen des Evangelischen Bundes*. Kirche und Konfession 25. Göttingen: Vandenhoeck und Ruprecht, 1986.

The volume treats the history and theology of the Evangelisches Bund which combines Reformation commitment with ecumenical zeal.

[723] Nagy, Gyula, ed. *Die konziliare Gemeinschaft: eine europäische theologische Diskussion über den Weg und das Endziel der ökumenischen Bewegung*. Konferenze Europäischen Kirchen, Studienheft 10. Frankfurt: O. Lembeck, 1978.

Five essays from Orthodox, Catholic, Anglican and Protestant perspectives comment on the notion of conciliarity or synodality. There is also a joint closing statement which formulates recommendations to the European churches.

[724] Nielsen, Niels C. *Revolutions in Eastern Europe: The Religious Roots*. Maryknoll, NY: Orbis, 1991.

In a rapidly evolving political setting, the author describes situations up to the summer of 1990 in Germany, Hungary, Poland, Czechoslovakia, Romania, Bulgaria, Albania and Russia. The final chapter is devoted to their recovering spiritual and humanistic traditions.

[725] Sánchez Vaquero, José. *Cristianos: Reconciliaos! (Salamanca:*

*30 años de Ecumenismo)*. Bibliotheca Oecumenica Salmanticensis 10. Salamanca: Universidad Pontificia, 1985.

Published by Salamanca's Centro de Estudios Orientales y Ecuménicos Juan XXIII which also publishes the journals *Diálogo Ecuménico* [105] and *Renovación Ecuménica* [153], this general study of ecumenism is particularly useful for its information about the Spanish context.

[726] Schmandt, Walther. *Keine Angst von Ökumene*. Mainz: M. Grünewald, 1972.

A TV commentator prepared this popular 123 page introduction to ecumenism for German-speaking countries.

[727] Segretariato Attività Ecumeniche, ed. *Ecumenismo Anni '80 [Atti della XXI Sessione di formazione ecumenica organizzata dal S.A.E., 1983]*. Negar-Verona: Editrice Il Segno, 1984.

Departing somewhat from the usual format of the meetings of the Italian Ecumenical Association, this session offered a critical summary of ecumenical activities in the 1980s (L. Sartori) and two talks on the church in God's design (B. Corsani and R. Fabris). Also summarized were two round table discussions.

[728] Van der Linde, Hendrik. *Rome en de Una Sancta: het oecumenisch vragstuk en de arbeid de hereniging der kerken*. Nijkerk: G.F. Callenbach, 1947.

Written by a Dutch Protestant, this study of Rome and the "Una Sancta" (meaning the world-wide communion of Christian churches) is well informed and a reliable source of information about the European scene in the 1940s. The lengthy bibliography cites mostly Dutch and German works (pp. 353-378). See also Mönnich [202].

[729] Verdoodt, Albert. *Les colloques oecuméniques de Chevetogne (1942-1983) et la réception par l'Eglise catholique de charismes d'autres communions chrétiennes*. Chevetogne: Editions de Chevetogne, 1986.

The annual ecumenical conferences held at the Chevetogne monastery, Belgium, have had a notable impact on the consciousness of church leaders and ecumenists.

# North America and Caribbean

[730] Beaubien, Irénée. *L'Unité au Canada*. Montreal: Bellarmin, 1955; *Towards Christian Unity in Canada*. Montreal: Palm, 1956.

> The French-Canadian ecumenist and founder of the Inquiry Forum and later of the Canadian Centre for Ecumenism (both of Montreal) published this modest introduction to the ecumenical movement for Catholics in both French and English editions. The English version (pp. 83-168) contains some personal reminiscences not found in the French original. The volume reflects Catholic ecumenism in its early stages.

[731] Bowman, David J., ed. *U.S. Catholic Ecumenism -- Ten Years Later*. Washington: United States Catholic Conference, 1975.

> The Jesuit researcher served on the staff of the National Council of Churches, specifically its Commission on Regional and Local Ecumenism (CORLE). He was commissioned to do this survey, ten years after Vatican II, to assess American Catholic involvement in church unity efforts.

[732] Brown, Robert McAfee, and Weigel, Gustave. *An American Dialogue: A Protestant Looks at Catholicism and a Catholic Looks at Protestantism*. Garden City, NY: Doubleday, 1960.

> The presentations by Brown (pp. 17-123) and by Weigel (127-208) were separately written without any attempt at synthesis. The volume is a fascinating sociological and cultural witness to a very early form of ecumenical exchange.

[733] Cavert, Samuel McCrea. *The American Churches in the Ecumenical Movement, 1900-1968*. New York: Association, 1968.

> This is an earlier version of *Church Cooperation* [734] sponsored by Union Theological Seminary in New York City. The author, previously general secretary of the National Council of Churches in the USA, was involved in church unity endeavors for over fifty years. The writer's focus is Protestant without taking into account Orthodox or Roman Catholic material. For a biography of Cavert see W. Schmidt [431].

[734] Cavert, Samuel McCrea. *Church Cooperation and Unity in*

*America: A Historical Review, 1900-1970.* New York: Association, 1970.

This is an updated version of the 1968 work *The American Churches* [733]. Especially useful is its comprehensive bibliography regarding church cooperation in America (pp. 354-396) as well as its chronology of union efforts from 1900 to 1970 (pp. 351-353). See also [431].

[735] Cuthbert, Robert W.M. *Ecumenism and Development: A Socio-Historical Analysis of the Caribbean Conference of Churches.* Bridgetown, Barbados: Caribbean Contact, 1986.

The time frame for this analysis is 1957-1977. It narrates the history of the Caribbean Conference of Churches founded in 1957 but which emerged as a powerful moral force in the 1970s. It is notable by having Roman Catholics as full members.

[736] Grant, J. Webster. *The Canadian Experience of Church Union.* Ecumenical Studies in History 8. Richmond: John Knox; London: Lutterworth, 1967.

The professor of church history at Emmanuel College, Victoria University, Toronto, and minister in the United Church of Canada describes the stages that led up to the formation in 1925 of that church by a merger of Methodists, Presbyterians and Congregationalists.

[737] Miller, Samuel H., and Wright, G. Ernest, gen. eds. *Ecumenical Dialogue at Harvard: The Roman Catholic-Protestant Colloquium.* Cambridge, MA: Harvard University, 1964.

Following the first session of Vatican II, this historic symposium took place at Harvard, March 27-30, 1963. The volume contains the three Stillman lectures on Christian unity by Augustin Bea and twelve papers given by Protestants and Catholics. Also included are the reports of the various seminar discussions.

[738] Nelson, J. Robert, ed. *Christian Unity in North America: A Symposium.* St. Louis: Bethany, 1958.

This volume records preparations for and actions subsequent to the North American Faith and Order conference held in Oberlin College, September 1957, on "The Nature of the Unity We Seek."

There are eighteen chapters composed by various Protestant authors including even Missouri Synod Lutherans, Southern Baptists and Mennonites. No Orthodox or Roman Catholics contributed to the project. See also [872].

[739] Sheerin, John B. *Christian Reunion: The Ecumenical Movement and American Catholics*. New York: Hawthorn, 1966.

In thirteen chapters the Paulist priest describes for a popular audience the history of tension among Christians in America and then analyzes the impact created by Vatican II on Christian relations.

# Middle East and Asia

[740] Achutegui, Pedro S. de, ed. *Towards A "Dialogue of Life": Ecumenism in the Asian Context. First Asian Congress of Jesuit Ecumenists, Manila, June 18-23, 1975*. Cardinal Bea Studies 4. Manila: Loyola School of Theology, Ateneo de Manila University, 1976.

This volume contains papers on the theme of evangelization and ecumenism in Asia today. Included are the major addresses, various lectures, reports and the final statement from the congress.

[741] *Christian Action in the Asian Struggle*. Singapore: Christian Conference of Asia, 1973.

These lectures in memory of D.T. Niles (1908-1970), Sri Lankan Methodist ecumenist who served as executive secretary for the Department of Evangelism at the WCC, includes an introductory lecture by M.M. Thomas and ten other contributions on ecumenism in Asia, Europe and Australia.

[742] Corbon, Jean. *L'Eglise des Arabes*. Paris: Editions du Cerf, 1977.

The member of the Melkite Catholic Church living in Beirut published this important work showing how the bonds of cultural and linguistic unity among Arab Christians lends a particular intensity to contacts between Orthodox and Catholic believers. See also, Zoghby [515].

[743] Hollis, Michael. *Mission, Unity and Truth: A Study of Confessional Families and the Church in Asia*. London: Lutterworth,

1967.

Bishop Hollis, sometime moderator of the Church of South India, asks whether the world confessional bodies are not stumbling blocks to ecumenism especially in the Asian context. He pleads for much more decision-making authority at local levels.

[744] Kaufmann, Ludwig. *Rencontre en Terre Sainte*. Lausanne: Editions Rencontre, 1964.

The Swiss Jesuit ecumenist and long-time editor of *Orientierung* accompanied Paul VI on the first trip of a pope outside the Vatican in modern times. This splendid art book contains hundreds of photographs of the papal trip to Jerusalem in 1964, culminating in the encounter between Patriarch Athenagoras and Pope Paul VI. There is also information on the religious and cultural history of the Holy Land. A German edition appeared as *Begegnung im Heiligen Land*.

[745] Perumalil, H.C., and Hambye, E.R. *Christianity in India: A History in Ecumenical Perspective*. Alleppey, India: Prakasam Publications, 1972.

This rare book contains twelve chapters on the origins of Christianity in India, its medieval history, Latin, Orthodox and Anglican missionaries, and modern Protestant and Catholic activities since the mid nineteenth century.

[746] Thangasamy, D.A. *India and the Ecumenical Movement*. Madras: Christian Literature Society, 1973.

The 56 page booklet contains a valuable account of the specific contributions of India to ecumenism. The survey goes up to 1973 the year of the author's death.

[747] Weber, Hans-Ruedi. *Asia and the Ecumenical Movement 1895-1961*. London: SCM, 1966.

The study describes the changes in Asia since 1895, the impact of the ecumenical youth movements such as the WSCF and YM/YWCA, foreign missions and the Asian churches, and finally Asian contributions to church unity. Also published is an annotated bibliography (pp. 293-306).

[748] Zachariah, Mathai, ed. *Ecumenism in India: Essays in Honour of the Rev. M. A. Thomas*. Delhi: Indian Society for Promoting Christian Knowledge, 1980.

> This *Festschrift* in honor of the Indian ecumenist Madathethu A. Thomas (1913-  ) contains contributions by twelve ecumenical collaborators familiar with the Indian context. Besides the strictly ecumenical material there is also discussion about inter-faith collaboration. On ecumenism in India see also [687, 768].

# Africa

[749] Kalu, Ogbu U., ed. *African Church Historiography: An Ecumenical Perpective*. Bern: Evangelische Arbeitsstelle, Oekumene Schweiz, 1988.

> The volume contains the papers in French and English given at an ecumenical workshop on African church history held in Nairobi, August 3-8, 1986.

[750] Roussouw, P.J. *Ecumenical Panorama: A Perspective from South Africa*. Pretoria: N.G. Kerk Sinodale Sentrum, 1989.

> The publication affords a rare glimpse into the shape of ecumenism in South Africa against the specific social and political challenges of the last decades.

[751] Utuk, Efiong. *From New York to Ibadan: The Impact of African Questions on the Making of Ecumenical Mission Mandates, 1900-1958*. New York: P. Lang, 1991.

> This doctoral dissertation for Princeton Theological Seminary by a Nigerian scholar outlines ecumenical birthpangs (1900-1910) in Africa, and then a gradual growth in the 1910s and 1920s. The final chapter covers the years 1939 to 1958 when ecumenical maturity is more noticeable. See also [754].

# South America

[752] Conferência Nacional dos Bispos do Brasil. *Guia Ecumênico: Informaçoes, Normas e Diretrizes sobre Ecumenismo*. 2nd rev. ed. Sao Paolo: Ed. Paulinas, 1984.

The principal author of this 297 page guidebook sponsored by the Catholic Bishops' Conference of Brazil is the Jesuit ecumenist Jesus Hortal Sanchez (1927- ). Besides describing Vatican II's Decree on Ecumenism and its subsequent documents, the volume offers short accounts of the ecumenical situation in Brazil.

# Third World (EATWOT)

[753] Ecumenical Association of Third World Theologians. *The Emergent Gospel: Theology from the Underside of History.* Eds. Sergio Torres and Virginia Fabella. Maryknoll, NY: Orbis, 1978.

The first theological consultation of EATWOT which met in Dar Es Salaam addressed the fact that most ecumenical research neglects, to its peril, the countries from the "underside of history."

[754] Ecumenical Association of Third World Theologians. *African Theology En Route.* Eds. Kofi Appiah-Kubi and Sergio Torres. Maryknoll, NY: Orbis, 1979.

The second theological consultation of EATWOT took place in Accra and concentrated on the African experience.

[755] Ecumenical Association of Third World Theologians. *Asia's Struggle for Full Humanity.* Ed. Virginia Fabella. Maryknoll, NY: Orbis, 1980.

The third theological consultation of EATWOT took place in Sri Lanka during 1979 and discussed particular challenges to ecumenism in the Asia context.

[756] Ecumenical Association of Third World Theologians. *The Challenge of Basic Christian Communities.* Eds. Sergio Torres and John Eagleson. Maryknoll, NY: Orbis, 1981.

The fourth EATWOT theological consultation met in Sao Paolo in 1980 and explored the ecumenical significance of basic Christian communities.

[757] Ecumenical Association of Third World Theologians. *Irruption of the Third World.* Eds. Virginia Fabella and Sergio Torres. Maryknoll, NY: Orbis, 1983.

The fifth theological consultation of EATWOT met in New Delhi in 1981 to discuss the way in which third world concerns have impacted ecumenical theology.

[758] Ecumenical Association of Third World Theologians. *Doing Theology in a Divided World*. Eds. Virginia Fabella and Sergio Torres. Maryknoll, NY: Orbis, 1985.

For the first time in its history EATWOT invited first world theologians to meet with them and to discuss doing theology in a divided world. This theological consultation, the sixth, was held in 1983 in Geneva.

[759] Ecumenical Association of Third World Theologians. *Third World Theologies: Commonalities and Divergences*. Ed. K.C. Abraham. Maryknoll, NY: Orbis, 1986.

The seventh theological consultation of EATWOT met in Oaxtepec, Mexico, in December 1986. Various reports and statements are here recorded, together with a final reflection. Prior to the gathering there was a meeting of the Women's Commission. See also Fabella [1285].

# 7

# Three Notable Documents

## Augsburg Confession (1530)

[760] *The Augsburg Confession: A Confession of Faith Presented in Augsburg by certain Princes and Cities to His Imperial Majesty Charles V in the Year 1530.* Anniversary edition. Philadelphia: Fortress, 1980.

> To mark the 450th anniversary of the formal presentation of the Augsburg Confession to the emperor on June 25, 1530, this new printing of the historic text was undertaken.

[761] Békés, Gerard J., and Meyer, Harding, eds. *Confessio Fidei: International Ecumenical Colloquium.* Studia Anselmiana 81. Rome: San Anselmo, 1982.

> In addition to this edition published in Rome which contains all the contributions in their original language (English, German, French) there is a German edition *Den einen Glauben bekennen* with all the essays in German. This publication contains the talks of the congress in Rome, November 3-8, 1980 sponsored by San Anselmo University and the Lutheran Institute for Ecumenical Research. The starting point was the pertinence of the Augsburg Confession today. Eleven contributors represented Catholic, Orthodox and Protestant views.

[762] Burgess, Joseph, ed. *The Role of the Augsburg Confession.* Philadelphia: Fortress, 1980.

> This is an American adaptation of the German *Katholische*

*Anerkennung des Augsburgischen Bekenntnisses.* Besides the original German contributions this volume contains additional studies by A. Dulles, H. McSorley and R. Jenson.

[763] *La Confession d'Augsbourg: 450e anniversaire: Autour d'un colloque oecuménique international.* Le point théologique 37. Paris: Beauchesne, 1980.

To celebrate the anniversary of the Augsburg Confession, an international colloquium was held in February 1980 in Paris. Eighteen Lutheran, Reformed, Roman Catholic and Orthodox speakers were assigned. Published here are seven ecumenical assessments of the historic Confession.

[764] Forell, George Wolfgang, and McCue, James F., eds. *Confessing One Faith: A Joint Commentary on the Augsburg Confession by Lutheran and Catholic Theologians.* Minneapolis: Augsburg, 1982.

This book is a translation of *Confessio Augustana: Bekenntnis des einen Glaubens* (1980). Besides the editors, twenty-two Protestant and Catholic scholars collaborated on this study. This work in twelve chapters is probably the best theological commentary published for the 450th anniversary.

[765] Fries, Heinrich, *et al. Confessio Augustana: Hindernis oder Hilfe?* Regensburg: F. Pustet, 1979.

At this 1978 meeting of the Katholische Akademie in Bayern and the Evangelische Akademie Tutzing, nine Catholics and Protestants presented historical and theological studies on the Augsburg Confession and its pertinence to the modern era.

[766] Garijo Guembe, Miguel M., ed. *La confesión de fé de Augsburgo ayer y hoy: Congreso internacional luterano-católico, Salamanca, 23-26 de setiembre de 1980.* Biblioteca oecumenica Salmanticensis 6. Salamanca: Universidad Pontificia, Centro de estudios orientales y ecumenicos "Juan XXIII," 1981.

At the international colloquium held in September 1980, seven Lutherans and seven Catholics addressed these issues: historical problems, confessional statements, justification, church, the Lord's Supper, ordained ministry and the Augsburg Confession. The work is especially valuable for those seeking information about ecumenism in Spain.

[767] Gaudy, Peter. *Katholisches Ja zum Augsburger Bekenntnis? Ein Bericht über die neuere Anerkennungsdiskussion*. Freiburg: Herder, 1980.

The Roman Catholic theologian from Freiburg outlines the genesis of the Augsburg Confession and recent discussions about the possibility of its recognition by the Catholic Church.

[768] Hoefer, Herbert E., ed. *The Augsburg Confession and Ecumenism in India*. Madras: Gurukul Luthcran Theological College and Research Institute, 1980.

These eight studies on the role of the Augsburg Confession in ecumenical dialogues underway in India are particularly valuable. Also included is a study guide relating the Confession to issues of mission theology. See also [687, 748].

[769] Hoffmann, Fritz, and Kühn, Ulrich. *Die Confessio Augustana im ökumenischen Gespräch*. E. Berlin: Evangelische Verlagsanstalt, 1980.

This is a collection of twelve essays on the Augsburg Confession which includes discussion about possible Roman Catholic recognition of the credal statement.

[770] Iserloh, Erwin, and Hallensleben, Barbara, eds. *Confessio Augustana und Confutatio: Der Augsburger Reichstag 1530 und die Einheit der Kirche*. Reformationsgeschichtliche Studien und Texte, no. 118. Münster: Aschendorff, 1980.

This volume contains fifty-two entries (some in summary form) drawn from an international symposium held in September 1979 at Augsburg. The contributions are often highly technical, touching upon mostly historical themes, but with some doctrinal discussion on ecclesiology and sacramentology.

[771] Kolb, Richard, ed. *Confessio Augustana: den Glauben bekennen: Berichte, Referate, Aussprachen*. Gütersloh: Gerd Mohn, 1980.

Over thirty ecumenical scholars from the German-speaking world, many of them recognized leaders in their field, contributed to this study of the Augsburg Confession from biblical, historical and theological perspectives.

[772] Lackmann, Max. *The Augsburg Confession and Catholic Unity*.

Trans. by Walter R. Bouman. New York: Herder and Herder, 1963.

This is one of the first in a series of works addressing the compatiblity of the Augsburg Confession and Catholic doctrine. The heart of the book (pp. 35-146) contains six theses on the document's theology that it is thought contain insights helpful to the entire church. The original German was entitled *Katholische Einheit und Augsburger Konfession* (1959).

[773] Lehmann, Karl, and Schlink, Edmund, eds. *Evangelium -- Sakramente -- Amt und die Einheit der Kirche: Die ökumenische Tragweite der Confessio Augustana*. Dialog der Kirche 2. Freiburg: Herder; Göttingen: Vandenhoeck und Ruprecht, 1982.

This volume reports on two meetings held in 1979 and 1980 and provides eight essays related to the Augsburg Confession from Catholic and Protestant perspectives. The volume concludes with two joint statements on the marks of unity of the church, and credal statement as a historical and ecclesial reality.

[774] Mastrantonis, George. *Augsburg and Constantinople: The Correspondence between the Tübingen Theologians and Patriarch Jeremiah II of Constantinople on the Augsburg Confession*. Brookline, MA: Holy Cross Orthodox Press, 1982.

This historical study of Ecumenical Patriarch Jeremiah II (1536-1594), contacted by a group of Tübingen Reformation theologians seeking support for the Augsburg Confession, is researched with care and thoroughness. The letters cited are given in English translation. See also Wendebourg [692].

[775] Meyer, Harding, and Schütte, Heinz, eds. *Confessio Augustana: Bekenntnis des einen Glaubens: Gemeinsame Untersuchung lutherischer und katholischer Theologen*. Paderborn: Bonifatius; Frankfurt: O. Lembeck, 1980.

This high level Catholic and Lutheran theological assessment of the doctrinal teachings of the Augsburg Confession is another major contribution to this much discussed topic. The work concludes with a five page summary statement (pp. 333-337). See also [776].

[776] Meyer, Harding, ed. *The Augsburg Confession in Ecumenical Perspective, with Anglican, Baptist, Methodist, Orthodox, Reformed*

*and Roman Catholic Contributions*. LWF Report 6/7. Stuttgart: Kreuz, 1980.

> This work, which also exists in German [775], reports on an ecumenical consultation held at Liebfrauenberg (near Strasbourg) in November 1978 to attempt a modern re-reading of the Augsburg Confession. Six non-Lutheran speakers gave assessments besides E. Schlink. See also [777, 778].

[777] Meyer, Harding, ed. *Lutheran / Roman Catholic Discussion on the Augsburg Confession: Documents 1977-1981*. LWF Report 10. Stuttgart: Kreuz, 1982.

> Following the 450th anniversary of the Augsburg Confession, the editor collected twelve major documents that addressed the theology of the text. These are in turn assessed by a Catholic (A. Klein) and a Lutheran (H. Meyer). See also [776, 778]

[778] Vajta, Vilmos. *Confessio Augustana 1530-1980: Commemoration and Self-Examination*. LWF Report 9. Stuttgart: Kreuz, 1980.

> For this 1979 consultation on the Augsburg Confession held in Liebfrauenberg, near Strasbourg, three major addresses were given by John Reumann, Sutan Hutagalung and Ulrich Kühn on various aspects of its significance. The work concludes with a statement: "Self-Examination: The Necessary Reflection." See also [776, 777].

# Leuenberg Agreement (1973)

[779] Asendorf, Ulrich, and Kuenneth, Friederich W., eds. *Von der wahren Einheit der Kirche: Lutherische Stimmen zum Leuenberger Konkordieentwurf*. Berlin: Spur, 1973.

> The Leuenberg Agreement (1973) declared church fellowship among the Lutheran, Reformed and United churches in Europe. This volume is a series of historico-critical and systematic essays explaining the importance of the Leuenberg ecumenical draft proposal leading up to a final text [780].

[780] Birmelé, André, ed. *Konkordie und Ökumene: Die Leuenberger Kirchengemeinschaft in der gegenwärtigen ökumenische Situation*. Frankfurt: O. Lembeck, 1988.

The European ecumenical agreement known as the Leuenberger Konkordie (1973) is here printed (pp. 161-170) together with a list of churches assenting to it (171-173). Five essays by various ecumenists evaluate discussions from 1981 to 1987 about the convenental agreement. For an English text of the agreement see [785].

[781] Lienhard, Marc, ed. *Lutherisch-Reformierte Kirchengemeinschaft heute: Der Leuenberger Konkordienentwurf im Kontext der bisherigen lutherisch-reformierten Dialoge.* Ökumenische Perspektiven 2. Frankfurt: O. Lembeck; J. Knecht, 1972.

The 1971 draft of what became the Leuenberg Agreement (1973) is reproduced here together with accounts of earlier regional and national meetings which paved the way for the final text.

[782] Lienhard, Marc, ed. *Zeugnis und Dienst reformatorischer Kirchen in Europa der Gegenwart: Texte der Konferenz von Sigtuna, 10. bis 16. Juni 1976.* Ökumenische Perspektiven 8. Frankfurt: O. Lembeck; J. Knecht, 1977.

This volume reports on the meeting held at Sigtuna to discuss the ongoing reception of the Leuenberger Konkordie, the text of which is here reproduced (pp. 13-22) Also included is an historical account of church communion among European Reformation churches. For an English text of the agreement see [785].

[783] Lohff, Wenzel. *Die Konkordie reformatorischer Kirchen in Europe: Leuenberge Konkordie: Eine Einführung mit dem vollen Text.* Frankfurt: O. Lembeck, 1985.

The booklet gives a brief commentary, the full text of the agreement, and a very useful chart showing the genesis of the document (p. 23).

[784] Mannermaa, Tuomo. *Vom Preussen nach Leuenberg: Hintergrund und Entwicklung der theologischen Methode in der Leuenberger Konkordie.* Arbeiten zur Geschichte und Theologie des Luthertums, NF, Bd. 1. Hamburg: Lutherisches Verlag, 1981.

The author, a Lutheran based in Helsinki, provides an excellent study of the genesis and meaning of the Leuenberger Konkordie from its early drafts through its final form.

**[785]** Rusch, William G., and Martensen, Daniel, eds. *The Leuenberg Agreement and Lutheran-Reformed Relationships: Evaluations by American and European Theologians*. Minneapolis: Augsburg, 1989.

This is the best and one of the rare commentaries on the Leuenberg Agreement (1973). There is an English translation of the text (pp. 139-154). Eleven Protestant theologians provide evaluations and several other Christian partners are brought into the discussion.

**[786]** Schieffer, Elisabeth. *Von Schauenburg nach Leuenberg: Entstehung und Bedeutung der Konkordie reformatorischer Kirchen in Europa*. Konfessionskundliche und Kontroverstheologische Studien 48. Paderborn: Bonifatius, 1983.

This massive 687 page doctoral dissertation (plus 223 pages of appendix) is an indispensable guide to the genesis and significance of the Leuenberger Konkordie adopted in March 1973. The Catholic author provides parallel columns comparing the 1971 and the 1973 versions.

# A Plan of Union (COCU)

**[787]** Consultation on Church Union (COCU). *A Plan of Union for the Church of Christ Uniting*. Princeton: COCU, 1970.

This booklet contains the plan commended to the churches for study and response by COCU in March 1970 at a meeting in St. Louis.

**[788]** Consultation on Church Union (COCU). *The Official Reports of the Four Meetings of the Consultation*. Cincinnati: Forward Movement, ca. 1966.

The first of the COCU meetings was held in 1962 and again in 1963, 1964 and 1965. Later meetings have published their proceedings and in more recent times the minutes are published in the journal *Mid-Stream* [133].

**[789]** Consultation on Church Union (COCU). *In Quest of a Church of Christ Uniting: An Emerging Theological Consensus*. Rev. ed. Princeton: COCU, 1980.

First published in 1976 this particular edition contains a new revised chapter on ministry (chapter seven).

[790] Consultation on Church Union (COCU). *Covenanting toward Unity: From Consensus to Communion: A Proposal to the Churches from the Consultation on Church Union.* Princeton: COCU, 1984.

This is a further text of the plan approved and recommended to the churches for study at the sixteenth plenary COCU session held in Baltimore in November 1984.

[791] Consultation on Church Union (COCU). *Churches in Covenant Communion: The Church of Christ Uniting.* Princeton: COCU, 1989.

This text represents the statement on covenanting agreed to at the seventeenth COCU plenary meeting.

[792] *Consultation on Church Union: A Catholic Perspective.* Washington: United States Catholic Conference, 1970.

Three Catholic ecumenists reacted to *A Plan of Union* published by COCU: J. Willebrands, W. Baum and G. Tavard. The introduction is by Paul A. Crow, Jr.

[793] *Consultation on Church Union 1967: Principles of Church Union, Guidelines for Structure, and a Study Guide.* Cincinnati: Forward Movement, 1967.

The booklet reports on the sixth meeting of the Consultation on Church Union held in Cambridge, Massachusetts, in 1967. It continues the reports of the earlier sessions as found in [788].

[794] Crow, Paul A., Jr., and Boney, William Jerry, eds. *Church Union at Midpoint.* New York: Association Press, 1972.

Some seventeen authors from Protestant, Anglican and Catholic perspectives address in this volume a whole congeries of issues raised in the early 1970s by *A Plan of Union for the Church of Christ Uniting.* There is a section on COCU and the future of ecumenism as well as a select bibliography (pp. 243-248).

[795] Day, Peter. *Tomorrow's Church: Catholic, Evangelical, Reformed.* New York: Seabury, 1969.

This publication is a valuable account of the nine churches that collaborated in the establishment of the Consultation on Church Union (COCU) to shape a church truly catholic, evangelical and reformed.

[796] Jameson, Vic. *What Does God Require of Us Now? A Resource for Study of a Plan of Union for the Church of Christ Uniting*. Nashville: Abingdon, 1970.

Written for the Consultation on Church Union (COCU), the book covers the years 1960 to 1970. It serves as a simple study guide to encourage grass roots involvement in the COCU plan. The booklet contains a sermon of Eugene Carson Blake.

[797] Moede, Gerald F., ed. *The COCU Consensus*. Princeton: COCU, 1985.

This helpful publication clearly outlines the various stages that the COCU plan had undergone by the year 1985.

[798] Moede, Gerald F. *Oneness in Christ: The Quest and the Questions*. Princeton: Minute Press, 1981.

The minister of the United Methodist Church who studied at Basel and worked for Faith and Order for seven years before serving as COCU's general secretary describes the discussions in the 1970s and the doctrinal issues that need to be addressed by those attracted to *A Plan of Union*.

[799] Osborn, Ronald E. *A Church for These Times*. Nashville: Abingdon, 1965.

This book is an open letter to American Christians by the dean and professor of church history at Christian Theological Seminary, Indianapolis. It is a plea for wider acceptance of COCU's *A Plan of Union*.

[800] Vassady, Bela. *Christ's Church: Evangelical, Catholic and Reformed*. Grand Rapids: Eerdmans, 1965.

The native Hungarian who was professor of theology at Lancaster Theological Seminary served as a member of the WCC in formation from 1938 to 1948. Inspired by Eugene Carson Blake's 1960 sermon, he argued for a church that would be evangelical, catholic and reformed, as does the COCU's *A Plan of Union*.

# 8

# Doctrinal Issues

## Visible Unity

[801] Achtemeier, Paul J. *The Quest for Unity in the New Testament Church: A Study of Paul and Acts*. Philadelphia: Fortress Press, 1987.

> The professor of New Testament at Union Theological Seminary in Richmond, Virginia, aims to show that the church from its beginning faced problems of division and disunity with the result that unity still remains a goal to be achieved.

[802] Achutegui, Pedro S. de, ed. *The Dublin Papers on Ecumenism: Fourth Congress of Jesuit Ecumenists*. Cardinal Bea Studies 2. Manila: Loyola School of Theology, Ateneo de Manila University, 1972.

> The fourth congress of Jesuit ecumenists took place August 16-20, 1971, in Dublin. Five papers touched on various aspects of church unity: the church and churches in the New Testament (P.-E. Langevin), unity and confessional statements (P. Fransen), the hierarchy of truths (P. O'Connell), the church and churches (A. Dulles) and the limits of papal primacy (W. de Vries).

[803] Adam, Karl. *The Roots of the Reformation*. Trans. by Cecily Hastings. London: Sheed and Ward, 1957.

> The famous German Catholic pioneer ecumenist Karl Adam (1876-1966) published here various lectures he had given at Stuttgart and Karlsruhe in 1947 concerning weakness in the church, Martin Luther, and the central question of unity in his day. The original title was *Una Sancta in katholischer Sicht*.

[804] Aland, Kurt, and Meurer, Siegfried. *Wissenschaft und Kirche: Festschrift für Eduard Lohse.* Texte und Arbeiten zur Bibel, Bd. 4. Bielefeld: Luther Verlag, 1989.

The volume published in honor of the New Testament scholar E. Lohse (b. 1924) includes reflections on unity and a list of his writings from 1948-1987 (pp. 371-404).

[805] Asmussen, Hans, and Sartory, Thomas. *Gespräch zwischen den Konfessionen.* Frankfurt: Fischer Bücherei, 1959.

This useful volume was completed by Easter 1959, shortly before the announcement of Vatican II and is the work of a Lutheran (Asmussen) and a Roman Catholic (Sartory) ecumenist. Fifteen doctrinal issues are treated from separate perspectives. The topics include: revelation, Scripture and tradition, Incarnation, Resurrection, Law and Gospel, grace, justification, ministry, etc. Later ecumenical methodology has favored joint texts such as the joint exposition prepared collaboratively in the Feiner/ Vischer work [1027].

[806] Aubert, Roger, et al. *Le Christ et les Eglises.* Paris: Editions universitaires, 1961.

These fourteen essays are organized into four sections: Eastern Christianity; churches of the Reformation; Anglicans and Free churches; and the ecumenical movement. The authors include well-known figures such as Olivier Rousseau, Georges Dejaifve, Pierre Michalon and Gustave Thils. This Catholic publication pre-dates Vatican II's Decree on Ecumenism and illustrates how much of the Council's ecumenical convictions were already present in writings of various theologians.

[807] Aubert, Roger. *Problèmes de l'unité chrétienne: Initiation.* New ed. Chevetogne: Editions de Chevetogne, 1961.

The first edition of this work appeared in 1952 and contains a preface by Lambert Beauduin, founder of the monastery of Chevetogne. One of the earliest works of Roman Catholic ecumenism, this volume, in small format (18 cm.), includes a section on Eastern Christianity, a separate entry on Anglicans, and one on Protestants in America. The appendix contains an account of the Faith and Order Conference at Lund (1952) by C. J. Dumont, O.P.

[808] Avis, Paul. *Christians in Communion.* Collegeville, MN: Liturgical Press, 1990.

The biblical notion of communion is used as a vehicle to explain reasons for the ongoing efforts at promoting Christian unity that have marked the twentieth century.

[809] Baker, Marion L. *On the Road to Unity: A Study Action Guide.* New York: Friendship, 1982.

This helpful, basic guide for teachers and group leaders draws heavily upon Paul A. Crow, Jr.'s *Christian Unity: Matrix for Mission* [1292] and Edward A. Powers' *In Essentials* [885].

[810] Bea, Augustin. *The Unity of Christians.* Ed. Bernard Leeming. New York: Herder and Herder, 1963.

This English version of *L'Unione dei Cristiani* (1962) is a work published during the Council deliberations on ecumenism by the man appointed by Pope John XXIII as first president of the Secretariat for Promoting Christian Unity. The English volume contains nineteen articles delivered or published at various times.

[811] Beauduin, Lambert, *et al. Eglise et unité: Réflexions sur quelques aspects fondamentaux de l'unité chrétienne.* Lille: Catholicité, 1948.

This volume is a valuable pre-Vatican II example of the first steps of Catholic ecumenism. The introduction and another essay (sanctity in the world) are written by Maurice Villain. Other pioneer Catholic contributors are Lambert Beauduin (unity of the church and Vatican I); Antoine Chavasse (true concept of papal infallibility according to Vatican I), and Pierre Michalon (the extent of the church). No non-Catholic writers were invited to contribute to the volume.

[812] Benning, Alfons. *Ökumenische Glaubensunterweisung: Perspektiven, Strukturen, Modelle.* Kevelaer: Butzon und Bercker, 1973.

The author, professor of Catholic theology at the Pädagogische Hochschule in Lörrach (Baden), treats three topics: foundations of ecumenical theology, structures of ecumenical education, and ways to achieve ecumenical awareness. Some practical information for German Christians is provided.

[813] Bent, Ans J. van der, ed. *Voices of Unity: Essays in Honour of Willem Adolf Visser 't Hooft on the Occasion of His 80th Birthday.* Geneva: World Council of Churches, 1981.

The *Festschrift* contains an introduction by Philip A. Potter and nine essays touching on issues such as: East and West church relations from 1966 to 1972, the work of the World Student Christian Federation (WSCF), trials and promises of ecumenism, political commitments of the WCC and finally the drive for church unity in Oceania, Latin America, the Caribbean and Asia. See also [867, 876, 877].

[814] Best, Thomas F., ed. *Instruments of Unity: National Councils of Churches Within the One Ecumenical Movement.* Geneva: World Council of Churches, 1988.

The Second NCC Consultation was held in Geneva, October 20-24, 1986 (the first since 1971) to discuss ecclesiological issues, the role of NCCs in promoting ecumenism, mission and dialogue, finance sharing, and the social and political contexts of national councils.

[815] Best, Thomas F., ed. *Living Today Towards Visible Unity: The Fifth International Consulation of United and Uniting Churches.* Faith and Order Paper 142. Geneva: World Council of Churches, 1988.

Following upon meetings held in Bossey (1967), Limuru (1970), Toronto (1975) and Colombo (1981), this consultation met in Potsdam, July 1987. Forty-five members from twenty-four countries were in attendance including Catholic and Orthodox observers. The eleven contributors studied visions of unity, unity and mission, and scenes from the lives of united and uniting churches. See also [853].

[816] Bevan, R.J.W., ed. *The Churches and Christian Unity.* London: Oxford University Press, 1963.

The professor at Durham edited this collaborative work which antedates the close of Vatican II. Jesuit ecumenist Bernard Leeming provided the groundwork and a possible explanation for Catholicism's aloofness to ecumenism. Other essays are by members of the Orthodox, Church of England, Baptist,

Congregational, Methodist, Presbyterian and South Indian churches.

[817] Biot, François. *En route vers l'unité*. Paris: Témoignage chrétien, 1965.

Dominican ecumenist Biot brought together in this volume various articles on unity previously published in the weekly *Témoignage Chrétien*. The material is intended for non-specialists. See also Biot's more detailed volume [189].

[818] Bismarck, Klaus von, and Dirks, Walter, eds. *Neue Grenzen: Ökumenisches Christentum Morgen*. 2 vols. Stuttgart: Kreuz; Olten: Walter, 1966-67.

These contributions were originally radio-talks for Westdeutsche Rundfunk. Volume one contains ten topics treated by at least two Christians of different confessions regarding the role of the Bible, church, situation ethics, peace, etc. Volume two treats social issues from religious and ecumenical perspectives. Final summaries are offered by W.A. Visser 't Hooft, Nikos Nissiotis and Johannes Willebrands.

[819] Blake, Eugene Carson. *The Church in the Next Decade*. New York: Macmillan; London: Collier-Macmillan, 1966.

At the time he published this volume Blake (1906-1985), an American Presbyterian, was begining his term as general secretary of the WCC. The last eight chapters are devoted to the new ecumenical Reformation.

[820] Boeckler, Richard, ed. *Welche Ökumene meinen wir? Die Bilanz der Ökumene seit Nairobi*. Beiheft zur ökumenischen Rundschau 32. Frankfurt: O. Lembeck, 1978.

In the period between the WCC's general assemblies at Nairobi (1975) and Vancouver (1983), six German-speaking ecumenists discussed here the nature of church unity as envisaged by the modern ecumenical movement.

[821] Boegner, Marc. *Le problème de l'unité chrétienne*. Paris: Je Sers, 1946.

A useful presentation (217 pp.) of how one of the leading modern

Protestant ecumenists (1881-1970) viewed the possibilities of church unity shortly after World War II.

[822] Bouillard, Henri. *Logique de la Foi. Esquisses dialogues avec la pensée protestante: approches philosophiques*. Paris: Aubier, 1964.

The French Jesuit philosopher and theologian was convinced that by illuminating the different emphases regarding the notion of faith in Soren Kierkegaard, Karl Barth, Rudolph Bultmann on the one hand and Gabriel Marcel and Maurice Blondel on the other he could make a contribution to Christian unity.

[823] Brantschen, Johannes, and Selvatico, Pietro, eds. *Unterwegs zur Einheit: Festschrift für Heinrich Stirnimann*. Fribourg, Switzerland: Universitätsverlag; Freiburg: Herder, 1980.

For the Swiss Dominican's sixtieth birthday, this large (942 pp.) *Festschrift* was prepared by colleagues and friends, many from the University of Fribourg where he taught. The third major section (pp. 571-929) treats ecumenism, eight studies on history and eighteen on systematic studies. A bibliography of Stirnimann's writings from 1945-1979 is appended.

[824] Bridston, Keith R. and Wagoner, Walter D., eds. *Unity in Mid Career: An Ecumenical Critique*. New York: Macmillan; London: Collier-Macmillan, 1963.

On the eve of Vatican II, these fourteen essays appeared. The authors are English-speaking Protestants (with the exception of the Orthodox professor Alexander Schmemann). The volume aims to explain to the non-specialist ("the Kansas City milkman") the ecclesial vision of the WCC in particular.

[825] Brouwer, Arie. *Ecumenical Testimony*. Historical Series of the Reformed Church in America. Grand Rapids: Eerdmans, 1991.

A record of ecumenical witnesses to church unity especially as they relate to the Reformed Church in America is here offered to a wider reading public.

[826] Burgess, Joseph A., ed. *In Search of Christian Unity: Basic Consensus / Basic Differences*. Minneapolis: Fortress, 1991.

Because there is so much confusion over what a "fundamental

consensus" in church dialogues actually means, the editor invited thirteen ecumenists from Orthodox, Catholic, Lutheran, Episcopalian, Methodist and Reformed churches to offer reflections which in turn are critiqued from another tradition.

[827] Casper, Josef, ed. *Um die Einheit der Kirche: Gespräche und Stimmen getrennter christlicher Brüder, in Verbindung mit Christen der römisch-katholischen, evangelischen und orthodoxen Kirche.* Vienna: F. Beck, 1940.

This fascinating book published during World War II extended to all German-speaking Christians a challenge to unite. The list of Protestant, Orthodox and Roman Catholic contributors included such ecumenical luminaries as R. Guardini, M. Pribilla, J. Lortz and M. Metzger.

[828] Congar, Yves. *Diversity and Communion.* Trans. by John Bowden. London: SCM, 1984; Mystic, CT: Twenty-Third Publications, 1985.

The volume is divided into three parts. Part one treats diversities in the New Testament era and the early church. Part two focuses on special issues separating Eastern and Western churches. Part three outlines concerns related to the Reformation churches. The French original *Diversités et communion* appeared in 1982.

[829] Congar, Yves. *Vocabulaire oecuménique.* Paris: Editions du Cerf, 1970.

To illustrate how Catholics and Protestants use various theological terms with different nuances, the author defines at some length thirteen words (e.g., sin, justification, merit, tradition, etc.). A final section compares theological methodologies.

[830] Congar, Yves; Bobrinskoy, Boris; and Bridel, Claude. *Communio Sanctorum: Mélanges offerts à Jean Jacques von Allmen.* Geneva: Labor et Fides, 1982.

This tribute to the professor of New Testament and ecumenism at the Faculty of Theology in Neuchâtel includes several on ecumenical topics. Also included in a complete bibliography of von Allmen's writings from 1939-1981.

[831] Coventry, John. *Reconciling.* London: SCM, 1985.

The English Jesuit and former Master of St. Edmund's College, Cambridge, gathers into this 136 page volume a series of ecumenical essays touching especially on the agenda of Anglican and Catholic discussions internationally such as ordained ministry, papal prerogatives, interchurch marriage, and eucharistic belief.

[832] Craig, Clarence Tucker. *The One Church in the Light of the New Testament*. New York; Nashville: Abingdon - Cokesburg, 1951.

Craig served for eight years on the American Theological Committee of Faith and Order and taught New Testament at Oberlin College for eighteen years. Here we have the ecumenical lectures he delivered at Southwestern University in Georgetown, Texas, July 1950.

[833] Cullmann, Oscar, and Karrer, Otto. *Einheit in Christus: Evangelische und katholische Bekenntnisse*. Zürich: Zwingli; Einsiedeln: Benziger, 1960.

One of the first serious books of its kind jointly authored by a Protestant and Catholic, this work still has pertinence today. It underscores different perceptions of ecumenism along confessional lines. Of special note is the list of "ten commandments" by Fritz Blanke (p. 57) for dealing with Christians of other confessions.

[834] Cullmann, Oscar. *Unity Through Diversity: Its Foundations and a Contribution to the Discussion concerning the Possibility of its Actualization*. Trans. by M. Eugene Boring. Philadelphia: Fortress, 1988.

This volume, a translation of *Einheit durch Vielfalt*, discusses unity and diversity in the New Testament, actualization of unity through diversity, and the author's reactions to the Fries-Rahner book [841], the Lima document and Taizé.

[835] Dumont, Christophe-Jean. *Approaches to Christian Unity: Doctrine and Prayer*. Trans. by Henry St. John. London: Darton, Longman and Todd; Baltimore: Helicon, 1959.

Not a scholarly study but a series of meditations, this pioneering work published first as *Les voies de l'unité chrétienne* (1954) stresses spiritual ecumenism.

[836] Dumont, Christophe-Jean. *Comment les chrétiens se sont-ils séparés?* Chevetogne: Editions de Chevetogne, 1962.

The 31 page pamphlet by the late Dominican ecumenist (1898-1991) and editor of the journal *Istina*, is a valuable expression of sensitive ecumenism well before Vatican II's Decree on Ecumenism.

[837] Enrique Tarancón, Vicente. *Ecumenismo y pastoral: carta pastoral.* Salamanca: Ediciones Sigueme, 1964.

Writing as Bishop of Solsona and secretary for the Spanish Episcopal Conference, the author published this 265 page pastoral letter on March 24, 1964. This highly clerical text reflects little of the deeper insights of Vatican II.

[838] Filthaut, Theodor, ed. *Umkehr und Erneuerung: Kirche nach dem Konzil.* Mainz: Matthias-Grünewald, 1966.

Shortly after the close of Vatican II, a number of German Catholic writers contributed essays on renewal (five contributions), on ecumenical tasks (four), and on the church in the modern world (seven).

[839] Fries, Heinrich. *Ökumene statt Konfessionen? Das Ringen der Kirchen um Einheit.* Frankfurt: J. Knecht, 1977.

Among the themes discussed in five chapters are: legitimate pluralism in the one church, and the need for confessions to become converted. See also the volume published by Fries in collaboration with Karl Rahner [841].

[840] Fries, Heinrich, and Pesch, Otto Hermann. *Streiten für die eine Kirche.* Munich: Kösel, 1987.

Especially insightful in this collaborative publication are the two articles by Pesch on the ecumenism of conversion and on the condemnations of the 16th century in light of today's ecumenical theology. See also [860, 861].

[841] Fries, Heinrich, and Rahner, Karl. *Unity of the Church: An Actual Possibililty.* Trans. by Ruth and Eric Gritsch. Philadelphia: Fortress; New York: Paulist, 1985.

This work received a great deal of attention in its German original (*Einigung der Kirchen - reale Möglichkeit*, 1983) and English version. Two German Catholic senior ecumenists proposed eight theses that if accepted mutually could, they felt, lead to a reunion of churches, especially Protestant and Catholic.

[842] Frost, Francis. *Oecuménisme*. Paris: Letouzey & Ané, 1984.

This 99 page introduction to ecumenism is a reprint from the lengthy article published in the encyclopedia *Catholicisme* (vol. 9, col. 1501-36; 10, 1-21). The main focus is on recent historical developments but some treatment is also given to the theology of ecumenism.

[843] Gassmann, Günther, and Meyer, Harding. *The Unity of the Church: Requirements and Structures*. LWF Report 15. Stuttgart: Kreuz, 1983.

The Lutheran World Federation's Department of Studies and Strasbourg's Institute for Ecumenical Research co-sponsored this work as a basis of discussion for the Vancouver WCC general assembly (1983) and the LWF assembly in Budapest (1984). The two ecumenists provided a draft (pp. 1-26) on the concept of unity in reconciled diversity.

[844] Groscurth, Reinhard, ed. *What Unity Implies: Six Essays After Uppsala*. World Council of Churches Studies 7. Geneva: World Council of Churches, 1969.

These excellent six essays by Protestants and Orthodox (all in English) address the theological implications of the search for unity.

[845] Guitton, Jean. *Unity Through Love: Essays in Ecumenism*. Trans. by Brian Thompson. New York: Herder and Herder, 1964.

Published on the eve of Vatican II, this work by a French theologian and friend of the late Pope Paul VI is a highly personal account of the need to respect the freedom of others in the search for Christian unity. The French original of this work was known as *Vers l'unité dans l'amour* (1963).

[846] Heiler, Friedrich, ed. *Neue Wege zur einen Kirche*. Munich: E. Reinhardt, 1967.

Theologian Friedrich Heiler (1892-1967) provided three of the
seven essays (on pioneer ecumenists and several aspects of the
New Delhi general assembly of the WCC in 1961). Other material
is drawn from the 10th International Congress on the History of
Religions. See also [216, 524].

[847] Herms, Eilert. *Einheit der Christen in der Gemeinschaft der
Kirche: Die ökumenische Bewegung der römischen Kirche in Licht der
reformatorischen Theologie: Antwort auf den Rahner Plan.* Kirche und
Konfessionen 24. Göttingen: Vandenhoeck und Ruprecht, 1984.

This response to the Rahner/Fries proposal [841] is written from
a strongly evangelical viewpoint. It addresses Bible-oriented
Christians in particular and raises a number of perceived
difficulties about ecumenism.

[848] Houssiau, André. *Voies vers l'unité: Colloque organisé à
l'occasion de l'éméritat de Mgr Gustave Thils, Louvain la Neuve, 27-28
avril 1979.* Cahiers de la Revue Théologique de Louvain 3. Louvain la
Neuve: Faculté de Théologie, 1981.

On the occasion of his retirement from the Louvain's Theology
Faculty, a colloquium was held to honor Thils, one of the major
theological influences on Vatican II. There is an assessment of his
career (R. Aubert) plus a bibliography of his published writings
from 1936 to 1980. Orthodox, Protestant and Catholic writers
reflect on church unity. Of particular note is the article on
patrology and ecumenism (A. de Halleux).

[849] Hunt, George Laird. *A Guide to Christian Unity.* Rev. ed. St.
Louis: Bethany, 1963.

The first edition of this basic guide book appeared the year after
the North American Faith and Order Conference in Oberlin
(1957). This revision includes an account of the Faith and Order
meeting in Montreal (July 12-26, 1963).

[850] Karrer, Otto. *Die christliche Einheit: Gabe und Aufgabe.*
Begegnung 5. Lucerne: Räber, 1963.

This short 84 page publication draws together several articles that
appeared in specialized journals. Karrer identifies theological and
non-theological divisive factors and offers practical suggestions
to promote unity. These essays pre-date Vatican II.

[851] Katholische Akademie Hamburg, ed. *Aspekte der Ökumene: Anregungen für Theorie und Praxis*. Hamburg: Katholische Akademie, 1984.

This book contains six contributions by Catholic, Protestant and Orthodox writers on the nature of ecumenism and on specific issues such as sacrifice, angels, papal infallibility, and Mary.

[852] Kean, Charles D. *Ecumenical Encounters in Christian Unity: Background Information*. New York: Seabury, 1963.

This ecumenical study guide was prepared under the auspices of the Department of Christian Education of the Protestant Episcopal Church of the USA.

[853] Kinnamon, Michael, and Best, Thomas F., eds. *Called to be One in Christ: United Churches and the Ecumenical Movement*. Faith and Order Paper 127. Geneva: World Council of Churches, 1985.

The introduction on united churches and the ecumenical movement by Thomas Best, executive secretary of the Faith and Order Commission, is excellent. There are eleven essays including some case studies from around the world. These proceedings of the WCC's Colombo Consultation include a narrative bibliography (pp. 73-77). See also [815].

[854] Kinnamon, Michael. *Truth and Community: Diversity and its Limits in the Ecumenical Movement*. Grand Rapids: Eerdmans; Geneva: World Council of Churches, 1988.

Kinnamon is dean and professor at Lexington Theological Seminary. In his study of multilateral dialogues he describes the dilemma in the ecumenical movement, the foundations of the ecumenical vision, doctrinal, social and confessional diversity, and the future agenda.

[855] Küng, Hans, and Tracy, David, eds. *Paradigm Change in Theology: A Symposium for the Future*. Trans. by Margaret Kohl. Edinburgh: T. and T. Clark, 1989.

Seventy scholars participated in this international ecumenical symposium held in Tübingen in May 1983 to explore new paradigms for theology. The volume contains the addresses and concluding remarks. The German original *Theologie - Wohin?* was published in 1984.

[856] Lambert, Bernard. *Ecumenism: Theology and History*. Trans. by Lancelot C. Sheppard. New York: Herder and Herder, 1967.

This 533 page English edition is a translation of the Dominican professor's two volume *Le Problème oecuménique* (1962). Conceived and written before Vatican II, it is one of the more enlightened Catholic expositions of ecumenism in that time period. The conceptual framework of the work, however, is dated.

[857] Lash, Nicholas, ed. *Doctrinal Development and Christian Unity*. London: Sheed and Ward, 1967.

The volume contains five essays by Catholics and one by an Orthodox on ecumenical theology. Also treated is the notion of development of doctrine and an ecumenical understanding of sacraments. In the USA this book appeared under the title: *Until He Comes: A Study in the Progress toward Christian Unity* (Dayton, OH: Pflaum, 1968).

[858] Lauret, Bernard, and Refoulé, François, eds. *Initiation à la pratique de la théologie*. 5 vols. Paris: Editions du Cerf, 1982-1983.

This series marks one of the high points of post-Vatican II theology in France. Although written mostly by Catholics, there are some Protestant contributors. The lengthy essays reflect ecumenical sensitivity. The most explicit treatment of ecumenism is J. Hoffmann's "La recomposition de l'unité" (vol. III, pp. 347-384).

[859] Leeming, Bernard, ed. *Towards Christian Unity: A Symposium*. London: Geoffrey Chapman, 1968.

Jesuit ecumenist B. Leeming (1893-1971) edited this account of the second conference on ecumenism held at Heythrop College (July 1967). Five of the nine speeches were given by non-Catholics. A total of fifty-six delegates from Catholic dioceses of England and Wales attended. See also the first Heythrop conference [467].

[860] Lehmann, Karl, and Pannenberg, Wolfhart, eds. *Lehrverurteilungen - kirchentrennend?* Vol. 1: *Rechtfertigung,*

*Sakramente und Amt im Zeitalter der Reformation und Heute.* Dialog der Kirchen 4. Freiburg: Herder; Göttingen: Vandenhoeck und Ruprecht, 1986. Vol. 2: *Materialen zu den Lehrverurteilungen und zur Theologie der Rechtfertigung.* Dialog der Kirchen 5. ibid, 1989. Vol. 3: *Materialen zur Lehre von den Sakramenten und vom kirchlichen Amt.* Dialog der Kirchen 6. ibid, 1990.

These scholarly volumes concerning the condemnations of the Reformation era are related to justification, sacramental theology, and the ordained ministry. The essays were written in collaboration by members of the Ökumenischer Arbeitskreis evangelischer und katholischer Theologen. The first volume has been translated into English [861]. See also Fries [840].

[861] Lehmann, Karl, and Pannenberg, Wolfhart, eds. *The Condemnations of the Reformation Era: Do They Still Divide?* Trans. by Margaret Kohl. Minneapolis: Fortress, 1990.

The first volume of the preceding publication [860] has been translated into English. This includes the section on justification (pp. 29-69), sacraments, especially the Lord's Supper (71-145), and ministry (147-159). The introductory material reviews the nature and content of the condemnatory pronouncements of the sixteenth century. See also Fries [840].

[862] Lengsfeld, Peter, ed. *Ökumenische Theologie: Ein Arbeitsbuch.* Stuttgart: W. Kohlhammer, 1980.

This is one of the most important books on ecumenical theology to have been published. The editor is Director of the Catholic Ecumenical Institute at the University of Münster. Fourteen authors collaborated to provide a theoretical introduction to ecumenical theology, historical studies on efforts at reunion, an analysis of non-theological factors (such as power), future perspectives and concrete proposals. A comprehensive bibliography (pp. 446-484) is included.

[863] Lescrauwaet, Josephus Franciscus. *Die Einheit der Ökumene: Perspektiven nach der Zweiten Vatikanischen Konzil.* Der Christ in der Welt. XII.14. Aschaffenburg: Pattloch, 1969.

The author is professor at the Theology Faculty in Tilburg. In 156 pages he offers seven chapters outlining the general principles of ecumenism. Especially useful are the sections on the ecumenical contributions of local churches and on unity in diversity.

[864] Link, Christian; Luz, Ulrich; Vischer, Lukas. *Sie aber hielten fest an der Gemeinschaft: Einheit der Kirche als Prozess im Neuen Testament und heute*. Zürich: Benziger, 1988.

This is a collection of studies comparing the notion of church unity in the New Testament period and in the modern church.

[865] Lovsky, Fadiey. *Un passé de division, une promesse d'unité*. Paris: St. Paul, 1990.

The author who is an historian argues that Christians at an early date learned division by the way they dealt with Judaism. Cardinal Albert Decourtray of Lyons wrote the preface to this study.

[866] Lowery, Mark D. *Ecumenism: Striving for Unity Amid Diversity*. Mystic, CT: Twenty-Third, 1985.

This book is meant to be a basic guide in small discussion groups. Besides a short history of ecumenism there are descriptions of the major Christian confessions. Each chapter provides discussion questions.

[867] Mackie, Robert C., and West, Charles C., eds. *The Sufficiency of God: Essays on the Ecumenical Hope in Honour of W.A. Visser 't Hooft*. London: SCM, 1963.

One of several *Festschriften* in honor of the noted ecumenist, this volume marks his twenty-five years of service for the WCC. There are fifteen essays by Orthodox, Catholics and Protestants from different parts of the world. See also [813, 876, 877].

[868] Macquarrie, John. *Christian Unity and Christian Diversity*. London: SCM, 1975.

This 118 page study of Christian unity outlines the theological principles related to the oneness and pluralism of the church. There are five *quaestiones disputatae* singled out for special attention concerning ministry, eucharist, marriage, mariology, and authority.

[869] Marchant, James. *The Reunion of Christendom: A Survey of the*

*Present Position*. London: Cassell, 1929.

In this early twentieth century publication, twelve church groups are identified and a representative churchman of each is asked to explain his church's teaching of church unity. Among them are Otto Dibelius for the Protestant Church of Germany, Metropolitan Germanos of the Orthodox Church, and Cardinal Francis Bourne of the Catholic Church.

[870] Mascall, E. L. *The Recovery of Unity: A Theological Approach*. London and New York: Longman, Green, 1958.

This collection of scholarly articles gave a variety of theological insights into the nature of church, liturgy, ministry and papacy. Mascall anticipated some of the vision associated with subsequent ecumenism.

[871] Michalon, Pierre. *L'Unité des chrétiens*. Paris: Artheme Fayard, 1965.

The short (124 pp.) but insightful book inspired by the work of Paul Couturier takes an irenic and sympathetic view of the doctrinal positions of Anglican and Protestant churches.

[872] Minear, Paul S., ed. *The Nature of the Unity We Seek*. St. Louis: Bethany Press, 1958.

The volume provides the proceedings of a North American Conference on Faith and Order held in Oberlin, Ohio, September 3-10, 1957. The conference addresses of ten ecumenists are here reproduced. There is also a brief statement by Orthodox on "Christian Unity as Viewed by the Eastern Orthodox Church" (pp. 159-163). See also [738].

[873] Morris, William, ed. *The Unity We Seek: Lectures on the Church and the Churches*. Toronto: Ryerson, 1962; New York: Oxford University Press, 1963.

This is a collection of fourteen lectures given by nine ecumenists at Huron College, University of Western Ontario, London (Canada) held shortly before Vatican II.

[874] Müller-Fahrenholz, Geiko. *Unity in Today's World: The Faith and Order Studies on Unity of the Church - Unity of Humankind*. Faith

and Order Paper 88. Geneva: World Council of Churches, 1978.

This is a retrospective study to 1937 with special attention to the Uppsala general assembly (1968) together with the draft text of 1969. The scope is then enlarged in light of contributions from groups and conferences as well as from ten individual written submissions.

[875] *Le Mystère de l'Unité.* Vol. 1: *Découverte de l'oecuménisme.* Vol. 2: *L'Eglise en plénitude.* Cahiers de la Pierre Qui Vire, NS 17-18. Paris: Desclée de Brouwer, 1961-1962.

Catholics, Orthodox and Protestants collaborated on these volumes written between the convocation of Vatican II and its opening. Volume one reviewed the history and experiences of the various churches; volume two reflected on the "mystery of unity."

[876] Nelson, J. Robert, ed. *No Man is Alien: Essays on the Unity of Mankind.* Leiden: Brill, 1971.

These thirteen essays on a variety of ecumenical and interreligious themes honor W.A. Visser 't Hooft. There is also a listing of his writings from 1918-1970 (some 1086 items!). The following German edition [877] omits four of the essays and replaces them with five others. See also [813, 867, 877].

[877] Nelson, J. Robert, and Pannenberg, Wolfhart, eds. *Um Einheit und Heil der Menschheit.* Frankfurt: O. Lembeck, 1973.

This is not strictly speaking a translation of the preceding volume [876] but an adaptation. Nine of the thirteen original articles are retained, but five new ones are added. The listing of Visser 't Hooft's publications noted above is expanded to include 1120 items (updated to 1973). See also [813, 867].

[878] Nelson, J. Robert. *One Lord, One Church.* New York: Association Press, 1958.

This 93 page booklet distinguishes between healthy diversity and unhappy divisions. The Methodist ecumenist then raised twelve vital questions facing the churches.

[879] Neuner, Peter, and Wolfinger, Franz, eds. *Auf Wegen der Versöhnung: Beiträge zum ökumenisches Gespräch.* Frankfurt: J.

Knecht, 1982.

This 302 page *Festschrift* in honor of Heinrich Fries contains a collection of German essays on a variety of historical and doctrinal themes and a list of his publications. See also [894].

[880] O'Brien, John A., ed. *Steps to Christian Unity*. Garden City, NY: Doubleday, 1964.

The research professor at the University of Notre Dame edited these twenty-six essays by a variety of churchmen on how best to achieve unity in the church. The authors cited are Anglican, Catholic, Orthodox and Protestant from both sides of the Atlantic.

[881] *The Old and the New in the Church: Two Interim Reports*. Minneapolis: Augsburg, 1961.

Following the Faith and Order meeting in Lund (1952) one of four theological commissions set up was asked to study "Christ and the Church." These two interim reports on tradition and traditions, and on institutionalism and unity are here published for reaction.

[882] Ouspensky, Léonide. *Vers l'unité*. Paris: YMCA, 1987.

The Russian Orthodox theologian wrote this short reflection on church unity by drawing out the spiritual significance of an icon depicting Pentecost as trinitarian theophany.

[883] Papandreou, Damaskinos; Beinert, Wolfgang A.; Schaferdiek, Knut, eds. *Oecumenica et patristica: Festschrift für Wilhelm Schneemelcher zum 75. Geburtstag*. Chambésy-Geneva: Centre Orthodoxe, 1989.

This collection of patristic and ecumenical articles pays tribute to Professor Schneemelcher and provides a list of his writings (pp. 397-404).

[884] Pesch, Otto Hermann, ed. *Einheit der Kirche - Einheit der Menschheit: Perpektiven aus Theologie, Ethik und Völkerrecht*. Freiburg: Herder, 1978.

In 1977 at the University of Hamburg, three authors, K. Rahner, F. Böckle and V. Scheuner, addressed dogmatic, ethical and juridico-political aspects of the theme of unity.

[885] Powers, Edward A., comp. *In Essentials, Unity: An Ecumenical Sampler*. New York: Friendship, 1982.

A 119 page resource of ecumenical reflections and prayers that intends to be a "map of the ecumenical territory." See also Baker [809] and Crow [1292].

[886] Raiser, Konrad. *Ecumenism in Transition: A Paradigm Shift in the Ecumenical Movement*. Trans. by Tony Coates. Geneva: World Council of Churches, 1991.

The former deputy secretary of the WCC (1973-1983) and professor of ecumenical theology at Bochum, Germany, devotes five chapters to analyzing shifts in ecumenism as regards goals, methods and leadership. He reviews the classic self-understanding of ecumenism and describes new challenges. There is also a thoughtful reflective essay on the oikoumene. The German original is *Ökumene im Übergang* (1989).

[887] Rusch, William G. *Ecumenism: A Movement Toward Church Unity*. Philadelphia: Fortress, 1985.

This account of the origins and goals of the modern ecumenical movement by the well-known Lutheran churchman is addressed especially to non-specialists. The book's thesis is that ecumenism is first and foremost a unity issue.

[888] Saayman, Willem A. *Unity and Mission: A Study of the Concept of Unity in Ecumenical Discussions since 1961 and its Influences on the World Mission of the Church*. Pretoria: University of South Africa, 1984.

The author is convinced that there is a basic relationship between unity and mission. One cannot sustain an either-or attitude but only a both-and attitude.

[889] Schilling, Othmar, and Zimmermann, Heinrich, eds. *Unio Christianorum: Festschrift für Erzbischof Dr. Lorenz Jaeger zum 70. Geburtstag am 23. September 1962*. Paderborn: Bonifatius, 1962.

The collection of essays in honor of Lorenz Jaeger, presented by the Philosophisch-Theologische Akademie and the Johann Adam

Möhler Institute for Ecumenics of Paderborn (which he founded), contains a number of studies, all in German, on the biblical, historical, ecclesiological and pastoral aspects of unity.

[890] Schlink, Edmund, and Peters, Albrecht, eds. *Zur Auferbauung des Leibes Christi: Festgabe für Peter Brunner*. Kassel: J. Stauda Verlag, 1965.

The *Festschrift* in honor of Peter Brunner includes a number of essays on the rebuilding of the body of Christ from a variety of methodological perspectives.

[891] Schreiner, Josef, and Wittstadt, Klaus, eds. *Communio sanctorum: Einheit der Christen - Einheit der Kirche: Festschrift für Bischof Paul Werner Scheele*. Würzburg: Echter, 1988.

This is a collection of eighteen essays composed in honor of Scheele for his sixtieth birthday. They cover a number of themes on unity ranging from the New Testament to modern times. See book by Scheele [500].

[892] Schütte, Heinz. *Ziel: Kirchengemeinschaft: Zur ökumenischen Orientierung*. Paderborn: Bonifatius, 1985.

The Catholic ecumenist and collaborator at the Johann Adam Möhler Institute for Ecumenics published this collection of essays on the notion of *koinonia*. He touches upon a wide assortment of ecumenical themes including new assessments of Martin Luther, the apostolic faith today, and consensus in international bilaterals.

[893] Schutz, Roger. *Unanimity in Pluralism*. Trans. by David Flood, *et al*. Chicago: Franciscan Herald, 1966.

Since 1940 Brother Roger Schutz (1915- ) has resided at Taizé's monastery dedicated to promoting Christian unity. This volume, originally entitled *Unaminité dans le pluralisme*, is a collection of his views on the religious dimension of life.

[894] Seckler, Max, *et al*., eds. *Begegnung: Beiträge zu einer Hermeneutik des theologischen Gesprächs: Festschrift Heinrich Fries*. Graz: Styria, 1972.

This 839 page collection of essays in honor of the ecumenist Heinrich Fries contains contributions in German, English and

French. Besides historical investigations on ecumenism, specific themes are addressed such as eucharist, ordained ministry and authority. T. F. O'Meara outlines stages in ecumenism in the USA from 1962-1972. See also [879].

[895] Segretariato Attività Ecumeniche, ed. *Ecumenismo e storia della salvezza [Atti della IV Sessione di formazione ecumenica organizzata dal S.A.E., 1966]*. Brescia: Morcelliana, 1967.

This year's theme for the Italian Ecumenical Association's meeting was ecumenism and salvation history and its bearing on the notion of unity.

[896] Segretariato Attività Ecumeniche, ed. *Ecumenismo e dialogo [Atti della V Sessione di formazione ecumenica organizzata dal S.A.E., 1967]*. Brescia: Morcelliana, 1968.

The 1967 meeting of the Italian Ecumenical Association studied the growing sense of unity that is emerging from the dialogue process.

[897] Segretariato Attività Ecumeniche, ed. *Ecumenismo e libertà religiosa [Atti della VI Sessione di formazione ecumenica organizzata dal S.A.E., 1968]*. Brescia: Morcelliana, 1969.

The 1968 meeting of the Italian Ecumenical Association explored the relationship between religious freedom and the ecumenical search for unity.

[898] Song, Choan-Seng, ed. *Growing Together into Unity: Texts of the Faith and Order Commission on Conciliar Fellowship*. Madras: Christian Literature Society, 1978.

This publication for Indian readers in particular gathers together a variety of Faith and Order texts of conciliar fellowship. There are also five essays by individual theologians on the same topic.

[899] Spinka, Matthew. *The Quest for Church Unity*. New York: Macmillan, 1960.

Spinka (1890-1972) was a lecturer at the Hartford Seminary Foundation. His discussion, addressed to Protestants of every persuasion, distinguishes between "federalists" and "ecumenists". Siding with the ecumenists, he argues that their hope is not for the establishment of a super organization but for an abiding spiritual unity.

[900] Stauffer, Richard, ed. *In Necessariis Unitas: Mélanges offerts à Jean-Louis Leuba.* Paris: Editions du Cerf, 1984.

Colleagues of the Swiss professor and founder of the journal *Verbum Caro*, who together with Philippe Menoud is credited as founder of the "school of Neuchâtel", published this collection of thirty-one articles (in English, French, German and Italian) for his seventieth birthday. A number of themes are touched upon including the role of the local church, ministry as articulated in bilateral dialogues, and academic theology.

[901] Struck, Guenther, ed. *Deshalb für den Menschen: Festschrift für Stanis-Edmund Szydzik.* Regensburg: Pustet, 1980.

This 380 page *Festschrift* contains a spectrum of articles touching on a variety of ecumenical themes particularly those with direct pastoral implications.

[902] Struve, Pierre; Beaupère, René; Ferrier-Welti, Maurice. *L'oecuménisme.* Eglises en dialogue no. 7. Tours: Mame, 1968.

This volume reflects the methodology commonly used in the 1960s. Three separate theologians (Orthodox, Catholic and Protestant) wrote three distinct essays on Christian unity without attempting jointly to form a synthesis.

[903] Thorogood, Bernard. *One Wind, Many Flames: Church Unity and the Diversity of the Churches.* Risk Books. Geneva: World Council of Churches, 1991.

The General Secretary of the United Reformed Church, London, produced this 71 page introduction to the ecumenical movement for non-specialist readers.

[904] Thurian, Max. *Visible Unity and Tradition.* Trans. by W. J. Kerrigan. Baltimore: Helicon, 1962; London: Darton, Longman and Todd, 1964.

Originally published as *L'unité visible des chrétiens et la tradition*, composed on the eve of Vatican II, the work stresses the considerable visible unity that already exists and the need for further spiritual conversion.

[905] Torrance, Thomas F. *Theology in Reconciliation: Essays Towards Evangelical and Catholic Unity in East and West.* London: Geoffrey Chapman, 1975.

The Scottish Presbyterian theologian outlines in six chapters his views on ecumenism, baptism, the Lord's Supper, liturgical worship, the theology of Athanasius, and the church in a new age.

[906] *Union et désunion des chrétiens.* Recherches oecuméniques 1. Bruges: Desclée de Brouwer, 1963.

Five Catholic authors contributed eight essays to illustrate the wide diversity among Christians in their liturgical, historical and doctrinal traditions. Also discussed are the Council of Trent as obstacle to reunion, and the ecumenism of Cardinal Mercier. The essays originated as lectures given at Louvain from 1960-1962 in honor of Pope Adrian VI (Adrian Florenszoon, formerly professor at Louvain).

[907] *L'Unità della Chiesa.* Milan: Vita e Pensiero, 1962.

While the future Pope Paul VI (Giovanni B. Montini) was still archbishop of Milan, a series of lectures was held there in February 1961 by six prominent ecumenists representing the Catholic, Orthodox, Anglican and Protestant traditions to describe hopes for reunion.

[908] Villain, Maurice. *Unity: A History and Some Reflections.* Trans. by J.R. Foster. London: Harvill Press; Baltimore: Helicon, 1963.

This book was translated from the third edition of *Introduction à l'oecuménisme.* It outlines the main stages of the ecumenical movement, various spiritual approaches within Protestantism and Catholicism, and what he called "technical ecumenism."

[909] Vischer, Lukas. *Veränderung der Welt - Bekehrung der Kirchen: Denkanstösse der Fünften Vollversammlung des Ökumenischen Rates der Kirchen in Nairobi.* Frankfurt: O. Lembeck, 1976.

Following the general assembly in Nairobi (1975) the former director of the Faith and Order Commission published these four chapters reflecting on witness, dialogue, political society, and conciliar fellowship.

[910] Vischer, Lukas, ed., *What Kind of Unity?* Faith and Order Paper 69. Geneva: World Council of Churches, 1974.

The project originated in a Faith and Order Consultation in Salamanca in 1973. Seven essays were prepared by Orthodox, Catholics and Protestants. The publication concludes with its report "Concepts of Unity and Models of Union" (1973).

[911] Visser 't Hooft, Willem A. *Ökumenische Bilanz: Reden und Aufsätze aus zwei Jahrzehnten.* Stuttgart: Evangel-isches Missionsverlag, 1966.

This volume contains some twenty speeches and essays composed between 1941 and 1966. Hanfried Krüger supplied the introductory essay. See also the companion volume [438].

[912] Visser 't Hooft, Willem A. *The Pressure of Our Common Calling.* Garden City, NY: Doubleday; London: SCM, 1959.

This early work of Visser 't Hooft contains the Taylor lectures of 1957 given at Yale Divinity School. He discussed the call to witness, to service, to fellowship in Christ and to unity in Christ.

[913] Wainwright, Geoffrey. *The Ecumenical Moment: Crisis and Opportunity for the Church.* Grand Rapids: Eerdmans, 1983.

Drawing upon two decades of involvement in the ecumenical movement and especially his work in editing the Lima document (BEM), Wainright argues that this is the opportune time for the visible expression of church unity.

[914] Webb, Pauline, ed. *Faith and Faithfulness: Essays on Contemporary Ecumenical Themes.* Geneva: World Council of Churches, 1984.

Designed as a tribute to the outgoing general secretary of the WCC, Philip Potter, this volume contains fourteen contributions from an internationally representative group of ecumenists. The editor provides a personal portrait of Potter.

[915] Whale, John S. *Christian Reunion: Historic Divisions Reconsidered.* London: Lutterworth, 1971.

Written in a popular style, this somewhat outdated work is still informative in giving an overview of the historical tensions among the churches, especially related to the Lord's Supper or eucharist. Disagreements between Lutherans and Reformed Christians are also discussed.

# Dialogue as Theology

[916] Amirtham, Samuel, ed. *A Vision for Man: Essays on Faith, Theology and Society in Honour of Joshua Russell Chandran*. Madras: Christian Literature Society, 1978.

On the occasion of his sixtieth birthday (his "Shastiabdapoorthi"), to honor J. R. Chandran, the well-known ecumenist and principal of United Theological College, Bangalore, a group of friends from Asia, Europe and America, published a collection of ecumenical essays concerning: theology and theological education; church and mission; and faith and society. Also included is a list of Chandran's publications arranged by E. Adiappa (pp. 19-25).

[917] Amirtham, Samuel, and Moon, Cyris H.S., eds. *The Teaching of Ecumenics*. Geneva: World Council of Churches, 1987.

These proceedings of an ecumenical colloquium held in the WCC's conference center in Bossey contain talks by eleven speakers drawn from widely geographic and cultural settings. Six discussion groups' views are summarized. The work includes an open letter to faculties of theology raising questions about whether or not theology is taught ecumenically.

[918] Barth, Karl, and Balthasar, Hans Urs von. *Dialogue*. Collection oecuménique 7. Geneva: Labor et Fides, 1968.

This book, originally published in German, contains a valuable record of ecumenical talks given on February 28, 1968 at Leuenberg (near Hölstein, Basel), Switzerland, by two influential theologians: Barth ("The Church on the Way to Renewal") and von Balthasar ("Unity in Christ"). Also published is the text of a round-table discussion on preaching by Barth and some Catholic priests that first appeared in *Orientierung* [147] on June 15, 1968.

[919] Baum, Gregory, ed. Vol. 1: *Ecumenical Theology Today*. Vol. 2: *Ecumenical Theology*. New York: Paulist, 1964-1967.

Volume one of this collection contains twenty-five essays originally published in *The Ecumenist* [111]. The articles discuss: problems of Vatican II, the Roman Catholic Church, ecumenical developments, ecumenical dialogue, Christians and Jews. Paul Broadhurst provides a 12 page briefly annotated bibliography (pp. 245-256) of mostly English books. Volume two has twenty-three articles on sacramental theology, ecclesiology, doctrinal development at Vatican II.

[920] Beaupère, René. *La trame de l'oecuménisme. Texte d'une série de cours donnée en 1970 à l'Institut supérieur d'études oecuméniques.* 3 vols. in 1. Paris: Editions oecuméniques; Editions St. Paul, 1970.

These pamphlets were produced by Beaupère, founder of the Centre oecuménique St. Irénée in Lyons, based on five lectures given at the Institut Supérieur d'Etudes Oecuméniques de Paris. The topics are: initiative and silence of the churches, spiritual ecumenism, doctrinal ecumenism, secular ecumenism, and the move from institutional ecumenism to ecumenism at all levels.

[921] Benignus, Emma Lou. *"All in Each Place": A Guide to Local Ecumenism.* Cincinnati: Forward Movement, 1966.

This popular guide aims to assist discussion and reflection on principles of self-conversion needed for ecumenism. Designed for private or group usage, this short (127 pp.) work was prepared by a former professor of the Episcopal Divinity School, Cambridge, Massachusetts.

[922] Birmelé, André, ed. *Local Ecumenism: How Church Unity is Seen and Practised by Congregations.* Geneva: World Council of Churches, 1984.

This publication is the final report of a four-year study suggested by the sixth assembly of the Lutheran World Federation in 1977 and carried out by the Institute for Ecumenical Research in Strasbourg. The material is organized around the topics: motivation, the role of church leaders, concepts of unity, doctrinal differences, and non-doctrinal factors.

[923] Böni, Josef. *Die Christenheit vor dem Entscheidung: Tatsachen zur konfessionskundlichen Aufklärung.* Trogen, Switzerland: Fritz Meili, 1968.

Composed just after the Uppsala general assembly of the WCC, this book tried in a somewhat apologetic vein to outline the essential differences between the beliefs of Catholics and Protestants in nine areas.

[924] Brosseder, Johannes. *Ökumenische Theologie: Geschichte - Probleme.* Theologische Fragen heute 10. Munich: M. Hueber, 1967.

The Roman Catholic author prepared this volume under the direction of Heinrich Fries at his Institut für Ökumenische Theologie in Munich. Although only 169 pages long, the volume is a solid piece of research that contrasts earlier forms of confessional activities (polemics, irenicism, prosyletism) with modern ecumenical goals.

[925] Buerkle, Horst, and Becker, Gerhold, eds. *Communicatio Fidei: Festschrift für Eugen Biser zum 65. Geburtstag.* Regensburg: F. Pustet, 1983.

In this 432 page collection of theological essays on how Christian faith is shared, several articles (those of K. Lehmann and K. Rahner) address this from a specifically ecumenical perspective.

[926] Callahan, Daniel J.; Oberman, Heiko A.; O'Hanlon, Daniel J. *Christianity Divided: Protestant and Roman Catholic Theological Issues.* New York: Sheed and Ward, 1961.

This early example of comparative theology invited a Reformation theologian and a Catholic theologian to address separately the following topics: tradition, the Bible, church, sacraments, justification, and classical controverted issues. The 335 page volume was translated into French as *Catholiques et Protestants: Confrontations théologiques* (1963).

[927] Centre Orthodoxe du Patriarchat Oecuménique, Chambésy-Geneva. *La théologie dans l'Eglise et dans le monde.* Etudes théologiques de Chambésy 4. Chambésy-Geneva: Centre Orthodoxe, 1984.

The annual ecumenical symposium sponsored by the Orthodox Center near Geneva devoted its sessions of May 28-June 20, 1983 to a study of the birth of theology, theology in the Middle Ages, and different streams of Orthodox theology today in the Ecumenical Patriarchate, Romania, Greece and North America.

[928] Cleary, Donald M., ed. *The Ecumenical Dialogue at Cornell University: September 1960 - September 1962*. Ithaca, NY: Cornell United Religious Work, 1962.

In the early 1950s the Cornell United Religious Work foundation awarded a two-year grant to bring ecumenical dialogue "out of the cloistered classrooms and theological tomes into the market place." Of special interest are the contributions of Edward J. Duff, S.J., (see also [230]) narrating his experiences as an official Roman Catholic observer at the WCC general assembly in New Delhi and of George Tavard on Catholic ecumenism in Europe.

[929] Cone, James H. *Speaking the Truth: Ecumenism, Liberation, and Black Theology*. Grand Rapids: Eerdmans, 1986.

The professor of systematic theology at New York City's Union Theological Seminary includes in his more comprehensive study an important section on "Black Ecumenism and the Liberation Struggle" (pp. 142-154).

[930] Cook, Martin L. *The Open Circle: Confessional Method in Theology*. Minneapolis: Fortress, 1991.

The associate professor of religious studies at Santa Clara University argues that an analysis of epistemology in the contemporary philosophy of science is useful to clarify contemporary theological diversity. He demonstrates the confessional nature of science and the spectrum of confessional theology.

[931] Cowan, Wayne H., ed. *Facing Protestant - Roman Catholic Tensions*. New York: Association, 1960.

This pre-Vatican II volume gives the views of fourteen Protestant and Catholic churchmen on a variety of controversial themes. The result resembles more a double soliloquy rather than a real dialogue.

[932] Desseaux, Jacques Elisée. *L'oecuménisme: Réflexions doctrinales et témoignages*. Paris: Editions Fleurus, 1969.

The author served as assistant secretary for the French Catholic Bishops' Committee for Unity and as director of the Centre Unité Chrétienne in Lyons. His six chapters focus on aspects of academic and spiritual ecumenism. There is an appendix on mixed marriages. See also his historical study *La rencontre oecuménique* [933].

[933] Desseaux, Jacques Elisée. *La rencontre oecuménique: Perspectives historiques, connaissance de nos frères*. Paris: Fleurus, 1969.

This companion volume to the previous work [932] is intended as a popular work for non-specialists which focuses on historical issues. Much attention is given to the separation of the Eastern and Western churches.

[934] *Dialogue East and West*. London: Faith Press, 1963.

These six lectures were delivered at a conference organized by the Fellowship of St. Alban and St. Sergius in Oxford, March 10, 1962. Orthodox, Anglican and Catholic churches were represented.

[935] *L'Eglise en dialogue*. Paris: Le Centurion, 1962.

This series was founded by the former bishop of Strasbourg, L.A. Elchinger while still a parish priest. This volume contains talks given in the program "Humanités chrétiennes" in November 1961. The four talks are by ecumenical experts: Paul Evdokimov, Bishop Cassien [Serge Besobrasoff], Marc Boegner, and Bernhard Alfrink.

[936] Froehlich, Karlfried, ed. *Ökumene: Möglichkeiten und Grenzen heute*. Tübingen: Mohr-Siebeck, 1982.

All of the essays are published in German but include submissions by non-German authors from a variety of confessional backgrounds. Especially useful among these eighteen contributions are those that study ecumenism in relationship to the Bohemian Reform, the Waldensian diaspora, and the "third world." The volume was presented to Oscar Cullmann on his eightieth birthday. See also [937].

[937] Froehlich, Karlfried, ed. *Testimonia oecumenica in honorem Oscar Cullmann octogenarii die XXV Februarii A.D. MCMLXXXII*. Tübingen: Refo-druck H. Volger, 1982.

Poorly bound and produced cheaply by photo-offset, this second

*Festschrift* includes a life of Cullmann (K. Froehlich) and a series of essays by Catholics and Protestants inspired by his research. Besides photographs there is also a two page tribute from colleagues and friends. See also [936].

[938] Greenspun, William B., and Norgren, William, eds. *Living Room Dialogues*. New York: National Council of Christian Churches; Glen Rock, NJ: Paulist, 1965.

The first of several volumes that contains non-technical discussions of how Orthodox, Protestants and Catholics might share their religious beliefs in informal settings. See also [939, 962].

[939] Greenspun, William B., and Wedel, Cynthia C., eds. *Second Living Room Dialogues*. New York: Friendship, 1967.

A continuation of a resource tool intended to facilitate informal exchange among separated Christians. The eight topics include discussion of the generation gap, human dignity, war and peace. See also [938, 962].

[940] Hild, Helmut; Hübner, Christian; and Appel, André. *Ökumene verändert die Kirchen*. Göttingen: Vandenhoeck und Ruprecht, 1976.

This brief 50 page collection gives three accounts of changes in Protestant and Catholic relations since the beginning of the modern ecumenical movement.

[941] Ishida, Yoshiro; Meyer, Harding; Perret, Edmond. *The History and Theological Concerns of World Confessional Families*. LWF Report 5. Stuttgart: Kreuz, 1979.

This account of the nature and activities of the World Confessional Families distinguishes between narrow confessionalism and confessionality that seeks to preserve one's specific historic confession to enrich the wider community of faith.

[942] *Itinéraires oecuméniques: Piste de recherches à l'intention des paroisses*. Geneva: Labor et Fides, 1982.

This Swiss text was prepared as a working document by three groups: the Conseil de la Fédération des Eglises Protestantes, the

Conférence épiscopale catholique-romaine, and the Conseil synodal de l'Eglise catholique chrétienne. In seven chapters it explores ways to promote ecumenism in local parishes.

[943] Küng, Hans, ed. *The Future of Ecumenism*. Concilium 44. New York: Paulist, 1969.

Eight writers, including bishops and theologians, address the question how ecumenism could be promoted in the 1970s. There is detailed documentation of ecumenical experiments in eleven specific countries.

[944] Leuba, Jean-Louis, and Stirnimann, Heinrich, eds. *Freiheit in der Begegnung: Zwischenbilanz des ökumenischen Dialogs*. Frankfurt: J. Knecht, 1969.

This volume was offered to Otto Karrer on his eightieth birthday and includes a list of his writings between 1959 and 1968. There are twenty-one essays covering numerous aspects of the ecumenical movement.

[945] Manns, Peter. *Dialog und Anerkennung: Hansfried Krüger zu Ehren*. Beiheft zur Ökumenischen Rundschau, 37. Frankfurt: O. Lembeck, 1980.

The honoree served as editor of the *Ökumenische Rundschau* [141] from 1956 and since 1954 had attended all the important international ecumenical meetings. Fourteen essays all in German are included. Of special interest are two: the social-political engagement of the WCC as a challenge to ecclesiology (H. Dietzfelbinger), and Roman Catholic membership in national councils of churches (B. Meeking).

[946] Meinhold, Peter. *Ökumenische Kirchenkunde: Lebensformen der Christenheit heute*. Stuttgart: Kreuz, 1962.

In this massive 652 page work based on years of research at the University of Kiel, the author outlines in ten chapters the distinctiveness of the major Christian bodies and suggests what each church could contribute not merely to its own confession but to the church universal.

[947] *The Nature of the Church and the Role of Theology*. Geneva: World Council of Churches, 1976.

These papers were prepared for a consultation between the WCC and the Reformed Ecumenical Council (formerly Synod), Geneva, 1975. The REC is a council of some thirty Reformed and Presbyterian churches in some eighteen countries.

[948] *Pluralisme et oecuménisme en recherches théologiques: Mélanges offerts au R.P. [Stanislas] Dockx, O.P.* Bibliotheca Ephermeridum Theologicarum Lovaniensium 43. Paris: Duculot, 1976.

For this 314 page *Festschrift*, twenty-one Lutheran, Orthodox, Reformed and Catholic scholars collaborate to comment on church history, sacraments and ministries, fundamental theology, and science and theology.

[949] Richter, Hans-Friedemann, ed. *Die kommende Ökumene: Theologische Untersuchungen.* Wuppertal: Brockhaus, 1972.

For this *Festschrift* in honor of Professor J.W. Winterhager, there are twenty-six various contributions on either social issues or on the history and theory of ecumenism. The book appeared during the twenty-fifth anniversary of the founding of the Ecumenical Seminar at the Kirchliche Hochschule Berlin.

[950] Segretariato Attività Ecumeniche, ed. *Ecumenismo e dialogo delle culture [Atti della XXVI Sessione di formazione ecumenica organizzata dal S.A.E., 1988].* Naples: Dehoniane, 1989.

This particular meeting of the Italian Ecumenical Association, under the presidency of Maria Vingiani, attracted a wide diversity of backgrounds. Four major addresses were given. Also included are round-table discussions, biblical reflections, and summaries of small group explorations.

[951] Segretariato Attività Ecumeniche, ed. *Ecumenismo oggi: Bilancio e prospettive [Atti della XIII Sessione di formazione ecumenica organizzata dal S.A.E., 1975].* Leumann-Turin: Elle Di Ci, 1975.

This is one of the more valuable volumes in the series of published acta of the Italian Ecumenical Association's meeting. It contains the views of Catholic, Orthodox, Anglican and Protestant theologians on doctrinal convergences and problems. There is an especially useful overview of the ecumenical situation in Italy.

[952] Séguy, Jean. *Les conflits du dialogue*. Paris: Editions du Cerf, 1973.

This study of ecumenical attitudes has a sociological focus. It analyzes resistance to ecumenism among Catholics, members of sects and neo-Pentecostals. It also explores the impact of ecumenical "informal groups" on unity movements.

[953] Sesboüé, Bernard. *Pour une théologie oecuménique: Eglise et sacrements, Eucharistie et ministères, la Vièrge Marie*. Cogitatio Fidei 160. Paris: Editions du Cerf, 1990.

The Jesuit collaborator who has been active for more than twenty years in the Group of Les Dombes has gathered into this volume some nineteen previously published essays on conversion, communio ecclesiology, apostolic ministry, and devotion to Mary. The 424 page volume typifies much of the finest in contemporary French Catholic theology.

[954] Thils, Gustave. *La "Théologie oecuménique": Notion, formes, démarches*. Bibliotheca Ephemeridum Theologicarum Lovaniensium, XVI. Louvain: E. Warny, 1960.

This astonishingly rich, though brief (83 pp.) pioneer work (1st ed. 1955) already reflects the influence of the WCC, as well as Protestant and Catholic ecumenists (especially Y. Congar and M. Villain). It identifies ecumenical theology as "existential confrontation", as a "dimension" of all theology, but also as a "particular discipline." See also [1007].

[955] Thomas, M.M. *Risking Christ for Christ's Sake: Towards an Ecumenical Theology of Pluralism*. Geneva: World Council of Churches, 1987.

The Indian ecumenist provides a survey of Catholic and Protestant approaches to pluralism especially in relationship to the writings of Raymond Pannikar and Paul Devanandan, two Indian Christians belonging respectively to the Catholic and Protestant context.

[956] Trautwein, Ursula and Dieter; and Gollin, Heidi and Jochen. *Mehr Hoffnung, mehr Einheit: Fünf Kapitel für den ökumenischen Hausgebrauch: eine Arbeitshilfe für die Gemeindepraxis*. Freiburg: Christophorus; Gelnhausen: Burckhardthaus, 1975.

Unfortunately there is no English equivalent to this creative
resource book (418 pp.) for use in home and local congregation.
The authors, two Protestant couples, working in the greater
Frankfurt area, prepared this aid for German churches with some
help from the Catholic theologian Karl Lehmann. The workbook
suggests liturgical services and questions for discussion groups.
See also Gleixner [61].

[957] Vischer, Lukas. *Ökumenische Skizzen: Zwölf Beiträge.*
Frankfurt: O. Lembeck, 1972.

Vischer, former secretary of the Faith and Order Commission,
collected here twelve essays previously published in journals.
Seven refer to ecumenical dialogue; five refer to the universality
of the church and the ecumenical movement.

[958] Wacker, Paulus. *Theologie als ökumenischer Dialog: Herman
Schell und die ökumenische Situation der Gegenwart.* Munich: F.
Schöningh, 1964.

This work on German ecumenist Herman Schell (1850-1906) was
sponsored by the Johann Adam Möhler Institute for Ecumenics
in Paderborn. It reproduces a *Habilitationsschrift* presented at
Würzburg. Especially useful is the chapter "Ecclesiology and
Ecumenical Dialogue" (pp. 271-392).

[959] Wallner, Leo, and Karner, Peter, eds. *Ökumene zum Weitergeben:
Ökumenische Morgenfeier im ORF.* Innsbruck: Tyrolia, 1980.

This book contains highlights from an ecumenical morning
broadcast series on Austrian Radio (ORF) from 1968 to 1980.
Wallner (Catholic) and Karner (Protestant) together exchanged
views about church dividing issues and ended each discussion
with a prayer.

[960] Wieser, Thomas, ed. *A Dialogue in the Transit Lounge of the
Ecumenical Movement.* Geneva: World Council of Churches, 1986.

This symposium in honor of Philip Potter's retirement from the
WCC in 1984 had as its theme cultures in dialogue. The topic is
organized into three sections: one earth, cultural transformation,
and action and icon (the "sacrament of ethics").

[961] Willaime, Jean-Paul. *Vers de nouveaux oecuménismes: les*

*paradoxes contemporains de l'oecuménisme: recherches d'unité et quête d'identité*. Paris: Editions du Cerf, 1989.

Produced in association with the Center for the Sociology of Protestantism at Strasbourg, this volume seeks to explain the sociological reasons for the shift in contemporary ecumenism. The author speaks of a secularization of ecumenism and identifies ethical heresy instead of doctrinal heresy.

[962] Young, James J. ed. and comp. *Bring Us Together: Third Living Room Dialogues*. Paramus, NJ: Paulist; New York: Friendship, 1970.

This volume, third in a series, continues the work begun under the auspices of the National Council of Christian Churches and the Confraternity of Christian Doctrine. This work suggests ways for Christian denominations to come to grips with cultural upheavals and to achieve conscientization. See also [938-939].

# Church in Ecumenical Perspective

[963] Académie internationale des sciences religieuses. *La portée de l'Eglise des apôtres pour l'Eglise d'aujourd'hui*. Brussels: Office Internationale de Librairie, 1974.

This volume contains the eight addresses given at the Ecumenical Colloquium held in Bologna, April 10-13, 1973 by Lutheran, Reformed, Orthodox and Catholic theologians. Theme of the meeting was the normative function of the apostolic church for today.

[964] Alberigo, Giuseppe, ed. *Les Eglises après Vatican II: Dynamisme et prospective. Actes du colloque international de Bologne, 1980*. Théologie historique 61. Paris: Beauchesne, 1981.

This volume which also appeared simultaneously in Italian contains the proceedings of an ecumenical symposium organized by the Institute for Religious Studies in Bologna, April 8-12, 1980. There are 18 contributions which touch on a variety of ecclesiological themes of interest especially to Catholics and Orthodox.

[965] Bäumer, Remigius, and Dolch, Heimo, eds. *Volk Gottes: Zum Kirchenverständnis der katholischen, evangelischen und anglikanischen Theologie. Festgabe für Josef Höfer*. Freiburg: Herder, 1967.

On the occasion of Höfer's seventieth birthday, a group of his colleagues collaborated to produce this *Festschrift*. Three essays are pertinent to ecumenism: ecumenical dialogue according to *Lumen gentium* (E. Schlink); early history of Lutheran/Catholic rapprochement (H. Asmussen); and the ecclesiology of the Faith and Order Commission compared to that of Vatican II. Also included is a bibliographical autobiography by the honoree (pp. 743-760).

[966] Baillargeon, Gaëtan. *Perspectives orthodoxes sur l'Eglise-Communion: L'oeuvre de Jean Zizioulas*. Montreal: Paulines; Paris: Médiaspaul, 1989.

This first major study of the ecclesiology of Orthodox ecumenist John Zizioulas is here undertaken by a Quebec Catholic theologian. The volume, based on a doctoral dissertation at the Institut Catholique de Paris, includes a special assessment of ecumenical perspectives in the Orthodox ecclesiologist. There is a list of his publications up to 1987 (pp. 395-403).

[967] Bea, Augustin. *The Church and Mankind*. Trans. by James Brand. London: Geoffrey Chapman; Chicago: Franciscan Herald, 1967.

This collection of eleven essays was originally published in Italian as *La Chiesa e l'umanità* (1967) which focuses on issues such as relationships between church and human society, individuals and those in authority, local churches and world-wide church. This volume was conceived as a continuation of *Unity in Freedom* (1964).

[968] Beinert, Wolfgang. *Um das dritte Kirchenattribut: Die Katholizität der Kirche im Verständnis der evangelisch-lutherischen und römisch-katholischen Theologie der Gegenwart*. 2 vols. Koinonia, Bd. 5. Essen: Ludgerus Verlag Hubert Wingen, 1964.

This is a definitive study of the concept of catholicity as applied to the church. Volume one begins with a lengthy analysis of the term "catholic" in the patristic and pre-Reformation periods as well as in early and classic Lutheranism. Volume two focuses on the Roman Catholic teaching. The scope is largely restricted to European theologians.

[969] Bermejo, Luis M. *Towards Christian Reunion: Vatican I, Obstacles and Opportunities*. Anand, India: Gujarat Sahitya Prakash,

1984.

As a contribution to the contemporary ecumenical dialogue, the Jesuit professor at the Pontifical Athenaeum in Pune wrote this reassessment of Vatican I (1869-1870) in light of its subsequent reception and non-reception. He also reviews the work of ARCIC-I's *Final Report* and relations with the Protestant communities.

[970] Bilaterale Arbeitsgruppe, ed., *Kirchengemeinschaft in Wort und Sakrament*. Paderborn: Bonifatius; Hannover: Lutherisches Verlagshaus, 1984.

The working group, established in 1976, is made up of representatives from the Catholic Deutsche Bischofskonferenz and the leadership of the Vereinigte Evangelisch-Lutherische Kirche Deutschland (VELKD). Its document on the notion of *koinonia* is 90 pages long. Most of the writing was done by H.J. Urban, A. Mauder and M. Kiessig.

[971] Bühlmann, Walbert. *Weltkirche: Neue Dimensionen, Modell für das Jahr 2001*. Graz: Styria, 1984.

The Swiss Roman Catholic author describes the move away from Western church hegemony to world-church contexts. His model for a church in A.D. 2001 calls for structural changes and a new vision of unity. The volume closes with a postscript by Karl Rahner on pastoral ministry for the future (pp. 220-234).

[972] Centre Orthodoxe du Patriarchat Oecuménique, Chambésy-Geneva. *Eglise locale et église universelle*. Etudes théologiques de Chambésy 1. Chambésy-Geneva: Centre Orthodoxe, 1981.

The first in a series of annual conferences under the sponsorship of the Orthodox Center near Geneva was devoted to the relationship between local churches and the world wide church. Twenty-one talks in French, German and Greek are here reproduced from a variety of ecclesial perspectives.

[973] *Church and World: The Unity of the Church and the Renewal of Human Community*. Faith and Order Paper 151. Geneva: World Council of Churches, 1990.

This text represents over six years labor by the Faith and Order

Study Program on "The Unity of the Church and the Renewal of Human Community." It invites Christians to assume a more holistic approach to ecumenism. The study concludes with a short but good bibliography (pp. 80-86).

[974] *Church as Communion*. London: Catholic Truth Society; Church House, 1991.

This booklet contains the second agreed statement of the continuation of the Anglican-Roman Catholic International Commission (ARCIC-II) on the theme of *koinonia*. See also ARCIC-II's statement on salvation [1020] and the final report of ARCIC-I [632].

[975] D'ercole, Giuseppe, and Stickler, Alfons M., eds. *Comunione interecclesiale, collegialità - primato - ecumenismo*. 2 vols. Communio 12-13. Rome: LAS, 1972.

The volumes contain the acts of the first international congress on the concept "care for all churches" (*sollicitudo omnium ecclesiarum*), held Sept. 25-30, 1971 in Rome. The term is traced to Leo the Great. Twenty-one studies in a variety of European languages on various aspects of *communio* are presented in a way that anticipates some of Vatican II.

[976] Dejaifve, Georges. *Un tournant décisif de l'ecclésiologie à Vatican II*. Le point théologique 31. Paris: Beauchesne, 1978.

The late Belgian Jesuit ecclesiologist published this volume that analyzes the paradigm shifts from Vatican I to Vatican II especially as they bear upon the possibility of church reunion.

[977] Dejaifve, Georges. *L'Eglise de Vatican I à Vatican II*. Rome: Pontifical Oriental Institute, 1976.

The volume contains reprints of articles mostly from the journal *Nouvelle Revue Théologique* from 1959 to 1966 studying Catholic ecclesiology especially as affected by ecumenical concerns.

[978] Dejaifve, Georges. *Una Sancta et confessions chrétiennes*. Rome: Pontifical Oriental Institute, 1977.

The volume contains reprints of articles on ecumenism published from 1952 to 1976. Special attention is given to relations between the Orthodox and Catholic churches.

[979] Dulles, Avery. *The Catholicity of the Church*. Oxford: Clarendon, 1985.

This book formed the 1983 Martin D'Arcy Lectures given at Campion Hall, Oxford. The American Jesuit ecclesiologist reviews the vast literature on the catholicity of the church and offers many new insights into the note's significance. One chapter explores whether Catholic and Protestant are contrary or complementary notions.

[980] Dulles, Avery. *Models of the Church*. 2nd rev. ed. Garden City, NY: Doubleday, 1987.

This volume since its first edition in 1974 has had conspicuous impact especially in the North American context. By showing how ecclesiology draws upon six distinctive models of church, as institution, mystical communion, sacrament, herald, servant and disciple, the author grounds a legitimate amount of theological and ecclesial pluralism.

[981] Erni, Raymund. *Die Kirche in orthodoxer Schau: Ein Beitrag zum ökumenischen Gespräch*. Fribourg, Switzerland: Kanisius, 1980.

The Swiss Catholic expert on Eastern theology describes Orthodox ecclesiology as eucharistic, trinitarian and pneumatological. He then comments on the impact that this theology of church has in the various forms of ecumenical dialogue among the Orthodox.

[982] Facoltà Teologica Interregionale Milano. *L'ecclesiologia dal Vaticano I al Vaticano II*. Brescia: La Scuola, 1973.

A theological symposium was held in Gazzada in 1970 to compare the ecclesiologies of the two Vatican Councils. The contributors, all Roman Catholic, were: G. Thils, A. Anton, G. Dejaifve, C. Vagaggini, U. Betti, W. de Vries and J. Hamer.

[983] Flew, R. Newton, ed. *The Nature of the Church: Papers Presented to the Theological Commission Appointed by the Continuation Committee of the World Conference on Faith and Order*. London: SCM, 1952.

This collaborative study undertaken by Protestants, Catholics,

Orthodox and members of the Free Church explores the essence of church in preparation for the upcoming Faith and Order meeting in Lund (1952).

[984] Fuerth, Patrick W. *The Concept of Catholicity in the Documents of the World Council of Churches 1948-1968: A Historical Study with Systematic-Theological Reflections.* Studia Anselmiana 60. Rome: Anselmiana, 1973.

Using primary sources and material from the WCC archives, this Canadian Catholic painstakingly analyzes the concept of catholicity from the first general assembly in Amsterdam through Uppsala.

[985] Gassmann, Günther, and Norgaard-Hojen, Peder, eds. *Einheit der Kirche: Neue Entwicklungen und Perspektiven: Harding Meyer zum 60. Geburtstag in Dankbarkeit und Anerkennung.* Frankfurt: O. Lembeck, 1988.

Thirteen colleagues of Harding Meyer published these studies in English, French and German on the unity of the church. The essays represent both Protestant and Catholic viewpoints. There is a list of the honoree's publications (pp. 164-177).

[986] Hahn, Ferdinand; Kertelge, Karl; Schnackenburg, Rudolf. *Einheit der Kirche: Grundlegung im Neuen Testament.* Quaestiones disputatae 84. Freiburg: Herder, 1979.

The three authors discuss the New Testament concept of *koinonia* and its importance for our present-day understanding of church unity.

[987] Hauschild, Wolf-Dieter; Nicolaisen, Carsten; and Wendebourg, D., eds. *Kirchengemeinschaft: Anspruch und Wirklichkeit: Festschrift Georg Kretschmar.* Stuttgart: Calwer, 1986.

The volume, a product of ecumenical cooperation, contains seventeen major studies by Germans on New Testament, patristic, historical and systematic aspects of church fellowship. Also included is a short biography of the honoree and a list of his publications.

[988] Herms, Eilert. *Von der Glaubenseinheit zur Kirchengemeinschaft: Pladoyer für eine realistische Ökumene.* Marburger Theologische

Studien 27. Marburg: N.G. Elwert, 1989.

Reflecting on several decades of ecumenical exchanges, the German scholar argues for a move from a unity in faith to a communion of churches. This still requires some paradigm shifts in Christian thinking.

[989] *In Each Place: Towards a Fellowship of Local Churches Truly United.* Geneva: World Council of Churches, 1977.

At the request of the Nairobi assembly, a small consultation was held in December 1976 in Geneva to study the ambiguous notion "local church." The booklet spells out the meeting's final report (pp. 3-12) and give four confessionally different background papers on the concept. Some examples from five different countries are cited.

[990] Johann-Adam-Möhler Institut, ed. *Die Sakramentalität der Kirche in der ökumenischen Diskussion. Referate und Diskussion eines Symposions anlässlich des 25 jährigen Bestehens des Johann-Adam-Möhler-Institut.* Paderborn: Bonifatius, 1983.

In March 1982 the Institute for Ecumenics, founded in 1957 by Lorenz Jaeger, celebrated its twenty-fifth anniversary. Five major addresses delivered then on the sacramental character of the church, as seen by Catholics, Orthodox and Protestants, are here reproduced.

[991] Küng, Hans. *The Church.* Trans. by Ray and Rosaleen Ockenden. New York: Sheed and Ward, 1967.

Perhaps the single most influential Catholic work of ecclesiology since Vatican II, this work appeared originally in German in the same year. The volume is markedly stamped with the perspectives of Vatican II and reflects a close familiarity with Reformation theology.

[992] *Laity Formation: Proceedings of the Ecumenical Consultation, Gazzada (Italy), September 7th-10th, 1965.* Rome: COPECIAL, 1966.

The informal ecumenical consultation on training of the laity was jointly sponsored by the WCC's Department on the laity and the Roman Catholic Permanent Committee for International Congresses of the Lay Apostolate (COPECIAL). This volume contains five addresses and summaries of the working groups' discussions.

[993] Leenhardt, Franz-J. *L'Eglise: Questions aux protestants et aux catholiques*. Geneva: Labor et Fides, 1978.

The former professor of New Testament and ecumenist at the University of Geneva composed these fourteen chapters with heavy biblical emphasis. Included are studies on *diakonia*, unity, and the ministry of unity in the New Testament.

[994] Lehmann, Karl. *Gemeinde*; Kauffmann, Franz-Xaver, et al. *Kirche*; Fries, Heinrich. *Konfessionen und Ökumene*. Christlicher Glaube in moderner Gesellschaft, Teilband 29. Freiburg: Herder, 1982.

The last part of this thirty volume mini-encyclopedia includes studies on community, church, and confessions in an ecumenical age.

[995] Lell, Joachim, and Menne, Ferdinand W., eds. *Religiöse Gruppen: Alternativen in Grosskirchen und Geselleschaft: Berichte, Meinungen, Materialien*. Düsseldorf: Patmos; Göttingen: Vandenhoeck und Ruprecht, 1976.

The volume reports on an ecumenical project undertaken at the instigation of the Deutscher Ökumenische Studienausschuss (DÖSTA) comparing participation in large churches versus small religious groups (pp.11-78). This is followed by a number of reactions and a series of background papers. There is a lengthy bibliography on the theme (pp. 183-204).

[996] Lessing, Eckhard. *Kirche - Recht - Ökumene: Studien zur Ekklesiologie*. Unio und Confessio, Bd. 8. Bielefeld: Luther Verlag, 1982.

The author offers a basic ecclesiology inspired by Lutheran theology and practice in light of modern ecumenism. He also draws upon the ecclesial convictions implicit in the Leuenberger Konkordie [779-786].

[997] Lubac, Henri de. *The Motherhood of the Church; Particular Churches in the Universal Church*. Trans. by Sister Sergia Englund. San Francisco: Ignatius, 1982.

These two separate studies were published in reverse order for the French original (1971). In his study of particular (or local) churches, the late Cardinal manifested his uneasiness with many structural changes in the Catholic Church since Vatican II.

[998] Madey, Johannes. *Die Kirche in der Sicht der Christenheit des Ostens und des Westens: Ein orthodox-katholisches Symposium.* Konfessionskundliche Schriften des Johann-Adam-Möhler Instituts für Ökumenik 12. Paderborn: Bonifatius, 1974.

The small book reports on a meeting in Paderborn of the working group "Begegnung mit den Kirchen des Ostens" held in October 1973. Six authors, Oriental Orthodox, Orthodox, and Catholic, describe their own communion's understanding of church and prospects for church unity.

[999] Mudge, Lewis S. *One Church: Catholic and Reformed Towards a Theology for Ecumenical Decision.* Philadelphia: Westminster, 1963.

The American member of the Reformed Church of Christ provides five chapters written at the WCC's headquarters. He addresess the role of theology for ecumenical decision, conciliar experiments, and the Reformation in church history.

[1000] Scharbert, Josef, ed. *Zum Thema: Eine Kirche, eine Menschheit.* Stuttgart: KBW, 1971.

These eight essays and three documents of an ecumenical working group address the question what role the church should play in helping to achieve God's intention to unify the world, a question also raised by Faith and Order at Bristol (1967).

[1001] Segretariato Attività Ecumeniche, ed. *La Chiesa mistero e signo di unità [Atti della II Sessione e della III Sessione di formazione ecumenica organizzata dal S.A.E., 1965].* Brescia: Morcelliana, 1966.

By way of exception this year's meeting of the Italian Ecumenical Association was held in two sessions. The theme of the meetings was the church as mystery of faith and as sign of unity.

[1002] Segretariato Attività Ecumeniche, ed. *Comunità locale ed ecumenismo [Atti della X Sessione di formazione ecumenica organizzata dal S.A.E., 1972].* Rome: Editrice A.V.E., 1973.

The acts of the tenth meeting of the Italian Ecumenical Association contain papers on local church and ecumenism, as well as reports on nine basic Christian communities in Italy, and summaries of discussions in small groups.

[1003] Segretariato Attività Ecumeniche, ed. *Laici, laicità, Popolo di Dio: l'ecumenismo in questione [Atti della XXV Sessione di formazione ecumenica organizzata dal S.A.E., 1987]*. Naples: Dehoniane, 1986.

The proceedings of this meeting of the S.A.E. contain three major addresses by L. Sartori, C.M. Martini, and G. Alberigo. Lay persons participated in the round table discussion which is here summarized.

[1004] Segretariato Attività Ecumeniche, ed. *Morte e risurrezione in prospettiva del Regno [Atti della XVIII Sessione di formazione ecumenica organizzata dal S.A.E., 1980]*. Leumann-Turin: Elle Di Ci, 1981.

The 1980 meeting of the Italian Ecumenical Association heard six presentations on the relationship of death and resurrection to the reign of God. Various Orthodox, Catholics and Baptists responded. Some 350 participants were in attendance.

[1005] Segretariato Attività Ecumeniche, ed. *Il Regno di Dio che viene [Atti della XIV Sessione di formazione ecumenica organizzata dal S.A.E., 1976]*. Leumann-Turin: Elle Di Ci, 1977.

The 1976 meeting of the Italian Ecumenical Association was devoted to the biblical, historical and liturgical significance of the notion "the coming kingdom of God."

[1006] Segretariato Attività Ecumeniche, ed. *Regno come comunione [Atti della XVII Sessione di formazione ecumenica organizzata dal S.A.E., 1979]*. Leumann-Turin: Elle Di Ci, 1980.

For this investigation of the biblical notion of communion, the Italian Ecumenical Association invited Catholics, Baptists, Waldensians, Methodists and a rabbi to present complementary perspectives. Even an interconfessional married couple (Catholic/Orthodox) was asked to speak.

[1007] Thils, Gustave. *L'Eglise et les églises: perspectives nouvelles en oecuménisme*. Paris: Desclée de Brouwer, 1967.

A Roman Catholic professor at the Catholic University of Louvain and a major influence at Vatican II wrote this work on the church of Christ and the Christian churches; the "elements" or "notes" of the church (especially holiness); and Catholic ecclesiology before the encyclical *Mystici corporis* (1943). See also [954].

[1008] Thurian, Max. *Aux sources de l'Eglise: Tradition et renouveau dans l'Esprit*. Taizé: Presses de Taizé, 1977.

This very important work contains five reflective essays on: the visible and invisible church; the Bible and tradition; the priesthood; eucharistic sacrifice; and Mary and the church. Thurian also includes a letter he wrote in 1957 in which he outlined as a member of the Reformed Church how he saw the "spiritual and ecumenical characteristics of Catholicism."

[1009] Tillard, Jean-Marie R. *Eglise d'Eglises: L'ecclésiologie de communion*. Cogitatio Fidei 143. Paris: Editions du Cerf, 1987.

The well known Dominican ecumenist and long time Catholic collaborator in the WCC's Faith and Order Commission published this 415 page work on ecclesiology that reflects his involvement with the Orthodox and Anglican international dialogues. The book's four divisions are: the church in God's design, communion among the people of God, the ministry for communion, and the visible communion of the churches.

[1010] Valeske, Ulrich. *Votum Ecclesiae*. I. Teil: *Das Ringen um die Kirche in der neueren römisch-katholischen Theologie*; II. Teil: *Interkonfessionelle ekklesiologische Bibliographie*. Munich: Claudius, 1962.

This work prepared at Göttingen's Evangelical Theology Faculty in the 1950s is now considerably outdated. The bibliography of English, French, German and Dutch works (II, pp. 1-210) is not well indexed although it follows an elaborate organizational schema.

[1011] Wagner, Harald. *Die eine Kirche und die vielen Kirchen: Ekklesiologie und Symbolik beim jungen Möhler*. Beiträge zur ökumenischen Theologie 16. Munich: F. Schöningh, 1977.

This *Habilitationsschrift* for the Catholic Theology Faculty at Munich under the direction of H. Fries establishes that J.A. Möhler, as early as 1825, was already researching confessionally divisive issues. He was familiar with the writings of Schelling and Schliermacher. The author also discusses modern perspectives on the same issues and provides an extensive bibliography.

[1012] Weissgerber, Hans. *Die Frage nach der wahren Kirche: Eine Untersuchung zu den ekklesiologischen Problemen der ökumenischen Bewegung.* Koinonia, Bd. 13. Essen: Ludgerus Verlag Hubert Wingen, 1963.

These reflections are based on the author's three years association with the Lutheran World Federation in Geneva and as lecturer in ecumenism at Göttingen. The three sections address historical and confessional presuppositions (the section on Catholicism is rather outdated), the church and its unity, and finally church, office and sacrament.

[1013] Wieh, Hermann. *Konzil und Gemeinde: Eine systematisch-theologische Untersuchung zum Gemeindeverständnis des Zweiten Vatikanischen Konzils in pastoraler Absicht.* Frankfurter Theologische Studien Bd. 25. Frankfurt: J. Knecht, 1978.

Prepared as a doctoral dissertation at the Catholic Theology Faculty of the University of Münster under P. Hünermann, this work analyzes the history of the term community (*Gemeinde*) and its gradual institutionalization; the concept in the preparatory documents of Vatican II; its use in the conciliar texts.

[1014] Winterhager, Jürgen Wilhelm. *Weltwerdung der Kirche: die ökumenische Bewegung als hermeneutische Ausgabe.* Zürich: Gotthelf, 1964.

The author worked for years with Dietrich Bonhoeffer on various commissions and also collaborated with Faith and Order. These thirteen reflective essays on ecumenism and the church are well informed, international in scope and well indexed.

# Other Doctrinal Issues
## Grace and Justification

[1015] Anderson, H. George; Murphy, T. Austin; Burgess, Joseph A., eds. *Justification by Faith*. Lutherans and Catholics in Dialogue 7. Minneapolis: Augsburg, 1985.

This is the seventh agreed statement in the series of US Lutheran/Catholic bilateral consultations. There are also sixteen background papers. See also [1019].

[1016] Küng, Hans. *Justification: The Doctrine of Karl Barth and a Catholic Reflection*. Trans. by T. Collins, E. Tolk, D. Granskou. New York: Thomas Nelson, 1964.

The original German edition *Rechtfertigung* appeared in 1957 with an introductory letter by Karl Barth. Küng's analysis of Barth's doctrine on righteousness is compared with the Catholic teaching formulated at the Council of Trent and later. It is argued that both positions are not in fact inimicable but are basically compatible.

[1017] Moeller, Charles, and Philips, Gérard. *The Theology of Grace and the Oecumenical Movement*. Trans. by R.A. Wilson. London: Mowbray; Paterson, NJ: St. Anthony's Guild, 1961.

A secret ecumenical meeting took place at Chevetogne in 1953 to discuss the theology of grace. The first five chapters report the views of the committee members (now identified). The final chapter summarizes Moeller's assessments. The French original *Grâce et oecuménisme* appeared in 1957.

[1018] Pöhlmann, Horst Georg. *Rechtfertigung: Die gegenwärtige kontroverstheologische Problematik der Rechtfertigungslehre zwischen der evangelisch-lutherischen und der römisch-katholischen Kirche*. Gütersloh: Gerd Mohn, 1971.

This 1969 Heidelberg *Habilitationsschrift* by a Lutheran pastor treats the historical and doctrinal issues associated with justification.

[1019] Reumann, John, ed. *"Righteousness" in the New Testament: "Justification" in the United States Lutheran - Roman Catholic Dialogue*. Philadelphia: Fortress; New York: Paulist, 1982.

These biblical essays are part of the background studies prepared from 1978 to 1981 to assist in the formulation of a common statement on justification by Lutherans and Catholics in the USA

[1015]. The lengthy study by John Reumann (pp. 1-192) is responded to by Joseph Fitzmyer (193-227); Jerome Quinn then describes the concept in the Catholic Epistles (229-238).

**[1020]** *Salvation and the Church.* London: Catholic Truth Society; Church House, 1987.

This booklet contains the first agreed statement of the second Anglican Roman Catholic International Commissision (ARCIC-II) on salvation. It includes an introduction by the co-chairs Cormac Murphy-O'Connor and Mark Santer. See the second agreed statement [974] and the final report of ARCIC-I [632].

**[1021]** Tavard, George H. *Justification: An Ecumenical Study.* New York: Paulist, 1983.

Drawing upon his participation in the US Lutheran/Catholic Consultation's effort to achieve an agreed statement on justification, the Catholic professor and ecumenist argues that Luther's doctrine is accurate and profound. He even suggests that Luther be called a doctor of the church. See also [1015].

## Apostolic Faith Today

**[1022]** Abbt, Imelda, and Jager, Alfred. *Weltoffenheit des christlichen Glaubens: Fritz Buri zu Ehren.* Bern: Haupt; Tübingen: Katzmann, 1987.

This *Festschrift* in honor of Fritz Buri (1907-  ) contains a number of philosophical essays and reflections on interreligious dialogue. J. Hersch contributes an essay in French on Christian ecumenical efforts looked at from the viewpoint of a non-Christian. There is also a list of Buri's writings from 1932 to 1987.

**[1023]** Centre Orthodoxe du Patriarchat Oecuménique, Chambésy-Geneva. *La signification et l'actualité du IIe Concile oecuménique pour le monde chrétien d'aujourd'hui.* Etudes théologiques de Chambésy 2. Chambésy-Geneva: Centre Orthodoxe, 1982.

To mark the sixteenth centenary of the second ecumenical council (Constantinople A.D. 381) the Orthodox Center near Geneva devoted its second annual conference in 1981 to this anniversary. A large number of talks in German, French and English from a variety of Christian confessional traditions is here published. See also [1031, 1035].

**[1024]** *Confessing the One Faith: An Ecumenical Explication of the Apostolic Faith as it is Confessed in the Nicene-Constantinopolitan Creed (381).* Faith and Order Paper 153. Rev. ed. Geneva: World Council of Churches, 1991.

This study document is the second stage in the ongoing process of preparing a more definitive text under the direction of the Apostolic Faith Today Steering Group of the WCC's Faith and Order Commission. An earlier version of the project was entitled *Confessing One Faith* (Faith and Order Paper 140, 1987).

**[1025]** *Confessing Our Faith Around the World, I-IV.* Faith and Order Papers 104, 120, 123, 126. Geneva: World Council of Churches, 1980-1985.

These contributions to the WCC's Apostolic Faith Today project describe how faith is perceived within various geographical contexts. Volume two reports on Africa, Asia, Australia, Europe and North America; volume three on the Caribbean and Central America; volume four on South America.

**[1026]** Echternach, Helmut. *Ökumenischer Glaube - - Heute: Dogmatik I.* Frankfurt: P. Lang, 1983.

The author (b. 1907) taught philosophy of religion from 1949 to 1975 at the University of Hamburg. He conceived this volume as an introduction to a longer doctrinal treatise. The fundamental and complex notion of faith is discussed from a strongly ecumenical perspective.

**[1027]** Feiner, Johannes, and Vischer, Lukas, eds. *The Common Catechism: A Book of Christian Faith.* New York: Seabury, 1974.

The German title better describes the intent of this ecumenical venture: *Neues Glaubensbuch: Der gemeinsame christliche Glaube* (1973). Over thirty-six collaborators, Protestant and Catholic, formulated a common articulation of the faith from the perspective of salvation history. A final section treats disputed questions.

**[1028]** Heim, S. Mark, ed. *Faith to Creed: Ecumenical Perspectives on the Affirmation of the Apostolic Faith in the Fourth Century.* Grand

Rapids: Eerdmans; New York: Friendship, 1991.

The monograph summarizes the Faith to Creed Consultation held in Waltham, Massachusetts, in 1989 as part of the ongoing research for the Apostolic Faith Today project. The meeting was sponsored by the Commission on Faith and Order of the National Council of Christian Churches in the USA.

[1029] Hultsch, Eric, and Lüthis, Kurt, eds. *Bekennendes Bekenntnis: Form und Formulierung christlichen Glaubens*. Gütersloh: Gerd Mohn, 1982.

Dedicated to the memory of the late professor of systematic theology at the University of Vienna, Wilhelm Dantine (1911-1981), the work was produced by fourteen collaborators. It includes a study by Dantine himself on the 450th anniversary of the Augsburg Confession [760 ff.] and one by K. Rahner on *fides qua* and *fides quae*. A list of publications by the honoree is included (pp. 231-237).

[1030] Le Guillou, M. J., *et al. Ecumenism and Religious Education*. Loyola Pastoral Series. Chicago: Loyola University, 1965.

The volume reproduces two issues of the Belgian catechetical journal *Lumen Vitae* 29 (1964) and adds two original articles. The challenge of ecumenism is described from pedagogical and psycho-sociological perspectives.

[1031] Lehmann, Karl, and Pannenberg, Wolfhart, eds. *Glaubensbekenntnis und Kirchengemeinschaft: Das Modell des Konzils von Konstantinopel (381)*. Dialog der Kirchen 1. Freiburg: Herder; Göttingen: Vandenhoeck und Ruprecht, 1982.

This is a further publication of the Ökumenischer Arbeitskreis evangelischer und katholischer Theologen. The group met in 1981 in Freiburg to commemorate the anniversary of the second ecumenical council. Besides individual essays there is a joint statement on the ecumenical significance of Constantinople I (pp. 120-125). See also [1023, 1035].

[1032] Link, Hans-Georg, ed. *Apostolic Faith Today: A Handbook for Study*. Faith and Order Paper 124. Geneva: World Council of Churches, 1985.

The present collection of texts originates in a decision of the
Faith and Order Commission to produce for the Apostolic Faith
Today Project a handbook containing texts from Lausanne (1927)
to Lima (1982) and outlines for further study. There are also
creeds from the ancient church and the sixteenth and seventeenth
centuries.

[1033] Link, Hans-Georg, ed. *One God, One Lord, One Spirit: On the
Explication of the Apostolic Faith Today*. Faith and Order Paper 139.
Geneva: World Council of Churches, 1988.

The former executive secretary of Faith and Order edited these
studies on the first three articles of the apostolic creed (Father,
Son and Spirit) as part of the on-going WCC project to explain
the "Apostolic Faith Today."

[1034] Link, Hans-Georg, ed. *The Roots of Our Common Faith: Faith
in the Scriptures and in the Early Church*. Faith and Order Paper 119.
Geneva: World Council of Churches, 1984.

This volume reports on a meeting of twenty ecumenical
theologians from different parts of the world who met in Rome,
October 1983, to explore the notion of apostolic faith in the New
Testament and early church. This project is part of the WCC
study "Toward the Common Expression of the Apostolic Faith
Today."

[1035] Piffl-Percevic, Theodor, and Stirnemann, Alfred, eds. *Das
gemeinsame Credo: 1600 Jahre seit dem Konzil von Konstantinopel*.
Pro Oriente 6. Innsbruck: Tyrolia, 1983.

The volume commemorates the anniversary of Constantinople I
(A.D. 381) with addresses given in Istanbul, Rome and Cologne.
There is also documentation regarding four bilateral consultations
between Oriental Orthodox Christians and Roman Catholics from
1971 to 1978 [627] and an account about an ecclesiological
colloquium in 1974 between Catholics and Orthodox on *koinonia*.
See also [1023, 1031].

[1036] Schlink, Edmund. *Ökumenische Dogmatik: Grundzüge*. 2nd ed.
Göttingen: Vandenhoeck und Ruprect, 1985.

This important interconfessional dogmatic theology is divided
into four parts: creation, salvation, new creation, and doctrine of

God. The Heidelberg professor relied on Professors Heinrich Fries (Catholic) and Nikos Nissiotis (Orthodox) to assist him. This is a veritable summa of ecumenical theology.

[1037] Segretariato Attività Ecumeniche, ed. *Ecumenismo e catechesi [Atti della XXIV Sessione di formazione ecumenica organizzata dal S.A.E., 1986]*. Naples: Dehoniane, 1987.

The twenty-fourth meeting of the Italian Ecumenical Association discussed how best to formulate the apostolic faith in catechisms designed for today.

[1038] *Towards a Confession of the Common Faith*. Faith and Order Paper 100. Geneva: World Council of Churches, 1980.

This short document reflects an early stage in the Apostolic Faith Today Project. It is basically the Commission's report as presented to the Joint Working Group of the Catholic Church and the WCC in 1979 and as revised in light of remarks and suggestions of a number of theologians.

# The Bible

[1039] Centre Orthodoxe du Patriarchat Oecuménique, Chambésy-Geneva. *L'Ancien Testament dans l'Eglise*. Etudes théologiques de Chambésy 8. Chambésy-Geneva: Centre Orthodoxe, 1988.

For the symposium held May 10-26, 1986, the ecumenical gathering of scholars discussed the importance of the Old Testament for the birth of Christianity, in the Fathers, and in modern currents. There is a section devoted to the meaning of the biblical creation accounts.

[1040] Cullmann, Oscar, and Karrer, Otto. *La Bible et le dialogue oecuménique*. Trans. by René Virrion. Mulhouse: Editions Salvator, 1967.

Contained in this volume are four essays, two by Catholics (Otto Karrer and Hans Urs von Balthasar) and two by Protestants (Peter Vogelsanger and Robert Leuenberger), outlining ways in which confessional adherence affects one's reading of the Bible. The German original was called *Die Bibel im Gespräch zwischen den Konfessionen*.

[1041] Flesseman-Van Leer, Ellen, ed. *The Bible: Its Authority and Interpretation in the Ecumenical Movement*. Faith and Order Paper 99. Geneva: World Council of Churches, 1980.

The 79 page study addresses issues such as guiding principles for interpreting Scripture, Scripture and tradition, hermeneutics as a challenge for ecumenism, the authority of the Bible, and the significance of the Old Testament for the New Testament.

[1042] Hedegard, David. *Ecumenism and the Bible*. Amsterdam: International Council of Christian Churches, 1954.

The title of this 251 page volume is somewhat misleading. Of the fifteen essays only the third specifically treats the Bible. Ecumenism is almost restricted to activities of the WCC. What the author presents are "ideas of the ecumenical movement in the light of the Bible."

[1043] Jones, Douglas Rawlinson. *Instruments of Peace: Biblical Principles of Christian Unity*. London: Hodder and Stoughton, 1965.

This short work explores the Bible not so much with the tools of historical critical method but with devotional conviction to discover the Scriptural foundations for church unity.

[1044] Segretariato Attività Ecumeniche, ed. *La parola di Dio e l'ecumenismo [Atti della IX Sessione di formazione ecumenica organizzata dal S.A.E., 1971]*. Rome: Editrice A.V.E., 1972.

The ninth meeting of the Italian Ecumenical Association held in Naples is reported in this volume on "the Word of God." Included are the major addresses as well as the conclusions of nine discussion groups. The Association's President is Professor Maria Vingiani.

# Christ

[1045] Asheim, Ivar, ed. *Christ and Humanity*. Philadelphia: Fortress, 1970.

This is an account of research on "The Quest for True Humanity and the Lordship of Christ" undertaken by a commission on theology of the Lutheran World Federation from 1964 to 1969. It includes studies on: the relation of Christian ethics to humanity;

critical revision of the much-discussed "doctrine of two kingdoms"; the relation of Christian ethics to existing and possible social and political orders including even revolution. The four collaborators attach a statement on "The Christian in a Post-Christian Context." The work also appeared in German as *Humanität und Herrschaft Christi: Zur ethischen Orientierung* (1969).

[1046] De Goedt, Michel. *Foi au Christ et dialogues du chrétien.* Présence du Carmel 10. Bruges: Desclée de Brouwer, 1967.

This work by a Discalced Carmelite is a reflective theological essay on the importance of dialogue and its relationship to faith in Christ.

[1047] Fries, Paul R., and Nersoyan, Tiran, eds. *Christ in East and West.* Macon, GA: Mercer University, 1987.

This volume reports on a consultation on Christology held in New York, April 26-27, 1985, by the Faith and Order Commission of the National Council of Churches (USA) with representatives of the Ancient Oriental Orthodox churches. Part one reproduces nine previously published articles on the theme; part two prints six Protestant papers prepared for the meeting. There is a concluding statement from the consultation (pp. 212-217).

[1048] Mbiti, John S., ed. *Confessing Christ in Different Cultures: Report of a Colloquium Held at the Ecumenical Institute, Bossey, 2-8 July 1977.* Geneva: World Council of Churches, 1977.

A large contingent of 110 participants explored together what the confession of faith in Jesus Christ means in the context of globalization.

[1049] Schlink, Edmund. *The Coming Christ and the Coming Church.* Trans. by I.H. Neilson, *et al.* Philadelphia: Fortress; Edinburgh: Oliver and Boyd, 1968.

This major contribution to the study of ecumenical theology was written prior to Vatican II by one who subsequently attended the Council as a Protestant observer. Among the topics treated are: dogmatic statements, Christ and the church, Protestant views on worship, apostolic succession, and East and West.

[1050] Simonson, Conrad. *The Christology of the Faith and Order Movement*. Oekumenische Studien X. Leiden: E.J. Brill, 1972.

The author compares the various stages in the Faith and Order's theology of incarnation and redemption. He describes an era of comparative Christology (1927-1948) and the post Lund period. In the later years it expanded its focus to include theological anthropology.

[1051] Torrance, Thomas F., ed. *The Incarnation: Ecumenical Studies in the Nicene-Constantinopolitan Creed A.D. 381*. Edinburgh: Handsel, 1981.

This useful ecumenical collaboration on the theology of the Incarnation originated from an international symposium held in Norwich, England, during 1978 (but whose papers were published only in 1981). Seven contributors, Orthodox, Anglican, Protestant and Catholic, explore the implications of the creed formulated in A.D. 381.

[1052] Weibel-Spirig, Rolf. *Christus und die Kirche: Das ökumenische Gespräch über die Kirche*. Zürich: Benziger, 1972.

This dissertation for the University of Fribourg, Switzerland, under the direction of H. Stirnimann, investigates the work of the commission established by Faith and Order in Lund (1952) to study "Christ and the Church" which gave its final report at Montreal in 1963. That report is compared here with similar statements by Catholic authors.

[1053] Willebrands, Johannes, and Ott, Heinrich. *Christus, Zeichen und Ursprung der Einheit in einer geteilten Welt*. Zürich: Benziger, 1970.

This 55 page booklet records an address given in December 1969 by Cardinal Willebrands to which Professor Ott responded in the Peterskirche, Zürich. Ott contrasts this exchange with the encounter in Augsburg, 1518, between Cardinal Cajetan and Professor Martin Luther.

# Holy Spirit

[1054] Académie internationale des sciences religieuses. *L'Esprit Saint et l'Eglise: L'avenir de l'Eglise et de l'oecuménisme*. Paris: Fayard, 1969.

The proceedings of this first symposium of the Académie internationale des sciences religieuses which met in Heverlee-Leuven, Belgium, in May 1966, aim to show how Catholics, Orthodox and Protestants from various countries draw upon their faith, tradition and theological heritage to understand how the relationship of the Holy Spirit and the church was seen in: Acts, Paul, liturgical prayer, Greek patristics, Augustine, and the *filioque* controversy. Other papers treat the church as epiphany, its mission, and Christian anthropology.

[1055] *Credo in Spiritum Sanctum. Atti del Congresso Teologico Internazionale di Pneumatologia.* Ed. José Saraiva-Martins. 2 vols. Vatican City: Libreria Editrice Vaticana, 1983.

These volumes make available papers given at a 1982 congress in Rome to commemorate anniversaries of two ecumenical councils: Constantinople I (1600th) and Ephesus (1550th). The 102 articles are in English, French, German, Italian and Spanish. Of all the aspects of pneumatology, the fourteen contributions on "The Holy Spirit and the Unity of Church and the Renewal of the World" are specifically ecumenical.

[1056] Davies, William Rhys. *Gathered into One: A "Charismatic" Approach to Unity.* Leighton Buzzard, UK: Faith Press, 1975.

This was the last of the "Lent Books" commissioned by Michael Ramsey as Archbishop of Canterbury before his retirement. In ten chapters on the Holy Spirit the author argued that each church, Catholic, Protestant and Pentecostal, has a special charism to contribute to the body of Christ.

[1057] Groupe des Dombes. *L'Esprit Saint, l'Eglise et les sacrements.* Taizé: Presses de Taizé, 1979.

This booklet contains the agreed statement of the Group of Les Dombes issued in 1979 on the Holy Spirit, the church and the sacraments. See also [699].

[1058] Putney, Michael E. *The Presence and Activity of the Holy Spirit in the Church, in the Studies of the Commission on Faith and Order (1927-1983).* Rome: Gregorian University, 1985.

The Australian Catholic published this 589 page doctoral dissertation under the direction of Jos Vercruysse. He studies in great detail the pneumatology explicit and implicit in the publications of Faith and Order.

[1059] Segretariato Attività Ecumeniche, ed. *Lo Spirito Santo pegno e primizia del Regno [Atti della XIX Sessione di formazione ecumenica organizzata dal S.A.E., 1981]*. Leumann-Turin: Elle Di Ci, 1982.

Among the presentations by members of the Italian Ecumenical Association on the Holy Spirit as pledge and first fruits of God's kingdom, there is a useful account on the ecumenical situation in Italy.

[1060] Vischer, Lukas, ed. *Spirit of God, Spirit of Christ: Ecumenical Reflections on the Filioque Controversy*. Faith and Order Paper 103. Geneva: World Council of Churches, 1981.

In 1978 and 1979 two consultations were organized by Faith and Order to study the *filioque* formula in the Niceno-Constantinopolitan Creed. The volume contains the official memorandum "The *Filioque* Clause in Ecumenical Perspective" (pp. 3-18). There are also two historical essays and nine essays on the importance of the issue for contemporary pneumatology. In French the volume was entitled *La théologie du Saint-Esprit dans le dialogue entre l'Orient et l'Occident*.

[1061] *Zweites Wissenschaftliche Konsultation der Societas oecumenica, 28. August bis 1. September im Schloss Sandbjerg, Sonderborg (Dänemark)*. Fribourg: Freiburger Zeitschrift für Philosophie und Theologie, 1983.

The theme of the second meeting of Europe's Societas Oecumenica was "The Holy Spirit and the Unity of the Church". Four papers delivered at this meeting are included. This volume is the sequel to the Society's first meeting. See also [1226].

# Prayer

[1062] Borrely, André, and Eutizi, Max. *L'oecuménisme spirituel*. Perspective orthodoxe 8. Geneva: Labor et Fides, 1988.

This joint publication by an Orthodox priest and a layman is not an academic study of the origin of spiritual ecumenism but rather a devotional reflection.

[1063] Cashmore, Gwen, and Puls, Joan. *Clearing the Way: En Route to an Ecumenical Spirituality*. Risk Books. Geneva: World Council of Churches, 1990.

> Two women, a British Anglican laywoman and an American Franciscan, now co-directors of a new ecumenical spirituality project of the British Council of Churches, in Surrey, England, narrate the origins of their collaboration and its specific goals.

[1064] Castro, Emilio. *When We Pray Together*. Risk Book Series. Geneva: World Council of Churches, 1989.

> The general secretary of the WCC, a Methodist minister from Uruquay, writes of the ecumenical significance of prayer, the various kinds of prayer, and how to pray ecumenically.

[1065] Chenu, Bruno. *L'Eglise au coeur: Disciples et prophètes*. Paris: Le Centurion, 1982.

> The nephew of M.-J. Chenu and director of the Le Centurion publishing house narrates his personal ecclesiological convictions in the manner of Marcel Légaut. He suggests seven ways for the church to divest itself of harmful tendencies.

[1066] De Fiores, Stefano, and Goffi, Tullo, eds. *Dictionnaire de la vie spirituelle*. French adaptation by François Vial. Paris: Editions du Cerf, 1983.

> Originally published by two professors in Italy, the large dictionary (1246 pp.) drew upon the expertise of many Catholic contributors from both sides of the Atlantic. Whereas the article "Eglise" is not ecumenically sensitive, the ones on "Orient chrétien", "Protestantisme" and "Oecuménisme spirituel" are more comprehensive in perspective.

[1067] *For All God's People: Ecumenical Prayer Cycle*. 2nd rev. ed. Geneva: World Council of Churches, 1983.

> This 234 page collection of prayers for the fifty-two weeks of the year and covering the various geographical areas has been replaced by a newer edition [1081]. In addition to the prayers of intercession there are historical information, maps and lists of churches associated with the WCC. See also Vischer [1079].

**[1068]** Heijke, John. *An Ecumenical Light on the Renewal of Religious Community Life*. Duquesne Studies, Theological Series 7. Pittsburgh: Duquesne University, 1967.

The Dutch Catholic ecumenist and professor of theology published this study on the meaning of membership in a "religious congregation" (with its three vows: communion of goods, celibacy, and acceptance of authority) and its specific pertinence to ecumenism.

**[1069]** Hurley, Michael, ed. *Praying for Unity: A Handbook of Studies, Meditations and Prayers*. Dublin: Gill and Son, 1963.

Twenty-one contributions by various ecumenists provide a useful source of prayers for parents and teachers especially apt for use during the Week of Christian Unity.

**[1070]** Michalon, Pierre. *"Spiritual Conversion."* Trans. by a Sister of the Order of the Holy Paraclete, Whitby. Lyons: Unité Chrétienne, 1961.

This English version of the classic *Oecuménisme spirituel* written by one of the principal proponents of spiritual ecumenism stresses the need for prayer and the "invisible monastery" of unity. The booklet includes an address on "Our Responsibilities" delivered at Brussels in March 1960.

**[1071]** Ryan, Noel J., ed. *Christian Spiritual Theology: An Ecumenical Reflection*. Melbourne: Dove Communications, 1976.

The editor is a professor of the United Faculty of Theology, Parkville, Australia, where twenty various speakers from six denominations gave brief introductory lectures on their understanding of spirituality. Included is a bibliography (pp. 367-382).

**[1072]** Schutz, Roger. *Unity Man's Tomorrow*. London: Faith, 1962.

This translation of *L'Unité, espérance de vie* (1962) contains reflections by Brother Roger, prior of the monastery at Taizé, largely on the role of prayer in the cause of ecumenism.

**[1073]** Suenens, Léon Joseph. *Ecumenism and Charismatic Renewal: Theological and Pastoral Orientations*. Malines Documents 1. Ann

Arbor, MI: Servant Books, 1978.

> This modern interpretation of spiritual ecumenism in terms of charismatic renewal is published by the now retired Cardinal Archbishop of Malines, Belgium.

[1074] *A Spirituality for Our Times: Report of a Consultation, Annecy, France, 3-8 December 1984.* Geneva: World Council of Churches, 1985.

> Published by the WCC's Sub-unit on Renewal and Congregational Life, this publication summarized the results of a meeting that responded to Vancouver's call for addressing spirituality. It identifies signs of our times and lists marks of a sprituality for today.

[1075] Thurian, Max. *Love and Truth Meet.* Trans. by C. Edward Hopkin. Philadelphia: Pilgrim, 1968.

> The well known ecumenist and monk of Taizé addresses three of the principal spiritual issues related to church unity under the headings: the truth, the way and the life. The original title was *Amour et Vérité se rencontrent* (1964).

[1076] Villain, Maurice, ed. *Oecuménisme spirituel: les écrits de l'Abbé Paul Couturier.* Tournai: Casterman, 1963.

> One of Courturier's successors in the French Catholic ecumenical movement here analyzes the meaning and significance of his "spiritual ecumenism." A number of his writings are cited with a commentary.

[1077] Villain, Maurice. *Pour l'unité chrétienne: Conférences.* Grenoble: B. Arthaud, 1943.

> Published during World War II, this volume is a collection of five spiritual exhortations on the need for prayer and interior renewal to achieve Christian unity.

[1078] Villain, Maurice. *La prière oecuménique.* Paris: Editions Paulines, 1970.

> This important book on prayer for ecumenism by Maurice Villain (1900-1977) shows how Catholicism moved from a highly apologetic mentality to a less rigid mentality at Vatican II. The

first three chapters are enlightening in exposing faulty presuppositions of prayer for the "Great Return."

[1079] Vischer, Lukas. *Intercession*. Faith and Order Paper 95. Geneva: World Council of Churches, 1980.

The book tries to articulate a theology of intercession understood in the sense of prayer for others. Among the aspects treated are Jesus Christ as Advocate, intercession in the church, the intercession of the saints. See also [1067, 1081].

[1080] Wakefield, Gordon S., ed. *The Westminster Dictionary of Christian Spirituality*. Philadelphia: Westminster, 1983.

Entitled *A Dictionary of Christian Spirituality* (London: SCM, 1983) in the United Kingdom, this joint venture was realized by some 150 collaborators. The editor is principal at Queen's College, Birmingham, England. Articles aim at ecumenical balance and Orthodox, Catholic and classical Protestant doctrines are explained. Non-European views are included as are issues of feminism, liberation theology, etc. The entries are rather short.

[1081] *With All God's People: The New Ecumenical Prayer Cycle, Orders of Service*. Geneva: World Council of Churches, 1989.

Intended as a revision of the earlier publication [1067], this 133 page collection of intercessory prayers for every week of the year covering most areas of the world is widely used internationally.

# Mary and the Saints

[1082] Bäumer, Remigius, and Scheffczyk, Leo, eds. *Marienlexikon*. St. Ottilien: EOS, 1988- .

Sponsored by the Institutum Marianum of Regensburg, this vast lexicon is still in production. Three large volumes have appeared as of 1992 (up to the entry "Laib"). The list of collaborators is lengthy. The entries are short but well informed and the bibliographies up to date. There are Orthodox and Protestant consultants.

[1083] Beinert, Wolfgang, and Petri, Heinrich, eds. *Handbuch der Marienkunde*. Regensburg: F. Pustet, 1984.

This mammoth (1042 pp.) one-volume encyclopedia on mariology was produced by fifteen collaborators. The material is organized into sixteen sections including: theological issues, spirituality, witness of art and literature, piety. A product of the post-Vatican II spirit, the work, although written only by Catholics, is ecumenically sensitive. Chapter IV (pp. 315-359) treats "Mary in Ecumenical Perspective".

[1084] Beinert, Wolfgang, *et al. Maria: Eine ökumenische Herausforderung*. Regensburg: F. Pustet, 1984.

Of these seven essays on the theology of Mary two are especially pertinent to ecumenism: "Shifts in Catholic Marian Devotion since the Reformation" (W. Beinert) and "Mary and the Unity of Christians" (H. Schütte).

[1085] Brown, Raymond E.; Donfried, Karl P.; Fitzmyer, Joseph A.; and Reumann, John, eds. *Mary in the New Testament: A Collaborative Assessment by Protestant and Roman Catholic Scholars*. Philadelphia: Fortress; New York: Paulist, 1978.

Encouraged by the success of their previous collaboration on *Peter in the New Testament* [1230], members of the US Lutheran/Catholic Dialogue undertook this similar study on the Mother of Jesus. Besides the New Testament material, they also include second century literature. Chapter ten enumerates the conclusions of their research.

[1086] Höfer, Lisolette. *Ökumenische Besinnung über die Heiligen*. Begegnung 1. Lucerne: Rüber, 1962.

The Swiss Catholic author prepared this series of lectures on the saints for delivery in the Lucerne and Zürich area. He included the New Testament understanding of holiness, a very brief historical overview (only three pages!), the definition of a saint, and what he calls saints "extra muros."

[1087] Küng, Hans, and Moltmann, Jürgen, eds. *Mary in the Churches*. Concilium 168. New York: Seabury, 1983.

Ten essays, one written by a Jewish scholar, comment on the role of the Mother of Jesus in the church. The Christian contributions enunciate Lutheran, Catholic and Orthodox perspectives.

**[1088]** O'Carroll, Michael. *Theotokos: A Theological Encyclopedia of the Blessed Virgin Mary.* Wilmington, DL: Michael Glazier; Dublin: Dominican Publications, 1982.

This ambitious project, completed by a single individual, an Irish theologian, contains a number of articles that are generally ecumenically sensitive. Some entries have excellent bibliographies. For readers of German the volumes by Bäumer [1082] and Beinert [1083] are more thorough and comprehensive.

**[1089]** Petri, Heinrich, ed. *Divergenzen in der Mariologie: Zur ökumenischen Diskussion um die Mutter Jesus.* Regensburg: F. Pustet, 1989.

Differing viewpoints in mariology are here surveyed especially within the context of German Catholic and Lutheran perspectives.

**[1090]** Riesenhuber, Klaus. *Maria im theologischen Verständnis von Karl Barth und Karl Rahner.* Quaestiones Disputatae 60. Freiburg: Herder, 1973.

In this comparative study of mariology in Barth and Rahner, attention is directed to biblical references to Mary, as well as her virginity, sinlessness, dormition, and role in salvation-history. This is a rare study of Barth's theology of Mary.

**[1091]** Stacpoole, Alberic, ed. *Mary and the Churches.* Dublin: Columba, 1987.

These nineteen articles written at the behest of the Catholic editor address a number of mariological themes. Several have ecumenical pertinence, namely, "The Place of Mary in Recent Ecumenical Documents" (J. Harding) and "Mary's Place in *Lumen gentium*" (A. Stacpoole). See also [1092].

**[1092]** Stacpoole, Alberic, ed. *Mary's Place in Christian Dialogue.* Middlegreen, Slough: St. Paul's, 1982.

These occasional papers given at meetings of the Ecumenical Society of the Blessed Virgin (1970-1980) cover eight areas including ecumenical studies. There is also a brief discussion of the Lima document [1175] as it relates to Marian devotion. See also [1091].

# Sacraments and Worship

[1093] Allmen, Jean-Jacques von. *Prophétisme sacramentel: Neuf études pour le renouveau et l'unité de l'Eglise.* Neuchâtel: Delachaux et Niestlé, 1964.

A collection of nine scholarly studies by the Swiss Reformed professor, previously published in the volume *1054-1954: L'Eglise et les églises* [665] and various journals. Among the topics treated in the volume are articles concerning: the prophetic significance of the sacraments; confessional loyalty and ecumenical commitment; the meaning of confirmation; remarriage of the divorced according to the New Testament; and the role of the Holy Spirit in worship.

[1094] Hempelmann, Reinhard. *Sakrament als Ort der Vermittlung des Heils: Sakramententheologie im evangelisch-katholischen Dialog.* Göttingen: Vandenhoeck und Ruprecht, 1992.

To illustrate differing emphases in Protestant and Catholic sacramental theology, the author illustrates complementarities in the thought of Karl Barth, Paul Tillich, Karl Rahner and Joseph Ratzinger. This work was a doctoral dissertation submitted to Heidelberg in 1989.

[1095] Hotz, Robert. *Sakramente im Wechselspiel zwischen Ost und West.* Ökumenische Theologie, Bd. 2. Zürich: Benziger; Gütersloh: Gerd Mohn, 1979.

The Swiss Jesuit collaborator on the biweekly *Orientierung*, an expert on Eastern theology, produced this 342 page study outlining the mutual influence of Eastern and Western sacramental theologies upon one another. He studies the Eastern use of "mysteries" over "sacraments" and highlights newer Orthodox theological emphases and Western influences.

[1096] Konstantinidis, Chrysostomos, and Suttner, Ernst Christoph. *Fragen der Sakramentenpastoral in orthodox-katholisch gemischten Gemeinden.* Regensburg: F. Pustet, 1979.

In order to assist pastoral workers especially in German speaking countries to appreciate the beliefs of Orthodox and Roman Catholic faithful, Metropolitan Chrysostomos (Orthodox) and Suttner (Catholic) jointly prepared this handbook. It treats of sacramental sharing and offers suggestions for overcoming potentially difficult pastoral conflicts.

**[1097]** Spisso, Mario. *Prospettive comunitarie ed ecumeniche nella teologia sacramentaria di Max Thurian (Vice Priore de Taizé)*. Agrigento: Padri Vocazionisti, 1965.
The Roman Catholic priest first reviews the origins of the Reformation monastic community at Taizé and then gives a sympathetic exposition of Max Thurian's sacramental theology (echoes of which can be seen later in the Lima document).

**[1098]** Swidler, Leonard J., ed. *Ecumenism, the Spirit and Worship*. Pittsburgh: Duquesne University, 1967.

The distinguished American ecumenist here collected twelve disparate essays on various aspects of ecumenism, the Holy Spirit and liturgical renewal from lectures given at Duquesne in the mid 1960s.

# Baptism

**[1099]** Carile, Sergio, ed. *I Battesimo: Riflessioni interconfessionali del Gruppo Misto di Studio per una cathecesi ecumenica collegato al S.A.E.* Leumann-Turin: Elle Di Ci, 1982.

The Segretariato Attività Ecumeniche (S.A.E.), the impressive Italian Ecumenical Association which has produced a number of valuable studies provides here a collection of ecumenical documents on baptism from 1970-1979 and gives the results of a questionnaire submitted to baptized persons and to ministers.

**[1100]** Hurley, Michael, ed. *Ecumenical Studies: Baptism and Marriage*. Dublin: Gill and Son, 1968.

This volume contains the proceedings of ecumenical conferences held at the Benedictine Abbey of Glenstal, Limerick (1966) and Greenhills, near Drogheda (1967) to discuss baptism (pp. 23-175) and marriage (176-240).

**[1101]** Rodger, Patrick C., *et al. All Are Called: Towards a Theology of the Laity*. London: Church House, 1985.

This 85 page work prepared by the Board of Education of the Church of England under the chairmanship of the Bishop of

Oxford studies the ministerial roles of the laity in light of baptism.

[1102] Suttner, Ernst Christoph, ed. *Busse und Beichte: Drittes Regensburger Ökumenisches Symposon.* Regensburg: Pustet, 1972.

The third in the Regensburg ecumenical symposia focused on penance and sacramental confession in its relationship to baptism. Eleven essays by Catholic, Orthodox, Lutheran and Old Catholic writers are included (seven other essays appeared in various journals). See also [1103, 1125].

[1103] Suttner, Ernst Christoph, ed. *Taufe und Firmung: Zweites Regensburger Ökumenisches Symposon.* Regensburg: Pustet, 1971.

Held in 1970, this second in the series of symposia included sixteen essays from different confessional viewpoints on the New Testament, patristic, mystical, liturgical and missiological aspects of baptism and chrismation or confirmation. See also [1102, 1125].

[1104] Wainwright, Geoffrey. *Christian Initiation.* Ecumenical Studies in History, no. 10. London: Lutterworth; Richmond: John Knox, 1969.

This historical and systematic study provides particularly useful background material for understanding the section on baptism in the Lima document [1175]. Especially pertinent is chapter 5: "Initiation and Unity" (pp. 57-70).

# Eucharist or Lord's Supper

[1105] Averbeck, Wilhelm. *Der Opfercharakter des Abendmahls in der neueren evangelischen Theologie.* Konfessionskundliche und kontroverstheologische Studien 19. Paderborn: Bonifatius, 1968.

In this massive monograph (846 pp.) prepared by the Osnabrück Dozent for Dogmatics, an ecumenical attempt is made to explain what Lutheran theologians have been saying about the sacrificial character of the Lord's Supper. Part one covers the period from the Reformation to the end of World War I; part two treats the years 1917-1958. The bibliography is notable (pp. 806-834).

[1106] Capieu, Henri; Greiner, Albert; and Nicolau, Albert, eds. *Tous invités: La Cène du Seigneur célébrée dans les Eglises de la Réforme.* Paris: Centurion, 1982.

The collection does not treat eucharistic hospitality or intercommunion as such but rather provides a contemporary account of the meaning of the eucharist in the Reformation tradition. A historical section reviews various texts of theologians from Calvin and Luther up to Karl Barth. Three ecumenical consensus statements from 1968, 1973 and 1981 are evaluated.

[1107] *A Critique of Eucharistic Agreement.* London: SPCK, 1975.

The booklet contains five Anglican critiques of the four eucharistic agreements published in the volume *Modern Eucharistic Agreement* [1118].

[1108] Echlin, Edward P. *The Anglican Eucharist in Ecumenical Perspective: Doctrine and Rite from Cranmer to Seabury.* New York: Seabury, 1968.

The Catholic researcher studied Anglican eucharistic doctrine from 1549 to 1789. From his research he concludes that with the Communion Service associated with Seabury all Roman Catholic requirements were fulfilled and that the rite is a legitimate form of the eucharistic prayer.

[1109] Empie, Paul C., and Murphy, T. Austin, eds. *Eucharist and Ministry.* Lutherans and Catholics in Dialogue 4. New York: USCC; New York: Lutheran World Federation USA, 1970.

The fourth of the agreed statements of the US Lutheran/Catholic Consultation is here published together with the background papers.

[1110] *Eucharistie und Priesteramt.* Beiheft zur Ökumenischen Rundschau Nr. 38. Frankfurt: O. Lembeck, 1980.

This volume provides the proceedings of the fifth bilateral theological dialogue between representatives of the Ecumenical Patriarchate and the Evangelische Kirche in Deutschland (EKD) held in Bonn, February 1978. Besides the minutes there are texts of the six papers (all in German) on eucharist and priesthood.

[1111] Garijo-Guembe, Miguel M.; Neugebauer, Eugenie; Riedel-Spangenberger, Ilona, eds. *Die Eucharistie im Gespräch der Konfession: Ein Beitrag zur Rezeption des Dokumentes "Taufe, Eucharistie und Amt" (Lima 1982).* Münster: Butzon und Bercker,

1986.

After a general commentary on the eucharistic section of BEM [1175], the Catholic writers under the sponsorship of the Münster Diocesan Commission for Ecumenical Questions provide a creative 200 page workbook designed for graduate seminars. Various ecumenical texts are organized to elucidate the Lord's Supper as sacrament, anamnesis, offering, epiclesis, presence, meal, communion, and as presided over by a minister.

[1112] Garijo-Guembe, Miguel M.; Rohls, Jan; and Wenz, Günther. *Mahl des Herrn: Ökumenische Studien*. Frankfurt: O. Lembeck; Paderborn: Bonifatius, 1988.

The collaborative publication of these studies on the eucharist in ecumenical perspective reflects the developments that were stressed in the Lima document.

[1113] Heron, Alasdair I.C., ed. *Table and Tradition*. Philadelphia: Westminster; Edinburgh: Handsel, 1983.

Given as the Kerr lectures at the University of Glasgow in 1978, these essays were published only after considerable delay and some revision. The author, now professor at Erlangen, Germany, discusses the eucharist in the New Testament and in the current Catholic-Reformed interpretations.

[1114] Groupe des Dombes. *Vers une même foi eucharistique? Accord entre catholiques et protestants*. Taizé: Presses de Taizé, 1972.

This is one of the series of agreements by the Group of Les Dombes. This consensus on the Lord's Supper can be found in English translation in *Modern Eucharistic Agreement* [1118]. See also [699].

[1115] Hönig, Elisabeth. *Die Eucharistie als Opfer nach den neueren ökumenischen Erklärungen*. Konfessionskundliche und Kontroverstheologische Studien 54. Paderborn: Bonifatius, 1989.

This 299 page carefully researched study reports on how the eucharist has been described in nine various ecumenical consultations. The author then explains in her conclusion what are the areas of agreement and ongoing controversy.

[1116] Lehmann, Karl, and Schlink, Edmund. *Das Opfer Jesu Christi und seine Gegenwart in der Kirche.* Dialog der Kirchen 3. Freiburg: Herder; Göttingen: Vandenhoeck und Ruprecht, 1983.

The sacrificial nature of the eucharist remains one of the thorniest issues in ecumenism. A joint ecumenical working group here published eleven major papers on sacrifice in the Old Testament, the New Testament, the early church, the Lutheran confessions, etc. The volume concludes with a lengthy joint statement: "Das Opfer Jesu Christi und der Kirche" (pp. 215-238).

[1117] Lies, Lothar, ed. *Praesentia Christi: Festschrift Johannes Betz zum 70sten Geburtstag dargebracht von Kollegen, Freuden, Schülern.* Düsseldorf: Patmos, 1984.

This collection of essays was offered to the Würzburg scholar known for his publications on the eucharist in the patristic era. The *Festschrift* contains a number of essays on confessional convictions about the presence of Christ in the Lord's Supper.

[1118] *Modern Eucharistic Agreement.* London: SPCK, 1973.

The booklet contains four agreed statements on the Lord's Supper, namely: Windsor ARCIC-I (1971), US Lutheran/Catholic (1967), Group of Les Dombes (1972), and Louvain Faith and Order (1971). For a critique of these texts, see [1107].

[1119] Rauch, Albert, and Imhof, Paul, eds. *Die Eucharistie der Einen Kirche: Eucharistische Ekklesiologie, Perspektiven und Grenzen.* Koinonia, Bd. 3. Aschaffenburg: Gerhard Kaffke, 1983.

Thirteen position papers from this Regensburg symposium held in July 1981 focus on differences and similarities between Eastern and Western ecclesiology and eucharistic doctrines.

[1120] Reumann, John. *The Supper of the Lord: The New Testament, Ecumenical Dialogues, and Faith and Order on Eucharist.* Philadelphia: Fortress, 1985.

Member of the US Lutheran/Catholic dialogue since 1965 and author of *"Righteousness"* [1019], the Lutheran professor outlines ecumenical agreements regarding the eucharist that have emerged from biblical studies or from bilateral dialogues and the Lima document [1175]. The history of communion practices is summarized.

[1121] Sartori, Luigi, ed. *Eucaristia, sfida alle chiese divise*. Padua: Edizioni Messaggero, 1984.

The volume contains the papers from an ecumenical symposium organized by the Istituto di Liturgia Pastorale de Santa Giustina, Padua, on the "Understanding of Eucharistic Celebrations in Various Christian Confessions". There is also a section evaluating the Lima document [1175].

[1122] Schäfer, Gerhard Karl. *Eucharistie im ökumenischen Kontext: Zur Diskussion um das Herrenmahl in Glauben und Kirchenverfassung von Lausanne 1927 bis Lima 1982*. Forschungen zur systematischen und ökumenischen Theologie 55. Göttingen: Vandenhoeck und Ruprecht, 1988.

Under the direction of Jürgen Moltmann at the Faculty of Evangelical Theology at Tübingen, the author completed this doctoral dissertation. He surveys the teachings on the Lord's Supper at seven Faith and Order conferences and points to elements not yet received by the churches.

[1123] Segretariato Attività Ecumeniche, ed. *Eucaristia e unità [Atti della XI Sessione di formazione ecumenica organizzata dal S.A.E., 1973]*. Rome: Editrice A.V.E., 1974.

There are papers by Catholics, Orthodox, Protestants and Anglicans in the acts of this congress devoted to the theme of eucharist and unity. The volume also contains Italian translations of four recent consensus statements on the eucharist.

[1124] Senn, Frank C., ed. *New Eucharistic Prayers: An Ecumenical Study of Their Development and Structure*. New York: Paulist, 1987.

The new eucharistic prayers introduced into the Roman rite are described and evaluated by a team of liturgists who are Catholic, Lutheran and Presbyterian.

[1125] Suttner, Ernst Christoph, ed. *Eucharistie, Zeichen der Einheit: Erstes Regensburger Ökumenisches Symposion*. Regensburg: Pustet, 1970.

This first in a series of symposia was attended largely by

Orthodox and Catholics. The published proceedings include two introductory essays and nine essays on the eucharist as sign of unity. See also [1102, 1103].

[1126] Swidler, Leonard J., ed. *The Eucharist in Ecumenical Dialogue.* New York: Paulist, 1976.

These papers were given at a consultation held in Philadelphia in 1976 and also appeared in *Journal of Ecumenical Studies* 13, no. 2 (1976) 191-344. The symposium explored conclusions and agreements on the eucharist reached by seven bilateral dialogues in which the Roman Catholic Church in the USA is involved with Orthodox, Anglicans, Lutherans, Reformed, Methodists, Baptists and Jews.

[1127] Thurian, Max. *The Mystery of the Eucharist: An Ecumenical Approach.* Trans. by Emily Chisholm. Oxford: Mowbray, 1983; Grand Rapids: Eerdmans, 1984.

This clear and insightful account of eucharistic theology was composed by a close collaborator of the Lima (BEM) document. He discusses for Christians of various ecclesial adherence what is the meaning of sacrifice, real presence, and invocation of the Spirit upon the eucharist.

[1128] Wohlmuth, Josef. *Realpräsenz und Transsubstantiation im Konzil von Trient: Eine historisch-kritische Analyse der Canones 1-4 der Sessio XIII.* Bd. 1: *Darstellung*; Bd. 2: *Anmerkungen und Texte.* Frankfurt: P. Lang, 1975.

For his doctoral dissertation at the Catholic Theology Faculty of Regensburg under J. Ratzinger, the author situated various methodological presuppositions of Catholic teaching on the real presence and transubstantiation that influenced the Council of Trent's formulation of canons 1-4 at its thirteenth session.

# Intercommunion or Eucharistic Hospitality

[1129] Baillie, Donald, and Marsh, John. *Intercommunion: The Report of the Theological Commission Appointed by the Continuation of the World Conference on Faith and Order Together with a Selection from the Material Presented to the Commission.* New York: Harper and Brothers, 1952.

Work on these nineteen historical and theological studies largely by Protestants regarding eucharistic hospitality began after the Faith and Order meeting of 1937 but was concluded only on the eve of the Lund meeting of 1952. Two Orthodox and one Catholic theologians contributed to the collection.

[1130] Blank, Josef, *et al. Was hindert uns? Das gemeinsame Herrenmahl der Christen.* Regensburg: F. Pustet, 1981.

The volume reproduces seven theological talks at a meeting held in May 1980 between the Katholische Akademie in Bayern and the Evangelische Akademie Tutzing concerning eucharistic hospitality or intercommunion.

[1131] Bobrinskoy, Boris; Heitz, Jean-Jacques; Lebeau, Paul. *Intercommunion: Des chrétiens s'interrogent: Eucharistie, Eglise, Unité.* Paris: Mame, 1969.

An Orthodox, Lutheran and Roman Catholic theologian present three expositions of their churches' teachings on the eucharist. These are followed by discussion (pp. 193-209) and concluding remarks (pp. 213-230).

[1132] Boeckler, Richard, ed. *Interkommunion, Konziliarität.* Beihefte zur ökumenischen Rundschau 25. Stuttgart: Evangelisches Missionsverlag, 1974.

This publication incorporates discussions by seven Protestants on historical and theological issues of intercommunion (pp. 5-127). The second part of the volume summarizes the results of a study group that met from 1970 to 1973 to study conciliarity, communion ecclesiology, ecumenical councils, and the catholicity of local churches.

[1133] Church of England. Commission on Intercommunion. *Intercommunion Today.* London: Church Information Office, 1968.

Fifteen Church of England theologians, and a few Roman Catholic, Methodist and Presbyterian observers discuss historical issues from the Reformation. Several recommendations are made regarding admission to Holy Communion in the Church of England. Especially notable is the section on "Local Ecumenical Commitment" (pp. 108-111).

**[1134]** Dock, Herman. *Intercommunione van Lund tot Uppsala.* Antwerp: Patmos; Roermond: J.J. Romen and Zonen, 1969.

The Flemish author began this work in Belgium and finished his research at the Lovanium in Kinshasa, Zaïre. He retraces the growth and shifts in theological reflection from the Lund Faith and Order meeting of 1952 to the Uppsala general assembly in 1968. The views of Orthodox, Anglicans, Protestant and Catholics are included.

**[1135]** Fries, Heinrich. *Ein Glaube, Eine Taufe, Getrennt beim Abendmahl?* Graz: Styria, 1971.

For the winter semester 1970/71 at the Ecumenical Institute of the University of Munich, Professor Fries asked why it is possible for Christians to share in one faith and one baptism and yet be separated at the Lord's Supper.

**[1136]** Huwyler, Christoph. *Das Problem der Interkommunion.* 2 vols. Bad Honnef: Bock + Herchen, 1984.

Under the direction of J. Finkenzeller, the author completed this doctoral dissertation at the Faculty of Catholic Theology in Munich in 1984. The concept of intercommunion, its historical development and place in numerous bilaterals are all treated. The bibliography is vast (II, pp. 839-893).

**[1137]** Kent, John, and Murray, Robert, eds. *Intercommunion and Church Membership.* London: Darton, Longman and Todd; Denville, NJ: Dimension Books, 1973.

This volume presents an account of the tenth Downside Symposium held in Bristol, England, April 1972, sponsored by the Catholic Theological Commission for England and Wales. Papers were given on the historical, theological and sociological factors hindering to eucharistic hospitality.

**[1138]** Kirchgässner, Alfons, and Bühler, Horst. *Interkommunion in Diskussion und Praxis: Eine Dokumentation.* Düsseldorf: Patmos, 1971.

The book contains documentation from various basic Christian communities regarding eucharistic hospitality, as well as texts from the "official" church, from theologians, and from several German sources. The information is now somewhat dated.

**[1139]** Krems, Gerhard, and Mumm, Reinhard, eds. *Evangelische-Katholische Abendmahlsgemeinschaft?* Veröffentlichung des Ökumenischen Arbeitskreises evangelischer und katholischer Theologen. Regensburg: F. Pustet; Göttingen: Vandenhoeck und Ruprecht, 1971.

At the thirty-first session of the ecumenical working group held in March 1970, the theme was eucharistic hospitality. The texts of individual theologians are provided and a summary is given by the editors.

**[1140]** Mumm, Reinhard, and Lienhard, Marc, eds. *Eucharistische Gastfreundschaft: Ökumenische Dokumente.* Kassel: Johannes Stauda, 1974.

These documents on intercommunion or eucharistic hospitality are drawn from WCC meetings in New Delhi, Uppsala and Louvain, plus from 16 other statements produced in the 1960s and 1970s, some of which from Old Catholic, Lutheran, Anglican sources (especially from Germany and France) are difficult to locate elsewhere.

**[1141]** Pigault, Gérard, and Schlick, Jean. *Eucharist and Eucharistic Hospitality; Eucharistie et hospitalité eucharistique.* International Bibliography 1971-1973 Indexed by Computer. RIC Supplément 10. Strasbourg: CERDIC, 1974; *Eucharist; Eucharistie.* International Bibliography 1971-1974 Indexed by Computer. RIC Supplément 17. Strasbourg: CERDIC, 1975.

The Center of Research and Documentation of Christian Institutions (CERDIC) undertook this amateurish retrospective search that yielded 490 entries for the years 1971-73. Unfortunately the material is poorly organized and not indexed. The second volume is much improved in arranging the material into fourteen areas. There are numerous typos and errors. See also [21].

**[1142]** Pruisken, Johannes. *Interkommunion im Prozess: Abendmahlsgemeinschaft als Zeichen und Mittel kirchlicher Einigung.* Koinonia, Bd. 13. Essen: Ludgerus Verlag Hubert Wingen, 1974.

This book supplies six chapters on the historical and theological issues related to Roman Catholic and Lutheran positions on eucharistic hospitality.

[1143] Reardon, Ruth, and Finch, Melanie, eds. *Sharing Communion: An Appeal to the Churches from Interchurch Families*. London: Collins, 1983.

This work addressed to non-specialists begins with the results of a questionnaire circulated in 1982 among some ninety couples of the Association of Interchurch Families. Citing from the responses, the authors argue for a rethinking among churches that do not permit intercommunion. There is a brief concluding statement by Catholic theologian John Coventry and excerpts from twenty-six pertinent official documents (1964-1982).

[1144] Stirnimann, Heinrich, ed. *Interkommunion: Hoffnungen - zu bedenken*. Ökumenische Beihefte 5. Fribourg: Universitätsverlag, 1971.

The fruit of the sixth ecumenical congress of German-speaking Switzerland (1970), this volume contains six essays on eucharistic hospitality or intercommunion between Catholics and Protestants. Also included is a proposal submitted to Catholic and Protestant leaders for consideration. A well indexed bibliography covering the years 1960-1970 is included prepared by Johannes Brantschen and Pietro Selvatico (pp. 77-149).

[1145] Thurian, Max; Klinger, Jerzy; Baciocchi, Joseph de. *Vers l'intercommunion*. Eglises en dialogue no. 13. Tours: Mame, 1970.

The three theologians, respectively Reformed, Orthodox and Roman Catholic, outline briefly the teachings of their churches regarding eucharistic hospitality.

[1146] Vajta, Vilmos. *Interkommunion - mit Rome?* Göttingen: Vandenhoeck und Ruprecht, 1969.

The volume contains four sections treating recent developments, eucharistic and ecclesial communion, Protestant and Catholic views on admission to communion, and spiritual reflections.

[1147] Ware, Kallistos [Timothy]. *Communion and Intercommunion*. Minneapolis: Light and Life, 1980.

The booklet contains a brief study of intercommunion based on the theology and practice of the Eastern Orthodox Church. The text also appeared in *Sobornost* 7, no. 7 (1978).

**[1148]** Zernov, Nicolas. *The Reintegration of the Church: A Study in Intercommunion.* London: SCM, 1952.

In this early work, Zernov (1898-1980), formerly lecturer at the University of Oxford, devoted twelve chapters to explaining the significance of eucharistic hospitality from a nuanced Orthodox perspective.

## Ordained Ministry

**[1149]** Allmen, Jean-Jacques von, *et al. El ministerio en el diálogo interconfesional.* Salamanca: Sigueme, 1976.

This collection of Spanish papers and documents was prepared for an interconfessional conference on ministry held in Madrid, May 19-23, 1975. There are eight major articles by Catholic, Orthodox, Anglican and Protestant scholars. Also included are various ecumenical documents on ministry including the US Lutheran/Catholic Consultation text and the Accra text that eventually led to the Lima document on *Baptism, Eucharist and Ministry.*

**[1150]** Baur, Jörg, ed. *Das Amt im ökumenischen Kontext.* Stuttgart: Calwer, 1980.

The volume contains essays by Anglicans, Catholics, Orthodox and Protestants on the New Testament concept of ministry. There are reports on the theology of ministry and a position paper (pp. 165-182) by the ecumenical commission of the Vereinigte Evangelisch-Lutherische Kirche Deutschlands (VELKD) and the Deutsche Nationalkommittee des Lutherischen Weltbundes.

**[1151]** Bläser, Peter, *et al. Amt und Eucharistie.* Konfessionskundliche Schriften des Johann-Adam-Möhler-Instituts, Nr. 10. Paderborn: Bonifatius, 1973.

These five ecumenical studies on ministry and eucharist treat the topics from the perspectives of the New Testament (P. Bläser), the early church (S. Frank), the theology of Martin Luther (P. Manns), the Council of Trent (G. Fahrnberger), and liturgical traditions (H.J. Schulz).

**[1152]** Burgsmüller, Alfred, and Frieling, Reinhard, eds. *Amt und Ordination im Verständnis evangelischer Kirchen und ökumenischer*

*Gespräche.* Gütersloh: Gerd Mohn, 1974.

The volume cites doctrinal texts on ordained ministry from Protestant and ecumenical sources. There is a useful summary of points of convergence and open questions (pp. 30-31).

[1153] Domínguez Sánchez, Benito. *El Ministerio y su repercusión en la unidad.* Valladolid: Imp. Benedictinas, 1984.

These six chapters treat ecumenical problems of ministry since 1927. There is also a comprehensive bibliography (pp. 511-522). The work contains little original material but makes current research more accessible to readers of Spanish.

[1154] *Episkopé and Episcopate in Ecumenical Perspective.* Faith and Order Paper 102. Geneva: World Council of Churches, 1980.

The Faith and Order Commission had posed seven questions to churches on *episkopé.* In Geneva, from August 13-16, 1979, five scholars from different churches (Raymond Brown, John Zizioulas, N.D. Rao-Samuel, M. Mbwana, and S. Escobar) explained various exegetical and historical aspects of this concept.

[1155] Ganoczy, Alexandre, *et al. Der Streit um das Amt in der Kirche: Ernstfall der Ökumene.* Regensburg: F. Pustet, 1983.

This is another volume recording the discussions of an annual meeting of the Katholische Akademie in Bayern and the Evangelische Akademie Tutzing in Munich (1982). This book focuses on ordained ministry through historical and theological analyses by one Anglican and several Protestants and Catholics. Among texts discussed are the international Lutheran and Roman Catholic statement on "Ministry in the Church" (1981) and the Lima document (1982).

[1156] Gassmann, Günther, and Meyer, Harding, eds. *Das kirchenleitende Amt: Dokumente zum interkonfessionellen Dialog über Bischofsamt und Papstamt.* Ökumenische Dokumentation, V. Frankfurt: O. Lembeck; J. Knecht, 1980.

After an introduction on pastoral office and episcopacy, there are German versions of the Groupe des Dombes text "Le ministère épiscopale" [1157], the US Lutheran and Catholic text on "Papal Primacy and the Universal Church " [1243] and the ARCIC-I statement on "Authority in the Church" [632].

[1157] Groupe des Dombes. *Le ministère épiscopal: Réflexions et propositions sur le ministère de vigilance et d'unité dans l'Eglise particulière*. Taizé: Presses de Taizé, 1976.

This agreed statement on *episkopé* understood as the ministry dedicated to promoting care and unity in the local church has been particularly well received in the wider ecumenical community. For an English text, see *One in Christ* 14 (1978) 267-288.

[1158] Groupe des Dombes. *Pour une réconciliation des ministères: Eléments d'accord entre catholiques et protestants*. Taizé: Presses de Taizé, 1973.

This is another in a series of consensus statements between French speaking Catholics and Reformed. For an English version of this text on the mutual recognition of orders, see *Modern Ecumenical Documents on the Ministry* [1161].

[1159] Haendler, Gert. *Luther on Ministerial Office and Congregational Function*. Trans. by Ruth C. Gritsch. Philadelphia: Fortress, 1981.

The material for this book originated in lectures from 1973 to 1975 in Rostock and Copenhagen. Eight chapters review research into the period prior to Luther, and then provide an analysis of Luther's own teaching on office and congregation. The short work (110 pp.) appeared originally as *Amt und Gemeinde bei Luther im Kontext der Kirchengeschichte* (1979).

[1160] Hahn, Ferdinand, *et al. Dienst und Amt: Überlebensfrage der Kirche*. Regensburg: F. Pustet, 1973.

The volume contains the acts of the 1972 joint meeting of the Katholische Akademie in Bayern and the Evangelische Akademie Tutzing. The biblical, historical and theological nature of church office are discussed by F. Hahn, B. Kötting, W. Joes, and H. Mühlen.

[1161] *Modern Ecumenical Documents on the Ministry*. London: SPCK, 1975.

The booklet contains four agreed statements on ordained ministry, namely: ARCIC-I (1973), US Lutheran/Catholic (1970), Group of Les Dombes (1973), and the Faith and Order Accra statement (1974) later reworked as part of the Lima document.

[1162] Mumm, Reinhard, and Krems, Gerhard, eds. *Ordination und kirchliches Amt.* Veröffentlichung des Ökumenischen Arbeitskreises evangelischer und katholischer Theologen. Paderborn: Bonifatius; Bielefeld, Luther Verlag, 1976.

The book contains five essays on various aspects of ordination in the Reformation and Catholic tradition delivered at an annual meeting of the working group held in Betzdorf in April 1974.

[1163] Rahner, Karl. *Vorfragen zu einem ökumenischen Amts-verständnis.* Quaestiones disputatae 65. Freiburg: Herder, 1974.

Rahner once complained that this book had received little serious attention. It aims to show the efficacious, salvific nature of ordained ministry in the divided churches. There is an excursus (pp. 79-93) on intercommunion.

[1164] Raiser, Konrad, ed. *Ökumenische Diakonie: Eine Option für das Leben.* Beiheft zur Ökumenischen Rundschau 57. Frankfurt: O. Lembeck, 1988.

The contributors to this book of essays ask what are the theological foundations for ecumenical diakonia. The articles are meant to contribute to the ongoing study of the WCC on this issue.

[1165] Rauch, Albert, and Imhof, Paul, eds. *Das Priestertum in der Einen Kirche: Diakonat, Presbyterat und Episkopat* Koinonia, Bd. 4. Aschaffenburg: Gerhard Kaffke, 1987.

This volume in the Regensburg series from the 1985 symposium contains thirteen reflections by Orthodox and Catholics on priesthood, the Lima document [1175] and the initial work of the International Catholic and Orthodox Consultation. See also [1102, 1103].

[1166] *Reform und Anerkennung kirchlicher Ämter: Ein Memorandum der Arbeitsgemeinschaft ökumenischer Universitätsinstitute.* Munich: C. Kaiser; Mainz: M. Grünewald, 1973.

Six university based ecumenical institutes at Bochum, Heidelberg, Munich (two), Münster and Tübingen jointly sponsored the memorandum containing twenty-three theses. [An English translation appears in *Journal of Ecumenical Studies* 10 (1973) 390-401.] This is followed by a series of background papers identifying reasons for problems in the ordained ministry.

[1167] Sanders, Wilm, ed. *Bischofsamt - Amt der Einheit: Ein Beitrag zum ökumenischen Gespräch*. Munich: J. Pfeiffer, 1983.

Based on communications given at Hamburg in 1982, these seven essays articulate various Orthodox, Catholic and Protestant understandings of the office of bishop. All the participants agreed that the bishop "remains constitutive" for the church. This joint working group's agreed statement is included.

[1168] Tavard, George H. *A Review of Anglican Orders: The Problem and the Solution*. Theology and Life Series 31. Michael Glazier Books. Collegeville: Liturgical Press, 1990.

Of the 167 pages in this study 113 are devoted to reviewing earlier discussions of the possible recognition of Anglican orders by the Roman Catholic Church. Tavard argues that Pope Leo XIII's view that Anglican orders are invalid has not passed into the *sensus fidelium*. He offers five proposals to solve the impasse.

[1169] Verghese, Paul; Leplay, Michel; Marcus, Emile. *Prêtres et pasteurs*. Eglises en dialogue no. 6. Tours: Mame, 1968.

This short 171 page work gives the viewpoints of a Syrian Orthodox, a Protestant and a Roman Catholic on the nature of the ordained ministry.

[1170] Vischer, Georg H. *Apostolischer Dienst: Fünfzig Jahre Diskussion über das kirchliche Amt in Glauben und Kirchenverfassung*. Frankfurt: O. Lembeck, 1982.

This doctoral dissertation for the Theology Faculty at the University of Basel is a useful overview of Faith and Order's ongoing discussions on apostolic ministry from Lausanne (1927) through Accra (1974). The volume helps one understand the genesis of the ministry section in the Lima document.

[1171] Vorgrimler, Herbert, ed. *Amt und Ordination in ökumenischer*

*Sicht.* Quaestiones Disputatae 50. Freiburg: Herder, 1973.

Ecclesiastical office and ordination are here discussed by a cross-section of Christian theologians in eight essays and two appendices.

# Ordination of Women

[1172] Field-Bibb, Jacqueline. *Women towards Priesthood: Ministerial Politics and Feminist Praxis.* Cambridge: Cambridge University, 1991.

Part one of this study contains documents over the last 200 years from English Methodist, Church of England, and Roman Catholic sources. Part two contains the author's interpretation which she analyzes in terms of undercurrents, strategies and interpretations.

[1173] Gössmann, Elisabeth, and Bader, Dietmar, eds. *Warum keine Ordination der Frau? Unterschiedliche Einstellungen in den christlichen Kirchen.* Munich: Schnell und Steiner, 1987.

Sponsored by the archdiocesan Katholische Akademie in Freiburg, a congress was held there in September 1986 to outline various confessional attitudes toward the ordination of women. Five talks are reproduced covering Lutheran, Orthodox and Catholic perspectives. There are also two concluding statements.

[1174] Parvey, Constance F., ed. *Ordination of Women in Ecumenical Perspective: Workbook for the Church's Future.* Faith and Order Paper 105. Geneva: World Council of Churches, 1980.

This consultation, sponsored by the WCC's Community of Women and Men in the Church, took place in Klingenthal, near Strasbourg, in August/September 1979. Starting point for the discussions was the acceptance of men and women as living images of God. There is a detailed bibliography on women's ordination covering the years 1960-1980 (pp. 75-94).

# Lima Document (BEM)

[1175] *Baptism, Eucharist and Ministry.* Faith and Order Paper No. 111. Geneva: World Council of Churches, 1982.

The famous Lima document (BEM) of the Faith and Order

Commission on the nature of baptism, eucharist and ministry was the culmination of over fifty years of ecumenical collaboration. Since its adoption in 1982 it has been the subject of many far ranging commentaries some of which are cited in the following entries.

[1176] *Baptism, Eucharist and Ministry, 1982-1990: Report on the Process and Responses*. Faith and Order Paper 149. Geneva: World Council of Churches, 1990.

After receiving some 186 official responses to the Lima document the Faith and Order Commission attempts in this volume to summarize the on-going process and to describe the major results and the tasks yet to be accomplished. See also [1193].

[1177] *Baptism, Eucharist and Ministry: Initial Reactions from Roman Catholic Dioceses in the United States*. s.l.: National Association of Diocesan Ecumenical Officers, 1986.

Some eighteen Roman Catholic dioceses responded to the request to state whether they recognized in the Lima document their own credal convictions. This publication gives a global summary of the reactions.

[1178] Church of England. General Synod. Board for Mission and Unity. *Towards a Church of England Response to BEM and ARCIC*. London: Church of England. General Synod, 1985.

This report by a committee of the Church of England addresses both the BEM document [1175] and the Final Report of ARCIC-I [632].

[1179] Fahey, Michael A., ed. *Catholic Perspectives on Baptism, Eucharist and Ministry*. Lanham, MD: University Press of America, 1986.

This collaborative work was commissioned by the Catholic Theological Society of America. It includes such studies as the genesis of the Lima document (M. Fahey), the BEM text's use of Scripture (P. Perkins), its ecclesiology (G. Worgul), its theology of baptism and eucharist (E. J. Kilmartin), and its theology of ordained ministry (W. Marrevee).

[1180] Fahlbusch, Erwin. *Einheit der Kirche - eine kritische*

*Betrachtung des ökumenischen Dialogs: Zur Reception der Lima-Erklärung über Taufe, Eucharistie und Amt.* Theologie Existenz Heute 218. Munich: Chr. Kaiser, 1983.

> The author contributes a long assessment of the Lima document giving special attention to the notions of *"kairos"* and "partners."

[1181] Gros, Jeffrey, ed. *The Search for Visible Unity: Baptism, Eucharist and Ministry.* New York: Pilgrim, 1984.

> This ecumenical collection, largely by theologians working in the USA but two visiting from India, provides a broad survey assessing the process of reception of the Lima (BEM) document. The papers were given at the Chicago conference on BEM Reception, October 12-14, 1983.

[1182] Houtepen, Anton W.J. *Bibiliography on Baptism, Eucharist and Ministry (Lima Text, 1982-1987).* IIMO Research Publications 23. Leiden: Utrecht: Interuniversitair Instituut voor Missiologie en Oecumenica, 1988.

> This 61 page bibliography of reactions to the Lima document covers most of the European languages.

[1183] Kinnamon, Michael. *Why It Matters: A Popular Introduction to the Baptism, Eucharist and Ministry Text.* A Risk Book. Geneva: World Council of Churches, 1985.

> This study guide to the Lima document also contains a glossary of theological terms used in BEM and the text of the Lima liturgy.

[1184] Konfessionskundliches Institut, ed. *Kommentar zu den Lima-Erklärungen über Taufe, Eucharistie und Amt.* Bensheimer Hefte 59. Göttingen: Vandenhoeck und Ruprecht, 1983.

> The commentaries are written from a Lutheran perspective as a guide for those trained in theology. Of the four essays two (the genesis of BEM, and its teaching on baptism) are written by E. Geldbach. The comments on eucharist are by W. Schöpsdau and on ministry by R. Frieling.

[1185] Lazareth, William H. *Growing Together in Baptism, Eucharist and Ministry: A Study Guide.* Faith and Order Paper 114. Geneva: World Council of Churches, 1982.

This booklet is intended to facilitate the process of reception of the Lima document by the wider membership of the churches. It tries to relate sections of the text to concerns of modern society. Discussion questions are also provided.

[1186] Limouris, Gennadios, and Vaporis, Nomikos Michael, eds. *Orthodox Perspectives on Baptism, Eucharist, and Ministry*. Faith and Order Paper 128. Brookline, MA: Holy Cross Orthodox Press, 1985.

The volume contains the proceedings and papers of an inter-Orthodox symposium on the Lima document held in Brookline, Massachusetts, June 11-18, 1985. Some forty-five hierarchs and theologians attended. There were nine major addresses and a six page final report (pp. 159-164). This also appeared in the *Greek Orthodox Theological Review* 30, no. 2 (1985).

[1187] McGuire, Joan Monica. *The Ministry Text in the Lima Report: A Comparison Study of Its Development, of Bilateral Statements and of Selected Reactions to Particular Issues, 1982-1985*. Rome: Angelicum, 1986.

This 313 page doctoral dissertation directed by Charles Angell traces the development of ministry studies from Lausanne (1927) through Lima (1982). The BEM document is compared to other bilateral statements and preliminary reactions to it from the churches are noted.

[1188] Price, Tony, ed. *Evangelical Anglicans and the Lima Text: An Assessment and Critique*. Bramcote, Nottingham: Grove Books, 1985.

The editor drafted this short but probing commentary on behalf of the Church of England Evangelical Council. There are a number of specific questions directed to the Faith and Order Commission about the Lima document's view of evangelism.

[1189] *The Reception of BEM in the European Context*. Geneva: Conference of European Churches [CEC], 1986.

The publication reports on four study consultations organized by the CEC in 1984 and 1985. Position papers were delivered by Harding Meyer, Grigorios Larentzakis, Alfonso Alvarez Bolado, Dumitru Popescu and Nikos Nissiotis as well as numerous responses. [available from St. Andrews Press, 121 George St., Edinburgh EH2 4YN, Scotland].

[1190] Schulz, Frieder. *Die Lima-Liturgie: Die ökumenische Gottesdienstordnung zu den Lima-Texten: Ein Beitrag zum Verständnis und zur Urteilsbildung.* Kassel: Johannes Stauda, 1983.

The text of this pamphlet appeared first in the *Jahrbuch für Liturgik und Hymnologie* 27 (1983). In 32 heavily annotated pages the author outlines the development of eucharistic consciousness at the WCC and the stages of composing the Lima liturgy.

[1191] Segretariato Attività Ecumeniche, ed. *La credibilità delle Chiese e il BEM (Battesimo - Eucaristia - Ministerio) [Atti della XXII Sessione di formazione ecumenica organizzata dal S.A.E., 1984].* Naples: Dehoniane, 1985.

This meeting of the Italian Ecumenical Association studied the Lima document in three major presentations and in an ecumenical round table discussion. The special focus was the credibility of the churches in light of BEM.

[1192] Seils, Michael. *Lutheran Convergence? An Analysis of the Lutheran Responses to the Convergence Document Baptism, Eucharist and Ministry of the World Conference of Churches.* LWF Report 25. Geneva: Lutheran World Federation, 1988.

The doctoral candidate at the University of Halle gathers and discusses the official views of twenty-seven Lutheran churches regarding the Lima document.

[1193] Thurian, Max, ed. *Churches Respond to Baptism, Eucharist and Ministry: Official Responses to the "Baptism, Eucharist and Ministry" Text.* 6 vols. Faith and Order Papers 129, 132, 135, 137, 143, 144. Geneva: World Council of Churches, 1986-1988.

As part of the process of reception on the Lima document, the study adviser to the Faith and Order Commission has collected and published a vast number of official church reactions.

[1194] Thurian, Max. *Ecumenical Perspectives on Baptism, Eucharist, Ministry.* Faith and Order Paper 116. Geneva: World Council of Churches, 1983.

These papers were prepared by scholars who had themselves been involved in the formulation of the Lima document. In 246 pages they review the genesis of the drafts and evaluate them from different doctrinal and theological traditions. Thurian provides an account and text of the Lima eucharistic liturgy.

[1195] Thurian, Max, and Wainwright, Geoffrey, eds. *Baptism and Eucharist: Ecumenical Convergence in Celebration*. Faith and Order Paper 117. Geneva: World Council of Churches; Grand Rapids: Eerdmans, 1983.

To help theologians and church leaders assess current understanding and practice of baptism and eucharist in their own churches, the two ecumenists have edited a representative collection of modern liturgical rites of baptism (Thurian) and eucharist (Wainwright). This volume also hopes to assist the reception process of the Lima document.

[1196] Voss, Gerhard, ed. *Wachsende Übereinstimmung in Taufe, Eucharistie und Amt: Hilfen zur Beschäftigung mit dem Lima-Erklärungen*. Freising: Kyrios; Paderborn: Bonifatius, 1984.

Prepared by the ecumenical commission of the Catholic dioceses of Bavaria, this high level study guide and assessment of the Lima document drew upon the work of seven experts. The German Catholic Bishops' Conference in 1983 studied this material and stressed the importance of study of the BEM text.

# Ecumenical Marriage

[1197] *Anglican-Roman Catholic Marriage: The Report of the Anglican-Roman Catholic International Commission on the Theology of Marriage and its Application to Mixed Marriages*. London: Church Information Office, 1975.

This publication is the fruit of some eight years' work by an international team of ecumenists from various English-speaking countries. The introduction is jointly composed by the former Archbishop of Canterbury, Donald Coggan, and the president of the Secretariat for Promoting Christian Unity, Johannes Willebrands. Included are the commission's proceedings, a discussion of relevant theological issues, reflections on defective marital situations, and advice on mixed marriages.

[1198] Beaupère, René, and Emery, Pierre-Yves, eds. *Mariages mixtes: témoignages de foyers, de pasteurs et de prêtres*. Eglise en dialogue 9. Tours: Mame, 1967.

The introduction to this volume is written jointly by a Catholic (Beaupère) and a Protestant (Emery, one of the brothers of Taizé). The book is divided into three parts: personal sharings about marriage, a statement of collective experience, and practical information (including an exposition of Orthodox regulations written by Pierre l'Huillier).

[1199] Böckle, Franz, *et al. Le problème des mariages mixtes: Colloque de Nemi.* Paris: Editions du Cerf, 1969.

Five Roman Catholic theologians from different backgrounds publish here their addressess given at a meeting in Nemi (near Rome) on theological, canonical and pastoral issues related to ecumenical marriages. This volume is a translation of the German *Mischehe in ökumenischer Sicht* (1968). See also [1200].

[1200] Böckle, Franz, *et al.*, eds. *Die Konfessionsverschiedene Ehe: Probleme für die Ökumene.* Regensburg: F. Pustet, 1988.

This further study of confessionally mixed marriage contains seven essays by Catholics and Protestants. There is a sociological essay on the life situation of mixed couples and comparisons of differing attitudes toward indissolubility and sacramental character. See also [1199].

[1201] Bressan, Luigi. *Il divorzio nelle chiese orientali: Ricerca storica sull'atteggiamento cattolico.* Nuovi Saggi Teologici, no. 11. Bologna: Dehoniane, 1976.

There are eight chapters on the history of divorce, ecclesiastical controversies regarding it, and Eastern attitudes from the Council of Florence up to the present. Other essays describe the pastoral practice of Eastern Catholic hierarchs. A long bibliography on the book's theme is appended (pp. 301-324).

[1202] *Eheverständnis und Ehescheidung: Empfehlungen des Interkonfessionellen Arbeitskreises für Ehe- und Familienfrage.* Mainz: M. Grünewald; Munich: C. Kaiser, 1971.

This short (74 pp.) work on pastoral problems relating to marriage and divorce was prepared by an ecumenical group from four different perspectives: sociological considerations, exegetical and historical dimensions, modern attitudes, and practical advice.

**[1203]** Engelhardt, Hanns, ed. *Die Kirchen und die Ehe.* Beiheft zur ökumenischen Rundschau, No. 46. Frankfurt: O. Lembeck, 1984.

The seven essays study Christian marriage from several ecumenical perspectives: Roman Catholic in light of the New Code of Canon Law (1983), Lutheran, Orthodox, Anglican and North American Protestant. There are also two African presentations one of which discusses polygamy.

**[1204]** Evangelische Kirche in Deutschland, Kirchenkanzlei, ed. *Ehe, Familie, Sexualität, Jugend.* Die Denkschriften der Evangelischen Kirche in Deutschland, Bd. 3 Gütersloh: Gerd Mohn, 1981.

This volume discusses marriage, sexuality and family life in light of the 1969 reform of the German Divorce Law and the EKD's reaction to it. This collection of documents includes the joint 1981 declaration of the EKD and the German Catholic Episcopal Conference's joint declaration. Also treated are: interconfessional marriage, sexual ethics, abortion, church and sport.

**[1205]** *Final Report: Theology of Marriage and the Problems of Mixed Marriages, 1971-1977. Dialogue Between the Lutheran World Federation, the World Alliance of Reformed Churches, and the Secretariat for Promoting Christian Unity of the Roman Catholic Church.* Washington: United States Catholic Conference, 1978.

Published in Venice, 1976, this thirty-nine page booklet summarizes five years of intense ecumenical dialogue among members of the three groups. The focus is both theoretical and pastoral.

**[1206]** *Gemeinsame kirchliche Empfehlungen für die Seelsorge an konfessionsverschiedenen Ehen und Familien.* Ed. Sekretariat des Deutschen Bischofskonferenz und Kirchenkanzlei der Evangelischen Kirche in Deutschland. Gütersloh: Gerd Mohn, 1981.

This is a brief 48 page review of basic pastoral issues peculiar to ecumenical marriages and the spiritual formation of children jointly written by the German Catholic Bishops' Conference and the secretariat of the EKD. A short inventory of available resources for Germany is included.

**[1207]** Harenberg, Werner. *Mischehe und Konzil: Chancen und Grenzen einer katholischen Reform.* Stuttgart: Kreuz, 1964.

The author wrote this volume during Vatican II while working as a journalist for *Der Spiegel*. He presents a historical account of attitudes by Protestants and Catholics toward mixed marriages prior to the Council. He then outlines various expectations raised by Vatican II as reflected in interviews with a cross-section of German Catholic bishops.

[1208] Heron, Alasdair. *Two Churches, One Love: Interchurch Marriage between Protestants and Roman Catholics*. Dublin: APCK, 1977.

The booklet by a British Protestant theologian now teaching at Erlangen covers the principal sources of tension in ecumenical marriages. He compares the older Roman Catholic directives in the 1918 Code of Canon Law to the decisions of Vatican II.

[1209] Hill, Philip W. *Mixed Marriages and their Pre-Requisites in the Light of Ecumenism*. Rome: Pontificia Università Lateranese, 1980.

This doctoral dissertation from the Lateran University outlines Catholic teaching on ecumenism and current canonical legislation on mixed marriages. The author concludes that even the new Code falls short of an ideal arrangement. A lengthy bibliography is included (pp. 368-397).

[1210] Hurley, Michael, ed. *Beyond Tolerance: The Challenge of Mixed Marriages*. London: Geoffrey Chapman; New York: Macmillan, 1975.

This record of an international consultation on ecumenical marriages held in Dublin in 1974 was edited by the founder of the Irish School of Ecumenics (f. 1970). It contains most of the papers and discussions representative of various Protestant and Catholic positions.

[1211] Kleemann, Jürg, and Nitschke, Horst, eds. *Ökumenische Trauungen: Predigten, Texte, Dokumente: Mit einem Beitrag zur kirchenrechtlichen Problematik*. Gütersloh: Gerd Mohn, 1973.

This resource book for mixed marriages contains sample orders of service, documents and sermons prepared by Catholic and Protestant preachers for such occasions. Most helpful from a scholarly point of view is its modest collection of documents from various ecumenical commissions and churches.

[1212] Krems, Gerhard, and Mumm, Reinhard, eds. *Theologie der Ehe*. Veröffentlichung des Ökumenischen Arbeitskreises evangelischer und katholischer Theologen. Regensburg: F. Pustet; Göttingen: Vandenhoeck und Ruprecht, 1969.

> At the twenty-ninth meeting of this ecumenical working group, two Catholics and two Protestants outlined the teaching of Scripture on marriage and sketched a theology of sexuality and marriage. The wedding liturgies of both churches are described and compared.

[1213] Lell, Joachim, and Meyer, Harding, eds. *Ehe und Mischehe im ökumenischen Dialog*. Ökumenische Dokumentation, IV. Frankfurt: O. Lembeck; J. Knecht, 1979.

> Two of the three documents quoted [632, 1197] are available in English elsewhere. But the volume provides a valuable German text of a consensus statement by Catholics and Lutherans entitled "Ehe und Familie in christlicher Sicht" (published September 1974).

[1214] Lengsfeld, Peter. *Das Problem Mischehe: Einer Lösung entgegen*. Kleine ökumenische Schriften, Bd. 3. Freiburg: Herder, 1970.

> This work grew out of three lectures given in Munich during 1969. It addresses problematic attitudes in the churches towards mixed marriages, theological views on interchurch marriage, and various suggestions in the form of fourteen short theses on what needs to be done.

[1215] Lüssi, Walter. *Kinder zwischen den Konfessionen: Religiöse Erziehung in der Mischehe als Herausforderung für die Ortsgemeinde*. Zürich: Theologische Verlag, 1983.

> Noting that one-third of Christian marriages are mixed marriages, the author explores in this 100 page study typical challenges especially in the spiritual formation of children. He develops the notion of a "charism of tolerance." There is a brief bibliography (pp. 95-98).

[1216] *Quinze ans de pastorale des Foyers Mixtes: Documents des Eglises*. Lyons: Foyers Mixtes, 1978.

This special double number of the journal *Foyers Mixtes* (nos. 37-38) focuses on ecumenical marriages. It contains an overview of 15 years of shared experience. Several confessional documents from Rome, France and Switzerland are included.

[1217] Stirnimann, Heinrich, ed. *Christliche Ehe und getrennte Kirchen: Dokumente, Studien.* Ökumenische Beihefte 1. Fribourg, Switzerland: Paulus, 1968.

In this new series the volume publishes three essays on the theology of marriage as well as three on problems in confessionally mixed marriages. A bibliography of some 650 titles was prepared by Johannes Brantschen (pp. 95-124).

# Authority, Sources and Expressions

[1218] Empie, Paul C.; Murphy, T. Austin; and Burgess, Joseph A., eds. *Teaching Authority and Infallibility in the Church.* Lutherans and Catholics in Dialogue 6. Minneapolis: Augsburg, 1980.

This sixth agreed statement from the US Lutheran/Catholic Consultation also includes fifteen useful background papers prepared for the dialogue.

[1219] Krems, Gerhard, and Mumm, Reinhard, eds. *Autorität in der Krise.* Veröffentlichung des Ökumenischen Arbeitskreises evangelischer und katholischer Theologen. Regensburg: F. Pustet; Göttingen: Vandenhoeck und Ruprecht, 1970.

The thirtieth meeting of the ecumenical working group focused on authority in the church. Two Catholic and two Protestant texts are provided.

[1220] Schuster, Josef. *Ethos und kirchliches Lehramt: Zur Kompetenz des Lehramtes in Fragen der natürlichen Sittlichkeit.* Frankfurter Theologische Studien 31. Frankfurt: J. Knecht, 1984.

This dissertation by a German Jesuit was written in Tübingen under the direction of the moral theologian A. Auer (1982). It includes a study of the expression *fides et mores* in Trent and Vatican I as well as the notions of the changeable and unchangeable in authoritative teaching. It explores what are the possibilities and limits of magisterial competence in ethical matters.

**[1221]** Weber, Wilhelm, ed. *Macht, Dienst, Herrschaft in Kirche und Gesellschaft*. Freiburg: Herder, 1974.

There are fifteen contributions to this lecture series held in 1972-1973 at the Catholic Theology Faculty of Münster on issues of power, service and lordship. Especially pertinent is the essay on "Power as a Factor in Ecumenical Processes" (pp. 222-237).

**[1222]** Yarnold, Edward J., and Chadwick, Henry. *Truth and Authority: A Commentary on the Agreed Statement of the Anglican-Roman Catholic International Commission "Authority in the Church", Venice, 1976*. London: CTS/SPCK, 1977.

Two members of the ARCIC-I group, E.J. Yarnold, tutor in theology at Campion Hall, Oxford, and H. Chadwick, Dean of Christ Church, Oxford, comment on the doctrinal statements of this agreed statement that was eventually incorporated into the *Final Report* [632].

# Reception

**[1223]** Alberigo, Giuseppe; Jossua, Jean-Pierre; and Komonchak, Joseph, eds. *The Reception of Vatican II*. Trans. by Matthew J. O'Connell. Washington: Catholic University of America Press, 1987.

Besides the original French and Italian editions, this volume also exists in German translation. Seventeen scholars addressed various aspects of the way Vatican II has or has not found "reception" in the Catholic community. Treated are the contexts and central themes of reception, as well as those themes taken further in reception and those insufficiently received. One chapter treats opposition to the Council. Avery Dulles comments in an appendix on the 1985 Roman Synod.

**[1224]** Beinert, Wolfgang, ed. *Glaube als Zustimmung: Zur Interpretation kirchlicher Rezeptionsvorgänge*. Quaestiones Disputatae 131. Freiburg: Herder, 1991.

Four theologians contribute to this collaborative study on reception: its meaning for the church (W. Beinert); reception and obedience (H.J. Pottmeyer); reception of the ecumenical councils in the first millennium (K. Schatz); and reception in the canonical tradition (F. Ochmann).

[1225] Hryniewicz, Waclaw, and Górka, Leonard. *Recepcja: Nowe Zadanie ekumenizmu [Reception: The New Task of Ecumenism].* Lublin: Redakcja Wydawnictw Kul, 1985.

Eight essays, all in Polish, treat modern issues related to the doctrine of "reception". Among the authors are several Orthodox and Protestant contributors besides the Roman Catholics.

[1226] Lengsfeld, Peter, and Stobbe, Heinz-Günther, eds. *Theologischer Konsens und Kirchenspaltung.* Stuttgart: W. Kohlhammer, 1981.

The volume contains the acts of the first consultation of the European Societas Oecumenica which met in Münster in 1980. All eleven essays are in German. They address various aspects of reception and consensus and offer a closing statement that proposes practical suggestions. See also [1061].

[1227] Rusch, William G. *Reception: An Ecumenical Opportunity.* Philadelphia: Fortress, 1988.

This brief 78 page book sponsored by the Lutheran World Federation addresses the theological meaning of the notion "reception" especially in relationship to bilateral and multilateral dialogues.

# Petrine Ministry

[1228] Allmen, Jean-Jacques von. *La primauté de l'Eglise de Pierre et de Paul: Remarques d'un protestant.* Cahiers oecuméniques 10. Paris: Cerf; Fribourg: Editions Universitaires, 1977.

This is an insightful collection of studies by the Swiss Reformed professor which includes essays on: the New Testament witnesses to Peter and Paul; historical examples showing how the Roman primacy was affirmed, contested and responded to, and including the text of the *Dictatus papae*, the twenty-seven theses of Pope Gregory VII (AD 1073-1085) on papal prerogatives; and a summary section which outlines five things that the Church of Rome should do to make the papacy acceptable.

[1229] Brandenburg, Albert, and Urban, Hans Jörg, eds. *Petrus und Papst: Evangelium, Einheit der Kirche, Papstdienst.* 2 vols. Münster: Aschendorff, 1977-1978.

Some of these studies appeared first in the journal *Catholica* [96] under the auspices of Paderborn's Johann Adam Möhler Institute for Ecumenics. These volumes include exegetical studies on Peter in the New Testament, Petrine ministry, the papacy in the bilateral documents, and as seen by Protestants (five essays) and by an Eastern Christian.

[1230] Brown, Raymond E.; Donfried, Karl P.; and Reumann, John, eds. *Peter in the New Testament: A Collaborative Assessment by Protestant and Roman Catholic Scholars*. Minneapolis: Augsburg; New York: Paulist, 1973.

Based on the discussions and collaboration of eleven biblical scholars working for the official US Lutheran/Catholic Consultation in preparation for its agreed statement on *Papal Primacy* [1243], this study represents an important exegetical account of the role of Peter in the various New Testament writings. See also similar study on Mary [1085].

[1231] Corsani, Bruno, and Ricca, Paolo. *Pietro e il papato nel dibattito ecumenico odierno*. Turin: Claudiana, 1978.

Both authors are professors at Rome's Waldensian Faculty of Theology. Corsani writes on the primacy of Peter and Petrine ministry according to the New Testament; Ricca describes the papacy as an ecumenical problem.

[1232] Cullmann, Oscar. *Peter: Disciple, Apostle, Martyr: A Historical and Theological Study*. Trans. by Floyd V. Filson. 2nd rev. ed. London: SCM, 1962.

Originally published in German in 1952, this study of the New Testament portrayal of Peter the Apostle strongly influenced the way subsequent biblical scholars and ecumenists addressed this question.

[1233] Journet, Charles. *The Primacy of Peter from the Protestant and from the Catholic Point of View*. Trans. by John Chapin. Westminster, MD: Newman, 1954.

This study translated from the French original of 1953 was in response especially to Oscar Cullmann's *Peter: Disciple, Apostle, Martyr* [1232]. It is informative to compare the methodology of this early work of Journet with the kind of ecumenical collaboration such as found in Brown [1230].

[1234] Lehmann, Karl, ed. *Das Petrusamt: Geschichtliche Stationen seines Verständnisses und gegenwärtige Positionen.* Munich: Schnell und Steiner, 1982.

The volume contains six articles on Petrine ministry in the New Testament, and in the first millennium, at Vatican I, in relationship to the doctrine of infallibility as perceived by Reformation churches. The editor provides a concluding essay on the disputed issues.

[1235] McCord, Peter J., ed. *A Pope for All Christians? An Inquiry into the Role of Peter in the Modern Church.* New York: Paulist, 1976.

Seven leading American theologians from various confessional traditions were asked to express their opinions regarding the possibility of an "ecumenical papacy." All but one of the theologians (the Baptist) would allow for the possibility of some primatial function for the pope.

[1236] Mund, Hans-Joachim, ed. *Das Petrusamt in der gegenwärtigen Diskussion.* Paderborn: F. Schöningh, 1976.

Five contributors prepared papers on Petrine ministry for this meeting organized by the Evangelisch-Ökumenische Vereinigung held in Kitzingen, September 1973: H.-J. Mund, J. Ries, H. Echternach, G. Kretschmar and K.C. Felmy.

[1237] Sartori, Luigi, *et al. Il Servizio di Pietro: Appunti per una riflessione interconfessionale.* Leumann-Turin: Editrice Elle Di Ci, 1978.

Besides the Venice statement on authority from the Anglican-Roman Catholic International Commission (ARCIC-I) [632], this volume contains nine essays on Petrine ministry as reflected in the New Testament and in modern ecumenical discussions.

[1238] Satgé, John de. *Peter and the Single Church.* London: SPCK, 1981.

The Anglican ecumenist is convinced of the closeness of views between Anglicans and Catholics regarding the Petrine office. He outlines for Anglicans what would be the consequences of formal recognition of and by the papacy.

# Papal Primacy

[1239] Aristi, Vasilios von; Blank, Josef; Fries, Heinrich, eds. *Das Papstamt: Dienst oder Hindernis für die Ökumene*. Regensburg: F. Pustet, 1985.

The volume contains the proceedings of an ecumenical consultation that discussed papal ministry from Protestant, Orthodox and Catholic viewpoints. In all there are nine essays treating issues raised by the papacy in the context of ecumenism.

[1240] Denzler, Georg, ed. *Das Papsttum in der Diskussion*. Regensburg: F. Pustet, 1974.

This volume contains seven essays on the papacy drawn from a theological forum held in Bamberg in 1973. The essay by U. Valeske is entitled "The Papacy and Ecumenism."

[1241] Denzler, Georg, ed. *Papsttum Heute und Morgen: 57 Antworten auf eine Umfrage*. Regensburg: F. Pustet, 1975.

The church historian Denzler administered a questionnaire among German-speaking Catholic and Protestant professional people to measure attitudes regarding the present and future role of the papacy. The fifty-seven responses are reproduced, each averaging some four pages.

[1242] Dvornik, Francis. *Byzantium and the Roman Primacy*. Trans. by Edwin A. Quain, S.J. New York: Fordham University Press, 1966.

Dvornik served as professor of Byzantine history at Harvard University's Dumbarton Oaks Center in Washington from 1949 until his retirement. This enlightened study, written after Vatican II, argues that the "only serious obstacle" between Orthodox and Catholics is the papacy, which needs to be studied as an historical and a theological problem.

[1243] Empie, Paul C., and Murphy, T. Austin, eds. *Papal Primacy and the Universal Church*. Lutherans and Catholics in Dialogue 5. Minneapolis: Augsburg, 1974.

The fifth agreed statement in this US Lutheran/Catholic

Consultation is here published together with thirteen background papers on papal primacy.

**[1244]** Giamberardini, Gabriele, *et al. Il primato e l'unione delle chiese nel medio oriente.* Studia Orientalia Christiana, Collectanea, No. 5. Cairo: Centro Francescano di Studi Orientali Cristiani, 1960.

This pre-Vatican II volume draws upon Coptic, Syrian, Armenian and Chaldean sources to argue the need for a more nuanced formulation of Petrine primacy in the church. Using Arabic, Coptic, Armenian and Syriac liturgical and theological documents, with French and Italian translations, the authors offer a series of proposed reforms.

**[1245]** Granfield, Patrick. *The Papacy in Transition.* New York: Doubleday, 1980.

This useful study by an American Benedictine professor shows how various "models" of understanding the papal office have been important in theological and ecumenical reflection. See also [1246].

**[1246]** Granfield, Patrick. *The Limits of the Papacy: Authority and Autonomy in the Church.* New York: Crossroad, 1987.

The Catholic author's second major study on the papacy outlines the claims of primacy and the limitations inherent in the papal office. Special attention is given to collegiality and local churches interacting with the church universal. Chapter 6 (pp. 169-193) discusses "The Pope and Other Christians." See also [1245].

**[1247]** Groupe des Dombes. *Le ministère de communion dans l'Eglise universelle.* Paris: Le Centurion, 1986.

The fifth in a series of agreed statements published by the Group of Les Dombes, this 117 page statement focuses on the ongoing Petrine ministry of pastoral solicitude for the church universal. See also [699].

**[1248]** Hardt, Michael. *Papsttum und Ökumene: Ansätze eines Neuverständnisses für einen Papstprimat in der protestantischen Theologie des 20. Jahrhundert.* Beiträge zur ökumenischen Theologie, Bd. 20. Paderborn: F. Schöningh, 1981.

This publication is based on a 1980 doctoral dissertation researched at Munich under the direction of Heinrich Fries. The author reviews the doctrine of papal primacy formulated at Vatican I (1870) and traces how it has been criticized by Protestant theologians before and after Vatican II.

[1249] Klausnitzer, Wolfgang. *Das Papstamt im Disput zwischen Lutheranern und Katholiken: Schwerpunkte von der Reformation bis zur Gegenwart.* Innsbrucker Theologische Studien, Bd. 20. Innsbruck: Tyrolia, 1987.

This work received the Karl Rahner Prize for Theological Research in 1987. Prepared as a *Habilitationsschrift* for Innsbruck, the volume gives a thorough coverage of the world-wide bilateral consultations on the papacy, comparing their viewpoints and offering a kind of synthesis.

[1250] Knecht, Sebastian [pseudonym]. *Un Pape, un jour...: Récit oecuménique.* Trans. by Pierre Homeyer. Chevetogne: Editions de Chevetogne, 1977.

This unusual contribution to the ecumenical discussions about the papacy is formulated in terms of what might be, a "dream" of what a future pope might do to enhance the credibility of Petrine ministry. The German original was *Die Vision des Papstes* (1975).

[1251] Meyendorff, John; Schmemann, Alexander; Afanassieff, Nicolas; Koulomzine, Nicolas. *The Primacy of Peter.* Essays 3 and 4 trans. by Katherine Farrer. London: Faith Press, 1963.

These four essays, first published in French, are still highly useful examples of Orthodox objections to papal primacy as practiced within the Roman Catholic Church.

[1252] Miller, J. Michael. *The Divine Right of the Papacy in Recent Ecumenical Theology.* Analecta Gregorians, vol. 218. Rome: Gregorian University, 1980.

The American Basilian priest covers the historical and theological background to the notion of *ius divinum*. He then outlines how it has been understood in Lutheran, Anglican and recent Catholic theology. He cites from Catholic bilateral conversations with Lutherans and Anglicans. The final section contains an evaluation and conclusions.

**[1253]** Ohlig, Karl-Heinz. *Why We Need the Pope: The Necessity and Limits of Papal Primacy*. Trans. by Robert C. Ware. St. Meinrad, IN: Abbey, 1975.

The title of the German original included a question mark: *Braucht die Kirche einen Papst?* The Catholic professor devotes half of his book to the origin and history of papal primacy and half to theological anlaysis. He includes a close study of Vatican I (1869-70). The author has appropriated a wide spectrum of ecumenical literature on this topic.

**[1254]** *Papsttum als ökumenische Frage*. Munich: C. Kaiser; Mainz: M. Grünewald, 1979.

The volume contains papers on papacy from an ecumenical meeting held in Heidelberg, October 1977, sponsored by the German university based ecumenical institutes. The topics range from the New Testament to the present day. The eight contributors are: E. Schlink, E. Grässer, J. Blank, W. de Vries, O. H. Pesch, H. Ott, J. Moltmann, H. Stirnimann.

**[1255]** *La Primauté romaine dans la communion des Eglises*. Paris: Editions du Cerf, 1991.

The Joint Committee of Catholics and Orthodox in France discussed for five years (1985-1990) the nature of the primacy of Rome. In this 128 page volume, seven background papers are reproduced. The book concludes with a mutual expression of convictions on ecclesiological perspectives and historical reflections that raise still unanswered questions.

**[1256]** Sartori, Luigi, ed. *Papato e istanze ecumeniche*. Scienze religiose 6. Bologna: Dehoniane, 1984.

The acts of this symposium in Trent, May 1982, contain four studies on Petrine ministry and papacy in the church as understood in official bilateral consultations.

**[1257]** Schwaiger, Georg. *Päpstlicher Primat und Autorität der Allgemeinen Konzilien im Spiegel der Geschichte*. Munich: F. Schöningh, 1977.

This historico-theological study of papal primacy and authority traces the development of the notions from the pre-Nicene synods up to modern times.

[1258] Stirnimann, Heinrich, and Vischer, Lukas, *et al. Papsttum und Petrusdienst.* Ökumenische Perspektiven 7. Frankfurt: O. Lembeck; J. Knecht, 1975.

> The volume contains seven articles by Protestants, Orthodox, Old Catholics and Roman Catholics on papacy and Petrine ministry. It also contains the German text of three documents: the US Lutheran/Catholic text on papal ministry, the Old Catholic statement on primacy, and seven brief theses of the International Old Catholic Theological Congress on primacy.

[1259] Tillard, Jean-Marie. *The Bishop of Rome.* Trans. by John de Satgé. London: SPCK, 1983.

> The Ottawa based French Catholic ecumenist organizes his creative and provocative reflections around three issues: the pope - more than a pope?, the pope - bishop of Rome, and the pope as servant of communion. The French original was *L'Evêque de Rome* (1982).

[1260] Vries, Wilhelm de, *et al. Rom und die Patriarchate des Ostens.* Orbis Academicus, Bd. III/4. Freiburg: Karl Alber, 1963.

> This major scholarly publication by the German Jesuit, former professor at Rome's Pontificio Istituto Orientale, discusses Rome's dealings with Eastern patriarchates up to the nineteenth century, as well as Rome's dealings with the Eastern churches in general. The bibliography contains useful primary and secondary literature (pp. 424-432).

# Councils

[1261] *Councils and the Ecumenical Movement.* World Council of Churches Studies 5. Geneva: World Council of Churches, 1968.

> The WCC study group here submits its report on the importance of the conciliar process in the ancient church for the ecumenical movement. Six background papers are then reproduced covering a wide spectrum of church history.

[1262] Fahey, Michael A. *Assembly 2000 A.D.: Preparing for a Truly Ecumenical Gathering of Christians.* Regina, Sask.: Campion College,

University of Regina, 1981.

The Catholic ecumenist outlines the desirability and possibility of planning for an eventual "ecumenical council" at which representatives of all Christian churches would be present.

[1263] Mühlen, Heribert. *Morgen wird Einheit Sein: Das kommende Konzil aller Christen: Ziel der getrennten Kirchen.* Paderborn: Schöningh, 1974.

This volume was one of the first to promote the goal for the future of a truly ecumenical council of all believers. It also explored the theological conditions for reception.

[1264] Tracy, David W.; Küng, Hans; and Metz, Johann B., eds. *Towards Vatican III: The Work that Needs to Be Done.* New York: Seabury, 1978.

From May 29 to June 1, 1977, a colloquium was held at the University of Notre Dame at which seventy-one theologians and social scientists outlined what might be the agenda for a symbolic "Vatican III." Twenty-seven papers from a cross section of the Catholic international community are here reproduced.

# Evangelism and Mission

[1265] Bria, Ion, ed. *Martyria / Mission: The Witness of the Orthdox Churches Today.* Geneva: World Council of Churche, 1980.

The Romanian Orthodox theologian associated with the WCC's Commission on World Mission and Evangelism edited this collection of essays enumerating the concerns and challenges of mission in the Orthodox world today. This is followed by a witness from each of the Orthodox and Ancient Oriental Orthodox churches. In the final section there are five Orthodox statements on mission emanating from recent consultations.

[1266] Castro, Emilio. *Freedom in Mission: The Perspective of the Kingdom of God: An Ecumenical Inquiry.* Geneva: World Council of Churches, 1985.

This study by the general secretary of the WCC was accepted as a doctoral dissertation by the University of Lausanne. Part one is the thesis proper on "A Biblical, Theological Discussion of the

Kingdom of God and its Missionary Implications" (pp. 1-126); part two contains a selection of his published articles on mission (129-330).

[1267] Castro, Emilio. *Sent Free: Mission and Unity in the Perspective of the Kingdom*. Risk Book Series. Geneva: World Council of Churches, 1985.

Dr. Castro explains that the church's mission is to proclaim the gospel to all nations, to express God's concern for the poor and powerless, and to repeat God's promise of a new day of justice and peace.

[1268] Margull, Hans Jochen. *Zur Sendung der Kirche: Material der ökumenischen Bewegung*. Theologische Bücherei, No. 18. Munich: C. Kaiser, 1963.

To show how commitment to the church's mission has been central to the modern ecumenical movement, the author cites a number of official texts dating back to Edinburgh in 1910. Most of these German texts were originally published in English.

[1269] *Mission in a Broken World: Report of ACC-8, Wales, 1990*. Ed. by Roger Coleman. London: Church House, 1990.

The Anglican Consultative Council (ACC) held its eight meeting in July 1990 to discuss the theme of mission. These proceedings contain the special papers, section reports and business minutes.

[1270] *The Missionary Obligation of the Church: International Missionary Council, Willingen, Germany, July 5-17, 1952*. London: Edinburgh House, 1952.

The 46 page booklet emanates from the International Missionary Council meeting held in Willingen. Of central importance are the two official statements: "The Missionary Calling of the Church" and "The Calling of the Church to Mission and Unity."

[1271] *Le Missioni e l'unità dei cristiani: Atti della decima settimana di studi missionari, Milano, 8-12 settembre 1969*. Milan: Vita e pensiero, 1970.

Held at Sacred Heart University, Milan, this congress addressed the challenges of combining missionary evangelization with ecumenical awareness. Among the addresses are texts on evangelization in Orthodox theology (E. Timiadis) and ecumenism and evangelization in India (M. Dhavamony).

[1272] Neill, Stephen; Anderson, Gerald H.; Goodwin, John, eds. *Concise Dictionary of the Christian World Mission.* London: Lutterworth, 1970; Nashville: Abingdon, 1971.

This massive 682 page encyclopedia on missions draws upon the expertise of 200 experts representative of an ecumenical spectrum of churches. Each entry, which is short, has a brief bibliography. The articles on the WCC and on the ecumenical movement were written by W.A. Visser 't Hooft.

[1273] Newbigin, Lesslie. *One Body, One Gospel, One World: The Christian Mission Today.* London: W. Carling, 1958.

Shortly before the merger of the International Missionary Council and the World Council of Churches, Newbigin (b. 1909), the former Bishop of Madurai and Ramnad who had been a driving force behind the creation of the Church of South India (1947), outlined the unchanging basis of mission and principles for action today. See also [423].

[1274] Segretariato Attività Ecumeniche, ed. *Ecumenismo ed evangelizzazione [Atti della XII Sessione di formazione ecumenica organizzata dal S.A.E., 1974].* Rome: Editrice A.V.E., 1975.

The 1974 session of the Italian Ecumenical Association published here its proceedings which contain Protestant and Catholic views on the theme of ecumenism and evangelization.

[1275] Seumois, André. *Oecuménisme missionaire.* Urbaniana 4. Rome: Urbaniana, 1970.

The Oblate Catholic priest explores in this 234 page volume the missionary origins of the modern ecumenical movement and the impact that ecumenism has had on the way Catholic missions are conceived and operated.

[1276] Stadler, Anton Paul. *Mission-Dialogue: A Digest and Evaluation of the Discussion in the Roman Catholic Church and Within the World Council of Churches, 1965-1975.* New York: Union Theological Seminary, 1977.

This doctoral dissertation studies a decade of official documents of the Catholic Church and the WCC to see how they express the relationship of the two concepts. The WCC is seen to gravitate more toward dialogue. Christian mission should be defined as dialogical apologetics whereby one communicates with others without seeking to dominate.

[1277] Stirnimann, Heinrich, ed. *Ökumenische Erneuerung in der Mission*. Ökumenische Beihefte 4. Fribourg: Paulusverlag, 1970.

This volume edited by the Swiss Dominican ecumenist contains five essays (all in German) outlining the need for renewal in missionary undertakings in light of newly acquired ecumenical sensibilities.

[1278] Van Dusen, Henry P. *One Great Ground of Hope: Christian Missions and Christian Unity*. Philadelphia: Westminster, 1961.

The former President of New York's Union Theological Seminary, who claimed to have attended every major ecumenical conference since 1937, writes about ecumenism yesterday, today and tomorrow. The volume is still amazingly pertinent thirty years later. Also included is a detailed chronology of efforts for Christian unity from 1795 to 1960 (pp. 159-185).

[1279] Wilson, Frederick R., ed. *The San Antonio Report: Your Will Be Done: Mission in Christ's Way*. Geneva: World Council of Churches, 1990.

The volume contains a record of the Commission on World Mission and Evangelism (CWME) conference held in San Antonio, Texas, May 1989. The CWME was previously known as the International Missionary Conference (IMC).

[1280] *Your Kingdom Come: Mission Perspectives: Report on the World Conference on Mission and Evangelism, Melbourne, Australia, 12-25 May 1980*. Geneva: World Council of Churches, 1980.

The conference of the Commission of World Mission and Evangelism (CWME), which succeded the International Missionary Council since its incorporation into the WCC, discussed: good news to the poor, the kingdom of God and human struggles, church witnesses to the kingdom, and the crucified Christ challenging human power.

# Women in Society and Church

[1281] Best, Thomas F. *Beyond Unity-in-Tension: Unity, Renewal and the Community of Women and Men*. Faith and Order Paper 138. Geneva: World Council of Churches, 1988.

> This volume reports on the Prague Consultation of 1985 which is intended to be a follow-up to the Sheffield report on "The Community of Women and Men in the Church" (1981) [1290]. The Consultation report is here reproduced (pp. 159-163).

[1282] Bliss, Kathleen. *The Service and Status of Women in the Churches*. London: SCM, 1954.

> This publication summarizes the WCC inquiry into the work and status of women in churches of some forty-five countries. The focus is not only on women's ordination but on their participation in church governance and voluntary service.

[1283] Crawford, Janet, and Kinnamon, Michael, eds. *In God's Image: Reflections on Identity, Human Wholeness and the Authority of Scripture*. Geneva: World Council of Churches, 1983.

> These studies are connected with the WCC project on the Community of Women and Men in the Church. Various reflections on the Sheffield report [1290] are offered. These are followed by systematic explorations on personal identity, human wholeness, theological anthropology, and finally Scripture and experience.

[1284] *The Deaconess: A Service of Women in the World of Today*. World Council of Churches Studies No. 4. Geneva: World Council of Churches, 1966.

> This document contains the proceedings of the consultation held in Presinge, near Geneva, September 5-8, 1965. Seven contributors outlined how the diaconate for women is understood and lived in different churches: Greek Orthodox, Anglican, Reformed, Free Church, younger churches. The consultation's report outlines areas of agreement and divergence (pp. 9-22).

[1285] Fabella, Virginia, and Oduyoye, Mercy Amba, eds. *With Passion and Compassion: Third World Women Doing Theology*. Maryknoll, NY: Orbis, 1988.

The two editors from the Philippines and Ghana summarized the proceedings of the Women's Commission of EATWOT (Ecumenical Association of Third World Theologians) following the theological consultation in Oaxtepec, Mexico, December 1986. See also [753-759].

[1286] Herzel, Susannah. *A Voice for Women: The Women's Department of the World Council of Chruches*. Geneva: World Council of Churches, 1981.

This is a chronological account of three decades (1950s through 1970s) outlining the struggles and gains by women in the ecumenical movement and in the WCC in particular. Included are interesting correspondence between Henrietta Visser 't Hooft and Karl Barth as well as three talks given by ecumenists of different confessional backgrounds. See also [1287].

[1287] Kaper, Gudrun, *et al. Eva, wo bist du? Frauen in internationalen Organisationen der Ökumene: Eine Dokumentation*. Gelnhausen: Burckhardthaus-Laetare, 1981.

This account of women in international ecumenism focuses on the Lutheran World Federation and the World Council of Churches over four decades. As does the book by Herzel [1286], it contains letters exchanged between Henrietta Visser 't Hooft and Karl Barth (1934 through 1948). The English language bibliography covers the years 1970 to 1979 (pp. 181-199).

[1288] May, Melanie A. *Bonds of Unity: Women, Theology, and the Worldwide Church*. AAR Academy Series 65. Atlanta: Scholars Press, 1989.

This publication was prompted by the WCC's study on "The Community of Women and Men in the Church." It includes two sets of voices: women who participated in the WCC from 1948 to 1975, and local groups of women reporting on their community studies. The author is a member of the Church of the Brethren. The bibliography is excellent (pp. 177-196).

[1289] May, Melanie A., ed. *Women and Church: The Challenge of Ecumenical Solidarity in an Age of Alienation*. Grand Rapids: Eerdmans, 1991.

The essays, all written by women, were published by the

Commission on Faith and Order, National Council of Churches of Christ in the USA. From a variety of Christian denominations, ethnic perspectives and professional experience, the twenty-five collaborators argue for a new ecumenical movement.

[1290] Parvey, Constance F., ed. *The Community of Women and Men in the Church*. Geneva: World Council of Churches, 1983.

The volume serves as the report of the WCC's conference on "The Community of Women and Men in the Church" held in Sheffield, England, 1981. The addresses given from the podium, representing voices from many corners of the earth, are reproduced. Also included are the Sheffield Recommendations (pp. 83-90) and section reports.

[1291] Thiering, Barbara, ed. *Deliver Us from Eve: Essays on Australian Women and Religion*. Sydney: Australian Council of Churches (NSW), Commission on Status of Women, 1977.

This collection of short essays on the status of women draws upon the experiences of nine women and two men (Christians, Jews and Muslims). Among the Christians there is a cross section of confessions and attention is given to the responsibilities incumbent on the churches.

# Ethical Issues
## General Studies

[1292] Crow, Paul A., Jr. *Christian Unity: Matrix for Mission*. New York: Friendship Press, 1982.

The author served from 1968 to 1974 as secretary of the Consultation on Church Union (COCU) and has served as editor of *Mid-Stream*. This "primer," prepared at the Ecumenical Institute of Bossey, identifies five major issues that divide the church today: the struggle for justice, poverty, racism, treatment of the handicapped, and sexism.

[1293] *Explorations in Theology 9: Ronald H. Preston*. London: SCM, 1981.

The volume contains a cross-section of writings by R.H. Preston, a leading British authority on social ethics and one-time professor of social and pastoral ethics at the University of Manchester. He argues that the years 1966-1968 witnessed a major breakthrough in formulating an ecumenical social ethic.

[1294] Hertz, Anselm, *et al.*, eds. *Handbuch der Christlichen Ethik*. 3 vols. Freiburg: Herder; Gütersloh: Gerd Mohn, 1978-82.

The first two volumes of this first-rate, collaborative publication appeared in 1978. The writers come from a wide spectrum of Christian backgrounds. Volume three appeared in 1982 with the assistance of twenty-five collaborators many of whom had not been involved in the earlier volumes. The last volume includes treatment of human rights, sexism, freedom, sports, etc.

[1295] Hochgrebe, Volker, ed. *Christliche Verantwortung: Eine ökumenische Bestandaufnahme zeitgemässer Ethik*. Würzburg: Arena, 1968.

The volume concentrates on four ethical areas: marriage and family, society, state and politics, and church. The contributions are radio talks given by both Lutherans and Roman Catholics.

[1296] Macquarrie, John, ed. *A Dictionary of Christian Ethics*. London: SCM, 1967.

Half of the contributors are from the Old World, half from the New World. Various Christian and Jewish authors wrote entries on basic ethical concepts, biblical and theological foundations, and a host of moral issues related to war, property, race, sex, etc.

[1297] Mehl, Roger. *Ethique catholique et éthique protestante*. Cahiers théologiques 61. Neuchâtel: Delachaux et Niestlé, 1970.

The professor at the Faculty of Protestant Theology, University of Strasbourg, analyzes the doctrinal and sociological sources of Catholic and Protestant ethics. He concentrates on their distinct views of natural vs. supernatural, natural law, secularization and sexuality.

[1298] Nelson, Claud D. *Religion and Society: The Ecumenical Impact*. New York: Sheed and Ward, 1966.

For many years associated with the YMCA movement and staff member of the National Council of Churches in the USA, the author here writes about responsibilities to social reform in the new ecumenical climate. Ethical issues touched upon include: racism, war, anti-Semitism, divorce, etc.

[1299] Segretariato Attività Ecumeniche, ed. *Questione etica e impegno ecumenico delle Chiese [Atti della XXIII Sessione di formazione ecumenica organizzata dal S.A.E., 1985]*. Leumann-Turin: Elle Di Ci, 1986.

Over 450 Italian ecumenists, including a number of non-Roman Catholics, attended the twenty-third meeting of the Italian Ecumenical Association, which addressed a spectrum of ethical issues bearing upon the ecumenical agenda.

[1300] Stoeckle, Bernard, ed. *Concise Dictionary of Christian Ethics*. London: Burns and Oates, 1979.

This volume is an abbreviated adaptation of *Wörterbuch Christlicher Ethik* (1975). The Benedictine editor was professor of moral theology at Freiburg beginning in 1970. The contributors include both Christian and non-Christian authorities.

[1301] Yannaras, Christos; Mehl, Roger; Aubert, Jean-Marie. *La loi de la liberté: Evangile et morale*. Tours: Mame, 1972.

To respond to various crises in morality today, it is here proposed by an Orthodox, Protestant and Catholic theologian that efforts be made to inspire Christian behavior by appeals to the Gospel.

# Peace

[1302] Bea, Augustin, and Visser 't Hooft, Willem A. *Peace Among Christians*. Trans. by Judith Moses. New York: Herder and Herder; Association Press, 1967.

This translation of *Friede zwischen Christen* (1966) contains ten talks given by Bea (President of the Secretariat for Promoting Christian Unity) and Visser 't Hooft (Secretary General of the WCC) in the first half of the 1960s. The volume received the Peace Prize of the German Publishers Association in 1966. Two valuable introductions by Johannes Willebrands and Eugene Carson Blake are included.

[1303] Centre Orthodoxe du Patriarchat Oecuménique, Chambésy-

Geneva. *Un Regard Orthodoxe sur la paix*. Etudes théologiques de Chambésy 7. Chambésy-Geneva: Centre Orthodoxe, 1986.

The annual Orthodox symposium held at Chambésy met in May 1985 to discuss Orthodox contributions to international peace efforts. Especially interesting are the reports on efforts by Orthodox (Todor Sabev), Catholics (René Coste), and Protestants (Martin Honecker).

[1304] Moltmann, Bernhard. *Militarismus und Rüstung: Beiträge zur ökumenischen Diskussion*. Heidelberg: Fest, 1981.

The volume draws upon research material prepared by the Evangelische Studiengemeinschaft of the EKD and describes the WCC's study program on disarmament.

[1305] *Peace and Disarmament*. Geneva: World Council of Churches, 1982.

This 254 page volume reports on the joint study by the WCC's Commission of the Churches on International Affairs and the Pontifical Commission "Iustitia et Pax." The volume cites documents from the first WCC's first five general assemblies and from papal statements from Pius XII through John Paul II.

[1306] Planer-Friedrich, Götz, ed. *Frieden und Gerechtigkeit: Auf dem Weg zu einer ökumenischen Friedensethik*. Munich: C. Kaiser, 1989.

The publication reviews the major stages in a developing ecumenical awareness of the ethical issues of peace.

[1307] Reuver, Marc. *Christians as Peace Makers: Peace Movements in Europe and the USA*. Geneva: World Council of Churches, 1988.

The Dutch author draws upon insights that emerged from the ninth assembly of the Conference of European Churches (CEC/KEK) that met in Stirling, Scotland, to explore the theme "Glory to God and Peace on Earth." In his 84 page booklet he also gives an account of Christian peace movements in Italy, Scandinavia, France and Eastern Europe.

[1308] Segretariato Attività Ecumeniche, ed. *Ecumenismo ed evangelizzazione della pace [Atti della VII Sessione di formazione ecumenica organizzata dal S.A.E., 1969]*. Brescia: Morcelliana, 1970.

The seventh volume of the acts of the Italian Ecumenical Association's annual congress is devoted to an examination of attitudes and teachings on peace in Catholic, Orthodox, Anglican and Waldensian traditions.

[1309] Segretariato Attività Ecumeniche, ed. *La pace sfida del Regno [Atti della XX Sessione di formazione ecumenica organizzata dal S.A.E., 1982]*. Leumann-Turin: Elle Di Ci, 1983.

There were three major presentations at this twentieth meeting of the Italian Ecumenical Association on the notion of peace as a challenge of God's kingdom. The biblical presentation was given by Carlo Martini. The acts conclude with a final statement by the membership.

[1310] Wischnath, Rolf, ed. *Frieden als Bekenntnisfrage: Zur Auseinandersetzung um die Erklärung des Moderamens des Reformierten Bundes "Das Bekenntnis zu Jesus Christus und die Friedensverantwortung der Kirche"*. Gütersloh: Gerd Mohn, 1984.

The volume records the lively discussion that followed upon the publication by the EKD of this position paper on the church's task to promote peace. Individual and corporate reactions are reproduced and theoretical issues regarding the prophetic role of the church are argued.

[1311] *The World Conference of Religious Workers for Saving the Sacred Gift of Life from Nuclear Catastrophe, Moscow, May 10-14, 1982*. Moscow: Moscow Patriarchate, 1983.

This volume serves as an official record of the 1982 conference including reports from the plenary sessions and working groups, together with its final position paper. All texts are given in English and numerous colored photos of the event are provided.

## Justice

[1312] Arruda, Marcos, ed. *Ecumenism and a New World Order: The Failure of the 1970s and the Challenge of the 1980s*. An Ecumenical Approach to Economics 1. Geneva: World Council of Churches, 1980.

This volume inaugurated a new publishing series for the WCC. It invites ecumenists to expand their horizons and to contextualize problems of church unity against the background of social justice issues.

**[1313]** Arruda, Marcos, ed. *Transnational Corporations, Technology and Human Development*. An Ecumenical Approach to Economics 2. Geneva: World Council of Churches, 1981.

This is a report of the third meeting of the WCC's Advisory Group on Economic Matters (AGEM) that met in Rome October 15-19, 1980. The WCC members belong to the Commission on the Churches' Participation in Development (CCPD). See also [1320].

**[1314]** Bent, Ans J. van der. *God So Loves the World: The Immaturity of World Christianity*. Maryknoll, NY: Orbis, 1977.

From 1963 to 1986 the author was director of the WCC's library in Geneva. This work records his impressions formulated in 1974 during stays in various parts of the "fourth world". Christian theology is presented as basically dialogical theology with a strong eschatological bent.

**[1315]** Derr, Thomas Sieger. *Barriers to Ecumenism: The Holy See and the World Council of Churches on Social Questions*. Maryknoll, NY: Orbis, 1983.

The volume seeks to explain the demise of SODEPAX which was to have coordinated common social concerns of the WCC and Rome. It does so by highlighting fundamental differences in their self understandings that impact their perception of issues such as the ethics of revolution, population, and women's issues.

**[1316]** Dejung, Karl-Heinz. *Die ökumenische Bewegung im Entwicklungskonflikt 1910-1968*. Studien zur Friedensforschung 11. Stuttgart: Ernst Klett; Munich: Kösel, 1973.

This work of a German Lutheran shows the roots of the conflicts between developed industrial nations and third world "underdeveloped" countries. Also treated is the relationship of Christianity and colonialism.

**[1317]** Duchrow, Ulrich. *Global Economy: A Confessional Issue for the Churches?* Trans. by David Lewis. Geneva: World Council of Churches, 1987.

This book is addressed to the affluent churches of the West

especially in Germany. It aims to show ways of their becoming an ecumenical people of God. The Barmen Theological Declaration of 1934 is used to illustrate the author's argument.

[1318] *Ecumenical Statements on Race Relations: Development of Ecumenical Thought on Race Relations, 1937-1964.* Geneva: World Council of Churches, 1965.

This publication reviews the history of shifting attitudes toward racial relations in this century as perceived by ecumenical statements.

[1319] *Empty Hands: An Agenda for the Churches.* Geneva: World Council of Churches, 1982.

This project of the WCC's Central Committee addresses the needs of disadvantaged persons and countries with "empty hands" and the necessity of our sharing resources with them both economically and spiritually. The practice of solidarity is seen as the ideal way to promote unity.

[1320] Gaspar, Diogo de; Espiritu, Caesar; Green, Reginald. *World Hunger: A Christian Reappraisal.* An Ecumenical Approach to Economics 3. Geneva: World Council of Churches, 1982.

This book contains the report to the fourth meeting of the WCC's Advisory Group on Economic Matters (AGEM) held in Washington, DC, October 1981. See also [1312, 1313].

[1321] Green, R. H. *The International Financial System: An Ecumenical Critique.* An Ecumenical Approach to Economics 4. Geneva: World Council of Churches, 1985.

The report of the WCC's Commission on the Churches' Participation in Development (CCPD) argues that the churches need to be concerned about the international financial system and to provide critique and appropriate action.

[1322] Preston, Ronald H. *Church and Society in the Late Twentieth Century: The Economic and Political Task.* London: SCM, 1983.

The author's revision of his Scott Holland Lecture (Manchester, England) given on Christian socialism criticizes the individualistic philosophy of members of the Radical Right such as Edward

Norman [242].

[1323] Santa Ana, Julio de, ed. *Towards a Church of the Poor*. Geneva: World Council of Churches, 1979.

This is a collective work of the WCC's Commission on the Churches' Participation in Development (CCPD). Following recommendations of the general assembly in Nairobi (1975) the group studied the plight of the poor, the relevance of the poor to the church and formulated proposals for the future.

[1324] Segretariato Attività Ecumeniche, ed. *L'annuncio del Regno ai poveri [Atti della XV Sessione di formazione ecumenica organizzata dal S.A.E., 1977]*. Leumann-Turin: Elle Di Ci, 1978.

This meeting of the Italian Ecumenical Association explored the notion of preaching the kingdom of God to the poor. This concept is examined in the Old Testament, the New Testament, the pre-Constantinean church and in the Franciscan emphasis on poverty.

[1325] Slack, Kenneth, ed. *Hope in the Desert: The Churches' United Response to Human Need, 1944-1984*. Geneva: World Council of Churches, 1986.

On the fortieth anniversary of the establishment of the WCC's Commission on Inter-Church Aid, Refugee and World Service, the editor collected thirteen essays to describe and evaluate its accomplishments. The activities are described as a new dimension of discipleship.

[1326] *Towards a Church in Solidarity with the Poor*. Geneva: World Council of Churches, 1980.

Published by the Commission on the Churches' Participation in Development (CCPD) as part of its research on poverty and the struggle of the poor, the illustrated booklet outlines the complex problem and offers recommendations to the member churches of the WCC.

[1327] Visser 't Hooft, W.A. *The Ecumenical Movement and the Racial Problem*. Paris: UNESCO, 1954.

The 70 pages of this earlier survey offer useful background

information for understanding later ecumenical statements on the evil of racism.

# Church and World

[1328] Baur, Jörg; Goppelt, Leonhard; Kretschmar, Georg, eds. *Die Verantwortung der Kirche in der Gesellschaft*. Stuttgart: Calwer, 1973.

This study-project of the ecumenical commission of the Vereinigte Evangelisch-Lutherische Kirche Deutschlands (VELKD) discussed the Church's social-political responsibilities. Several non-Lutheran guests participated including a Jesuit philosopher from Munich (Walter Kerber). The volume contains ten contributions and a final statement in seven theses (pp. 225-226) which include: political theology and preaching, colonialism and help for development, and eschatology from a social-ethical viewpoint. See also [703].

[1329] Bent, Ans J. van der. *Christian Response in a World of Crisis: A Brief History of the WCC's Commission of the Churches' on International Affairs*. Geneva: World Council of Churches, 1986.

The former librarian at the WCC outlines here the origins and purpose of the WCC's CCIA. He describes its work in promoting peace and disarmament, defending human rights and religious liberty, and other ecumenical involvements. Included are its bylaws and a bibliography (pp. 76-80). See also [1332].

[1330] *Christian Social Ethics in a Changing World*. New York: Association; London: SCM, 1966; *Responsible Government in a Revolutionary Age*. New York: Association; London: SCM, 1966; *Economic Growth in World Perspective*. New York: Association; London: SCM, 1966; *Man in Community*. New York: Association; London: SCM, 1966.

These four volumes were published together as preparatory documents for the World Conference on Church and Society, Geneva, 1966. See also [1345].

[1331] *Church and State: Opening a New Ecumenical Discussion*. Faith and Order Paper 85. Geneva: World Council of Churches, 1978.

In August 1976 representatives of various church traditions and of different political, social and cultural contexts met for a study conference in Bossey to continue a topic last raised at the Life and Work Oxford Conference on "Church, Community and State" [1337]. Six papers are here reproduced together with the report of the colloquium.

[1332] *The Churches in International Affairs: Reports 1974-1978; 1979-1982; 1983-1986; 1987-1990.* Published quadrennially. Geneva: World Council of Churches, 1979-1990.

The quadrennial reports of the Commission of the Churches on International Affairs (CCIA) describe its activities to promote human rights, peace and disarmament, and the United Nations. These are followed by statements, arranged by continent, on regional and national issues. See also [1329].

[1333] *Faith, Science and the Future.* Ed. by Paul Abrecht. Geneva: World Council of Churches, 1978.

This volume contains preparatory readings for the world conference organized by the WCC's department Church and Society scheduled for meeting at Massachusetts Institute of Technology (MIT), Cambridge, July 12-24, 1979. See also [1334].

[1334] *Faith and Science in an Unjust World.* Ed. by Paul Abrecht. Geneva: World Council of Churches, 1980.

This companion volume to the preceding [1333] contains the report of the WCC Conference on Faith, Science and the Future held at MIT, Cambridge, USA, July 1979. There are ten section reports and additional reports and resolutions.

[1335] Hudson, Darril. *The Ecumenical Movement in World Affairs.* London: Weidenfeld and Nicolson; Washington: National Press, 1969.

This volume summarizes research undertaken at the London School of Economics where Hudson served as a research fellow. It shows that many of the pioneers in ecumenism had a notable interest in political, social and economic problems. Discussed are issues of peace and the thrust of the Life and Work movement. The focus is on Protestant initiatives. There is a fine bibliography (pp. 255-272). See also [236].

[1336] Lange, Ernst. *Kirche für die Welt: Aufsätze zur Theorie kirchlichen Handelns.* Munich: Kaiser; Gelnhausen: Burckhaus, 1981.

This volume was edited and published posthumously by Rüdiger Schloz after Lange's death in 1974. It includes his inaugural lecture at the Kirchliche Hochschule in Berlin (1965) and other essays on the relationship of church and world that show the influence of D. Bonhoeffer. He also wrote about the deficit of ecumenical consciousness.

[1337] *The Oxford Conference: Official Report.* Ed. by J.H. Oldham. Chicago: Willett, Clark, 1937.

The Life and Work Conference of Oxford 1937 discussed church and community, church and state, church and state in relationship to the economic order, in relation to education, and the church universal and the world of nations. See also [1331].

[1338] Srisang, Koson, ed. *Perspectives on Political Ethics: An Ethical Enquiry.* Geneva: World Council of Churches,; Washington: Georgetown University, 1983.

Published by the WCC's Commission on the Churches' Participation in Development (CCPD), this volume contains eleven articles outlining the major issues facing political ethics.

[1339] Segretariato Attività Ecumeniche, ed. *Ecumenismo e secolarizzazione [Atti della VIII Sessione di formazione ecumenica organizzata dal S.A.E., 1970].* Brescia: Morcelliana, 1971.

The eighth meeting of the Italian Ecumenical Association heard seven talks on secularization and spiritual ecumenism. Also included are summaries of discussions by nine study groups.

[1340] Segretariato Attività Ecumeniche, ed. *Regno di Dio e città terrena [Atti della XVI Sessione di formazione ecumenica organizzata dal S.A.E., 1978].* Leumann-Turin: Elle Di Ci, 1979.

The sixteenth session of the Italian Ecumenical Association continued its explorations of the kingdom of heaven, this time discussing its relationship to the earthly city. Besides papers by the Catholics, Orthodox and Protestants, there is an interesting account of the history of the first sixteen meetings of the association (pp. 175-184).

[1341] Stirnimann, Heinrich, ed. *Kirche im Umbruch der Gesellschaft: Studien zur Pastoralkonstitution "Kirche in der Welt von heute" und zur*

*Weltkonferenz "Kirche und Gesellschaft".* Ökumenische Beihefte 3. Fribourg: Paulusverlag, 1970.

> The volume contains articles in French and German on the relationship betweeen church and society in light of Vatican II's Pastoral Constitution on the Church in the Modern World (*Gaudium et spes*) and the Geneva Conference on Church and Society (1966). A bibliography of over 600 titles was prepared by Philippe Reymond (pp. 105-132).

[1342] Thomas, Madathilparampil M., and Abrecht, Paul, eds. *Christians in the Technical and Social Revolutions of Our Time.* Geneva: World Council of Churches, 1967.

> The 141 page account of the World Conference on Church and Society held in Geneva in July 1966 was edited by an Indian and European theologian. See also [1345].

[1343] Thomas, Madathilparampil M. *Towards a Theology of Contemporary Ecumenism: A Collection of Addresses to Ecumenical Gatherings (1947-1975).* Geneva: World Council of Churches; Madras: The Christian Literature Society, 1978.

> This collection of talks by the Indian ecumenist dates back in part to 1947 and includes fourteen essays on the Church's mission as response to Christ in the world, and seven on the need for theological integration in the ecumenical movement.

[1344] Visser 't Hooft, W.A. *The Fatherhood of God in an Age of Emancipation.* Philadelphia: Westminster, 1982.

> This work is an analysis of the process of liberation from patriarchal ways of living and thinking that involve family, church and society. He examines young people's struggle to escape from authoritarian parents and women's quest for liberation.

[1345] *World Conference on Church and Society, Geneva, July 12-26, 1966: Official Report.* Geneva: World Council of Churches, 1967.

> The conference proceedings report on the four sections: economic development in a world perspective, the nature and function of the state, the struggles of international cooperation, humans and community in changing societies. See also [1330].

# Author Index

All index entries refer to bibliographic item numbers.

# Title Index

All index entries refer to bibliographic item numbers.

# Subject Index

All index entries refer to bibliographic item numbers.

## About the Compiler

MICHAEL A. FAHEY, S.J., is Dean and Professor in the Faculty of Theology, University of St. Michael's College. He has served for over twenty years on the Orthodox/Roman Catholic Consultation in the United States and is a consultant to the Anglican Church of Canada. He is past president of the Catholic Theological Society of America. He has authored several books, and his articles have appeared in *Theological Studies, Anglican Theological Review, Ecumenism,* and the *Journal of Ecumenical Studies.*